The Sacrificed

The Sacrificed Generation

Youth, History, and the
Colonized Mind in Madagascar

Lesley A. Sharp

UNIVERSITY OF CALIFORNIA PRESS
Berkeley   Los Angeles   London

University of California Press
Berkeley and Los Angeles, California

University of California Press, Ltd.
London, England

Portions of this book have been published in less developed form as
follows: chapter 1, as "Youth, Land, and Liberty in Coastal Madagascar: A
Children's Independence" *Ethnohistory* 48 (2001): 1–2, 205–36; chapter 4, as
"Royal Difficulties: A Question of Succession in an Urbanized Sakalava
Kingdom," *Journal of Religion in Africa* 27, 3 (1997): 270–307, subsequently
reprinted, with minor revisions, as "Royal Difficulties: The Anxieties of
Succession in an Urbanized Sakalava Kingdom," in *Ancestors, Power and
History in Madagascar,* ed. K. Middleton, 101–41 (Leiden, Netherlands: Brill,
1999); and chapters 3 and 7, as "Girls, Sex, and the Dangers of Urban
Schooling in Coastal Madagascar," in *Contested Terrains and Constructed
Categories: Contemporary Africa in Focus,* ed. G. Bond and N. Gibson (Boulder,
Colo.: Westview Press, 2002).

Library of Congress Cataloging-in-Publication Data
Sharp, Lesley Alexandra.
   The sacrificed generation : youth, history, and the colonized mind
in Madagascar / Lesley A. Sharp.
      p.   cm.
Includes bibliographical references and index.
   ISBN 0-520-22950-9 (Cloth : alk. paper)—ISBN 0-520-22951-7
(Paper : alk. paper)
   1. Youth—Madagascar.   2. Education—Madagascar.   3. Youth—
Madagascar—Political activity.   4. Imperialism.   I. Title.
HQ799.M25 S53   2002
305.235'09691—dc21   2001007074
                                                               CIP

Manufactured in the United States of America
12 11 10 09 08 07 06 05 04 03 02
10 9 8 7 6 5 4 3 2 1
The paper used in this publication is both acid-free and totally chlorine-
free (TCF). It meets the minimum requirements of ANSI/NISO
Z39.48–1992 (R 1997) (*Permanence of Paper*). ●

This book is, first,
for Alexander,
and for Julio, Franck,
Claré, Rachida, Nora,
Armelle, Lalaina, and Mirana, too,
each one circulating in his or her own
unique educational sphere.
You bring great delight.
And for wise and thoughtful Zoko,
who had little chance in life
but who never ceased to astound us all.

CONTENTS

ILLUSTRATIONS

FIGURES

MAPS

TABLES

ACKNOWLEDGMENTS

This study marks a commitment to long-term research based in northwest Madagascar, with activities extending back to the late 1980s. My original work focused on the interplay of gender, migration, and religious experience in Ambanja and the Sambirano (Sharp 1993). Although at the time I was most concerned with adults' lives, a theme that emerged repeatedly involved adults' concerns for school youth (Sharp 1990). In fact, numerous informants, while simultaneously highly supportive of my interest in local culture, nevertheless encouraged me to return in order to investigate the more pressing social problems that plagued their children's lives. This current book is the end result of a promise I made to the community to return with this specific goal in mind.

I am therefore deeply indebted to a number of institutions and individuals who have made this second research project possible. Generous funding was provided for the field component by the American Philosophical Society; an Academic Grant from Butler University; and the Joint Committee on African Studies of the Social Science Research Council and the American Council of Learned Societies with funding from the National Endowment for the Humanities and the Ford Foundation. An association with L'Institut des Civilisations at the Musée d'Art et d'Archéologie in Antananarivo, under the helpful guidance of its director, Jean-Aimé Rakotoarisoa, made this work both possible and enjoyable. Two faculty grants from Barnard College and a Richard Carley Hunt Fellowship from the Wenner-Gren Foundation for Anthropological Research (Grant No. 6047) have offered invaluable support for writing and for complementary archival research in Berkeley, Cambridge, New York, and Aix-en-Provence, France. In Aix, I am especially indebted to Jean Villon, whose kindness, patience, and archival expertise greatly facilitated this phase of research.

Many other individuals have been of immense help throughout various stages of this work. Gillian Feeley-Harnik, Kathleen Kilroy-Marac, William Lambert,

Nancy Scheper-Hughes, Paula Sharp, and an anonymous reviewer all offered expert advice on earlier drafts. I have profited greatly from discussions with Charlanne Burke, Lisa Colburn, Robert Dewar, Stephen Foster, Ron Kassimir, Susan Kenyon, Michael Lambek, Shirley Lindenbaum, Maman'i'Franck, Mohamed Mbodj, Daniel Raherisoanjato, the Ralaizonias, Hanta and Chris Rideout, Tsiaraso Rachidy IV, Marcia Wright, and Arab, Mariamo, and Neny. Kathleen Kilroy-Marac and Sarah Sasson assisted with French translations, as did Tiana Ralaizonia and Annie Rabodoarimiadona with those from highland Malagasy. Also, Heather Fisher, Anna Gavin, Evi Rivera, and Chomee Yoon proved invaluable as research assistants at Barnard. Moral and other forms of support have been offered with great kindness, love, and fortitude by Andy and Alex Fox (without whom, frankly, I would not have accomplished this project), as well as my parents and my siblings, Paula and Erik. One could not hope for better friends and colleagues than those I have had at Barnard: Marco Jacquemet, the late Morton Klass, Brian Larkin, Abe Rosman, Nan Rothschild, Paula Rubel, Paul Silverstein, and Maxine Weisgrau have all been wonderfully supportive. I am grateful to Burton Benedict, Elizabeth Colson, and Frederick Dunn for their expert mentoring, and to Jean and John Comaroff, who share my interest in youth identity politics in Africa. I am forever indebted to many people in Ambanja, both old and young, who welcomed me into their schools and homes, offering shelter, good company, and precious interview time, too. Last but not least, I thank my editor, Stanley Holwitz, whose persistent interest in youth has made this published work a reality, alongside other gifted staff at the Press who handled this project with such care, including Rachel Berchten, Peter Dreyer, Diana Feinberg, Kristen Cashman, and Marian McKenna Olivas. *Misoatra tompokô lahy sy tompokô vavy. Merci ê jiaby.*

NOTES ON THE TEXT

The letters *c, q, u, w,* and *x* do not exist in Malagasy.

The letter *o* is pronounced like a long *u* or *double-o* in English (thus "tromba" is pronounced "troomba," "Antandroy" as Antandroo-y).

The letter *j* is pronounced like a *z* or *dz* (as in Ambanja).

The nasal *n* sounds (both velar and palatal) of northern Sakalava (as in tsiñy) are written as *ñ*, following current (and now widely standardized) preferences shared by other scholars working in northern Madagascar. (In earlier publications I have written this as *ṇ*, as is done in Ambanja's schools.) The sound in English which approximates this is the *ng* in "sing."

In Malagasy, there is no difference between singular and plural noun forms. The term *ampanjaka* (royal, royalty), for example, may refer to one or several individuals, so throughout the text I have sought to clarify the number.

Unless otherwise stated, all foreign terms are given in the Sakalava dialect (which includes a wide range of borrowed terms, especially French). The following abbreviations are used to specify different dialects or languages: SAK: Sakalava dialect; HP: High Plateaux (generally Merina); OF: official Malagasy, the bureaucratic language of the island put into use in the 1970s; FR: French. The most important terms appear in the glossary.

The national currency of Madagascar is the Malagasy franc, or franc malgache (FMG). Throughout the first half of 1987, the exchange rate was approximately FMG 750 / U.S.$1.00; in mid July 1987, the FMG was devalued to 1,300. In mid 1993, the rate was approximately 1,890; a year later, in July 1994, the FMG was again devalued, so that the exchange rate became 3,530. In mid 1995, it was around 3,400 (updated from Sharp 1993, xv). As of January 2002, U.S. $1.00 was equivalent to FMG 6,621.

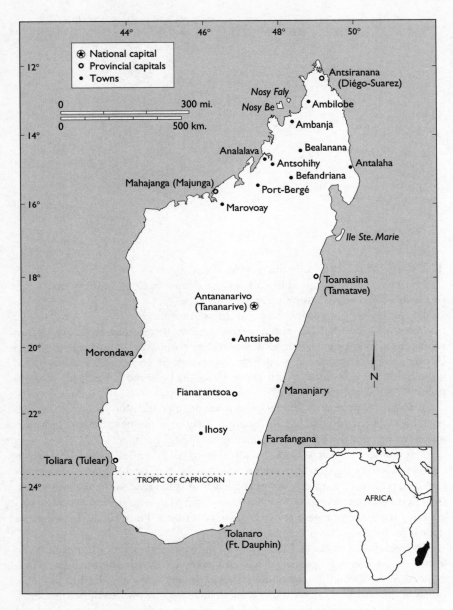

Map 1. Madagascar. *Sources:* After Sharp (1993: xx) following Bunge (1983: 51),
Madagascar-FTM (1986), and Société Malgache (1973: 2). Adapted from map drawn
by Christine Flaherty.

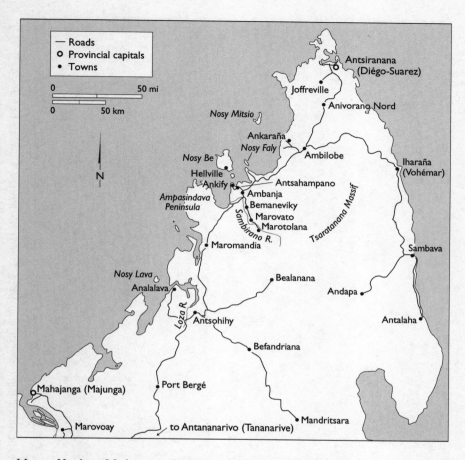

Map 2. Northern Madagascar. *Source:* After Madagascar-FTM (1986). Adapted from map drawn by Christine Flaherty.

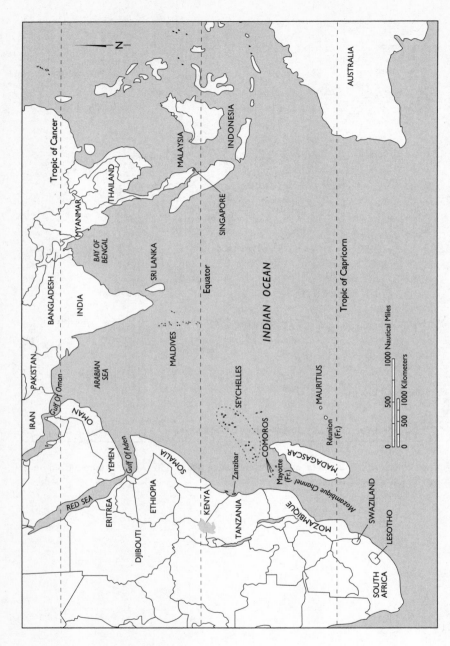

Map 3. The Indian Ocean Basin. *Source:* After Bunge (1983: xii–xiii). Adapted from map drawn by Christine Flaherty.

PART ONE

The Reconstruction
of a Children's History

Introduction

ALTERNATIVE VISIONS

In June 1993, I returned to Madagascar following an absence of six and a half years, and by the end of my first day back, my head was swimming. The recent shift from isolationist socialism to open market trade was evident everywhere in the central highland capital of Antananarivo. The streets were choked with new cars and trucks, many of them pricey all-terrain vehicles, including the one my friends had borrowed in order to pick me up at the airport. Colorful billboards lined our route, some with three-dimensional frames capable of automatically displaying a repetitive series of images. For an instant, I thought I was in the French countryside. As we reached the outskirts of town, the air seemed terribly polluted, the car fumes burning my eyes, nose, and throat. The neighborhood where I regularly stay was full of new construction projects, yet it also swarmed with more *katramy* (the homeless) than I remembered. This was not the island nation I remembered from 1987, and I found myself staring out the car window in wonder. By the end of the day, I was exhausted. I had arrived at 6:00 A.M., after nearly twenty hours of flying; followed by a full day of carousing with old friends and surrogate kin, I was so tired I could hardly stand. Around 7:00 P.M., a group of us sat down in the family parlor in order to watch television before dinner, as had sometimes been our habit when I had lived here before. I settled into a comfy armchair, hoping to take a brief nap before we reassembled at the table.

I had anticipated either a stilted presentation of the national news or a boring and sappy historic drama imported from Brazil, a soap-opera-style program aired over the course of many nights, the characters' lives hopelessly entangled and plagued by unrequited love, infidelity, greed, treachery, and murder. In 1987, there had been only one, government-controlled television station in Madagascar, and the programming was predictable, with shows sometimes running uninterrupted for hours at a stretch. By 1993, however, national television had clearly undergone radical changes, as I soon realized as I watched the screen. For one, there was talk of more than one station. Furthermore, and much to my surprise, the broadcast opened with a series of ads for items that were of foreign origin yet produced locally on the island. The most memorable involved a scenario intimately familiar to all inhabitants of Madagascar: a group of strangers traveling together suddenly find themselves stranded, their van having broken down on an unpaved rural road. Everyone piles out to await repairs. The driver searches for a pen to jot down some notes, and a passenger reaches into his pocket for a brand-new BiC® pen. Another man, realizing they may be stuck there for a long time, rummages through in his travel bag until he finds what he's looking for: his BiC® razor, with which he begins nonchalantly to shave, without soap and water. Meanwhile, the transport's crew have discovered a flat tire. They open the back of the van and unearth a brand-new spare, still encased in its yellow factory wrapping. They strip this from the tire and toss it on the ground, so that we viewers can read the label—the tire, too, is a BiC® product. By the end of the commercial, the room is in an uproar of laughter.

"What has happened to Malagasy TV?" I later asked a young friend.

"Ahh, Lisy! This is [President Zafy's] Third Republic," she responded. "We young people don't listen to the radio any more—it's old-fashioned, it's not cool."[1]

"But why?"

"Because we have nothing else to do! . . . You know, the politicians and journalists, they call us *la génération sacrifiée*—we are Madagascar's 'sacrificed generation.'"

La génération sacrifiée, "the sacrificed generation": I would hear this phrase repeatedly throughout the next three years of research as I probed the experiences of Madagascar's educated youth. Students of a range of ages were regularly described by adults as "sacrificed," "massacred," "forgotten," and "neglected," their current lives judged emblematic of a comprehensive political experiment gone awry. Frequently, too, such critiques were laced with adult fears of the corrupting nature of mass media of foreign—and especially, Western—origins. More specifically, these powerful terms were used to describe rural and coastal youth, regarded as the island's most innocent and vulnerable inhabitants. The coast in particular offers evidence of long-term national suffering: plagued for twenty years by material shortages of all kinds, a decrepit infrastructure, and poorly funded schools, it epitomizes the greatest failures of the socialist revolution in Madagascar.

In this light, this current study concerns those deemed this nation's most gravely affected victims: marginalized, coastal youth, many of whom were born in the early 1970s and schooled during the next twenty years under Madagascar's unique form of socialism. Their experiences are also emblematic of more widespread forms of disparity. For one thing, their lives differ radically from elders who experienced colonialism firsthand; furthermore, their current predicament parallels that of children born elsewhere during Africa's early postindependence years (cf. Atteh 1996 and other works cited in this volume). Framed by adult readings, such children commonly emerge on a global scale as suffering under a host of politicoeconomic crises, the expression "lost generation" often being employed to underscore the extreme nature of their plight. This study, however, refutes this dominant paradigm, questioning the assumed helplessness of Madagascar's sacrificed youth. An important point of departure involves a significant methodological shift: in contrast to a pervasive anthropological approach, this study places youth at the center of analysis, where they, not adults, are the primary informants. By insisting upon the legitimacy of children's voices (cf. Coles 1971, 1986), this work thus ultimately challenges current understandings of youth and, more particularly, of young people in postcolonial settings. As we shall see, Madagascar's students do, indeed, inhabit a highly marginalized realm, for this tropical island is consistently ranked among the poorest nations in the world. Nevertheless, throughout this work, coastal youth emerge as savvy social critics and significant political actors in contexts where failure seems inevitable. In turn, their readings of colonial history are intrinsic to shaping their collective understanding of their nation's current predicament and the active roles they play in transforming it. A central assumption, then, that drives this work is that autobiography and national history are inextricably linked and must be read in tandem. Furthermore, it is in the schoolroom that historical and, ultimately, political, consciousness are forged. Thus, students' shared critical vision (that is, what Freire 1985 refers to as *conscientização*) of their personal trials, of the colonial past, and of the current nation are rooted in a dialectic of state ideology and pedagogical praxis. In the end, students' narratives expose the provocative and potent nature of collective memory in forging political consciousness and action in youth.

As such, this work is intended simultaneously to be a rich ethnographic account of a particular community, and a comparative study of youth, history, and political agency in francophone Africa. Key here are the life narratives of a cohort of *lycée* (high school) students from the coastal northwest. These students' education largely coincided with the nation's radical socialist era and terminated at the very moment when, through their own collective action, socialism in Madagascar came to an abrupt halt. Central to this now defunct era was the nationalist ideology known as malagasization (FR: *malgachisation*), whose architects forged strident critiques of colonial occupation and of subsequent neocolonial policies following the island's independence in 1960. The architects of malagasization rejected Francocentric readings of history that had remained in place since the colonial era. By the mid 1970s, history lessons no longer began with "Nos ancêtres les Gaulois . . . " ("Our ancestors the Gauls . . . "); instead, they gave pride of place to Madagascar's precolonial past and, more generally, to the many indigenous institutions that had been misunderstood, ignored, or denigrated by the French. Central to malagasization was a more general desire to generate nationalist pride. Unlike many of their elders, who might have experienced as much as seventy years of foreign occupation, school youth of the 1970s could envision Madagascar as a fiercely independent African nation.

Such aspirations necessitated sacrifice throughout the entire country, since this vision insisted that the nation break free of former relationships that fostered political and economic dependency. Within this framework, France emerged as an especially oppressive former ally. Madagascar's socialist leanings also led to the systematic withdrawal of other Western countries, so that material scarcity rapidly became a daily experience on an island where members of the elite and middle class had formerly been able to travel relatively freely to Mauritius, Réunion, and Europe to purchase coveted goods and have access to medical and other services unavailable at home. By the mid 1980s, however, the lovely villas of the past stood weathered and unpainted; medicines of every kind were difficult to find or were simply nonexistent; automobiles and electrical appliances were expensive and scarce; and the shelves of stores both large and small were frequently bare, or displayed only a limited array of Chinese, North Korean, and Malagasy-produced goods of shoddy quality. Nowhere, however, was scarcity more evident than in the nation's coastal schools. Madagascar as a whole now suffered from a dearth of schoolbooks, the most basic of school supplies, and competent teachers. These problems were even more severe on the coast, where one could search in vain for printed materials, wall maps, blackboards, and even stable desks or chairs, and where instructors stood unprepared to teach a nationally mandated curriculum (Clignet and Ernst 1995).

Ironically, as a result of their particular predicament, coastal youth emerge as far more critically aware of the origins of disparity, and of the significance of sacrifice and suffering, than do their counterparts in the nation's capital, Antananarivo. Most striking is their deep collective awareness of what Frantz Fanon (1963) and others refer to as the "colonized mind" (cf. Jinadu 1980; Mannoni 1990; Memmi 1965; Ngugi 1986). Coastal students are far from passive victims of the colonial legacy or of their nation's brand of socialism. Rather, their reconstructions of the past in particular reflect a self-reflexive stance, where they and their forebears emerge as significant players who have actively shaped their nation's destiny. Young coastal informants are likewise conscious of the effects of more recent economic and political changes upon their lives. Schooled under socialism, they await with anticipation the consequences of the most recent educational and social reforms, as their country, like so many others now, embraces idealized models of democracy and capitalism. As such, they are *willing* victims of the postindependence era.[2]

A Neglected Nation

In the United States, and in the English-speaking world in general, Madagascar is a largely neglected, if not invisible, nation. As a scholar of Madagascar, I am sensitive to its absence from our consciousness: the campus where I work is frequently littered with fliers that sport maps of Africa on which no hint of Madagascar appears, and so I am regularly impelled to pen in its shape before moving past local bulletin boards. Those who have heard of the island know of it primarily for its unique flora and fauna (and especially its array of lemur species), yet of its people they know little or nothing at all. Furthermore, Madagascar is frequently confused with other African countries, especially with those whose names begin with the letter *M:* colleagues refer me to books written about the region where I work; upon further investigation, however, I often discover that they are about Mozambique.

Such pervasive lack of interest among Americans always strikes me as odd, given Madagascar's enormous size: it is, after all, the fourth largest island in the world, spanning approximately 1,500 kilometers from its northern to its southern tip. American reactions stand in stark contrast to those I encounter in France, of whose colonial empire Madagascar was once a prized possession. During the late nineteenth century and throughout much of the twentieth, Madagascar defined an important segment of a web of global relations for France, and French colonial officers and even African soldiers moved frequently between France, the Maghreb, West and Equatorial Africa, Indochina, and this "Great Red Island" (Stratton 1964). Far from being viewed as an isolated and little-known, ocean-bound terrain, Madagascar figured prominently as an exemplary colonial model, and many French acquaintances boast of kin who lived there as military men, administrators, missionaries, merchants, doctors, or schoolteachers and university professors. Furthermore, given the complex origins of the Malagasy people—whose ancestors hail from such diverse regions as Southeast and South Asia, East and Central Africa, and the Arabian peninsula—the island emerges as a fascinating enigma that defies, in this instance, a French propensity for racial categorization. In the Musée de L'Homme in Paris, for example, an exhibit on Madagascar has long occupied the troublesome border zone between the two halls reserved for displays on "white" (that is, *blanche, Arabe,* or northern) and "black" (*noire,* or sub-Saharan) Africa.[3]

In Madagascar itself, a localized myopia is pervasive, too, ultimately shaping understandings of margin and metropole. As noted above, great disparities are assumed to exist between the central highlands, where the capital of Antananarivo is located, and the island's extensive coast. Such constructions reflect long-standing assumptions about the original peopling of the island, the diverse cultural array of its current population, and French racial categories. These complex constructions are not only embedded in the colonial record but have been reinforced by a propensity among scholars, until very recently, to focus nearly exclusively upon the central highlands to the neglect of other regions.[4] From a coastal perspective, however, the national picture changes radically, and my work to date has been driven by the desire to assert coastal understandings of Madagascar.

More specifically, this work is based in the town of Ambanja, the bustling urban center of a prosperous plantation region known as the Sambirano Valley. My earliest research in this town spanned 1987, and I returned there for the purposes of this study in 1993, 1994, and 1995. From the perspective of Antananarivo, Ambanja and the Sambirano Valley occupy a marginal zone by virtue of their location: they lie in the far northwest, near the ocean, and approximately 950 kilometers by rough roads from the nation's capital. In contrast to so many other severely economically depressed regions of this nation, however, this is a highly productive area economically, one where severe hunger is rare. Ambanja, with a population of approximately

30,000, is unlike many other towns its size. Its boutiques burst with foreign goods; it has not one, but two large daily markets; its main street is paved; it lies near the crossroads of a national route; and it has its own small airstrip nearby. Here one also finds a stately Catholic cathedral, five mosques, and a wide assortment of Protestant churches; two hospitals (one state-run, the other part of the Catholic Mission), as well as a private clinic primarily serving plantation employees; it not only has a strong city government *(firaisana)* but it is also a county seat *(fivondronana)*; and it plays host to an assortment of many other businesses and associations, including three banks, numerous ethnic and burial associations, a branch of the Alliance Française, and a newly formed Lions Club. Such prosperity is closely bound up with the success of the large-scale plantations that have dominated the Sambirano Valley for over a century, which first grew manioc and sugarcane for export and now produce cocoa, coffee, and perfume plants. Ambanja also serves as an imposing educational center for the region, offering an impressive array of public and private schools that extend from the elementary through the lycée levels.

Structurally speaking, Ambanja is difficult to map. On the one hand, the valley's terrain is dominated by large holdings of export cash crops, and thus local plantations exert significant power in the region's political arena. The local city and county governments are, nevertheless, significant institutions as well, a situation further complicated by the fact that the Sambirano delineates the boundaries of the ancestral kingdom of the Bemazava-Sakalava, a once semi-dormant dynasty that has begun in recent years to reassert its power. As detailed in a previous study (Sharp 1993), other localized forms of contention are also at work here: as a result of its prosperity, the Sambirano is a long-standing destination for labor migration within the island, so that Ambanja's population is split nearly evenly between indigenous Sakalava *teratany* (literally, "offspring" or "children of the soil"), and myriad Malagasy-speaking migrant *vahiny* ("guests") who come here in search of work, wealth, and, perhaps, even land. Such constructions of indigenous versus migrant identities are complex, pervasive, and essential to understanding localized constructions of history. As will become clear in the chapters that follow, this complex history is particularly important in pedagogical contexts, since schoolteachers and students alike struggle with conflicts over national—and inevitably highland—constructions of history versus those that foreground coastal experience.

Politics and Pedagogy

Here in northwest Madagascar, one may speak of border wars of the mind, where pedagogical battles are waged over the schooling of children as a key strategy for nation building. In Ambanja, malagasization has radicalized pedagogical praxis. More specifically, through local reconstructions of history, personalized and collective suffering have been redefined in reference to this local community's struggles with the paired forces of foreign domination and racism set in place during— and perpetuated well beyond—the colonial era. This history is framed by events that have occurred within the past 150 years, involving, first, the failed invasions of coastal territory by other Malagasy of highland origin; second, the conquest of the entire island by the French; third, the constant influx of non-Sakalava strangers; and, fourth, several periods of political upheaval since independence in 1960.

How Ambanja's youth position themselves in such contexts hinges on their ability to retell and, thus, reformulate events that shaped the lives of their elders, who have been manual laborers, foot soldiers, prisoners, and nationalists. As this book will show, school youth of an array of ages and from different epochs have frequently played significant roles in their island's history, often instigating political change through open, public protest. This history has generated a particular body of local knowledge, where a retelling of the past proves transformative, yielding a new sense of collective identity, shaped by critical understandings of the roles youth play in shaping their nation's destiny. Although this is a study of Madagascar first and foremost, students' tales prove essential to a comparative study of African colonial policy, particularly in francophone territories. Madagascar typified French colonial aggression, occupation, and governance, and this study's ethnographic concerns are thus inevitably relevant to other former colonies as well. By focusing on the power of collective memory, nationalism, and local knowledge, this work insists that we must reconsider the assumed political impotence of youth throughout Africa.

HISTORICAL AND POLITICAL CONSIDERATIONS

How, then, are we to reconstruct a children's history within this complex nexus of island events, experiences, and regions? The primary purpose of this introduction is to map the theoretical and methodological terrains so essential to this question. To assist readers unfamiliar with Madagascar, I first offer a general overview of the political history of the island in anticipation of a more detailed discussion in chapter 1. Of special concern is the importance of introducing key terms and concepts that will appear throughout the work (see also the glossary). This section is then followed by a description of anthropological models of childhood and their shortcomings in reference to this project. I then conclude with a review of methodological approaches employed throughout my research with school youth, ending with an overview of the study as a whole.

Island Politics

The origins of Madagascar's sacrificed generation lie in the political and economic changes that have shaped this island's recent history. Drawing upon rhetoric reminiscent of the French Revolution (and thus of the former colonizing power), Madagascar's politicians now divide their nation's postcolonial history into four regimes. The First Republic (Première République) emerged after independence in 1960 under the leadership of President Philibert Tsiranana, who maintained a close alliance with France. The early 1970s, however, marked the beginning of a radical departure from Tsiranana's policies. Protests initiated by university students eventually toppled Tsiranana's government, and following a period of great unrest, Didier Ratsiraka emerged as the president of what is now referred to as the Second Republic (Deuxième République). Ratsiraka, who led Madagascar under two decades of socialism, was a strong proponent of self-sufficiency, and attempts to achieve this resulted in a period of intense isolationism. Then, in the early 1990s, lycée and university students again banded together with peasants, this time to overthrow Ratsiraka, and there followed what is generally referred to as the transitional period *(période transitionelle)*. In 1993, Madagascar elected President Zafy Albert,[5] who, as the leader of the new Third Republic (Troisième République), reembraced an open-door, capitalist agenda in an attempt to free Madagascar from two decades of self-imposed isolation. Zafy's presidency, however, was short-lived. Following Zafy's impeachment in 1996, Ratsiraka was reelected and sworn into office in 1997. He now advocates continuing many of Zafy's economic policies, although this stance has been qualified by federalist leanings that privilege regional decentralization, and he also favors foreign aid that targets the island's ecology. Ratsiraka's return marked the beginning of the Fourth Republic (Quatrième République). This study extends from the precolonial era into mid 1995, concluding in the second of three years of Zafy's Third Republic, by which time malagasization had met its final demise.

These periodic political shifts are perhaps most keenly felt in Madagascar's schools, because each time the nation realigns itself politically, it also imposes new educational reforms on its children. As noted earlier, a cornerstone of the socialist era was malagasization, of which Ratsiraka was the key architect. In the early years, the application of malagasization as a state policy focused on the expulsion of French advisors, who had continued to play crucial roles in the island's government since independence in 1960. By the mid 1970s, however, it quickly evolved into a nationalist ideology that emphasized the centrality of indigenous culture in the construction of a new collective identity. An important element was the development of a national language that, like kiSwahili in Tanzania and Bahasa in Indonesia, could unite Madagascar's diverse groups of Malagasy speakers. Malagasization had an immediate impact on Madagascar's schools, because within only a few years *malagasy iombonana,* or official Malagasy (in French, *Malagasy officiel*) became the language of instruction. Up to this point, curricula at all levels had been derived from French models. Under malagasization, France was no longer the central focus in lessons in history, geography, and politics but was, rather, displaced by studies that explored Madagascar's own history and its position in the larger arena of geopolitics dominated by First and Second World powers.

Zafy's educational policies launched a direct assault on the architecture of Ratsiraka's Second Republic, because Zafy advocated democratic process, anti-isolationism, and the promotion of capitalist modes of production through privatization and foreign investment. Within one year of Zafy's instatement in March 1993, French quickly assumed its former role, replacing official Malagasy as the language of instruction in primary and secondary schools. This has remained the case notwithstanding Ratsiraka's reelection in 1997.[6] Under Zafy, the same school-age youth who had successfully joined forces with peasants and older university students to overthrow the socialist Ratsiraka now had to confront their collective destiny as a failed experiment in their nation's history. Far from being naïve victims of this process, many of them demanded and fought passionately for this transition, even though they foresaw the self-sacrifice it entailed. As members of this nation's sacrificed generation, students on the brink of completing lycée offer compelling critiques of the meaning of political change, their perceptions of individual and collective failure, and their hopes for pedagogical redemption.

Pedagogical Considerations

Myriad paradoxes underlie these political transitions. Among the most significant are those arising from the problems associated with malagasization. At its onset, malagasization embodied the vision of a nation that sought to free itself from the chains of foreign domination, building a strong national identity by drawing on indigenous institutions. In retrospect, however, it is viewed by many as an abysmal failure. This sentiment is expressed in especially virulent terms on the coast, where malagasization is perceived as having only exacerbated regional differences, rather than having created a cohesive sense of collective national identity. Official Malagasy draws most heavily from the dialects of highland groups that dominated the island politically in late precolonial and then colonial times. As a result, under Ratsiraka's Second Republic, students living in the island's central highlands (and particularly in or near Antananarivo) quickly mastered official Malagasy, whereas those on the coast (and even their teachers) struggled to learn what was essentially a foreign dialect, based on the language of the hated highland oppressors (see Sharp 1990; 1993, 222–44). National educational programs thus followed a trend established during the colonial era (1896–1960), when educational policies likewise favored highland students, particularly those living within easy access of the capital. As early as the 1970s, elite highland parents perceived malagasization as an isolating force, and many therefore quickly placed their own children in private French schools. Today, Madagascar is faced with a vast majority of coastal children who have never fully mastered official Malagasy, in contrast to a small highland elite whose offspring have been prepared for advanced training overseas or who now aspire to fill newly vacated posts under this island's current regime.

A second paradox that characterizes the lives of coastal students in this study is their peculiar social status. Many are children of rural origins who have relocated to Ambanja to complete their schooling, living alone or renting small houses with a sibling or with friends, where they are responsible for their own welfare. Some begin this new urban life when they are as young as ten years old, for their adult kin are peasants who must remain in the countryside partially in order to raise enough food to feed their offspring in town. Thus, these young students should not be viewed as social castaways. Rather, they have at least initially succeeded where others have failed: the majority of their peers found their studies too difficult, and so they were forced to abandon schooling and remain in their villages. Such rural inhabitants have since assumed duties associated with adult status, fulfilling roles as young parents, laborers, and peasants.

In contrast, Madagascar's educated coastal students appear at first glance to be suspended in a phase of prolonged childhood (cf. Ariès 1960; Minge 1986). However, this approach is overly simplistic. In terms of age alone, many are hardly young children, having been obliged to repeat one or more years of schooling; as a result, few complete lycée before the age of twenty. Furthermore, from a Malagasy point of view, adulthood depends on an individual's productive and reproductive capacities. The manner in which youth develop such skills not only varies enormously between village and urban contexts but hinges as well upon whether one lives an independent existence. It is urban-based students who specifically live under the watchful eye of adult kin who are most likely to experience a suspended phase of childhood. A larger question that looms over the lives of all coastal students is the fact that many find themselves occupying a tenuous status that now leads nowhere. The immediate goal of the most successful of these students is to complete their final *(terminale)* year and pass the post-lycée *baccalauréat*, or "bac," exam—one based on the French model, retained by all four Malagasy republics—in order to continue their studies at a national university. Few succeed, however, and even fewer have parents or other relatives who possess the economic means that would enable them to complete their studies at this advanced level. Moreover, Madagascar offers its educated youth few employment opportunities. These are, of course, trends that typify much of Africa and other formerly colonized regions of the world as well.

Children, History, and the Colonized Mind

This study is concerned with a particular moment in Madagascar's history: of special importance is the transitional period of the early 1990s that falls between the Second and Third Republics of Presidents Ratsiraka and Zafy. Central to this project is the assumed power of collective memory for defining identity; second, that such power is often embodied in storytelling; and, third, that personal and social histories are malleable. The power of memory to shape oral narratives does not lie simply in the truthfulness of the tales. More important, historical reconstructions embody contemporary concerns and values that inform individual and collective representation and action.[7] The reflections of an unusual cohort of youth in Madagascar reveal deep understandings of their colonial origins, the power of nationalism, and their personalized conceptions of their collective destiny as students. Their narratives also tell us much about the experiences cross-culturally of children who are too young to have experienced colonialism firsthand, yet whose lives have nevertheless been shaped by a problematic past.

Of particular theoretical importance here are Frantz Fanon's writings on the colonized mind (Fanon 1963, 1966, 1967), for he has had a profound influence on nationalist movements throughout Africa; in turn, his work has shaped early analyses of independence movements by scholars as well. Fanon's works had a particularly strong impact on francophone nations, and in Madagascar, his writings followed in the wake of a localized interpretation of the psychology of colonization by Octave Mannoni (1999), discussed in greater detail in chapter 1.[8] As I discovered in the course of my fieldwork, critiques offered by students of the French conquest of Madagascar often echoed Fanon. These students had no access to his writings, but Fanon's ideas had been relayed to them orally by their schoolteachers.

For the past two decades, Fanon's works have been used primarily by scholars (and it is noteworthy that he is once again academically fashionable), but in Madagascar, his writings continue to provide a framework for self-analysis by the colonized. We therefore need to take another close, critical look at his significance in the formation of neonationalist movements in Madagascar and elsewhere. Finally, this study analyzes, from an anthropological perspective, the significance of nationalism as a force that shapes daily action, even decades after formerly colonized nations have won their independence.[9] It differs from the current literature on nationalism in that it foregrounds children as social critics and political activists.

CHILDHOOD RECONSIDERED
The Reification of Adolescence

An assumption that typifies current academic writings on children is that adolescence, as a dominant social category, signifies an incomplete and liminal status. That is, adolescents are assumed to occupy a transitional phase of life, suspended between childhood and adulthood. No author has been as influential as Philippe Ariès (1960) in the rendering of this category: as he argued four decades ago, the institutionalization of schooling defines a pervasive force that transformed the socioeconomic significance of the child in European history. In essence, the child's life is framed by the boundaries set by schooling and the now overlapping category of adolescence. Through formalized education, young people are caught in a suspended state of childhood, so that the training, expectations, and associated knowledge of adulthood are delayed until the close of the teenage years.

In anthropology, adolescence has, sadly, become reified as an assumed category of social experience cross-culturally and even universally. As Alice Schlegel writes in her introduction to a collection of essays on adolescence, for example,

> There is growing evidence that social adolescence not only is a near-universal or universal feature of human organization but that it also characterizes many higher primate groups. . . . Like any other stage in the life-cycle, it merits study: by psychological anthropologists as a further step in the socialization process; by social anthropologists as one of the sex-age categories into which human communities are

divided for purposes of organization and action. In addition, as anthropology joins its sister disciplines of psychology and sociology in contributing to applied interventionist programs, the study of adolescence within and across cultures can illuminate some of the problems and issues of contemporary adolescence. Although the contexts vary, the issues are the same: how children move from the dependency of childhood to the greater autonomy and responsibility of adulthood; how the sexuality of reproductively capable but unmarried young people is managed; how social groupings of adolescents, the peer groups, contribute to social well-being or turbulence; how adolescents' skills can best be trained, both to prepare them for adult occupations and to give them a sense of competence in this stage of their lives. (Schlegel 1995a, 3–4)

I quote this passage at length because it provides a detailed rendering of many of the assumptions that characterize the dominant yet horribly myopic ways in which young people are viewed within the social sciences, typifying how adolescence is so often reified and, in turn, essentialized. The following assumptions are particularly troubling: that marriage is a cultural universal, that full-fledged productivity is characteristic of *adult* behavior, and, further, that a distinct and identifiable pre-adulthood phase is more often than not marked by turbulence or, at the very least, by an underlying sense of incompetence (and by implication, ennui, if not anomie). Adolescence therefore warrants not only study but intervention by adults. Adolescents are also described in terms of deficiencies: unlike adults, they are not yet married, they remain unsettled, and they are not yet competent in skills that mark them as fully socialized human beings. When viewed as such, the category of adolescence is devoid of subtlety. What such a model also implies is that one can clearly demarcate its boundaries to determine where childhood ends or adulthood begins, even though each status paradoxically flanks a fluid and ill-defined one that lies in between.

Another artifact of this dominant approach is that adolescence, as a social category, is rarely historicized in any depth beyond comparisons that span two or perhaps three generations of experience. Thus, history, or, as it is more typically labeled, "tradition," also becomes reified within the context of adolescence studies. This is especially troubling, given the care with which Ariès himself sought to historicize the transformation of childhood over several centuries in Europe (and, more particularly, France). As a result, there is a disturbing telescoping of knowledge, whereby the collective voice of living elders is far too often legitimized by scholars as being truly representative of past ways of doing things. That is, elders' personal memories pass for a deep rendering of history. In essence, the lived experiences of parents and grandparents shape constructions of history that adolescents are inevitably assumed to confront. Yet elders themselves may have challenged a radically different order only two generations before. Absent from these studies, too, is acknowledgment that each generation of children may potentially incorporate and creatively transform such narratives to redefine their own sense of collective self in ways that can persist beyond their teenage years. In essence, then, each generation potentially retells and thus redefines the significant elements of the historicized past. Sadly, current models overlook this as a possibility. Children are assumed incapable of generating coherent critiques of injustice, formulating radical change, or making social history, and thus adults remain the only legitimate authorities. For reasons such as these, children remain virtually invisible historically.

This uncritical approach has also led social scientists to universalize adolescence as intrinsic to our human (and primate) nature. A reliance on shallow ethnographic databases only serves to perpetuate this flawed approach, since the information on which one must rely has often been gathered by researchers who themselves did not challenge the paradigm (see Schlegel 1995b). I must stress that it is not my intention to single out Schlegel as the primary culprit; a quick review of the anthropological literature underscores that many of these assumptions are deep-seated within the discipline and span several decades of intensive research by numerous authors.[10] However flawed it may be (Freeman 1983; Grant 1995; Holmes 1987), Margaret Mead's work stands in contrast to this; oddly, however, her 1928 study of adolescence in Samoa (Mead 1961) is neglected today, even though she sought energetically to prove how difficult it is to generate universal statements about children's experiences. Although she embraced the label *adolescence,* Mead nevertheless illustrated that the teenage years did not necessitate a distinct tumultuous phase of life preceding adulthood. She herself asserted that a great variety of experience characterized Samoan and American lives, challenging the assumption that adolescence is, in fact, a universal category of experience (Mead 1939), let alone measurable by urban, capitalist, postwar North American standards.

The propensity to generate social categories is, nevertheless, inherent in anthropology, for without a means to label, the comparative method that drives the discipline proves extremely difficult if not impossible to apply. In this study, I hope to remain true to social categories operative in Ambanja itself, and, for the reasons outlined above, I reject the term *adolescence.* I prefer instead to use *youth,* which I feel more accurately conveys the flexible nature of identity as it is experienced by school-age informants. Such factors as socioeconomic standing, migrant versus town-based status, and gender are highly effective in determining the manner in which their capabilities develop and how they are evaluated (and misinterpreted) by adults.

Understanding Youth in Ambanja

In the context of northern Madagascar, *adolescence* is in any case a category of little value. The lives of students in Ambanja in particular underscore the limitations of this form of social labeling. Their experiences are so highly varied that it can be difficult to identify key moments or events that typify obvious and shared shifts in status. As shown in greater detail in chapters 3 and 8, children as well as adults move slowly and steadily through various statuses throughout their lifetimes. Nevertheless, the manner in which change is experienced varies radically from one life to another and is further framed by individual experience and talent. Some transitions are marked explicitly through ritual and may also be mapped upon the body. For Sakalava children, for example, several transitions call for celebration: postpartum bathing and other associated practices assert a child's maternal and paternal links during the first four to six weeks of life (Sharp 1993, 108 ff.; 2000); the arrival of the first tooth precedes the first meal of true food, which is, inevitably, rice; the first hair cutting helps to distinguish the animal-like infant from its childhood potential; and circumcision and menarche signify yet other transitions for older boys and girls. But Sakalava lives are not marked solely by these events and their associated public celebrations. One's status within a political hierarchy further determines how significant such events are: special rituals typify royal teething and hair cuttings, whereas these are far more low-key and even mundane events among Sakalava commoners.

Even more important on a daily basis is the manner in which a child's capabilities are measured, where valued skills include dexterity, the ability and willingness to work hard in the fields and the domestic sphere, facility with numbers and other skills relevant to the marketplace (cf. Friedl 1992; Schildkrout 1981), and the mastery of schoolwork (cf. Le Vine et al. 1986; Serpell 1993). In northwest Madagascar, the value or worth of a child is expressed through an array of Sakalava terms, including: *mahay:* communicates a high level of (generally learned) capability and skill; *hendry:* innate social wisdom; and *miasabe* and *miasa mafy:* the ability to work hard. Children are, in a sense, born, raised, and cultivated. As I illustrate throughout this work, children reveal their capabilities in increasingly sophisticated forms, so that they ultimately move through the staggered statuses assigned to babies *(zaza, zazakely)*, children *(tsaiky)* and, eventually, toward the adult statuses of women and men *(mañangy, lahy)*; together these eventually render them full-fledged people, or human beings *(ny olo, ny olombeolo[na])*.

A question that arises, then, is what are we to make of the years in Madagascar that Ariès, Schlegel, and others would ultimately label *adolescence?* Schooling undoubtedly has a significant effect on a child's upbringing: the knowledge and skills that characterize a village-raised child with only a few years of primary schooling have, on the face of it, little in common with those of an urban-schooled lycée graduate. Contrary to assumptions generated by Ariès, one cannot assume, however, that students in urban Ambanja are suspended in adolescence, and that the relatively unschooled children in rural villages make a more direct and integrated transition to adulthood. From a Sakalava point of view, each child is *mahay*, or "capable," in his or her own distinct ways. These distinctions do not end with urban and rural differences: migrant schoolchildren reveal other possibilities. For example, the reader might easily assume that if a child raised in the countryside were to change places with one from urban Ambanja, neither would fare particularly well in the other's milieu. As I argue in chapter 3, however, solitary school migrants who live in town without adult supervision in fact share much in common with their village-based peers, because they are saddled at an early age with the double burdens associated with the domestic sphere and the classroom. As a result, they, like their rural counterparts, move more quickly toward adult status than do urban children raised by adults. This is by virtue of the fact that the solitary school migrant is more highly skilled *(mahay)* in a wider variety of contexts and, thus, for Sakalava, he or she ultimately may possess more wisdom *(hendry)* at an earlier age than do many students raised by their parents in urban households.

In response to urban and related developments, there is a label in common usage in Ambanja that seems at first glance to correspond roughly with the Western category of adolescence. This is *tanora*, or "youth," a term of highland origin that has been applied in the northwest throughout this century, particularly in contexts where children's lives are framed by institutions of Western origin. For example, children who sing in church choirs, as well as students, are often referred to collectively as *tanora*, because they represent a congregation's youthful membership, or, in political discourse, the nation's children (and thus, its future potential).

What must be understood, however, is that in Ambanja, *tanora* nevertheless retains the elasticity of other local social labels applied to children: one does not abandon youth status once one reaches a particular age, or after one completes school. *Tanora* can as easily be applied to people in their late twenties as to ten-year-olds. One essentially remains a baby, a child, or a youth until one proves *capable* of certain abilities, particularly through one's reproductive, economic, and/or ritual capacities. Adulthood is truly a slowly and very subtly achieved status in northern Madagascar.

Naming practices further emphasize the transitional and elastic quality of identity: a child can remain unnamed for days, weeks, or even longer, receiving a name only after he or she appears healthy and safely out of the reach of infant mortality. Most often, an infant only receives its first name after its mother emerges from confinement. Religious affiliation may also dictate the need for additional names: many Sakalava are at least marginally Catholic, and their children are often given additional saints' names when they are baptized and, potentially, confirmed. A sickly child, or one whose mother has experienced the loss of other offspring, may be disguised, too: young boys in particular are given girl's hairstyles, clothes, and names to avoid attracting the attention of jealous neighbors or spirits. Because the state of Madagascar mandates that all inhabitants carry identity cards, surnames are often invented for this purpose (Sharp 1993, 106–8). Even colleagues and neighbors may be ignorant both of one's bureaucratic name and those bestowed by one's parents, however, because upon the birth of a first child, mothers and fathers adopt teknonyms (i.e., assume new names that reflect their relationship to the child). Thus, "Franck's Mother" is addressed as Maman'i'Franck by her friends, co-workers, neighbors, and kin. Nicknames may also be equally important in daily discourse: among my neighbors in 1987 was a woman known by all simply as Maman'i'Tsara Zanaka or "Mother of the Beautiful Children." Much later in life, elders adopt such honorary titles as Dady or Dadilahy to signify that they are "Grandmothers" or "Grandfathers," or they may revert back to one of the many given names of their youth: thus, another grandmother and elderly neighbor of mine was Mama Soa ("Mother Soa" or more literally "Sweet Mama"). To summarize, Sakalava (and Malagasy more generally) adopt, grow into, shed, and invent names throughout the course of their lives, names that often reflect changes in status. They may also reflect personal whims, or an open desire to alter one's public persona.

As we shall see, not even elected rulers *(ampanjakabe)* are able to appropriate their own status. Instead, they, like children, grow slowly into their roles, a process that is symbolized by an elaborate series of rituals designed to instate them gradually in their rightful place. The transitional nature of these events was particularly well illustrated in late 1993 when a young, unmarried "man-child" *(tsaiky lahy)*, aged twenty-five, was selected as the new ruler of the Bemazava-Sakalava kingdom of the Sambirano Valley following the sudden and unexpected death of his father. Later, throughout the first days of his official instatement, he rarely spoke, because he was still considered a child who lacked the knowledge of a full-fledged ruler. When the time came for him to inhabit the royal palace, he had to be carried on the back of an experienced old man as if he were a mere baby. Rulers are marked in their transitions through life and, ultimately, in death, by the adoption of new names. Born Parfait, this young king assumed the new title of Tsiaraso Rachidy IV once he was fully instated as ruler. When his life inevitably comes to a close, he will, like his forebears, discard the names he bore in life and be given a sacred praise name *(filahiaña)* that proclaims his achievements to posterity, rendering all other former names taboo. Thus, his father, Tsiaraso Victor III, is now referred to only by his praise name, Andriamanaitriarivo, "The Ruler Who Surprised Many." The new young ruler's story is the primary focus of chapter 4.

Youth and the Politics of Culture

The history of the Sakalava is shaped by the actions of their royalty, memorialized in *tromba* spirit possession performances, as I have noted extensively elsewhere (Sharp 1993, 144 ff.; 1995; 1999). Thus, the young living ruler Tsiaraso Rachidy IV embodies several forms of collective history in the making, being both a newly appointed ruler and, by virtue of his age and schooling, a member of the sacrificed generation. But what of the more mundane aspects of everyday life as it affects commoners, migrants, and youth? A central purpose of this book is to explore the ramifications of Ambanja's lycée students as political and, therefore, historical actors and critics, in contrast to royalty and adults. As I have argued above, dominant understandings of childhood and adolescence deny the possibility of such a project, since their assumed proto-adult status automatically renders them incapable of such power.

A troublesome question, then, is how to approach the question of children's political consciousness and action. An inherent problem is that much of the existing literature either portrays children as passive, vulnerable victims of political and economic forces (Mendelievich 1979; Scheper-Hughes 1987 and 1992; UNICEF-U.K.

1988), or as dangerous hooligans (Donal Cruise O'Brien 1996; Comaroff and Comaroff 1999; Scheper-Hughes 1995). Only a few studies explore the lives of urban
children, but these similarly address the extreme margins of life, where they are the
victims of abandonment, famine, warfare, or the untimely deaths of kin (Ennew
and Milne 1990; Reynolds and Burman 1986; UNICEF 1987). "Children most often come under public scrutiny," write Stevi Jackson and Sue Scott, in circumstances where adults are suddenly more aware of new social risks. Children define
relevant categories when they are perceived either as in danger or as endangering
others (1999, 92, after Thorne 1987). Both stances ultimately undermine their autonomy when adults step in to protect or police children (ibid. 1992, 91, 93–94). In
turn, such polarized constructions of their collective identity and social worth ultimately trap children in a theoretical double bind.

Against this background, African youth in particular occupy an especially troubled position: in the West, it is assumed that African children are regularly abandoned, they starve, or they are transformed into fighting machines because of the
violence and danger said to characterize their continent. If African youth are politically motivated, they are inevitably portrayed as the disenfranchised who resort
to chaotic forms of violent mob behavior as they rip away at the fragile social fabric that binds people together. Media portrayals of Africa as a continent fraught
with drought, disease, and warfare only further exacerbate this. African youth therefore shoulder a double burden in Western interpretations of their lives: as children
(or adolescents), they are judged incapable of transformative action; and as
Africans, they are confined geographically to societies that seem to place little value
on civil society and, thus, their lives are threatened the moment they are born.

The paired themes of murder and warfare are especially pervasive in the literature on African children, as reflected in titles such as *Small Wars* (Scheper-Hughes
and Sargent 1998), "Who's the Killer?" (Scheper-Hughes 1995), *A Different Kind of
War Story* and *Girls and War Zones* (Nordstrom 1997a and 1997b), and *Fighting for the
Rain Forest: War, Youth and Resources in Sierra Leone* (Richards 1996). My point here is
not to challenge the quality of these stellar works nor to deny the horrors of war
but, rather, to underscore a dominant academic preoccupation with Africa as a site
of violence meted out by youth. In the end, Africa's youth inevitably emerge as
"lost" generations who can occupy only one of two extremes: they are either powerless victims of structural violence or the perpetrators of physical assault upon the
continent's citizenry. Accordingly, they are perceived as incapable of sophisticated
social critique or organized and sustainable political action.

A refreshingly alternative approach can be found in the edited works of Sharon
Stephens (1995b) and Vered Amit-Talai and Helena Wulff (1995), who challenge the
stances outlined above by reframing discussions of children in terms of their cultural
agency (cf. Durham 2000). This act of reframing exposes yet another set of assumptions implicit in much of the existing literature: that children, as an incomplete social
category, can only be understood as members of a substandard and, ultimately, sub-
servient and subcultural category. The dominant paradigm assumes that children can

only react to, but not generate or transform, dominant cultural forms. Lacking knowledge, wisdom, and political prowess, they are incapable of generating sustainable ideas or action, which are the monopoly of those who can claim full adult status.

As Stephens has asserted, however, in many circumstances children are, in fact, often powerfully transformative "social actors in their own right" (1995a, 23). Children may initiate protest in the face of massive injustices, sacrifice their lives for such causes, or enter lifelong careers as political activists in response to actions taken earlier in their lives. A particularly striking innovative approach characterizes the work of Paul Richards (1994, 1996), whose writing on child soldiers in Sierra Leone integrates interpretations of both exploitation *and* agency at the extreme margins of human existence (cf. Nordstrom 1997a and b on Mozambique). Pamela Reynolds has shown how, in 1976, Soweto schoolchildren organized one of the first successful protests against the racist South African state, marking an important "symbolic divide" not only in their own lives but for the nation itself (Reynolds 1995b, 223; see also Brooks and Brickhill 1987; Ndebele 1995). "[T]o dub youth, as is often done, as the 'lost generation' is to demean their contribution and to deny the inventiveness inherent in processes of inheritance and change," Reynolds observes (1995b, 224). This study similarly rejects portrayals of youth as inevitably lost, helpless, and lacking political awareness or agency.

Political Activism

The case of Madagascar challenges the current literature in yet another way, since it offers a more subtle understanding of political activism than do the examples noted above. As we shall see, activism need not be so dramatic or violent as the civil wars of Sierra Leone and Mozambique or the school protests in Soweto. Set against literature that focuses on violence, Malagasy youth may at first glance appear passive or extraordinarily reserved, and, ultimately, some readers may be disappointed by this. Yet such reserve is a quality that frequently characterizes Malagasy activism. In Madagascar, demonstrations involving tens of thousands of protesters are at times virtually silent affairs. As one European observer remarked to me in 1993, what shocked her the most about recent street protests in Antananarivo was that the loudest sound of all was produced by the persistent shuffling of crowds of feet. Nevertheless, Malagasy youth of the past and present have been extraordinarily active—and repeatedly *successful*—as political actors throughout the twentieth century. Students in Madagascar have repeatedly abandoned their classrooms and taken to the streets to protest oppressive policies, helping to topple two regimes in less than forty years. Readers will, I anticipate, inevitably respond in various ways to this study depending on how much they privilege physical and psychic suffering, violence, and armed struggle in the context of political upheaval. These themes emerge repeatedly in students' critiques of a brutal colonial past, but they do not characterize their own actions against the state.

A key assumption that informs this work as a whole is that schooling provides an important referent for children's experiences (cf. Hostetler and Huntington 1992; Pomponio 1992; Simpson 1998; Dijk 1998; Willis 1977). Furthermore, the rhetoric and consciousness associated with malagasization as nationalist pedagogy generates compelling critiques of the past, allowing for the shaping of future visions. Forms of radical pedagogy generate a language through which school youth articulate the nature of suffering and transform these understandings into action. Among the most profound exercises is the rereading of history. Thus, within this study, children are given a voice so that they may tell their own tales. These tales are not merely symbolic—and thus oblique and unfulfilled—challenges to oppression (cf. Comaroff 1985; Comaroff and Comaroff 1993; Pred and Watts 1992; Ong 1987). Rather, they are carefully constructed narratives that illustrate a heightened level of personal and collective awareness of the effects of such forces as colonial rule, capitalist exploitation, and race relations. These are stories of their own choosing, and ones that reflect particular moments in the island's tumultuous history. Their rendering of the past underscores an astute collective consciousness of their multiple peripheral statuses: as youth, as coastal, as Malagasy, and as Africans. It is through these careful readings that they ultimately generate new ideological forms, which, in turn, shape their own brand of political activism.

METHODOLOGICAL CONUNDRUMS
Children as Informants: An Interactive Approach

Children form close to half of the population of Madagascar (Andriamihamina et al., 1987; Covell 1987, xvi–xvii; Madagascar [Census Data]1950–71; Population Reference Bureau 1990), a trend that characterizes many other Third World countries, yet their lives often remain undocumented. This study seeks to rectify that discrepancy by granting them a voice to articulate their own concerns. Conducting fieldwork among youth is, nevertheless, a difficult enterprise; this was a lesson that took some time to learn (and overcome). The data reported here are drawn primarily from three seasons of research, spanning the northern hemisphere's summer seasons of 1993, 1994, and 1995. When I first conducted research in Ambanja in 1987, I worked primarily with adults, and 1993 proved a frustrating year. The nation had been in great turmoil for the past eighteen months, and, as with my arrival in Antananarivo, I hardly recognized Ambanja either. Although lycée students were the focus of this new study, I slowly realized that those who fell within the target age of fifteen to twenty-four did not respond well to a structured interview format. Early interviews seemed to go nowhere or would end abruptly when the informant became bored or disenchanted with the line of questioning. I returned to the United States in the fall of 1993 to struggle with my data.

As Allison James notes, research that focuses on the lives of youth may ultimately necessitate "learning to 'talk'—again" (James 1995, 47), a process that certainly characterized my own subsequent field experience. When I returned to Ambanja in the summer of 1994, a series of events led to my developing strong rapport with a cohort of students primarily from the state-run lycée who were preparing for that year's bac exam. Here, the tables were turned: soon these students, individually and as a group, were interviewing me about topics central to their exam preparations and that, ironically, formed the core of my own research. Their key questions concerned, for example, the impact of colonialism in a postindependence state; the dilemmas faced by youth in African nations; the trials of urban life; the nature of racism in Madagascar and elsewhere; the psychological significance of, in their words, *la mentalité colonisée* ("the colonized mind"), and, more generally, the meaning of history for colonized peoples. This interactive interview format, reminiscent of the consciousness-raising approach of the Brazilian educator Paulo Freire (1970), yielded much deeper cultural understandings of one another than would have been possible had I relied on more orthodox anthropological research methods that insist on objectivity and a distanced stance between investigator and informant. Often the most compelling data did not arise out of structured interviews (which now ran smoothly), but from my informants' interviews of me following these scheduled—and more structured—encounters. The data generated by these interactive interviews form the core of this study. Thus, the primary data for this research in Ambanja are drawn from individual and group interviews with twenty lycée-level students and an additional fourteen enrolled in a more specialized seminary track at the town's private Catholic Mission Academy (see appendix 1). Complementary data have also been assembled from a host of interviews with students' elders; schoolteachers and administrators; a small sample of elite highland children from the national capital; and government officials at the local and national levels. Additional archival research was conducted in national libraries in Antananarivo; the Centre des Archives d'Outre-Mer (CAOM) in Aix-en-Provence, France; and the holdings of Barnard College, Columbia University, the University of California–Berkeley, and the Tozzer Library at Harvard University.

I am deeply indebted to Mme. Tsarahita (referred to in other works as HT), with whom I have worked closely since 1987.[11] As a research assistant, her knowledge and field skills have proved invaluable, as has, similarly, a level of kindness and patience that one expects only from the dearest of friends. When we first met, I was still a graduate student and she an unemployed lycée graduate who had passed her bac the year before. As the daughter of a Sakalava mother and a migrant father, her insights into localized constructions of identity are sophisticated, and she thus proved an important guide throughout my earlier work on migration and religious experience. We have since collaborated on this project as well; yet, again, she has been an important partner, because not only was she schooled in the Sambirano Valley during the Second Republic, but she has subsequently acquired a part-time post at one of the town's schools and is involved on a daily basis in overseeing the schooling her own sons, her younger siblings, and several sisters' children.

History Reconstructed

A problem inherent in this project is, of course, the complex issue of what, in fact, constitutes history, or, more specifically, legitimate narratives of the past (cf. Cohen 1994; Davidson and Lytle 1992; Dirks 1992, esp. 9 ff.; Said 1978; Stoler 1985; Wolf 1982). As emphasized earlier, what matters here is not the ability to formulate a true and thus pristine narrative of past events; instead, this study is driven by the premise that the tales recounted here are valid by virtue of the fact that they reflect what is valued by the teller of the tale. Of greatest importance is the nature of the voice, and this study takes as its central charge the legitimation of coastal youths' perspectives. Thus, it is students' narratives that are foregrounded throughout this work. Other voices—of parents and other elders, teachers, and government officials, for example—serve to complement their tales, without supplanting them. After all, these complementary voices are the sources of knowledge from which students themselves draw, and which they may then reshape. Colonial documents in turn have proved invaluable in allowing me to contextualize students' narratives.

A trend that has struck me repeatedly throughout the course of this project centers on the foci that students themselves identify as most relevant to their lives, as opposed to what scholars regularly consider the nation's most important events. For example, I was surprised at first that students did not dwell on the insurrection of 1947, a time that always figures prominently in adults' (and textbook) accounts of the colonial period. Whereas 1947 is most strongly associated with the island's east coast, Ambanja's youth frequently focused instead upon highly localized moments of resistance from the Sambirano's own history.[12] Furthermore, they were far more concerned with events and themes that underscored quotidian forms of exploitation. The theme of enslavement is especially prominent, uniting discussions of royal power, colonial wartime conscription, and corvée labor as imposed by a foreign power (these themes correspond to chapters 4, 5, and 6 in Part 2). In such contexts, enslavement also assumes a highly charged metaphorical value, because it refers to power exerted not only over physical bodies but over minds and territories, too.

Another important question involves defining who, exactly, these young informants are. As will become clear in Parts 2 and 4, Ambanja's students are drawn from a variety of geographic and ethnic backgrounds. Interestingly, regardless of whether or not they consider themselves indigenous Sakalava tera-tany, as students from the northwest they identify strongly with coastal concerns. In Ambanja, this then necessitates understanding their island's history from a highly localized perspective. By default, they often embrace the centrality of indigenous Sakalava communities in building this script. If, in fact, they are not Sakalava by birth, they nevertheless use this point of reference from which to extrapolate the significance of oppression in the lives of marginal coastal peoples.

In this regard, they also offer an important contrast to arguments so central to my earlier work (Sharp 1993). Ambanja's youth seem to experience and understand identity in more malleable terms than do adults, since the latter rely heavily on categories that separate insiders from outsiders. Many school youth move frequently between town and countryside in ways that defy strict categorization. Their schooling also plays a part, so that students may be more sensitive to the racist and Eurocentric undertones of dominant social categories. In interviews, all students, regardless of their (or their parents') origins also privileged coastal history, underscoring their personal identities as linked to this region. Finally, rather than embracing a highland rhetoric that privileges the Asian origins of the Malagasy, Ambanja's youth seize upon Africa as central to their identities. They thus assume that their history parallels those of other African subjects who have lived under the shadow of the French colonial empire.

The Complexity of Language in a Coastal Migrant Community

Fluency in local languages is central to the success of the anthropological enterprise. In a polycultural community such as Ambanja, this is a complicated issue in both linguistic and political terms (two domains that, as we shall see, are inseparable). Malagasy, which is recognized as the national language of the vast island of Madagascar, is divided into anywhere between eighteen to twenty or more dialects (depending on the era and who is doing the counting). When asked what they speak, Malagasy people will typically reply that they "speak Malagasy" *(teny gasy)*, which sets them apart from other foreigners. The reply "I speak European" *(teny vazaha)*, or "white" (in French, *parler blanc* [cf. Gueunier 1993]) implies that one speaks French *(Franzay)*. Unless the context requires it, Malagasy generally do not specify their dialect. As an anthropologist who works almost exclusively on the northwest coast, however, I am often required to clarify my linguistic abilities and deficiencies. When moving about in Antananarivo, for example, I often state, "Aza fady tompokô, fa tsy mahay tsara teny Merina aho. Izaho teny Sakalava ê!" ("Please excuse me sir/madame, but I don't speak Merina well. I speak Sakalava!"), a self-parodying statement that generally causes my listener to smile broadly or even snort a bit with laughter, because, as any Malagasy speaker will recognize, it is a crudely composed statement that opens with a bookish-sounding highland Merina phrase and closes with a colloquial coastal Sakalava one. Linguistic differences truly complicate this study, because it is set within a migrant town in the northwest, where all ethnic groups live, and thus all dialects are spoken.

To simplify this matter for readers, it should be understood that northern Sakalava serves as the standard dialect for this book. What must be stressed, however, is that Sakalava, as it is spoken in Ambanja, is a *mélange-be* ("big mixing")—as one of my Sakalava friends once joked—of coastal Sakalava with other Malagasy dialects (such as Tsimihety, Antankaraña, and official Malagasy) with French (of which the term *mélange-be* is itself a humorous example), English, Arabic, kiSwahili, Comorean, and other foreign tongues. Official Malagasy, an artificial, pan-Malagasy bureaucratic language that was perfected in the mid 1970s, is often of central importance to this book, since it figures prominently in schools. From a Sakalava point of view, it closely resembles highland dialects, especially Merina. Throughout this book, the dialect spoken should be clear from the context. Where the dialect is ambivalent, I employ a method from my previous work (although it requires embracing a form of coastal ethnocentrism): SAK refers to the dominant Sakalava dialect of Ambanja; HP designates high plateaux and primarily Merina expressions; OM, official Malagasy; and FR, French.

The naming of villages, towns, provinces and their capitals can be similarly confusing to the novice. Five of Madagascar's seven provinces have both Malagasy and French names, which they share with their respective urban capitals. These are Antananarivo (FR: Tananarive), Fianarantosoa (same in French), Toamasina (FR: Tamatave), Tolanaro (FR: Fort Dauphin), Toliara (FR: Tulear), Mahajanga (FR: Majunga), and Antsiranana (FR, but of Portuguese origin: Diégo-Suarez). Malagasy often use these terms interchangeably, although preference certainly varies according to the region where one lives (as well as one's age, since those schooled during the colonial era are more likely to use the French term). Ambanja, for example, lies within the province of Antsiranana, but one rarely refers to its provincial city by this same name; instead, nearly everyone speaks of the city of Diégo-Suarez or, more commonly, Diégo. To simplify this matter for readers, I generally use the Malagasy names; where a quotation makes use of the French name (as in passages drawn from colonial documents), I have included the Malagasy name in brackets. In my desire to remain loyal to local northern ways of speaking, I use "Diégo-Suarez" or "Diégo" to refer to the provincial city, whereas "Antsiranana" specifies the province as a whole. Three maps have been provided to assist readers unfamiliar with Madagascar.

I have also chosen to remain loyal to certain Malagasy grammatical forms and expressions. As an Austronesian language, Malagasy does not distinguish between singular and plural noun forms. To preserve the poetry and sound of the language, I have chosen to do the same. Thus, such labels as Malagasy, Sakalava, and so on, may designate one or several people; the context should make it clear whether I refer to one or more. It is also necessary to clarify the manner in which I refer to the indigenous inhabitants of the Sambirano Valley: to simplify matters, I generally refer to them simply as the Sakalava. Only in cases that necessitate references to the local royal dynasty do I use the more specific form Bemazava-Sakalava, or simply Bemazava. Finally, to underscore the expansiveness of the central highlands, I follow national practice and refer to this region using the plural form "high plateaux" rather than the singular "plateau."

THE ORGANIZATION OF THE STUDY

This study is organized into four general sections, which alternate between history (parts 1 and 3) and contemporary ethnography (parts 2 and 4). Part 1, "The Reconstruction of a Children's History" (consisting of this introduction and chapter 1, "Youth and the Colonized Mind"), provides a comprehensive review of this book's theoretical, methodological, and historical frameworks. Coastal Madagascar offers a rich terrain for exploring academic, bureaucratic, and lived constructions of identity among school-age youth. Their peripheral status exposes a host of problems inherent in the study of the politics of education cross-culturally. More specifically, their experiences typify those of many other young Africans born and raised during the continent's postindependence era. An examination of the fortitude, ills, and paradoxes that characterize their lives necessitates questioning the manner in which anthropology considers children. This approach ultimately requires politicizing the discipline's dominant models to a much greater extent than is usually done.

Given that lycée-level students are central to this study, education is necessarily a primary focus of analysis. This work, however, is not intended as an examination of schooling in Madagascar per se. Rather, a central concern is the mutable quality of pedagogy as an ideological enterprise. As such, schooling in Madagascar must be understood in reference to the complexity of sociopolitical forces set within a historical framework. Because the majority of readers will be unfamiliar with Madagascar, chapter 1 begins with a detailed history of education on this island; it then offers a more deeply nuanced analysis of concepts central to the remainder of the study. Of particular importance are localized constructions of the colonized mind, homeland and nation, and, finally, sacrifice.

Part 2, "The Perplexities of Urban Schooling: Sacrifice, Suffering, and Survival," marks a shift in presentation that is more radically ethnographic. Chapter 2, "The Sacrificed Generation," grounds the preceding detailed analysis of chapter 1 in a particular coastal context, exploring the nature of education as it is practiced, so to speak, in Ambanja and the Sambirano Valley. Schooling in this polycultural plantation region emerges at times as exemplary of education in Madagascar and, at others, as exceptional. Chapter 3, "The Life and Hard Times of the School Migrant," offers portraits of the everyday experiences of Ambanja's school-age youth, contrasting the realities of their lives with the assumptions about them. At the lycée level, students' lives exhibit a surprising array of experiences, mediated by such forces as social class and urban versus rural residence or origin. Here the school migrant emerges as a particularly compelling category in a town where insider-outsider statuses dominate everyday discourse about identity. Unlike their adult counterparts, students do not fall as neatly into the opposed categories of indigenous Sakalava (tera-tany) and migrant "guests" (vahiny) that are so pervasive in this community (Sharp 1993). Instead, these two social categories are rendered even more complex and malleable when applied to youth. Furthermore, the geographic requirements of schooling are operative in an unusual sense. First, students of non-Sakalava origins who have lived in Ambanja most of their lives are considered by their peers to be tera-tany; yet when the children of indigenous rural-based Sakalava tera-tany relocate to town, they are transformed into vahiny if they lack town-based adult kin. Clearly, child migrants—and especially *school* migrants—define unusual social categories that demand careful analysis here and cross-culturally.

Part 3, "Freedom, Labor, and Loyalty" marks a return to historical narratives, albeit of another sort. Chapters 4, 5, and 6 focus specifically on topics and events of students' choosing, and enslavement and resistance are the dominant themes throughout. In these chapters, students' readings of exploitation vary radically according to the time frame and arena of power in question, with significant contrasts centering on royal versus colonial forms of authority. In addition, these discussions are consistently set against the local political economy of the Sambirano, a region that is simultaneously an established kingdom and a region long exploited by plantations that are neither owned nor run by Sakalava. Within the collective consciousness of lycée youth looms a prioritizing of labor history as a way to critique the onslaught of colonial power and its aftermath.

Part 3, then, concerns the effects of French conquest and colonial domination on the lives of royalty. As illustrated in chapter 4 ("The Resurgence of Royal Power"), authority demands loyalty, and in the royal context this collective sentiment is expressed through willing participation in various forms of ritual service (*fanompoaña*). Associated tasks are difficult by virtue of the love and devotion required by rulers, rendering loyalty simultaneously a great virtue and a form of enslavement. Furthermore, the royal context underscores indigenous understandings of the past, given that, for the Sakalava, it is royal action that shapes history (see Sharp 1993, 1995). Past and present royalty thus figure prominently in students' critiques of local history. The fact that the newly instated young king Tsiaraso Rachidy IV is simultaneously a member of Madagascar's sacrificed generation further underscores the potential of youth to make history.

Chapters 5, "Our Grandfathers Went to War," and 6, "Laboring for the Colony," build on these themes of conquest, labor, and enslavement, likewise focusing on past events that Ambanja's youth identify as central to understanding the effects of the colonial legacy. These chapters' respective foci are, first, forced army conscription during World War I and, then, the colonial demand for labor during peacetime. The historical narratives that appear in these chapters foreground the brutality of conquest and the economic demands placed on inhabitants of an especially fertile and productive region. Of central importance here are the injustices associated with colonial (versus royal) forms of enslavement and, in turn, indigenous defiance of exploitative practices.

The book's focus then shifts once again from history to the ethnographic present. Whereas part 3 concerns historical themes that inform contemporary readings of everyday suffering, part 4, "Youth and the Nation: Schooling and Its Perils," explores the contemporary urban problems of the postindependence era. Of special importance here are the dangers associated with mass media, sex, and magic, all of which potentially imperil school success. Chapter 7, "Girls and Sex and Other Urban Diversions," explores adults' assumptions versus the lived realities of Ambanja's school youth, where television, video cinemas, and discotheques are said to corrupt the lives of unsupervised migrant school youth. Students in turn voice their own opinions on sexuality, where foreign aid (particularly in the form of "population control") emerges as a neocolonial agenda. Relevant here is AIDS, which is described as an insidious form of foreign hegemony. By focusing on sexuality, this chapter also underscores the gendered nature of urban dangers in Ambanja and its social and educational consequences. Finally, chapter 8, "The Social Worth of Children," explores localized readings of success and failure in school and beyond. This chapter opens with the sudden death of a former classmate who falls victim to lethal magic (*fanafody raty*) used against him by an anonymous rival, underscoring the fragility of school success. The chapter then considers forms of success that lie beyond the schoolyard, noting those values that render children so precious. The book's conclusion ends the work with a concise review of the dialectic of pedagogy and political ideology in Madagascar and beyond.

CHAPTER I

Youth and the Colonized Mind

Vive Madagascar "Tsy Mandohalika"

["Long Live Madagascar—'We shall not go down on our knees'"].

DIDIER RATSIRAKA, *Ny Boky Mena*

The political consciousness of youth is a complex affair. One of the guiding premises of this study is that students' understandings of their collective destiny hinge on unified interpretations of the past and their own significance in shaping their nation's political trajectory. The purpose of this chapter, then, is to explore the historical dimensions of this process. It thus begins with a detailed review of recent political developments in Madagascar's postindependence period, where students constitute a vanguard whose demands ultimately have transformed the state not once, but twice since the 1970s. Central to this review is a discussion of the key ideological assumptions of Madagascar's First and Second republics. Of special significance here are Malagasy understandings of a neocolonial and capitalist President Tsiranana versus an isolationist and socialist President Ratsiraka. As we shall see, the rhetoric and practice of Ratsiraka's malagasization played a decisive role in politicizing Madagascar's coastal youth.

Although students' political visions are most certainly anchored in recent island politics, they cannot be fully deciphered without a careful analysis of this nation's troubled pedagogical history either. Education in Madagascar is deeply rooted in missionary activities that predate the French conquest in 1895–96. Of great significance here is that highland and coastal experiences diverged in response to competing Protestant versus Catholic forces. Once French colonial hegemony was asserted, this was then paired with highland structures. Together, these were imposed on other regions, especially in pedagogical spheres. The assertion of highland and essentially Merina culture as a national one has become only further entrenched in the postindependence period: ironically, although President Ratsiraka, who was originally from the coast, envisioned malagasization as a means to unify Madagascar, coastal inhabitants viewed the newly created national language of official Malagasy as the linguistic arm of highland-based power. Thus, whereas malagasization generated a powerful rhetoric through which to critique colonial violence, it failed to unify the nation because of its own troubled origins. In essence, then, a pedagogical dilemma that plagues Madagascar is Merina linguistic hegemony. Such failures inevitably shape who is part of this nation's sacrificed generation.

The discussion then turns to an analysis of the important ideological concepts of sacrifice, nation, and homeland. These highly nuanced terms are entangled in competing French, highland, and coastal understandings of each, rendering their decipherment highly problematic. As Fanon and other revolutionary theorists have argued, the colonial encounter is deeply troubled and affects the psyches of colonized and colonizer alike. In Madagascar, this complex relationship is not simply demonstrated by a review of pedagogical history but emerges as well in students' critiques of the concept of the "colonized mind" *(mentalité colonisée)*. In such contexts, localized readings of the past and independence converge. A particularly compelling example of this relationship arises in the Independence Day celebrations in Ambanja, performative events that draw simultaneously from Merina, French, and coastal understandings of community and nationhood. The chapter concludes with students' candid discussions of homeland, where their use of the indigenous term *tanindrazaña,* or "ancestral land," underscores the struggles they face in shaping their own unique vision of the nation.

REVOLUTION AND NATIONAL TRANSFORMATIONS

The year 1972 saw the full-scale, public emergence of Madagascar's youth as a revolutionary force in the postindependence period. The nation had been independent for over a decade, long enough for the oldest of its children to witness—and comprehend—the contradictions that characterized its leaders' political ideals versus life's realities in the wake of colonialism. As they neared the end of their lycée years, many school youth recognized the hypocrisies of education, its flaws rendering them victims of an insidious colonial *mentalité*. Schooled to accept a particular foreign vision of the world without question, they were forced to swallow a rhetoric that stressed the pride one should feel in being Malagasy, when simultaneously one's own language, history, and a staggering array of cultural institutions were denigrated as inferior to things French. Language was an especially potent symbol of this denigration, for the Malagasy tongue was deemed inadequate by the French for indigenous educational needs. Furthermore, from a colonial perspective, the Malagasy as a people were assumed to be ill equipped to fill upper-level positions of power even within their own nation, so that expatriates continued to occupy the most coveted positions in educational, financial, political, and military spheres. This section offers a review of such developments, focusing more specifically on Madagascar's political history following independence, foregrounding the relevance of youth within that history.

TABLE I An Abbreviated Political Timeline

July 14, 1789		Storming of the Bastille in Paris.
1787–1810		Reign of the Merina ruler Andrianampoinimerina, who, assisted by European entrepreneurs, reorganizes the army and considerably expands the kingdom of Imerina.
1810–28		Reign of the Merina ruler Radama I (son of Andrianampoinimerina), who continues his father's campaign to conquer the entire island.
1818		Members of the London Missionary Society (LMS) arrive on the east coast of Madagascar; in 1820 the LMS establishes itself in Antananarivo, capital of Imerina.
1820	NW	Andriantompoeniarivo, founding ruler of the Bemazava-Sakalava dynasty, arrives in the Sambirano Valley.
1840–41	NW	In July 1840, Queen Tsiomeko, the ruler of the Bemihisatra-Sakalava, abandons her rights to territory that includes the two offshore islands Nosy Be and Nosy Komba, as well as part of the neighboring mainland. Unable to secure assistance against the Merina from the sultan of Zanzibar, she seeks help from the French. By 1841, her territory (located near the Sambirano) becomes an official protectorate of France.
1860	NW	Catholic missionaries establish a settlement on the small offshore island of Nosy Faly, sacred territory to the Sakalava and their Antankaraña neighbors to the north.
1828–61		Reign of the isolationist Merina Queen Ranavalona I (the widow of Radama I). Missionaries and other Europeans are expelled from Imerina.
1861–63		Reign of the Merina King Radama II (Prince Rakoto, son of Ranavalona I). British and French missionaries are once again welcomed into the Merina kingdom. His reign comes to an abrupt halt when he is strangled by an adversary.
1868–83		Reign of the Merina Queen Ranavalona II (Princess Ramoma), the first Merina ruler to convert to Christianity. Protestantism is proclaimed the official state religion.
1895–96	NW	Under General Duchesne, the French seize Antananarivo. French troops spread throughout the island as part of a colonial pacification strategy under General Gallieni, reaching the Sambirano in 1895. In 1896. Madagascar is officially declared a colony of France.
1885–96		Reign of the Merina Queen Ranavalona II. Following the conquest of the island, the French abolish the monarchy and exile her. She dies in Algiers in 1917.

Continued on next page

TABLE I *(continued)*

1912		The VVS (Vy Vato Sakelika, or "Iron Stone Network") is created by nationalist medical students in Antananarivo.
1921	NW	First Catholic baptism performed in the Sambirano.
1936	NW	Catholic cathedral completed in Ambanja.
September 28, 1958		Madagascar becomes a self-governing republic within the French Community.
June 26, 1960		Independence is declared.
1960–72		First Republic of President Philibert Tsiranana.
May 14, 1972		"The May Revolution." Protesters march on the presidential palace in the capital of Antananarivo, and President Tsiranana is forced to resign only four months after being reelected, and two weeks after his inauguration.
May 1972– June 1975		Interim period of military rule.
May 1972– February 1975		General Gabriel Ramanantsoa serves as president; he resigns on February 5, 1975.
February 11, 1975		Colonel Richard Ratsimandrava is assassinated after serving as president for less than a week. Martial law is declared, and the country is governed by an eight-man military directorate under General Andriamahazo.
June 15, 1975		End of the "Trial of the Century," aimed at identifying those responsible for the assassination of Ratsimandrava. The directorate dissolves itself, and Didier Ratsiraka is declared president.
1975–91		Second Republic under Didier Ratsiraka; also referred to as the period of the socialist revolution.
1991–93		Transitional period. Didier Ratsiraka is voted out of office in 1993.
1993–96		Zafy Albert wins the presidential election against Ratsiraka in February 1993 and is instated as president of the Third Republic shortly thereafter.
late 1996		Zafy Albert is successfully impeached and removed from office.
1997–present		Didier Ratsiraka is reelected president. He is sworn in on February 9, 1997, marking the beginning of the Fourth Republic.

NOTE: NW designates an event relevant to the northwest.

The Awakening of the Consciousness of Youth

In May 1972, students at the medical school at Befelatanana in Antananarivo took to the streets, and they were soon joined by workers, peasants, and other students much younger than they. This was not the first time the nation's youth had played a crucial role in a nationalist movement; the activism of university students and journalists in particular is deeply entrenched in Madagascar's history and has become emblematic of uprisings and resistance. As early as 1912, the Vy Vato Sakelika ("Iron Stone Network"), or VVS, was formed by students at the medical school at Befelatanana in Antananarivo, and among its members were numerous future nationalists. As we shall see in chapter 5, one of its celebrated leaders was the poet Ny Avana Ramanantoanina, and the tenor of his sacrifice was communicated poignantly through poetry now favored by Ambanja's literate youth. More immediate inspiration for the May Revolution of 1972 came from the 1968 student uprising in France; the Civil Rights Movement in the United States; the writings of Maoist intellectuals; and a heightened awareness of the needs of myriad constituencies within their own nation, including merchants, small-scale planters, and a landless urban underclass. Demands for educational reforms lay at the heart of the May Revolution. Students insisted on dismantling a system that favored a small, educated elite, where the poor faced barriers that included a rigid national examination system, expensive private schooling, and limited places at the lycée and university levels. Access to significant positions of power was further limited by a heavy reliance on expatriate "technical assistants," particularly French-born educators, administrators, and military personnel. So important were the 60,000 or so who remained in Madagascar that President Tsiranana referred to them as the nation's "Nineteenth Tribe" (Paillard 1979, 306). French expatriates filled over half of all senior positions, and approximately 4,000 foreign paratroopers alone were employed for national defense purposes (Covell 1987, 36–38).[1]

Colonial education bore much of the responsibility for promoting a strong sense of moral[2] inferiority among Malagasy and, paired with it, dependence on the former colonizer, for as one advanced through the grades, Malagasy educators were increasingly underrepresented, a trend that had become firmly entrenched during the colonial era. Although the French trained many accomplished Malagasy as schoolteachers, the majority remained confined to primary and middle schools. Furthermore, they were far better represented in coastal and rural settings, a trend that perpetuated—albeit insidiously—an assumed hierarchy where race, region of origin, and nationality determined social worth and were marked by an array of specialized terms that persist today. Thus, white (FR: *blanc,* HP: *fotsy*) was valued over black (FR: *noir,* HP: *mainty*); highland (Merina, and, to a lesser extent, Betsileo)[3] over coastal (FR: *côtier*); and French *(vazaha)* over Malagasy. In essence, the French perceived the Malagasy intellect to be limited and thus well suited to training young children. Advanced knowledge, however, was best imparted by those who were expatriate, French, and white. This trend was particularly pronounced at the university level and persisted throughout the first decade following independence. As Maureen Covell explains,

> The university had a further significance as an essential component in the perpetu-ation of the neocolonial basis of the Tsiranana regime and as a place where French domination of the regime was demonstrated and even exaggerated. Although 80 per cent of the 1,000 students were Malagasy, 200 of 250 professors were French. The au-thoritarian style of professor-student relationship against which French students had revolted in 1968 had survived in Madagascar. When the professor was French and the student Malagasy the relationship reproduced the colonial era; when the professor was Malagasy the relationship underlined the point that only Malagasies who became like the French could command other Malagasies. Degrees given by the university were French degrees and the research and teaching of the university reproduced that of a French establishment . . . the point was clear: it was through learning about France, not Madagascar, that one had to pass to aspire to even the subordinate posi-tion in the system for which Malagasies were destined. (Covell 1987, 37)

In pedagogical terms, it was not simply at the upper educational level that Mala-gasy suffered; many were denied the most basic right to elementary schooling. The needs of the nation's underclass became increasingly obvious, especially in An-tananarivo, whose population had doubled in size within a decade of indepen-dence, as the rural poor, denied access to arable land, flooded into the city.[4] Many were of slave (HP: *andevo*) origins and thus were the poorest of the poor. Over 60 percent of those in the city's slums were under twenty-five years of age, representing a neglected generation of children who were increasingly denied access to over-enrolled state schools and prohibitively expensive private establishments (Covell 1987, 38–39).[5]

A newborn awareness of these social conditions and their historical origins fur-ther fueled an already deep-seated hatred of French dominance, especially among Madagascar's youth. The larger political events that made a student revolution pos-sible in the early 1970s are complex, rendering a full-scale account beyond the scope of this discussion (but see Althabe 1972, 1980; Bouillon 1973; Covell 1987; Raha-jarizafy 1973; Rajoelina 1988). Of concern here is the manner in which such events shaped a newly awakened political consciousness among youth in this African na-tion and the significance of education as a strong focus of contention. Thus, a num-ber of events are worth noting (what follows is a highly cursory review of those significant to this particular discussion).

By 1970, Tsiranana had served as president for a decade, and the country was in turmoil. The year before, a series of cyclones had hit the island, with the econ-omy already suffering from the 1967 closure of the Suez Canal. In February 1970, Tsiranana had a stroke while attending a conference in Yaoundé, Cameroon, and was then hospitalized in Paris, where he remained for seven months. His absence enabled his adversaries to reposition themselves politically. In March 1971, the coun-try witnessed a series of strikes involving secondary school and university students.

In April, peasants in the arid and anthrax-stricken south seized control of administrative offices and state police posts *(gendarmeries)* in regional villages and towns. Tsiranana's government responded with repressive measures that resulted in as many as 1,000 dead, 1,500 arrests, and over 500 deportations to the offshore island of Nosy Lava (which houses a prison). The rival MONIMA[6] party was implicated in this and other actions, and its leader was likewise arrested and deported (Covell 1987, 43–45; Paillard 1979, 322 ff.).

These and other related events culminated in the May Revolution of 1972. Its most striking characteristics include, first, the manner in which it was a revolution of youth, and, second, how quickly members of the underclass also became actively involved. The revolution is often said to have begun when medical students went on strike in January; in March, they were joined by much younger students from the city's state-run middle schools *(collèges)* along with those from numerous private schools; and, then, in April, by lycée students. Other groups soon followed, most notably the urban poor and labor unions. On May 14, 1972, which is now honored as the official Day of the Revolution, approximately 100,000 people marched to the presidential palace to demand the ouster of Tsiranana, who only four months before had been reelected by a supposed 99.7 percent of voters. Tsiranana's inauguration occurred on May 1; less than two weeks later, he witnessed the end of what is now referred to as his First Republic. The popular revolution that toppled Tsiranana's regime was followed almost immediately by a military coup on May 17 (Covell 1987, 45, 47–48; Paillard 1979, 327 ff.).

The period from May 1972 to June 1975 was one of great turmoil, characterized by continued economic failure, accusations of corruption, rumors of attempted coups, and ever-shifting alliances. Tsiranana's immediate successor was General Gabriel Ramanantsoa, who later resigned his post on February 5, 1975. Today, this is often regarded by historians of Madagascar as a lengthy interim period. Covell, for example, refers to the years between the First and Second republics as "the Ramanantsoa interval" (1987, 51), whereas Yvan-Georges Paillard offers a far blunter reading, stating that during the first two years of military rule, "Madagascar seemed to be leaderless" (1979, 338). Ramanantsoa named Colonel Richard Ratsimandrava as his successor, but the latter was promptly assassinated only a few days later, on February 11. The following morning, an eight-man military directorate was formed under General Andriamahazo, who declared martial law. As Covell explains, the group's mission was "to hold the ring while factions and personalities struggled for power. Maintaining this façade of collective rule was simplified by the fact that public attention was focused on the trial of Ratsimandrava's accused assassins, [referred to as] the 'trial of the century' with 297 defendants" (Covell 1987, 57). Among the more powerful voices to emerge as part of the nation's new military vanguard was Didier Ratsiraka, a junior naval officer who had served as Ramanantsoa's foreign minister. With the close of the trial on June 15, the military directorate officially pronounced Ratsiraka president and then dissolved itself. Thus began sixteen solid years of Ratsiraka's socialist revolution, or Second

Republic, when the Malagasy Republic (FR: République malgache) assumed its new name, the Democratic Republic of Madagascar (OM: Repoblika Demokratika Malagasy).[7]

Ratsiraka's Madagascar

Ny Boky Mena ("The Red Book") (Ratsiraka 1975) is Ratsiraka's revolutionary charter, a text that assembles a series of radio broadcasts he made in August 1975 as part of a campaign that culminated in his being elected president for an initial seven-year term (Covell 1987, 59; Paillard 1979, 343, 244). In it, Ratsiraka envisioned a newly emergent and truly independent nation, built upon premises inspired by Mao and other socialist visionaries. Ratsiraka's early public support was overwhelming. According to Covell, "of those eligible to vote, 92.6 per cent did and 94.7 per cent of those voted 'yes' for Ratsiraka" (Covell 1987, 59; cf. Rajoelina 1988, 57 ff.). Ratsiraka took the oath of office in January 1976 and moved into the palace formerly occupied by the French embassy, establishing himself as the secretary-general of a single national party, the Antokin'ny Revolisiona Malagasy, or AREMA (FR: Avant-Garde de la Révolution Malgache, or "Vanguard of the Malagasy Revolution").[8] As Paillard wrote in 1979, "Although only a prophet could predict the Second Malagasy Republic's future it is clear that the pace of history in Madagascar had accelerated within the last four or five years; that in just a few months' time decolonization had progressed more than during the dozen preceding years" (1979, 346). Important changes included a move toward economic independence through state capitalism, whereby large-scale foreign-owned concerns were nationalized; the elimination of foreign technical (generally French) assistance in schooling, the military, and other arenas; the breaking of ties with (and economic dependence on) South Africa; and the promotion of a strong nationalist ideology, referred to as malagasization (see Paillard 1979).

My own experience of Ratsiraka's Second Republic is limited primarily to the period from late December 1986 to early January 1988, when I first conducted anthropological field research in Madagascar.[9] Later, in 1993, 1994, and 1995, I witnessed localized responses to Ratsiraka's failure during what was then dubbed the transitional period, and, then, the first year of the Third Republic under the newly elected President Zafy Albert.[10] Throughout 1987, I was keenly aware of the silencing of political dissent and the omnipresence of AREMA: it was the party of and for everything, serving as the official and only representative, for example, of labor unions, state employees, and even school sports teams. In Ambanja, no one spoke openly of politics and, in particular, of Ratsiraka's political rivals. Such matters came up rarely and only in private, hushed conversations at home at night, when doors and windows were shut tight. Everyone publicly proclaimed their allegiance to Ratsiraka—to do otherwise put one's safety in serious jeopardy. I was among the few social scientists allowed into Madagascar at this time, and I was the target of intense scrutiny, my work documented on a weekly basis for the national police by one of my local informants. On several occasions, veiled warnings were issued to me by other academics, all of whom told a seemingly apocryphal tale of an anthropologist who, a decade before, had been "eaten by fish" (the corpse having been found abandoned in an unspecified body of water). Wary of the danger associated with dissent, I made it a point never to engage in political discussions with friends or informants for fear of the harm that might befall them—and me. My husband, nevertheless, was a witness to (and felt compelled to end) a police interrogation of a petty thief, an event that confirmed our own shared sense that the potential for political violence meted out by the state lay close to the surface of daily life. Like all Malagasy, I was constantly aware of Ratsiraka's presence, as he looked down upon us from his framed portrait in banks, post offices, schoolrooms, and government foyers, dressed, ironically, in garb reminiscent of a French commander (a theme to which I shall return below). Corruption (HP: *riso-riso*, lit. "zig-zag") was pervasive, especially in the form of bribery and black market trade, since illicit commerce was often essential to survival in a nation experiencing intense economic isolation from much of the rest of the world.[11] The island's middle class and elite bemoaned their inability to travel abroad for coveted goods and services, as had been possible (and affordable) under Tsiranana; and everyone, regardless of status or origin, suffered the consequences of shortages of such basic items as laundry soap, kerosene, and textiles. In Ambanja, nearly all construction had come to a halt, for there were no tools, no nails, no cement or paint to be found in any shops in the province. Goods that were available were usually of inferior quality, manufactured in nationalized factories.

During Zafy's brief three-year presidency, I found that, suddenly, even some of Zafy's strongest supporters would speak of Ratsiraka's initial popularity with great nostalgia, for Ratsiraka's charisma is legendary. As one friend, in her thirties and raising children of her own, explained to me one afternoon in 1995:

> Look, I know that things changed drastically as the years went by. Ratsiraka promised many things that never materialized. His greed for power and wealth got the best of him—look at him now, hiding out in a mansion in Ivato [a suburb near the Antananarivo airport], too afraid to move, knowing that someone might pop him for what he did to his own people! Now he's an old, blind, paranoid man. But you know, when he first emerged as a political presence, he was so moving, he had such a vision! He would talk about the power the French held over us as colonized people, and the need for a *true* kind of freedom—that we were living in a state of neocolonial oppression. And his vision for the schools, it was remarkable, really. Official Malagasy [i.e., the language] may have been a failure, but it didn't have to be—it wasn't the idea that failed, but the manner in which it was applied. It could have worked. We really believed in Ratsiraka. We all had to read the *Boky Mena*. My friends and I, we would stay up late at night, talking about Ratsiraka's ideas. It was truly an exciting time.

"[I]ndependence, and more precisely political independence, does not simply happen ipso facto. It requires the end of colonialism and the advent of a more just society," the *Boky Mena* proclaimed.[12] From Ratsiraka's perspective, the nation could not experience its true independence until it had freed itself from the intellectual, emotional,[13] political, and economic shackles of foreign dominance. In her historical overview of the First Republic, Covell exposes the complacency characteristic of the Tsiranana era:

> Supporters of [Tsiranana's] . . . First Republic considered it a perfect example of successful decolonization, in that [the transition was calm and without incident] . . . the First Republic is . . . a classic example of a neo-colonial regime in which an elite, selected and prepared by the departing colonial power, moves into government positions, exchanging its protection of the interests of the former colonial power for that power's protection of its own position.[14]

In contrast, for Ratsiraka, the true independence of the nation (versus the "formal" independence of 1960) corresponded with the founding of his own regime on June 16, 1975 (Ratsiraka 1975, 14). "[T]he Revolution is a daily struggle," he stressed,[15] a battle that had to be fought consistently at all levels of society if freedom were to endure. In 1987, during my first period of field research, the practical application of this rhetoric was evident in nearly every sphere of life: on an island long regarded as a hardship post, French and U.S. embassy staffs were now skeletal, and USAID presence was hardly more than a shadow. If one sensed any foreign presence at all, it was that of the Eastern Bloc, and especially in the context of infrastructural renovations. Chinese and North Koreans were heavily involved, for example, in the rehabilitation of roads and ports (cf. Rajoelina 1988, 59), and students who received foreign scholarships typically went to universities in Moscow or Czechoslovakia. In many homes, one could also find books by Libya's Muammar al-Qaddafi, a close colleague and friend of Ratsiraka, and so French renditions of Qaddafi's writings were distributed freely to state employees and students. Throughout the island, European expatriates were scarce, and typically belonged to small settlements of missionaries, who funded and staffed the island's better rural hospitals and private schools. I myself was often assumed to be a Catholic sister, because in Ambanja the only Europeans were the few French, Italian, and German priests, nuns, and doctors who worked at the imposing mission complex.

Ratsiraka's *Boky Mena* generated a language that became pervasive throughout the Second Republic, shaping the content and tone of political discourse and school curricula for the next fifteen years. It is also, significantly, the language employed by members of the sacrificed generation, and the following passage is exemplary:

> Specifically, this requires a revolution of minds *[mentalités]*, a coherence between the doctrine and reality, between speech and action, between governmental action and that of the people. In short, all the nation's driving forces must be unified and focused on the same goals—to create a new Malagasy people, and to build a better society under the direction of the laboring urban and rural masses. We know that the struggle will be difficult, and will require that many sacrifices be made. We understand that the path will be littered with obstacles. There is no question that it will be necessary to come up against and conquer each of these in turn and one by one. . . . We have

only one choice: we must fight to exist, or we will disappear. We have chosen an independent existence, with liberty, dignity, justice, and peace—whatever the cost to
us may be....

    ... The national Malagasy revolution is not the end result of a parthenogenesis;
it has its roots in the Malagasy soul, it is objectively determined both by its history of
colonial domination and by its strategic geographic position.[16]

Ratsiraka sought above all to revolutionize and transform the Malagasy mind, or
mentality (FR: *mentalité*), where collective action involving the integration of political praxis into people's daily lives could bring about significant change. From this
would spring a new sense of what it meant to be Malagasy. Such a transformation
was possible, however, only through great collective sacrifice (a theme I address in
greater detail below). Within this context, it was the labor of the rural, landed peasant that was especially valorized, these particular citizens being recognized as the
backbone of a primarily agricultural nation, where approximately 80 percent were
employed in the agricultural sector, providing approximately 40 percent of the nation's domestic product (World Bank 1980, 1, based on data assembled in 1978; see
also Razafimpahanana 1972, 11). An important tenet of this revolution was that
only with true independence and liberty are justice and dignity possible. And, finally
(contrary to a deep-seated racism espoused by colonial French), it was affirmed that
foreign dominance over the Malagasy did not spring from an inherent weakness
of the Malagasy spirit (FR: *l'âme*) but was, rather, the product of a set of relations
rooted in the historical conditions of the colonial encounter. Madagascar had been
conquered and held onto by the French because it was of global strategic (and, as
Ratsiraka argued consistently elsewhere, economic) value: it not only lies at the intersection of important trade routes but commands one of the naval approaches
to the Gulf of Aden and, beyond it, the Suez Canal.[17]

    Ratsiraka insisted on self-sufficiency as the key to building a cohesive national
identity and collective vision. Important reformist policies included the rejection of
old colonial alliances in favor of those with socialist nations (an approach that had
also characterized Ratsiraka's work as Ramanantsoa's foreign minister); the (re)vi-
talization of the nation's infrastructure through construction projects; and a more
general desire to transform society from its assorted and often contentious geographically, ethnically, and class-based factions, into a united national front of Malagasy. Social and economic isolation was put forth as a key strategy, since only when
secure from the grip of stronger world powers could Madagascar develop into a
truly viable independent nation. Ratsiraka envisioned a country well equipped to
sustain itself through the twentieth century and beyond, freed of the intellectual,
economic, and political fetters that had, up to this point, weighed so heavily upon
Malagasy as colonized peoples.

    It was not simply Ratsiraka's ideas that inspired Malagasy to follow him but also
the power of his language in a nation whose people as a whole value political oratory (OM: *kabary*). The essence of the revolution was communicated through com-

pelling rhetorical phrases; the slogan "We shall not go down on our knees," for example, offered a striking allusion to the cultural values that opposed self and other in pan-Malagasy fashion. This phrase referred both to the symbolic subordination of the colonized and, quite literally, to the action of kneeling. Throughout the island's many indigenous communities, the human head is considered sacred, and its placement in social contexts is evidence of rank. One lowers oneself before others in humble respect and, ultimately, subjugation: youth before their elders, commoners before royalty, and the living before their ancestors (when the latter speak through spirit mediums). *Under* the French, however, this action was seen as a forced, and thus involuntary, form of public humiliation.

The power of Ratsiraka's slogan is rendered all the more obvious in a photo reproduced in a frequently distributed copy of the *Boky Mena* (Ratsiraka 1975, 15), where three Malagasy men can be seen kneeling on an unprotected patch of earth (fig. 1). To the right stand four armed soldiers (three upon a plank, as if to avoid muddy ground). These two small groups are situated before a small, shaded grandstand, on which five European men and a woman stand and sit. Nearby stand three Malagasy men who hold their hats and wear suit jackets (two of them wear men's waist wraps). The Europeans address an unseen audience through two microphones. At the very back of the platform are five turbaned soldiers, their national origin unclear, although one appears to be European. Such graphic images, invoked by powerful rhetorical references, kindled political awareness of oppression and generated a language for addressing it. This convergence of memories and associated imagery took their firmest hold in the educational sphere through malagasization. This cornerstone of Second Republic reforms instilled a new political and historical consciousness into the nation's youth. This stands, however, in stark contrast to the previous history of pedagogy on the island, to which I now turn.

LINGUISTIC HEGEMONY
Empowerment through Language

The French term *malgachisation* has its roots in the colonial period, when it was used to describe the transition from colonial to indigenous rule under Tsiranana in the late 1950s (Covell 1987, 30–31). The variant *malagasization* was later adopted as an important slogan of Ratsiraka's indigenous socialist revolution.[18] As Covell explains, its focus shifted over time and expanded:

> [It] had originally been a demand for an education in the national language reflecting the national culture, but in the course of the [1972] uprising its meaning widened to include the ouster of the French technical assistants, and then the real departure of the French and the regime they had installed: a second independence and the vindication of the sacrifices of the martyrs of 1947. As the slogan acquired new meanings, new groups joined the movement: urban workers, middle-class elements and finally the armed forces [came together to form the May Revolution]. (Covell 1987, 45–46)

Figure 1. Malagasy subjects kneeling before the French. From Ratsiraka 1975, 15.

Subsequently, throughout Ratsiraka's Second Republic, this expression gained a more global meaning that became significant in many arenas, affecting myriad aspects of everyday life. No sphere, however, was as strongly affected as education. Among the first and most profound reforms involved the creation of a national language, Malagasy iombonana (*iombonana* means "joint effort"), or official Malagasy, which was designed to undermine the hegemony of French while simultaneously acknowledging the significance of the island's many subethnic categories of Malagasy speakers (FR: *races, ethnies;* OM: *karazana*). Official Malagasy defined not only the legitimate language of political discourse; it was also central to the revitalization of school curricula at all levels. By late 1975, Madagascar's children had experienced major transformations in their schools: suddenly history, geography, literature, philosophy and, at times, even the sciences,[19] were being taught in this new language. More important, ideologically, school lessons were transformed almost overnight to emphasize the strength of Malagasy character and the centrality of the island's history for understanding one's position both within the nation and beyond. As Mme. Vezo, a thirty-six-year-old lycée teacher, explained:

> You see, when I went to school [under Tsiranana] it was strange—for us it was a sort of sickness, really, when I think back on [how we were taught]. I'm older and now I understand these things better. Think of it: when we studied history our lessons al-

ways started with the statement "Our Ancestors the Gauls." Why should I care about the Gauls?! I've never been—nor will I ever be able to go—to France, and I certainly wasn't destined to be French. As a child I would find myself looking at these books and being puzzled—why the Gauls? I have my own *razana* [ancestors]. But I kept my mouth shut. I studied, I got high marks. Now I myself am a history [and geography] teacher. What pleasure it gave me when I first started teaching [in the Second Republic], and I, as a Malagasy, could begin my own lesson, "Our Ancestors the Vazimba. . . . "[20] It gave me such pleasure. And I was good at official Malagasy, too, from the start. In fact, I teach it now at the high school level. Others found it difficult, but I love our language, and I really enjoy being able to pass it on to our children.

In contrast, other teachers found the transition devastating. So explained Mr. Victor, who has taught both middle school and lycée students:

> *Mr. Victor:* The transition to official Malagasy? It was terrible. Truly terrible. I can say this to you now because we are reverting back to French [under President Zafy]. The experiment failed. I was terrified as a teacher—I spent several years studying at the university, and I did all right, you know. I felt I was prepared to assume my first post. And then there I was, teaching in a coastal town, with no schoolbooks—I only had my class notes in French, and I was told I could only speak in official Malagasy. But I had never really studied it.
>
> *LS:* What did you [and others like you] do?
>
> *Mr. Victor:* We did the best we could. I knew the Merina dialect pretty well, because I had lived in Antananarivo while attending university. And so I spoke that in the classroom—it's pretty close, you know, to official Malagasy.
>
> *LS:* How did the students react?
>
> *Mr. Victor:* They of course hated it. It was the same as it is here. If you speak Merina, or even official Malagasy, the students will refuse to speak to you. They might say to your face, or more likely, behind your back, "That *ramsay* [teacher], he's just a *borzany*" [highly derogatory term for Merina]. But I'm not, you know! My parents are Betsimisaraka, and I grew up on the east coast. So over the years I've learned to speak a combination of languages in the classroom: I first cover the subject matter in a combination of French and official Malagasy, and then I go over the lesson again, this time in [the local] Sakalava [dialect], which I speak with ease now. I know of no other way to make sure my students understand their lessons. And even then it may not get through to them, because they are unsure of what language to use when they take notes in class.

These competing accounts from Mme. Vezo and Mr. Victor exemplify the range of experiences of teachers trained at the end of Tsiranana's First Republic. Mme. Vezo represents a minority of eager teachers, since she not only excelled in her studies but adapted quickly to the language shift. In fact, when she later learned of Mr. Victor's trials, she responded as follows: "What? Oh my, no, what he says isn't altogether true. We were in school together and, you know, we all had to study Malagasy as part of the required university curriculum at that time. Perhaps it wasn't exactly the same as what we use now, but if he can't speak official Malagasy, well, then, he should have worked harder at his studies!" The struggle described by Mr. Victor nevertheless reflects the extreme difficulties encountered by the majority of teachers posted to unfamiliar coastal communities to fend for themselves without preparation or guidance. After all, although Mme. Vezo teaches history and geography in official Malagasy, she is also responsible for teaching it as a foreign language in a separate class period. Furthermore, since she is of Vezo descent and thus from the distant southwest, she is perceived by her students as being Sakalava (although other Vezo may not see her as such; see Astuti 1995). The problems Mr. Victor encounters in the classroom are far more typical: the majority of teachers I have known since 1987 have always lamented the resistance and even surprising levels of insubordination they encounter among students who typically refuse to engage in any dialogue that requires official Malagasy. Many instructors recount firsthand experiences from the early Ratsiraka years when tensions were especially pronounced. Several found themselves caught in the midst of schoolroom epidemics of spirit possession whose timing coincided with the first national examinations to be issued in official Malagasy rather than French, and the most direct targets of this anger were their instructors (Sharp 1990).

Faith and the Politics of Language

The development of official Malagasy has its own peculiar history, rooted in the larger history of religious education on the island. Although French, British, Portuguese, and Dutch attempts (and failures) to colonize and missionize the island date back several centuries,[21] the arrival of the London Missionary Society (LMS) in 1820 in the central highland kingdom of Imerina is most relevant to tracing the development of Western-derived education. As P. M. Mutibwa explains, the willingness of the Merina to embrace British Protestantism (especially as opposed to French Catholicism) grew out of preexisting relationships with British technicians, whose skills as engineers and military men the Merina greatly admired (Mutibwa 1974, 165–66). The first highland LMS school was established during the reign of King Radama I (r. 1810–28) in late 1820 and targeted royal and then noble Merina children. In the following year, nine youths returned from England, where, as part of a treaty agreement, they had been sent to be schooled. Eyewitnesses registered shock during the public reading of a letter from Radama I to the LMS on this occasion, an event that did much to emphasize the power of the written word.[22] Although initially the LMS encountered much resistance to and fear of education among the Merina, by September 1824, the missionaries could boast of twenty-two new schools, where 2,000 children were enrolled, all within a radius of thirty-two kilometers of Antananarivo. Schooling was primarily religious, concentrating on Bible translation, catechism, and the composition of Malagasy hymns (weekend sermons were held in English, French, and Malagasy). By 1826, much of the New Testament had been translated, as had a considerable portion of the Old. Language was nonetheless a source of great contention: LMS missionaries struggled to master French, a language already spoken by Merina elites as a result of earlier contact with French traders and other professionals. The greatest ideological battles, however, centered on the alphabet itself, an issue that created factions within the LMS community. Even as English speakers, they could not agree on a phonetic system, since some insisted on Welsh orthography; and men of French and British descent likewise bickered. Radama I put an end to this by dictating that consonants would follow English pronunciation, the vowels French, a decision that encouraged additional debate within the LMS community back in England (Brown 1978, 152–60; Belrose-Huyghues 1974; Dandouau and Chapus 1952, 183–84; Mutibwa 1974, 21 ff.).

In contrast to the welcome the LMS initially received in Imerina in 1820, the subsequent period marked by the reign of Queen Ranavalona I (r. 1828–61), the widow of and successor to Radama I, grew to be one of anti-European sentiment and isolation. This period is marked by purges of rival factions (the mother of Radama I, among others, was executed), missionaries (who were expelled from the island), and Christian converts (many of whom were thrown from cliffs). Schools remained open, but enrollment declined because of lack of support from the queen (Brown 1978, 167 ff.). In short, Ranavalona I is described by some historians as tyrannical and xenophobic, but in more recent reconstructions, she emerges as an early traditionalist and nationalist who refused to tolerate foreign occupation of her kingdom.[23] The expulsion of LMS and other missionaries marked the end of British influence as a primary foreign force on the island. A handful of French traders (some were Catholic priests from Nosy Be in disguise) won the favor of the queen and, secretly, of her son (Heseltine 1971, 113–15). This paved the way, albeit very slowly, for French occupation of the highlands later in the century.

Nevertheless, Catholic attempts to gain a firm hold in Imerina were mostly unsuccessful. When Radama II (r. 1861–63) succeeded his mother on the throne, Catholic missionaries from Nosy Be were among the first to arrive in the Merina kingdom to congratulate him (La Vaissière 1884, 1: 230–40). They remained, however, far less influential than Protestants throughout much of the second half of the nineteenth century, for the latter had already won converts among royals and elites, a hold that survived even through the isolationist period of Queen Ranavalona I. Protestantism became even more firmly entrenched in the highlands when Queen Ranavalona II (r. 1868–83) declared it the state religion of Imerina (and thus of the island) in 1869. The French read this as a solid rejection of their own religious influence (Heseltine 1971, 11; Mutibwa 1974, 54–57, 164–80). As a result, French Catholic activity became more firmly rooted among more peripheral people of slave descent (HP: *andevo*) in Imerina (cf. Bloch 1994), in the southern highlands among the Betsileo, and along the coast. As Covell explains, throughout the colonial period the Catholic Church's position remained ambivalent. Most colonial administrators favored a secular orientation and were suspicious of religious activities, even though Catholic clerics were generally French (Covell 1995, 53–54).

Mission groups have continued to battle with one another for territory and souls, and today the divisions outlined above remain firmly entrenched throughout much of the island, delineated along geographic, ethnic, and even class or former caste lines. Official agreements have been drawn up repeatedly under a series of Merina, French, and Malagasy administrations that designate religious boundaries (see Rabenoro 1986, 100–101). Such territorial and ecumenical wars have also shaped the construction of Malagasy as a written and spoken language and, in turn, the form education has assumed. Thus, the history of official Malagasy must be traced alongside a religious and, ultimately, a colonial one and set against highland and coastal perceptions. An early trend that continues to be relevant today is that Catholics and Protestants rely on different translations of the Bible (cf. Rafael 1992). Today in the north, Catholic priests and nuns are usually of Sakalava origin or, if they are European, they speak Sakalava fluently. The majority of Protestant ministers, on the other hand, are from the highlands and thus they remind their congregations of their origins linguistically each time they publicly address a group. Given that Merina territory has remained a stronghold of Protestant activity, official Malagasy's bureaucratic origins must be understood as being rooted in early LMS activities, efforts that then launched the subsequent Merinization of a pan-Malagasy lingua franca. Such Merina hegemony was even further secured by the fact that by the 1870s, the LMS and Quakers were responsible for training a literate Merina elite, who sat poised to assume civil service positions (Gow 1979, 136–39).

Thus, education in Madagascar is framed by this history of Christianity's expansion, where the most pronounced rift is defined by coastal/highland and Catholic/Protestant divisions. If we turn to the Catholic coast, we find different sets of circumstances dictating the trajectories of language and education than existed in Imerina. Significant to coastal developments are early ecumenical agreements that divided the island into Catholic and Protestant spheres. Whereas the Merina state embraced British Protestantism, by the mid nineteenth century, French Jesuits were well established on the coast, especially in such regions as the northern Sakalava territory of Nosy Be; this offshore island had become an active plantation zone and port for the French by the early nineteenth century and a French protectorate in 1840–41, following an agreement with the young Sakalava[24] Queen Tsiomeko, who feared a Merina invasion, after she had failed to secure arms from Sultan Seyid Said of Zanzibar (Brown 1978, 177; Rajemisa-Raolison 1966, 360; Stratton 1964, 113).[25] By the 1850s, Nosy Be was without question a center of French Catholic activities, with small chapels established throughout this and on smaller offshore islands. Islam, nevertheless, presented a significant barrier to missionization, since the northwest had recently become a stronghold of Islamic activity, affected in part by its commerce with Muslims on the island of Mayotte in the Comoros. Here French Catholics had less success than they did on the island of Sainte Marie off the northeast coast. By 1860, Catholics were negotiating with the northern sovereigns for rights to expand missionizing activities. Soon a small contingent of priests and nuns established a small mission on the sacred royal Sakakava island of Nosy Faly (La Vaissière 1884, 1: 315–17).

The earliest coastal European schools were shaped by a French Catholic trajectory, one that was wholly conscious of British Protestant efforts in Imerina. As Father de la Vaissière's personal account reveals, Catholic education on Nosy Be began in the 1840s and required overcoming several linguistic hurdles. First was the need to develop a dictionary and grammar suitable for use in the north. This inevitably involved integrating the work of Pierre Dalmond (1840, n.d.), who had studied Sakalava, along with efforts to translate existing English texts into French. This lack of materials necessitated sending the first contingent of students from Nosy Be to Bourbon (Mauritius) (La Vaissière 1884, 1: 93 ff.).

These initial efforts—both missionizing and pedagogical—were limited, however, and in the northwest, Catholics were unable to penetrate the interior of the Bemazava-Sakalava kingdom, located in the Sambirano on the main island, until French armies established a military post and began to clear this valley for plantations at the end of the nineteenth century. The first Catholic baptism was performed in Ambanja in 1921, and the stately rose-colored cathedral was completed in 1936. As La Vaissière (1884, 1: 299–302) explains, it was *French* schooling that would provide the key to undermining Islam and winning Catholic converts, particularly by targeting Sakalava children. His prediction eventually proved true: as described in chapter 4, royal Sakalava children were schooled at the mission school and among them was the future King Tsiaraso Victor III (r. 1966–93). As a result, by the mid twentieth century, a strong local alliance was formed between the Catholic Mission and Sakalava royalty of the Sambirano, even though the majority of royalty here, on Nosy Be, and in Antankaraña territory to the north remained Muslim.

Today, the Catholic Mission in Ambanja is a large complex, housing a private academy and seminary, a productive printing shop and, most recently, an impressive hospital, which includes surgical and dentistry services, as well as a leprosy outpatient service. In contrast, when I first arrived in Ambanja in 1987, the relatively new Lutheran Mission was small and unimpressive, the Lutheran Church only having been allowed, by virtue of an islandwide ecumenical agreement, to establish missions in the north a few years before. Although the Lutheran Church has never done well in Ambanja, it flourishes to the north in the provincial capital of Diégo-Suarez, where there is a much larger contingent of laborers from the south and educated highlanders, who together make up the vast majority of Lutherans nationwide.[26] Save for two small, part-time Islamic schools, the Catholic Academy is the only full-time religious educational institution in Ambanja. It is also, without question, the best.

The force of French conquest provided the impetus for subsequent missionary activities, and their religious and educational services have often been shaped by typically French values. Conquest began with the military occupation of Antananarivo by General Duchesne in 1895 (Kent 1962, 58–59); the following year, the island was declared a colony of France. Armies quickly fanned out throughout the island as part of the colonial pacification process. With the establishment of the Merina city of Antananarivo as the new French colonial capital, Merina linguistic hegemony was rendered secure. Throughout the colonial period, one finds documents recorded in French as well as in a standardized form of Merina that is rooted in the LMS translation and alphabetization campaign. Archived petitions to the colonial state signed by coastal Sakalava rulers, for example, are written neither in French nor in Sakalava, but in Merina. Other written evidence similarly makes it clear that both French and Merina were considered appropriate bureaucratic languages even along the northwest coast. A reporter's transcriptions of interrogations might lapse into Merina regardless of whether the parties were speaking Sakalava. Thus, romanized Merina was already the standard.

A Linguistic Revolution

This religious and educational history is key to more recent developments within the independent state, since language remains central to national ideology. In the 1970s, malagasization emerged as an important thrust of Ratsiraka's reforms in the educational sphere, forming the third arm, as it were, of a tripartite system (he identified the other two as democratization and decentralization). In Ratsiraka's words, the malagasization of education was deemed essential to the "the imperatives of the Revolution [which include] building a state that is [both] socialist and truly Malagasy."[27] Ratsiraka recognized the difficulty of this task, stressing that a newly formulated language must recognize Malagasy as the ancestral tongue of all of the island's inhabitants while also acknowledging the effects French had had on the way Malagasy was currently spoken. The process of malagasization was described as a simultaneous construction, reconstruction, and destruction of language, one that required codification, modernization, and enrichment by drawing from all dialects and incorporating useful technical and scientific knowledge of foreign origin. A nation that saw itself as francophone was one that succumbed to paternalism; true bilingualism, however, could be a powerful tool of liberation (Ratsiraka 1975, 85). For the next fifteen years, French would take a back position in state education, yet in fact the majority of the nation's children were fluent neither in official Malagasy nor in French.

Malagasy people of different origins have persistently understood official Malagasy in a variety of ways, because its goals and the realities are so different. As one exasperated civil servant from Antananarivo exclaimed, "[Contrary to what others tell you] it is not Merina at all! Many terms may sound Merina, but they actually bear meanings from elsewhere—a word can have one meaning if you're speaking Merina, but in official Malagasy, it could easily be Antandroy [from the far south]. You have to think carefully about the language. It's very complicated, you know. You really see this in the technical language that was developed for the sciences—it can make your head spin, it's very complex!" In contrast, coastal sentiments occupy another extreme. Mme. Vezo provided this precise explanation: "[I]t's beautiful what they tried to do—the idea was to give equal shares to all Malagasy dialects. What's so sad is that it's really about 80 percent high plateaux and only 20 percent coastal, and the coastal part must represent many more dialects than the highland part." Mme. Vezo's sorrow was shared by the principal of one of Ambanja's larger primary schools, a man who is now in his late fifties and who was trained as a teacher under the French: "I was among those who fought for the idea of official Malagasy. It was a wonderful plan. But look—it resembles Merina far too much. And, so, you know, this is where we failed in our mission. But it didn't have to be so." It is therefore hardly surprising that when the interim government announced its plan to replace French with Malagasy in secondary schools in the early 1970s, there were anti-Merina riots in a number of coastal cities, and many Merina fled to the highlands (Covell 1995, 134–35). In the opinion of many informants, official Malagasy's inability to unite Malagasy linguistically, and, thus, ideologically, was among the revolution's greatest failures.

Schooling and Scarcity

Malagasization also mandated structural reforms designed to fill the needs of rural schoolchildren. The failure of these measures, too, ultimately undermined the initial faith that Malagasy had in Ratsiraka's educational proposals. Although funds were funneled into construction projects from the late 1970s into the mid 1980s, many of these ultimately failed. In the northern province of Antsiranana, in which Ambanja lies, numerous schools were shut down and abandoned only a few years after being built. In some instances, this was because of faulty and, ultimately, dangerous construction practices. Several schools I visited had collapsed internally, although their concrete exteriors looked deceptively smooth and strong; corrupt construction companies had saved money by packing sand behind thin walls, and even beneath second- and third-story floors. In many other cases, schools closed simply because the state decided to cancel teachers' assignments in small or remote communities, once again leaving rural children with no access to schooling. In Ambanja, no problem is noted more often than the *total absence* (not shortage) of curricular materials. If, in 1987, one wandered from bookshop to bookseller in Antananarivo, one could often find a variety of secondary and postsecondary materials for sale, albeit often at prices beyond what students and even instructors could pay. In the north, however, such supplies simply did not exist. Furthermore, no informants who attended public school had ever had the financial means or the social networks that would have enabled them to acquire school texts, maps, or workbooks (had they known where to locate them). In an isolated nation plagued by shortages of all sorts of essential items—including chalk, erasers, ink, paper, pencils, maps, and soccer balls—it is hardly surprising that schoolbooks would similarly be rare commodities.[28]

Teachers therefore had to be not only clever but enterprising, which unfortunately was true of only the most devoted. On their meager salaries, all were so demoralized—and poor—that they felt driven to put their greatest efforts into daily survival, be it by supplemental farming or petty trade. All teachers made use of old college notes recorded at a time when they had no idea how valuable they would later become. Only a few books existed in town that could serve in any way as reference materials for local instructors, so that textbooks were among the most cherished of all commodities in town. When a philanthropic organization from Réunion donated outdated history and science books to Ambanja's schools, these quickly vanished, sold by corrupt state employees to itinerant booksellers. When such underhanded dealings became known, lycée and, soon, middle school students went on strike for weeks at a time until at least some texts were recovered and returned to local schoolrooms.

Many parents are currently at a loss to understand their children's experiences in school, since they themselves completed only perhaps a few years at the primary level before returning home to assist their parents in their fields. Thus, it is the town's educated elders who comprehend most intensely the painful shortfalls of Ratsiraka's failed educational experiment. Mr. Pascal, who has watched eight of his children pass through local schools, expressed the depth of his frustration one afternoon. A lively intellectual now in his sixties, he was identified at a young age as a gifted student. During the colonial era, he was trained first as a scribe, then as a teacher, and, as a young adult, he was sent to France and, later, to Israel to study law and economics. For many years, he has held the coveted job of personal secretary to the founder and sons of one of the island's oldest private and foreign-owned plantations. He also practices law on the side. Today, in his limited spare time, he can sometimes be found sitting quietly at home in an armchair or at his desk reading from volumes of French literature, philosophy, or in economics or political science. The day we had the following conversation, I had spotted him on his porch, deeply involved in a book entitled *Les Français de Ravensbrück*. Despite his high level of education, he finds he is often unable to assist his own children in their studies:

In 1972 we formed a parent-children's association and demonstrated against the idea of *malgachisation* in Diégo. Really! We made a great deal of trouble! There were quite a few of us who were dead set against this idea. [But it triumphed] and look what has happened: my children have had to study everything including such things as math in Malagasy! And I can't help them with their homework. Why? Because I don't understand all of these terms they've made up to explain technical things. [Slapping his hand repeatedly on the chair arm for emphasis:] *We have sacrificed our children! An entire generation, massacred!* And now what? Well, we're going to have to wait—our only hope lies in a generation from now.

... When one has kids one is obliged to understand what happens with them in school. We had problems before with the changes [in the 1970s]—we changed all the priorities of teaching. And now we're doing it again! That means that teachers don't understand how to go forward with their work, with these internal changes, or how to adopt to these changes and how to help our children. *This* is what rests at the bottom of all our problems now. . . . And now [we have new problems]. My oldest daughter, she is at the university in Antananarivo right now. She is having terrible problems! She cries when she talks to me about how she is learning, all of this TV teaching [where lessons are broadcast on monitors]. This isn't enough—you can't ask any questions. *This is the robotisation of education*—it is so very, very sad. The bastardization of education, I tell you—changes, always, always, always these changes. My youngest child, she's six, and she loves to learn—she's just like my oldest. Already in school the teachers show no interest in her abilities. So I've told all my kids, "Hands off!—she's *my* domain." I don't want them to destroy her love of learning. Only my oldest daughter is allowed to teach her, because she was the same way, they are so much alike. Schooling in Madagascar?—*it is a travesty.*

Sacrifice and Perpetual School Failure

Mr. Pascal was among the first to alert me to the complex tragedies of the sacrificed generation. As he asserts, these pedagogical reforms are now perceived as having devastated an entire era of learning in this nation, to the extent that it wreaked havoc on the lives of all whom it touched. One of the most striking trends to emerge in the course of this study is that informants did not necessarily agree on who actually made up the sacrificed generation. All those who had lived through malagasization potentially perceived themselves as being its victims. An especially embittered thirty-three-year-old young woman from Nosy Be named Fleur explained:

> You know, *drakô* [my friend], I'm always hearing you ask others, "Who do you think belongs to the sacrificed generation?" Well, I'll tell you who: *we* are, it's *our* generation that was sacrificed. Because amid all of this, we are the ones who went through the schools, got the good marks, only to find no employment in the end. You want to know what is truly the greatest problem of this nation of ours? It's the unemployment, *drakô*, that's what has truly devastated us. These children you're now studying, well, they are simply the second wave of that devastation.

The majority of informants concurred, however, that it was those children who were schooled during the late 1980s and early 1990s who endured the greatest tragedies, because their academic careers exclusively spanned the years of the Second Republic, and they knew no other reality. More specifically, this category best encompassed students enrolled in state-run schools whose ages ranged between fifteen and twenty-four, the younger end representing those who had excelled in their studies, whereas older students were those who had repeated one or several years of schooling but who, nevertheless, had persevered throughout and thus made it to the *terminale*, or final year of lycée.

PAST SACRIFICES

Memory and the Power of History

In order to comprehend the significance of Ratsiraka's educational experiment as it was lived, and is now imagined and remembered, entails deciphering indigenous meanings of sacrifice. The concept of "the sacrificed generation" was, in fact, never expressed to me in Malagasy, but always in French; and although I often asked for a Malagasy version, the only responses I ever received were clumsy, impromptu attempts at translation. The concept of sacrifice is understood as a pervasive and complicated one throughout Madagascar, with its own particular meanings in the northwest. Each localized context generates a set of collective memories that shape the interpretation of ritualized sacrificial forms. As such, sacrifice, as ritualized historical memory, is often highly politically charged (Apter 1992, 1993; Bloch 1986, 1989; Ellis 1985; Kramer 1993).

Thus, in order to understand sacrifice as a *historicized* ideological construct in Madagascar, we must first consider the intertwining of memory and historical event. More specifically, how are stories (re)told? In what contexts and through which media? To answer these questions first necessitates understanding the Malagasy term *taloha*.[29] Roughly translated as "the past," it can refer to any action, event, or deed that precedes others. Thus, one might use this word to express, for example, that "although I now live in Ambanja, *before [taloha]* I grew up in Antananarivo"; or, "I am now a school principal; *formerly [taloha]* I led the simple life of a peasant." As used here, *taloha* implies transition, change, and contrast. In a more powerful sense, *taloha* operates as a referent to a time of long ago, of past experiences recorded and preserved through the memories of elders, and, as is often the case, transmitted orally over many generations. Thus, an important journal for historical studies in Madagascar bears the title *Taloha* (published by the Institut des Civilisations at the Musée d'Art et d'Archéologie in Antananarivo). So named, it conveys a sense of tradition, or its role in preserving the memory of Malagasy traditions (*fomba-gasy* "Malagasy customs," or *fombandrazana*, "ancestral customs"). For Sakalava, this more deeply nuanced sense of taloha embodies not only written and oral memories of the colonial era but, more important, the deeds of precolonial sovereigns *(ampanjakabe)*, including those who founded the local Sambirano's Bemazava-Sakalava dynasty in 1820, as well as the early Maroseranana dynasty of the far south, for whom knowledge (oral, written, and archeological) extends as far back as the sixteenth century (Kent 1968).

The storytelling media that reference the past are vast. In addition to school lessons, spirit possession ceremonies and royal dances convey official versions of highly localized royal history. Furthermore, many young adults recall with great nostalgia spending evenings huddled around elderly grandparents who would tell bedtime stories that perhaps focused on the meanings of particular proverbs, or folk or historical tales *(tantara)* of rulers and their customs *(fomba)* (Paes et al. 1991; Gueunier n.d.; for the Merina, see Callet 1974), as well as of events drawn from their own lives as conquered subjects, including their early memories of the arrival of the French, or as conscripted soldiers during the two great wars in Europe. As will become clear in part 3, these tales supply a rich repertoire of meanings through which youth ultimately sense the power of history and its relevance in defining what it means to be Sakalava, Malagasy, and African today.

Contextualizing Sacrifice

As a medium for ritualized gesture and action, the sacrificial act ultimately encapsulates a distant past, recording ancestral events in codified form. Thus, sacrifice is historically referential, reiterating in liturgical form the significance of the past. It also lends itself to the (re)formulation of what is valued in the present; as Andrew Apter (1992) has argued in the case of the Yoruba, it may even contest, and therefore supply counterhegemonic commentaries on, established orders. Because of their power to define reality and legitimate authority, ritual forms and their associated regalia regularly undergo transformation. In other instances, they are deliberately co-opted in various attempts to usurp their associated power.

A clear example of the appropriation of ritual form in northwest Madagascar is the *joro*, a collective ceremonial request or giving of thanks for ancestral blessing through the sacrifice of a bull.[30] The joro is a pan-Malagasy practice. In northern Sakalava territory, the bull is most often offered as a gift to benevolent royal spirits *(tromba)* who serve as collective ancestors *(razaña)*. Thus, typically, a joro is staged at important royal ceremonies, including the circumcisions of male royalty and the various stages of a new ruler's instatement. During the latter, subjects confirm their loyalty through the sacrificial act of giving valuable beasts as gifts to the ruler; he or she in turn then sacrifices these animals, feeding ancestors and royal subjects alike with their blood and flesh. Many royal subjects flock to these events from diverse regions of the kingdom to publicly proclaim their devotion. As we shall see in chapter 4, the difficulty of expressing and sustaining devotion, love, and service to rulers is what makes this relationship so dear. Such royal events thus expose the paradoxical nature of contemporary *secular* readings of sacrifice when citizens are required to subject themselves to the nation-state. Coastal students' readings of the ancestral land *(tanindrazana)*[31] only further underscore this dilemma, a topic that concludes this chapter.

The symbolics of the joro are significant nationally, since this ceremonial form has been neatly incorporated into state rituals. During the Second Republic, the joro was practiced as a means to sanctify the nation as a collectively defined tanindrazana—that is, as one belonging to *all* Malagasy. This occurred especially in contexts relevant to the economic development of Madagascar: the fences surrounding newly erected factories often bore the magnificently horned skulls of sacrificed zebu cattle, a sight one would often see not only in the capital of Antananarivo but in various locations throughout the Sambirano. In the valley, state-sponsored joro were staged at the opening of a new coffee factory and the expansion of a new

plantation warehouse. As described elsewhere, malagasization as a political movement mandated the honoring of local ancestors and ritual practices as central to
state activities in the Sambirano and its neighboring waters (Sharp 1993, 165–70;
Sharp 1999). The notion of the island as a unified tanindrazana (rather than a collective of many regional ancestral lands) is yet another significant theme that reveals how the Malagasy state was imagined during the Second Republic. The presence of bovine skulls on fences and walls long after joro had occurred
communicated the long-term blessing of a host of local ancestors, now reimagined
as national ones (cf. Beard 1994).

Personal and collective sacrifices assert themselves as well in the daily world of
the living, serving as potent reminders of a treacherous past, memories shaped by
the onslaught of Merina conquest that preceded French occupation. The possession ceremonies of a specific category of Sakalava tromba spirits commemorate
the self-sacrifice of royalty who willingly drowned themselves in the Loza River[32]
when faced with Merina conquest. These memories are embodied in the dress, gestures, and words of mediums during possession episodes. They also surface repeatedly in daily life, because their spirit mediums must forever refuse to eat the
very fish that fed upon their royal corpses. Other prohibitions that perpetuate the
separation of coastal Sakalava from highland Merina insist that Merina may not
attend these spirits' ceremonies, that it is forbidden to speak the Merina dialect in
their presence, and even that people of Merina descent may not come into physical contact with unpossessed mediums, out of fear of the wrath of angered spirits
(see Sharp 1993, 185–87).

Sakalava, as they recall their own past through such ritualized forms of historical narrative, repeatedly stress the theme of sacrifice, a ritual gesture that reflects
that the most pronounced forms of love and devotion are reserved for royalty.
Bemazava-Sakalava speak with pride of their ability to thwart Merina hegemony
in the late eighteenth and early nineteenth centuries. They also lament the decision of the neighboring Bemihisatra-Sakalava kingdom of Nosy Be to form an alliance with France in 1840 to stave off the Merina. Such accounts underscore the
anger and frustration associated with replacing one conqueror with yet another,
particularly since, for over a century, the French had considered the Sambirano an
impenetrable territory guarded by fierce warriors. Thus, the Sambirano's inhabitants assert their own unique history of resistance, a theme that will be pursued in
detail throughout part 3.

Resistance and sacrifice are similarly paired in accounts of early nationalist
movements. Four in particular receive the greatest attention in historical texts and
school lessons. One is the early uprising of the Menalamba ("Red Shawls," or burial shrouds) against both British and French invaders during the 1890s (Ellis 1985;
Rasoanasy 1976). Another is the VVS secret society, formed in 1912 by medical students and journalists, who were arrested and sentenced to long-term or life imprisonment, or deported (Bunge 1983, 2; Covell 1995, 251–52). Jean Ralaimongo's
attempts to establish a communist party in the 1930s constitute the third (Randri-

anja 1990). Finally, there is the 1947 insurrection, a time when perhaps 100,000 Malagasy died and many others hid in fear for their lives.[33] Colonial records from the north are thick with descriptions of incarcerations, interrogations, and spying in paranoiac response to these movements. Through these and other more quotidian events, coastal school youth link their own sacrifices to those of past Malagasy nationalists.

RECONFIGURING THE NATION

What, then, is meant by independence in Madagascar? Further, how significant are school youth to shaping this nation's trajectory? Postcolonial survival is plagued by paradoxes, where contemporary citizens must bear the weight of colonialism's legacy. Nowhere is this more evident in Madagascar than in the nationalist rhetoric that draws simultaneously on indigenous notions of power and French republicanism, configuring the state both as the collective tanindrazana (ancestral land) of its people and a contemporary *république.* This perplexing hybridity is manifest as well in formal displays of power, such as the Independence Day celebrations staged annually throughout the island. As we shall see, children figure especially prominently in such contexts, since it is they who collectively embody the future of the nation.

A Shadow upon the Land

Collective identity in Ambanja is firmly rooted in highly localized and historicized readings of the homeland, as embodied more specifically in the term *tanindrazana,* or "ancestral land."[34] As students reflect upon this term, they inevitably sift through Sakalava encounters with Imerina, colonial France, and now the independent state of Madagascar. The meaning of this term is inherently complex, because it must draw from such a wide variety of historical references. Throughout Madagascar, individual identity is conveyed through this term. For example, if one wishes to identify another's ethnicity *(karazana)* one asks, "Where is your ancestral land?" (HP: "Aiza ny tanindrazanao?"). The answer necessitates that the speaker assert his or her rootedness to a particular region, community, kin group, and tomb (see Bloch 1971). Thus, for the state—be it colonial or independent—to speak of itself as a collective tanindrazana is a radical move, for it implies several things. First, that the island as a whole is the homeland of all Malagasy speakers. Second, that in making such a claim, the state is not unlike a ruler *(ampanjakabe)* who embodies the collective power of the ancestors *(razana)* and the government *(fanjakana)* of the people. As the overseer of the lives of its subjects, the state, like a ruler, emerges simultaneously as a protective and exploitative force.

The central concept of tanindrazana has remained intact throughout the numerous permutations of Madagascar's national slogan. Under President Tsiranana's First Republic, the ethos of the nation was embodied in the slogan "Tanindrazana—Fahafahana—Fandrosoana" ("Ancestral Land, Liberty, and Progress"). Under President Ratsiraka's Second Republic, a new slogan reflected the transformation of the state: the nation now celebrated "Tanindrazana—Tolompiavotana—Fahafahana" ("Ancestral Land, Revolution, and Liberty"). Under Zafy's Third Republic, it experienced yet another transformation, becoming "Tanindrazana—Fahafahana—Fahamarinana" ("Ancestral Land, Liberty, and Justice"). Following his reelection in 1996, Ratsiraka reverted to Tsiranana's original "Tanindrazana—Fahafahana—Fandrosoana."[35] In each version, tanindrazana is primary and linked to fahafanana, liberty, but the relationship between these two ideals varies radically; they are shaped in turn by progress, by revolution, and by justice, and then by progress again.

Another irony is how the independent state of Madagascar is reimagined in reference to France. Efforts to define the nation inevitably draw upon the language of the French Revolution as it asserts its own unique identity, for the national slogan has been consistently reworked in mimetic fashion as a reformation of France's own "Liberté, Egalité, Fraternité." The inherent paradox is that Madagascar's liberty must inevitably be framed historically and rhetorically in reference to its colonizer. Further, this island's model of a republic is, ultimately, confined to French one.[36] As M. Esoavelomandroso (1990) has argued, this paradox is hardly new, for by the 1860s royal and other elite Merina struggled with how to conceive of France as simultaneously an advocate of the rights of man and a colonizing nation. Such rhetoric inevitably shapes the imagining of the homeland: for just as France places much value on the concept of the *patrie* or *pays maternelle,*[37] the concept similarly resurfaces in the constantly reworked Malagasy imagining of the *tanindrazana.*

The referential quality of the nationalist agenda is similarly evident in the manner in which Madagascar conceives of historical periods as *republics,* a theme remarked upon as well by Jacques Tronchon (1990). On September 28, 1958, France adopted the constitution of the Fifth Republic under Charles de Gaulle, and on that same day Malagasy considered a referendum that determined their own future as a nation. The vote transformed the colony into a self-governing republic within the French Community, the Malagasy Republic, or République Malgache. Two days later, Tsiranana was elected as the first president by the newly formed National Assembly, and June 26, 1960, marks the colony's official date of independence (Bunge 1983, 24; Paillard 1979, 301). Like postrevolutionary France, Madagascar has, to date, passed through its respective First, Second, Third, and Fourth republics.[38] The shadow of the French mode of historicizing is further evident in the common practice of referring to the past (especially Tsiranana's First Republic) as the *ancien régime,* as the French call their own prerevolutionary history.

The 200th anniversary of the storming of the Bastille in 1789 (it was also just shy of the 100th anniversary of the French conquest of Madagascar in 1895–96) was marked by a conference in Madagascar that addressed the relevance of French ideology in shaping Malagasy constructions of revolution, the republic, and the state. As the papers by Manassé Esoavelomandroso, Guy Jacob, Françoise

Figure 2. Didier Ratsiraka in presidential regalia.
From Ratsiraka 1975, frontispiece.

Raison-Jourde, Jeannine Rambeloson-Rapiera, Yvette Sylla, Jacques Tronchon, and Claude Wanquet in *Ravao ny "La Bastille": Regards sur Madagascar et la Révolution française* (Jacob 1990) underscore, throughout the nineteenth century, the French Revolution was a popular topic of discussion among educated Malagasy, French, and British inhabitants of the island. Tronchon (1990) in turn argues that the ideals of French republicanism were planted in Madagascar as early as 1789 (and have been sustained well beyond independence). The French struggled to construct a portrait of an indigenous Malagasy character in reference to Enlightenment ideals, one whose racist overtones ultimately challenged their own charter on the International Rights of Man. Another source of tension involved definitions of a civilized versus a romanticized primitive man (Rousseau 1992) where firsthand experience with the vibrant kingdom of Imerina proved particularly perplexing. As Rambeloson-Rapiera, writing of the colonial French, reminds us, "Observing the other always leads one to examine oneself."[39] One might argue the same of the Malagasy, who, in confronting the image of the colonizer are continually forced to take a careful look at themselves.

Formal presidential portraits illustrate this. During the Second Republic, Ratsiraka is generally pictured wearing a European-style military tuxedo, with a colorful

Figure 3. Merina King Radama II (r.
1861–1863). From Jacob 1990, pl. 4,
between 112–13.

sash, a five-crested star on his chest, and an elaborate chain-link necklace, all emblematic of state authority (fig. 2). His dress is reminiscent not only of nineteenth-
century French military uniforms of the sort worn by Napoléon III (r. 1852–71) but
of the attire of the Merina King Radama II (r. 1861–63) (fig. 3). Ratsiraka thus embodies the images of both the imperial French military state and precolonial Merina
royal power.[40] This contrasts with the simplicity of dress considered emblematic of
Zafy Albert, who has often been photographed wearing a simple suit and a peasant-
style hat.

What, then, are we to make of the self-referential quality of the nation as embodied by the president, where the state displays its power through symbols appropriated from the symbolic repertoire of the conqueror? Madagascar clearly
struggles with the weight of its colonial legacy, where symbolic and rhetorical inspiration are drawn predominantly from French writers and theorists. As such,
French intellectual history becomes the history of Malagasy intellectuals, too (cf.
Domenichini 1990, Raison-Jourde 1990, Tronchon 1990). This is one of the traps
of postcolonial survival. It is also a foundation that must be acknowledged in the
search for meaning in discussions among youth and their participation in more general public displays that commemorate independence on this African island.

Staging Autonomy and National Unity

"[Only] the ocean divides my rice paddies" ("Ny ranomasina no valam-parihako"), proclaimed the Merina monarch Andrianampoinimerina (r. 1787–1810), who conceived of the entire island as his royal domain (K. Raharijaona, personal communication, November 1996; cf. Rajemisa-Raolison 1966, 57). Under this ruler, Malagasy would be united in the Merina state by force, regardless of territorial or ethnic affiliation.[41] Northern Sakalava were among the few non-Merina peoples who successfully resisted the onslaught of Merina armies. The Sakalava, as state builders in their own right, still figure prominently in the histories of other peoples who in turn resisted *their* hegemony (Astuti 1995; Wilson 1992). As the preserved tales of drowned Sakalava ancestors reveal, localized Sakalava memories contradict nationalist readings that idealize unification. For Sakalava, unification (be it under the Merina, French, or the independent nation) tarnishes a now distant period of their own precolonial splendor.[42]

Unfortunately, Madagascar's history is far too frequently written as that of Imerina, regardless of whether the intended audience is Malagasy schoolchildren or foreign scholars. Relatively little has been written about the Sambirano Valley, and so, throughout 1987, I invested considerable time in reconstructing a local past through oral historical accounts, since little had been written about northern Madagascar (Sharp 1993, 144 ff.; see also Dandouau and Chapus 1952, 19–34; Verin 1986). Malagasization in many coastal schools has, from a local perspective, simply transformed the history of conquest from the French ("our ancestors the Gauls") to the Merina ("the descendants of Imerina").[43] It is no wonder, then, that Ambanja's teachers struggle to reconstruct a Malagasy history in national terms, simultaneously engaging in linguistic battles with students who view official Malagasy as simply a poorly disguised rendering of the dominant Merina dialect.

Ritualized state performances offer contexts where tensions over autonomy and the nation's precarious unity are manifest. Among the most striking examples are those that celebrate Madagascar's Independence Day, June 26.[44] In Ambanja, children figure prominently in these events. As a fleeting resident of Ambanja, I have witnessed these celebrations in four different years, the first in 1987 under Ratsiraka, the second during the transitional period in 1993, and in two subsequent years under Zafy in 1994 and 1995. As I shall show, the annual parade is particularly emblematic of the paradoxes of nationhood.

Independence celebrations span a variety of events in Ambanja. Sometimes, for example, a grandstand is constructed in the town square, and for a week or more children (and sometimes, adults) from diverse regions perform regional songs and dances. More impressive, however, is a regular event that always occurs during the early evening of June 25. Once it is dark, young children congregate near the town's center, bearing delicate paper lanterns illuminated by candles. These children then form a silent procession that begins at the local county seat (*fivondronana*); moves down main street to the central market, pauses at city hall (*firaisana*), and, afterward, climbs the neighboring steep hillside to the mayor's residence, one originally inhabited by the colonial governor. Seeking the blessings of local authorities, Ambanja's children map out the local stations of state power.

On the morning of Independence Day on June 26, brigades of older school-children now fill the streets. Organized by their individual schools, they goose-step through town, making their way to the region's largest annual event: a two-hour Independence Day parade that, in 1987, occurred on the grounds of the newly completed state-run Lycée Mixte Tsiaraso I,[45] and, subsequently in 1993–95, before the grandstand of the town's large soccer field. Throughout this event, local dignitaries sit together on a shaded grandstand, safe from the oppressive midday heat and the great dust cloud created by a mass of shuffling feet. The day's events culminate in a lively soccer game and, sometimes, a biking competition whose participants race throughout the Sambirano Valley in an event reminiscent of the Tour de France. Later that evening, local discos, the Catholic Academy, royalty, and the city government host grand disco parties that end in the early morning hours of June 27.

During all four years when I have been present, the basic format of the parade has been the same. Although there is a military presence, it is clear that this is very much a children's holiday. Like the evening before, youth dominate the parade and constitute the majority of the audience. The official opening of the event is announced with the raising of the Malagasy flag, often to the tune of a poorly recorded military march (in 1993, it was the Battle Hymn of the Republic). The procession is always led by local gendarmes who man the town's prison, their entrance signaled by the broadcasting of more music, played by a brass marching band, the same tune blaring loudly throughout. The gendarmes are followed by a small rag-tag band of forestry employees of Rano sy Ala (the "Water and Forest" department), and then a small troop of Boy Scouts.

Behind the military appear nearly a dozen brigades of schoolchildren, and among the most striking aspects of their style is that they, too, goose-step as they march (fig. 4). The rank and file of town youth simultaneously shrink in height and increase in number as students pass by, moving from the town's state-run lycée to the middle school and six urban and rural primary schools. Other contingents represent the private Catholic Academy and the exclusive French Elementary School. At times, too, there is a small assemblage from the Technical High School, which is located at the edge of town. The order of the high school students is reflective of the year: in 1987, the state-run lycée led the parade's students, presumably in celebration of its first anniversary; but by the 1990s, the Catholic Academy always appeared first, its students and teachers dressed neatly in matching uniforms made especially for the occasion, so that by comparison the poverty of the other schools was obvious. Parade membership and order also change according to the year and, thus, the republic: in 1987, labor groups from state-run plantations were heavily represented; and in some years a small band from the town's center for the disabled has joined the parade. By the mid 1990s, the workers' ranks had shrunk considerably, and they had fallen to the rear of the parade, while new interest groups had emerged, including several unlicensed remedial schools and a small Islamic school.

Every year a few soccer teams bring up the rear, along with kung-fu aficionados. The appearance in 1987 of one such kung-fu group, although small in number, was regarded as a bold move, because President Ratsiraka had only recently outlawed the sport in Antananarivo, perceiving it as a front for rival political parties seeking young supporters (Covell 1995, 54; Rajoelina 1988, 79–80). Everyone always eagerly awaits these clubs, whose members display a brief yet fabulous array of moves before the town's dignitaries. By 1994, kung-fu had become so popular that their appearance created a stampede, as many public viewers broke past measly police barriers to bolt en masse toward the grandstand to view them. The economic shifts of 1995 were manifest here as well: other more elite groups had emerged, including a handball club, which brought up the rear and, in the grandstand itself, a new chapter of the Lion's Club, which made its own dramatic entrance prior to the festivities, mounting the platform in unison, dressed in matching vests of vibrant yellow satin.[46] By the end of the procession, several thousand people will have filed by the grandstand, the majority being children. Nearly an equal number stand by patiently along the sidelines to watch them in the oppressive heat beneath a cloudless sky. As such, the parade itself generates a lively display of the town's many factions of school youth, ranked by age, school affiliation, and religion.

Such groupings, however, define simply one aspect of these processions. One need only watch the televised broadcasts of Bastille Day from France (as I did with friends in Ambanja in 1994, the year that a satellite antenna was installed in town) to realize that portions of Ambanja's Independence Day events mirror this celebration of French nationalism. On the surface, they emerge as blind parodies of French military strength, and, thus, an unselfconscious rendering of a supposedly defunct colonial presence. When I remarked on the similarities between Malagasy and French military marching styles,[47] informants responded with an air of obvious yet unquestioning familiarity. Absent was any blatant challenge to French hegemonic symbols, and I nowhere saw any intentional public parodying of state power of the kind so beautifully described by Achille Mbembe (1992) in the case of Cameroon. In contrast, Faranirina Esoavelomandroso describes Malagasy peacetime reactions in 1908 as sarcastic and characterized by despair and shows that criticism was also fierce after World War II (F. Esoavelomandroso 1990, 149, 154–57).

Were we to end the critique here, such celebrations in Ambanja would inevitably emerge as inherently weak displays of national independence. As I argue extensively elsewhere (Sharp 2001a), however, careful scrutiny of the colonial past uncovers yet other readings. If we step back a century, we find that early French celebrations of Bastille Day (July 14) in Antananarivo were themselves characterized by ambiguity. Briefly, the French themselves struggled to construct celebrations that could assert French hegemony in Imerina, appropriating symbolism associated with the most important indigenous event, the Fandroana, or Royal Bath, the annual renewal ceremony when subjects of Imerina proclaimed their allegiance to the ruler. The last Fandroana under the architect of the French conquest, Governor-General Joseph-Simon Gallieni (1886–1905), occurred in November 1896; the fol-

Figure 4. Independence Day parade in Ambanja.

lowing February, Gallieni abolished the Merina monarchy (Rajemisa-Raolison 1966, 126–27; Stratton 1964, 217 ff.), and Bastille Day was proclaimed the true "celebration of all freed people."[48] This displacement of the Royal Bath necessitated the merging of French and Merina celebratory forms.

Among the most striking aspects of these events involved the widespread participation of children (again, see Sharp 2001a). For example, on the eve of the Fandroana in Antananarivo in the 1890s, one could witness a lit procession that included children. Among Malagasy, this procession signified life and the perpetuation of Merina lineages. There were also children's games, and dance and singing competitions between villages, again involving children. Some other practices characteristic of the Fandroana included public displays by warriors recently returned from royal expeditions, and groups of children imitated the military style of the *marakely*, or young soldiers who served under Queen Ranavalona II (r. 1868–83). The French then embellished upon children's involvement in the Merina context by including a range of sports events and games during the island's Bastille Day celebrations (Faranirina Esoavelomandroso 1990, 146, 151; cf. Rajemisa-Raolison 1966, 126–27). As advertised on a poster from Antananarivo, dated July 1909, these included children's foot and sack races, water games, and theater events (see Jacob 1990, pl. 8, between pp. 112–13).

The mimetic quality (cf. Taussig 1993) of these displays of state power must, then, be understood as complexly malleable and multifaceted, allowing for readings of cultural meaning on multiple layers. In this light, the Independence Day parade uncovers a rich ground for indigenous reflection. As Fritz Kramer (1993) stresses, appropriation is not so much about succumbing to or capturing the power of the other, but about drawing upon difference as a means to reflect on an indigenous ego. Furthermore, it is at those very moments where appropriation seems so very *in*appropriate that the power of such constant (re)mirroring is so startling. The more problematic forms associated with Independence Day ultimately underscore the fact that French and Malagasy alike were both actors and victims of appropriation, defining a dialectical layering of sorts, as one group's borrowing also served to squelch the legitimacy of its own predecessor. In essence, each year that children march in Ambanja's parade, they must inevitably conform to displays of power whose potency rests on layers of appropriated references to Merina, French, and nationalist hegemonic power. Nothing more clearly shows these contradictions than the red, white, and green bands of Madagascar's flag, the nation's most prominent symbol. The flag of the now defunct Imerina kingdom was red and white, and in October 1958, a green band was added as the "color of the *côtiers*" (Paillaird 1979, 302). In Ambanja, this embellishment only further underscores the sense that the coast was added onto a hybrid Merina-French empire.[49]

YOUTHFUL REFLECTIONS

The "colonial" is not looking for profit only; he is also greedy for certain other—psychological— satisfactions, and that is much more dangerous.
OCTAVE MANNONI, *Prospero and Caliban: The Psychology of Colonization*

La Mentalité Colonisée

Clearly, complex forms of appropriation uncover a rich ground for indigenous reflection on self and other. Frantz Fanon, a psychiatrist and revolutionary from Martinique, was one of the most important authors to explore this murky terrain. This political critic and visionary has experienced a recent revival among North American scholars, who draw from his work for theoretical inspiration. Four decades ago, however, his writings inspired political praxis on a global scale, including revolution in a host of quarters. In Madagascar, too, Fanon's ideas have generated careful critiques of colonial and international relations, even reaching students in Ambanja who are inspired by lectures delivered by a handful of articulate and politicized instructors. These students' astute remarks reflect both an acute understanding of the history of colonial relations and, in turn, of the transformations instituted by Ratsiraka. More specifically, Fanon's critiques of the exploitative nature of colonialism and neocolonialism offer a foundation for young informants' discussions of history and nationhood. As will become clear throughout this book, this level of awareness is especially pronounced among those schooled not simply during Ratsiraka's Second Republic but, more specifically, far more so among students enrolled in state-run institutions than those from elite, well-equipped private schools. As Paulo Freire argues, education is an inherently political process (1985; cf. Ferro 1984). In northwest Madagascar, it is precisely the students the state schooled who developed the most sophisticated knowledge and language by which to critique past and current state-based hierarchies.

Madagascar has been a significant site for explorations into the psychology of colonization, where the experience of the colonial subject is captured by the French expression "the colonized mind" *(la mentalité colonisée)*. This phrase surfaced frequently in interviews I had with young and adult informants, and in archival writings by French colonial administrators. The potency of this phrase is evident when set more generally against colonial schooling in Africa, for its frequent use underscores a deeply entrenched preoccupation with mental capacity and ability in the colonies. As such, it is a phrase that is highly charged politically. Finally, it signifies an awareness that parallels or is directly inspired by the works of Fanon and other writers as they reflect on their colonial experiences in Africa and elsewhere (Césaire 1970; Fisher 1985; Memmi 1965; Ngugi 1986; Soyinka 1988).[50]

During the colonial period, the French assumed that they were superior to all Malagasy. The island as a whole, however, presented a puzzling mosaic of peoples that mandated precise categorization and, ultimately, hierarchization. Nowhere was the need to explore the effects of *la mentalité indigène* (the "indigenous [Malagasy] mentality") greater than in arenas framed by forms of political and economic organization. The French were most impressed with the highland Merina and Betsileo, the former for their state organization (represented by the kingdom of Imerina, centered in Antananarivo), the latter for their tiered rice paddy cultivation. Other groups (subsequently categorized and thus petrified by ethnic labeling) fell into lower ranks, where aspects of their culture were reduced to predictable behaviors. These categories were also frequently linked to a French privileging of the assumed Asian origins of highland peoples over the supposed more African Malagasy coastal populations; these, in turn, were codified according to French readings of social sophistication and economic value. The Tandroy pastoralists of the south were thus considered far more primitive than highland agriculturists, although valued for their willingness to work as wage laborers even when faced with the most backbreaking of tasks (Sharp 2001b). Against this backdrop, the Sambirano presented a complex case: the Sakalava impressed the French with their array of west coast kingdoms and their formidable legions of warriors, yet they were also a continual source of frustration in their refusal to labor for the foreign-owned plantations that dominated their local sacred territory. As a result, within two decades of conquest, the Sambirano became an important destination for laborers from the distant south and southeast, as it continues to be today (see Sharp 1993).

Madagascar has provided the impetus for a number of critiques of the psychology of colonization, the most noteworthy authors being Mannoni (1990) and Bouillon (1981), who write respectively from the perspective of the colonial and postindependence periods. Mannoni is especially pertinent here. His work preceded

Fanon's and was later criticized by Fanon himself (see Maurice Bloch's foreword in Mannoni 1990, vii, and Fanon 1967, ch. 4). Writing in the wake of the 1947 insurrection in Madagascar, Mannoni, who was a psychiatrist like Fanon, argued that colonialism fostered a mutual dependency between the colonized and colonizer not unlike that between child and parent. Such dependence is particularly virulent in a political context, since it is perpetuated by the colonial encounter without fostering any sort of break or initiative on the part of the colonized subject. Mannoni argued that this "dependency complex" was inherent in the Malagasy psyche, and thus, whenever the colonizer attempted to withdraw and allow more freedom, the colonized would experience abandonment and might, potentially, retaliate (an interpretation that led to bizarre readings of why the 1947 insurrection occurred). Mannoni recognized this relationship as reciprocal, implicating the colonizer as well as the colonized. In fact, he expressed serious contempt for the Frenchman who was attracted to colonial service, regarding him as inferior or "mediocre" (1990, 24), a type of European whose psyche required that he dominate other races. Ultimately, the colonizer's downfall was his assumption of superiority.

The French, too, thus suffered from the colonial relationship (ibid., 18). Mannoni thus intended his book as a mirror (ibid.) of sorts for colonial readers, although he realized only a few would embrace its arguments, the majority being blinded by their arrogance. As he stressed, intrinsic to the colonial relationship was the pairing of two seemingly symbiotic yet wholly different personality structures (ibid., 23). Whereas the colonizer, on the one hand, hungered to dominate others, the character flaw of the Malagasy was that he was caught in a perpetual state of infantile dependence (ibid., 48). Much of Mannoni's evidence was drawn from his own very limited experiences with Malagasy (primarily with his tennis coach!), and he misread the significance of the ancestral dead as yet another category of parental figure upon whom Malagasy were deeply dependent (ibid., 49 ff.). To illuminate his critique, Mannoni drew on the archetypal figures of Prospero and Caliban in Shakespeare's *The Tempest*. "When thou camest first / Thou strok'dst me, and mad'st much of me ... / ... and then I lov'd thee," Caliban says to his master, and Mannoni added: "and then you abandoned me before I had time to become your equal. ... In other words: you taught me to be dependent, and I was happy; then you betrayed me and plunged me into inferiority" (ibid., 76–77). Mannoni argued that such remorse and resentment over abandonment could quickly turn to anger (ibid., 137). In other words, as soon as the colonizer eased his grip on the colonized, he was faced with the potential threat of revolutionary violence, necessitating the tightening, rather than loosening, of controls.

Mannoni's critique is certainly disturbingly flawed, particularly when viewed from the vantage point of the colonized. It stands in a glaring contrast to the better-known works of Fanon, whose concerns similarly focused on the psychology of colonization, especially in Algeria, where he served as a psychiatrist for both Algerian subjects and colonial officers. Fanon, too, argued that it was the oppressive nature of forced subordination that undermined the psyche of the colonized. He offers a far more compelling critique than Mannoni, however, since he recognized that colonial brutality—be it physical or psychic—led some to assume the mask of the colonizer and then to turn such violence upon their own kind. Unlike Mannoni, Fanon also recognized that such brutality could also provide the impetus for insubordination and, ultimately, bloody revolution (Fanon 1963, 1967).

Misguided though it is, Mannoni's work is valuable, because his racism rawly exposes the danger of his assumed liberal stance.[51] Furthermore, his arguments repeatedly underscore how destructive this reciprocal relationship is to the colonizer. Although blind to his own deep-seated paternalism and racism, Mannoni was repulsed by the colonial drive to subjugate others, and he underscored the centrality of the mirroring of the self by the other in the context of the colonial encounter. As Mannoni himself stated, "The negro, then, is the white man's fear of himself" (1990, 200).

A point on which both Mannoni and Fanon agree is that the colonial encounter is fraught with ambivalence and that it is inherently pathological for all parties (Fanon 1967, 83–84). Where they part company is in their reading of the origins of such pathology and in their interpretations of its aftermath. Mannoni assumes that dependency was inherent in the Malagasy (or, more generally, colonized) psyche; Fanon (1967, 85, 97) instead asks why we should assume that internalized inferiority predated colonialism. What sort of society makes an inferiority complex possible? Fanon also warns how dangerous it is to blindly assume that, in Mannoni's words, "France is unquestionably one of the least racialist-minded countries in the world" (quoted in Fanon 1967, 92). Here, Fanon stresses, Mannoni is making "a mistake that is at the very least dangerous. In effect, he leaves the Malagasy no choice save between inferiority and dependence. These two solutions excepted, there is no salvation" (ibid., 93). Furthermore, unlike Fanon, Mannoni evinces no grasp of the economic situation that creates inequality and racism and the accompanying fears and desires (see ibid., 88, and Fanon 1963).

Both Fanon and Mannoni were trained as physicians, and both relied heavily on psychoanalytic readings to expose the more disturbing aspects of the colonial encounter. Each drew on personalized accounts from informants as they explored the psychology of colonial domination (Mannoni by offering examples of children's dreams, and Fanon through case studies of "reactionary psychoses" among his Algerian patients). Although in my opinion neither presents a particularly compelling critique of their respective informants' fears, Fanon was certainly far more keenly aware of the raw and twisted nature of colonial violence (cf. Mannoni 1990, 89–93, and Fanon 1963, 249 ff.). Fanon, like Mannoni, reveals a dark irony: that the tortured and the torturer both suffer from their encounters with one another (Fanon 1963, 264–70). Furthermore, as we shall see, it is not only the colonizer who inspires terror, but also a particular kind of foreign soldier: in the case of the French colonial empire, these were most often Senegalese conscripts forced to do the dirty work of the French on foreign soil (Fanon 1963, 267–70, case no. 5).[52]

Children's experiences expose the degradation colonialism inflicts on human beings in the writings of both Fanon and Mannoni. Fanon describes, for example, a child in Algeria who had to endure the screams of her father's torture victims in her own house. Mannoni summarizes the dreams of four children in which foreign soldiers, robbers, and charging bulls emerge as terrifying images. Although Mannoni acknowledges the fearful quality of such images as "objectively justified" (1990, 93), he nevertheless views them as symbolic renderings of oppressive father figures, whom he inevitably (mis)interprets in sexual terms, along with their guns and horns. Fanon read Mannoni and recognized these and related images for what they were: clear impersonations of the colonial violence that characterized the French response to the 1947 insurrection in Madagascar. Given such conflicts in interpretation, the dreams of four Malagasy children as reported by Mannoni are worth reprinting here:

> *Dream of a thirteen-year-old boy, Rahevi.* "While going for a walk in the woods, I met two black men. 'Oh,' I thought, 'I am done for!' I tried to run away but couldn't. They barred my way and began jabbering in a strange tongue. I thought they were saying, 'We'll show you what death is.' I shivered with fright and begged, 'Please, Sirs, let me go, I'm so frightened.' One of them understood French but in spite of that they said, 'We are going to take you to our chief.' As we set off they made me go in front and they showed me their rifles. I was more frightened than ever, but before reaching their camp we had to cross a river. I dived deep into the water and thanks to my presence of mind found a rocky cave where I hid. When the two men had gone I ran back to my parents' house."

> *Dream of a fourteen-year-old boy, Razafi.* He is being chased by (Senegalese) soldiers who "make a noise like galloping horses as they run," and "show their rifles in front of them." The dreamer escapes by becoming invisible; he climbs a stairway and finds the door of his home.

> *Raza's dream.* In his dream the boy heard someone say at school that the Senegalese were coming. "I went out of the school yard to see." The Senegalese were indeed coming. He ran home. "But our house had been dispersed by them too."

> *Dream of a fourteen-year-old boy, Si.* "I was walking in the garden and felt something like a shadow behind me. All around me the leaves were rustling and falling off, as if a robber was in hiding among them, waiting to catch me. Wherever I walked, up and down the alleys, the shadow still followed me. Suddenly I got frightened and started running, but the shadow took great strides and stretched out his huge hand to take hold of my clothes. I felt my shirt tearing, and screamed. My father jumped out of bed when he heard me scream and came over to look at me, but the big shadow had disappeared and I was no longer afraid." (Mannoni 1990, 90–93)

Fanon amplifies the power and the terror of these images, drawing on testimony given elsewhere by Malagasy men tortured for their assumed involvement in the 1947 insurrection. In so doing, Fanon's interpretation exposes the absurdity of Mannoni's blindness: "[T]he rifle of the Senegalese soldier is not a penis but a genuine rifle, model Lebel 1916," and the soldiers are clearly agents of colonial violence, including those who followed the orders of French torturers in maiming the bodies of their Malagasy victims (Fanon 1967, 103–7). As chapters in part 3 of this study will show, the Senegalese soldier looms prominently in coastal students' re-constructed memories of colonial oppression, as do the French soldiers who raided villages and towns in their constant search for laborers and soldiers during both peacetime and war. It is older boys and young men who were the constant targets of these sorts of patrols, which for Sakalava evoke the terror of slave raids. Thus, both authors (albeit Mannoni far more naïvely) underscore the complexity and am-bivalence of the colonial encounter, where Mannoni emerges as the voice of the assumed liberal colonizer, whereas Fanon's ideas inspire the revolutionary rheto-ric of malagasization. The ambivalence inherent in the colonial encounter was refl-ected at times in the narratives of the students I interviewed in Ambanja, who, al-though clearly inspired by Fanon's powerful critiques, nevertheless occasionally offered readings far closer to Mannoni's in moments of confusion and doubt.

Imagining the Tanindrazaña

I wish to conclude this chapter with a brief discussion of how Ambanja's school youth imagine their nation thirty-five years after its independence and how they situate themselves within this context. Of particular importance is how Ambanja's school youth understand what it means to be Malagasy and how they interpret the tanindrazana (SAK: tanindrazaña) as both an ancestral land and the nation. As will become clear from their responses below, students shift between registers of meaning—particularly between the local and national—as they struggle to define who they are, often by opposing their own sense of belonging in a grounded com-munity against what it means to be a citizen of a nation once colonized by France.

When asked what it means to be Malagasy, the majority of students stressed first and foremost that this entailed a deep-seated respect for—as well as knowledge and practice of—indigenous fomba (customs). Furthermore, Malagasy customs are unique, and it is thus the fomba that serve to distinguish Malagasy from all other people. As Lucien,[53] aged twenty, succinctly put it, "[To be Malagasy] means I speak Malagasy. [And] I know the fomba." His sentiments were echoed by Pauline, also aged twenty: "[What does it mean] if I say I'm Malagasy? It means that my fomba are not the same as those of the vazaha ["stranger," generally applied to whites of European origin]." Clearly, both students stress the importance of the fomba, but whereas for Lucien this entails linguistic affiliation, Pauline defines her identity in opposition to an extreme category of Other.

When couched in local terms, however, these definitions become more complex. Inhabitants of Ambanja are quick to distinguish between indigenous Sakalava (gen-erally referred to by the term tera-tany, "children" or "offspring of the soil") and vahiny ("guests," and thus migrants). There is much tension in the way these terms are defined locally, because even people born and raised in the Sambirano, and who may constitute a third generation of long-term settlers who are entombed lo-cally, may still be considered vahiny by Sakalava (Sharp 1993). Such rigidity of iden-tity is particularly evident in statements made by young members of the Sakalava royal family who are without question "children" of the Sambirano. Hazaly, aged twenty-four, whose mother is royalty, defined *tera-tany* as follows: "If I go away it means I can always come back here." When I asked the same of Sidy and Lucien, both of whose parents are royalty, Lucien answered first, declaring: "[What am I?] I'm tera-tany! *Izaho citoyen*! . . . I'm a citizen of the Sambirano. I follow the fomba of the Sambirano. I work the land here. Here you can't work the land on Tuesdays and Thursdays—these days are taboo. This is what it means to follow the fomba of the Sambirano."[54] To this, twenty-year-old Sidy added, "And you work to help your kin *[havaña]*, or the ruler, but no one else."

Although Jaona, aged nineteen, is not of royal Sakalava descent like Hazaly, Lucien, and Sidy, his knowledge of royal custom is vast: he has spent much of his life in Ambanja, his father is Antankaraña from the north, and his mother, with whom he lives, is of royal Betsimisaraka descent (from the east coast). Jaona always displays a keen interest in the local fomba, and he answered as follows: "Look, for us there are two parts to our identity, two realities: the mental [OM: *fanahy*] and the body [OM: *vátana*]. . . . [It is] the mental part of who you are [that] doesn't die. This is the way it is with royalty [SAK: *ampanjaka*], for example, and their advisors [SAK: *manantany*]. The spirit of the ruler lives on, and comes to the *manantany* in dreams, giving messages, saying what it thinks. *This is Malagasy.*" Jaona offered the most localized response of all, merging what he has learned from philosophy lectures at school with his own understanding of royal tromba possession, an institution central to Sakalava identity (Sharp 1993).

If we turn to responses to questions posed regarding the meaning of the tanindrazaña, it becomes clear that individual interpretations are in conflict with one another; and, furthermore, that particular individuals struggle to offer concise definitions of this complex term. Royalty have the clearest sense of where their allegiance lies: the tanindrazaña, in local terms, is the Bemazava-Sakalava kingdom of the Sambirano Valley. As Hazaly explained, "[T]he tanindrazaña, it's like something that's independent. A country that has its own laws and rights and power . . . [and then, after some thought, he added:] But of course Madagascar comes first and then the tanindrazaña." This sentiment echoes Lucien's proclamation, "Izaho citoyen!" They both stress their local allegiance first. Among other (nonroyal) Sakalava students, the concept inspires strong sentiments of love and devotion. As Dalia, aged twenty-one, explained: "It means I'm devoted to the tanindrazaña, to the land. It makes me think of the importance of the tombs." For Pauline, such devotion is historically based and rooted in a sense of taloha, or "long ago": "It means the people of the past. The ancestors. The place where the ancestors live." Similarly, Félix, aged eighteen, explained tanindrazaña as follows: "It is the territory of my grandparents, and my nation—[one that encompasses respect for the] *fomba malagasy*—this is what it means to be Malagasy. [The tanindrazaña and Malagasy] are one and the same. . . . Tanindrazaña [refers to] the land where we are interred, and it is the land where there are tombs. It is the land of our ancestors."

Hasina quickly recognized the deeper meanings rooted in this term. Although he is nineteen years old, he looks much younger, being small, with an impish face. Hasina's own background is complex: his father is Merina, and he was born just outside Antananarivo, but he has spent most of his life in the Sambirano with his mother and siblings. He has no memory of his father or of the highlands. Thus, sentimentally, he feels himself to be tera-tany, although locally—and especially by adult Sakalava—he will always be considered to be Merina because of his paternal heritage. The fact that he is Protestant only further complicates his predicament, because Sakalava typically are Catholic, Muslim, or follow the fombandrazaña, which entails honoring local royalty, especially through participation in tromba possession ceremonies (see Sharp 1993, 1994). Hasina's favorite school subject is philosophy. Bright and articulate, he nevertheless reported that several teachers had made it clear they had no interest in what he had to say, news that saddened me deeply. When asked what the tanindrazaña meant to him, he replied as follows:

> *Hasina:* Well, first of all, it makes me think of my island. I'm Malagasy. My fomba come first. It means that in spirit *[esprit]* I am Malagasy. If I'm in France then I think I should [still] probably speak Malagasy.
>
> *LS:* OK, but if you're Adventist, what are your fomba? What if I said you're not Malagasy because you follow a religion of foreign origin that has made Malagasy fomba taboo *[fady]*?
>
> *Hasina [thinking]:* Well, it's true that foreign ideas destroyed many of the Malagasy fomba. But I think I'd still have a Malagasy spirit [here he uses both the terms *esprit* (FR: spirit) and *saina* (HP: mind, intellect)] if I'm an Adventist. And I think that the love for others—*fihavanana*—matters here, too. Lots of Malagasy, for example, adore the[ir] royalty *[ampanjaka]* but then if you do bad things to others you don't have a Malagasy spirit. So, I think being Malagasy involves [three things:] *fihavananany*—[OM; that is,] loving others, the sense of the *patrie* [FR: fatherland], and a spirit that is Malagasy to the core.

As this brief exchange reveals, Hasina struggles to make sense of the ambiguities created by his own overlapping yet conflicting identities. Furthermore, he reconstructs his understanding of French and Malagasy national slogans to encompass his own ideas of one's heartfelt love for the nation. Not only do both the French word *patrie* and the Malagasy term *tanindrazaña* articulate the idea of the nation, but the French nation's brotherhood *(fraternité)* has been transformed into the official Malagasy term for Christian love, *fihavanana*.[55]

In addition to one-on-one interviews, I often engaged in both scheduled and spontaneous group discussions with a cohort of lycée informants, of which Dalia, her boyfriend Foringa Josef (aged twenty-three), Félix, Jaona, and Hasina were the liveliest participants (and often the organizers). These discussions would take place, typically, outside on the grounds of the state-run lycée or at Dalia's home. Among the more animated discussions was one that centered on defining the tanindrazaña and what it meant to be Malagasy. My research assistant Tsarahita also often attended. A circumspect woman in her thirties, she has generally masked, in outstanding fashion, her personal sentiments on the host of research topics we have pursued together for nearly a decade. Even she, however, was drawn into the following debate, offering her own opinions, many of which she had formed during the past two years as a teacher.

LS: How would you define *tanindrazaña*?

Foringa Joseph [looking at Tsarahita with an expression that could only mean, "She asks hard questions!"]: For me? Well, it means I'm tera-tany Malagasy. I'm not vazaha. I'm not Chinese. I'm not Comorean. I was born here.

Tsarahita [unusually excited]: But there are vazaha who are born here!

LS: OK, so let's consider Mr. Q[56]—What about him?

Foringa: Right. Mr. Q is tera-tany—his mother is Malagasy!

Tsarahita: So what does it means to be Malagasy? What are you saying? For me it means my mother and father were both born here, that both are Malagasy.

Foringa: Wait [SAK: *ambesa*] ! No, wait [FR: *attendez*]! It could be a vazaha, too. You can be vazaha and born here. OK, it's like if you have a ruler *[ampanjakabe]*, for example. What if he follows French customs *[ny fomba-vazaha]*. Then he's not Malagasy. If you follow the fomba, then you're Malagasy.

LS: What if you're Malagasy, but you're born in and you die in France?

Foringa: He's Malagasy if his spirit [FR: *esprit*] is Malagasy.

Tsarahita: But I don't agree!

LS: Why?

Tsarahita: First of all, a vazaha is white, has light hair.

Foringa: And a big head and big spirit, ha ha!

Tsarahita: No, no, listen. Second, vazaha don't have the same spirit [FR: *esprit*] of being Malagasy. Their customs—their fomba—they don't follow Malagasy customs.

LS: So, what if you're born and die in France but decide to be buried in Madagascar?

Tsarahita: I'm not sure.

Dalia and Foringa J., together: No! I don't think that's what makes you Malagasy.

Dalia: How can they be Malagasy if they don't know the fomba?

[Tsarahita ponders this question; everyone falls silent.]

LS: What about the idea of the tanindrazaña, what is this, ultimately?

Tsarahita: For me it means you were born here, you speak the Malagasy language, you die here, you know the fomba, then you're Malagasy.

Foringa: It means [this is] something I adore—it's something that is very precious. It's part of my heart. It's what is valued. And so Ambanja is my tanindrazaña.

LS: What about your tomb, where is that?

Foringa: It's [much farther north] in Antsakoamanondro, where my grandfather lives.

As this lively discussion reveals, an array of heartfelt sentiments are at work that confound the pursuit of providing a clear and concise meaning for the tanindrazaña, the homeland, the nation. There is a layering of definitions that coincide with ideas of self and other, insider and outsider, as well as values (adoration, love, and the fomba) that are central, in a Malagasy context, to imagining the homeland. These concepts are only further complicated by disjunctures that are historically based, where the encroachment of foreigners (be they French or migrants of Malagasy origin) undermines localized definitions of community and territory. Dalia, Foringa Josef, Hasina, and Tsarahita all grasp the complexities of personalizing a localized tanindrazaña, since their parents' origins are highly varied. Thus, their ties to the tanindrazaña (representative of a specific location, such as the Sambirano, or the nation) are enforced through language, burial practices, and devotion to the fomba, but also by something more deeply inherent in the individual that encompasses both one's spirit and one's unwavering love and devotion to the land, its ancestors, and its customs. Of special note is the fact that, over time, I have witnessed the radicalization of Tsarahita's own ideas. Perhaps this stems in part from her commitment to this project. But I believe other factors figure in more prominently. These include working at the Catholic Academy, where teaching official Malagasy has forced her to confront what, in fact, it means to be Malagasy. And I know, too, that she struggles periodically with an ambivalence she feels in working with me as a vazaha who, with each visit, seems more entrenched than ever as a member of her precious community.

A central purpose of this chapter has been to lay the groundwork for subsequent discussions of the past among Madagascar's youth. As such, it has required detailed reviews of very particular moments in Madagascar's history. Of primary importance are the first three decades following independence, for it is during this period that Ambanja's lycée-level students were born and raised, as were, only slightly earlier, their own schoolteachers. The collective experiences of these two groups are radically different in key ways, since teachers, on the one hand, are products of President Tsiranana's First Republic, whereas the youth who form the core of informants for this book were schooled during the socialist era under President Ratsiraka. Teachers and students have converged in the schoolroom, where together they have been forced to confront the realities of colonial oppression and the transformed independent state. Themes that emerged as central to their dialogue include both psychic and physical dangers of European racism; the denigration of the colonized subject in reference to all things French; the significance of the colonized mind; and the centrality of the homeland—as indigenous territory as well as nation—for colonizer, Malagasy citizen, and the Sambirano's local inhabitants.

It is these themes and their associated lessons that have provided the impetus for the politicization of Ambanja's youth, a process that ultimately has fueled—and confounded—the repeated reimagining of Madagascar as a nation. As the early history of literacy and schooling reveals, however, perceptions of a persistent Merina hegemony impede Malagasy unification. From the onset, agents of European knowledge and power favored Merina structures, an impenetrable chauvinism that continues to marginalize coastal inhabitants. Given the weight of linguistic history in Madagascar, even malagasization, as an attempt to overcome these barriers, is itself rife with contradictions, which are played out on a daily basis in the classroom. Nationalism, malagasization, unification—all of these ideological constructs are plagued by ambiguities, which are central to the remainder of this book. As this chapter has shown, schooling and identity in Ambanja are shaped by differences of region and ethnic affiliation. As will be illustrated in part 2, class and gender only further complicate this picture.

PART TWO

The Perplexities of Urban Schooling: Sacrifice, Suffering, and Survival

Figure 5. *Lambahoany* (body wrap) depicting students involved in an islandwide literacy campaign as part of their National Service. School youth who have passed their baccalauréat examinations are shown instructing older peasants in the official Malagasy alphabet (there is no *c, q, u, w,* or *x*). The inscription "Tanora Malagasy mianara taratasy" means "Malagasy youth teach letters."

Schooling is not simply about learning, for pedagogy is intrinsically linked to the ideological concerns of the state—be it colonial or independent. Madagascar, as a former French colony, bears the weight of this legacy, one that affects all quarters of education. A question that constantly perplexes educators is: What precisely does it mean to be Malagasy? Students likewise grapple with this concern, their answers framed by how they imagine their tanindrazaña, or homeland.

As illustrated in part 1, education in Madagascar is characterized by sacrifice and suffering, as students, parents, and educators alike struggle for success. In an effort to expose their daily struggles, part 2 addresses these historical and ideological concerns by grounding them in the experiences of contemporary schooling in Ambanja. As such, chapters 2 and 3 are about the logistics of academic success. As will be shown in chapter 2, economic scarcity is commonplace throughout Madagascar, a reality that undermines quality schooling, especially in rural and coastal regions. In this regard, Ambanja emerges as an especially compelling case. As a coastal town, its schools typically lack even the most basic resources, yet in other ways, it is exceptional. With its impressive array of state-run and elite as well as inferior remedial institutions, it is among the largest (and strongest) educational centers in the north. As such, it may be viewed as a microcosm of island schooling.

Chapter 3 then examines daily survival in this urban center, focusing on a special category of students: school migrants, and especially those of rural origin. Migrant strangers are suspect in Ambanja, so young people drawn from afar struggle to survive on their own. This chapter examines the quandaries of their daily experiences and offers comparative data from the lives of town-based peers. The myriad obstacles that characterize schooling nevertheless do little to squelch the dreams and aspirations of this astonishing cohort of youth.

CHAPTER 2

The Sacrificed Generation

If 100 students enter kindergarten together in Madagascar, only 10 percent from the same class will ever take the bac, and only 1 percent will pass it.

From a scrap of newspaper of unknown origin, dated July 14, 1994 (Bastille Day), wrapped around a loaf of bread from a bakery in Ambanja

AFRICAN INEQUALITIES

"Africa is experiencing an educational crisis of unprecedented proportions," writes Samuel Atteh (1996, 36); although he speaks specifically of education at the university level, his statement is just as pertinent to discussions of primary and secondary school opportunities. Schools across the continent currently are plagued by a host of problems. These include poor infrastructural support, inadequate schoolroom facilities, gross disparities in educational access, poorly trained teachers and support staff, and increased unemployment among upper-level graduates, as public expenditures on education shrink with each decade. The significance of such critical shortages can similarly be understood in financial terms. According to a World Bank report, "the allocation of public expenditure on education in forty-nine sub-Saharan African countries fell from $10 billion in 1980 to 8.9 in 1983, while school enrollments increased more than 50 percent. Comparatively, military expenditures in most African countries have increased at faster rates than expenditures for basic human needs such as education, health, and shelter" (World Bank 1989, 12, quoted in Atteh 1996, 36). Clearly, education is a luxury that many African countries feel they can ill afford.

One might therefore argue that sacrifice—as a national gesture, action, or policy—dominates current understandings of education not only in Madagascar but throughout much of Africa. This theme is central to this chapter, which explores the nature of education under the Second Republic and the subsequent demise of Ratsiraka's vision during the transitional period of the early 1990s. The innovative restructuring of education under his brand of socialism was plagued by inadequate public financial support, because although the architects of malagasization astutely identified the ideological faults of colonial pedagogy, funding for many of the island's most basic educational needs was not forthcoming. The price associated with financial abandonment (of which former regimes were also guilty) has always been felt most acutely in the island's coastal and rural regions. During the Second Republic in particular, teachers and students together blindly struggled to comprehend the ideological dictates of malagasization as they forged viable curricula from the ruins of Tsiranana's toppled First Republic.

With these problems in mind, this chapter has several goals. The first is to provide a detailed overview of schooling in the Sambirano Valley in order to illustrate the effects of French colonial pedagogy. The second is to assess the quality of education in this region. Schooling in the Sambirano is simultaneously representative of education throughout Madagascar and exceptional when compared to other coastal and rural areas. A common problem that typifies discussions of African schooling is the paucity of supportive quantitative material that can uncover long-term national trends. Such is, unfortunately, the case for Madagascar as well. The chapter thus provides a detailed overview of existing data culled from the Sambirano and elsewhere.

An exceptional work in this regard is Rémi Clignet and Bernard Ernst's *L'École à Madagascar* (1995), a detailed study of Madagascar's primary schools, conducted in 1991 as part of a new Franco-Malagasy partnership, which provides a rough baseline for this chapter's reconstruction of secondary schooling.[1] When Clignet and Ernst conducted their study, the island's isolationist policies were coming to an end, and Madagascar now looked beyond its borders for pedagogical assistance, turning once more to French scholars for help. Clignet and Ernst initially targeted 191 schools, scattered throughout the island's six provinces, and their study generated comprehensive data for 2,356 students from 74 schools. In addition to conducting interviews with administrators and teachers, distributing questionnaires, and making site visits to numerous schools, the authors administered a standardized test to students enrolled in their final year of primary school in order to assess their knowledge and abilities in three academic areas: mathematics, French, and Malagasy. Two of their findings are especially pertinent here: students in the central province of Antananarivo scored highest across the board; and although there was much to differentiate the quality of schooling within and across regions, the northern province of Antsiranana, in which the Sambirano lies, generated an overall and pervasive picture of mediocrity. Its schools were geographically located the farthest from one another; they were most lacking in supplies; and collectively their students scored the lowest in all three disciplines (see Clignet and Ernst 1995, esp. 12 ff.).

In light of these findings, educational opportunities in the Sambirano are relatively impressive, for in many other coastal and rural areas there is often no middle school *(collège)*, much less a high school, or lycée. Ambanja presents the greatest opportunities, since it houses both private and state-run institutions whose offerings extend from the primary level up through lycée (for an overview of local schools, see appendix 4). The valley is thus an exception to many of the disparities that Clignet and Ernst identified for this neglected province. Although Ambanja's educational infrastructure suffers from many problems, it is, nevertheless, a model that embodies the island's potential. It is striking that its schools are able to produce *any* lycée graduates who pass their baccalauréat (bac) exams, and that some of these then go on to study at the university level. The fact that only roughly 1 percent of schoolchildren will ever accomplish this goal, as the epigraph to this chapter indicates, is sadly typical of the current state of educational affairs in the Sambirano, in Madagascar, and throughout much of Africa today.

A third goal of this chapter is to explore the inequalities of schooling in Madagascar. The previous chapter explored the limitations of the Tsiranana era and the alternatives offered by Ratsiraka as part of his socialist revolution. This chapter addresses the shortfalls of Ratsiraka's vision and the aftermath of the transitional period and Zafy's brief presidency during the Third Republic. As will be shown, such shortfalls cannot simply be defined in material terms (most obviously in the shortage of school supplies, adequately trained teachers, and classroom space). They are also structural. This chapter therefore analyzes the manner in which economic reforms and their associated educational policies are manifested in terms of gender, social class, and regional hierarchies. When viewed through this lens, a key question that arises is, who in Madagascar has truly been sacrificed?

A central concern of this study is the centrality of ideological concerns for shaping education (cf. Colonna 1997; Hall 1995, esp. 249 ff.; Shiraishi 1995; Willis 1977; and see also Nelson 1996), a theme that emerges in this chapter's concluding section. As stated earlier, this book is not so much about daily schooling in Madagascar as it is a portrait of educational policy and, thus, of pedagogical morality. The ideological shifts that have redefined Madagascar's ongoing educational project have been among the most problematic aspects of the nation's recent political upheaval. As described in chapter 1, much of Ratsiraka's inspirational power lay in his ability to expose the rampant inequalities of Tsiranana's administration. This chapter focuses on the consequences of this vision, not only in terms of its material limitations, but in reference to how curricula were restructured in light of a new nationalist agenda. Questions drawn from post-lycée bac exams render this agenda explicit, especially through a comparison of questions from the First and Second republics and the transitional period. As will become clear, education is, indeed, an ideological enterprise.

ENCOUNTERING EXTREMES
A Town Transformed

Among the most striking themes that has emerged in the course of this research is the manner in which social distinctions frame disparate notions of history and political consciousness in Madagascar and, more specifically, among Ambanja's youth. Drawing upon field observations made in 1987 during the Second Republic, I argued earlier (Sharp 1993) that the paired forces of ethnicity and regionalism were far more significant than social class in shaping cultural constructions of difference in the Sambirano, for the majority of elite inhabitants were almost exclusively high-landers who had been posted here to serve as directors for large state-run agricul-tural plantations of colonial origin.[2] Indeed, I still maintain that this was so dur-ing Ratsiraka's socialist regime. For although there were obvious disparities between rich and poor (most evident in material possessions and the quality and perma-nence of building materials), by the late 1980s, all of Ambanja's inhabitants felt the weight of scarcity. In essence, Ratsiraka's isolationist state capitalism worked as a social equalizer. Even the richest landholders lived in shabby dwellings, for there was no paint to be found anywhere, no skilled electrician or plumber in town, and, worse yet, there was a severe shortage of every conceivable housing supply, rang-ing from wiring, to bolts, to faucet washers.[3] My own hammer, screwdriver, wrench, and all-purpose pocket knife were highly prized, scarce items in a town where many homes stored coveted yet long broken and damaged appliances and other posses-sions such as electric irons (supplanted by heavy charcoal-heated ones), gas stoves (replaced with charcoal braziers), rotary egg beaters (which gave way to spoons), and motorbikes (people moved about more frequently than ever on foot). Only a few merchants in Ambanja had the money and other necessary means to travel abroad, and although a few homes in this large town had functioning television sets, these were useless given the poor quality of reception. As a result, they stood idle, ornamented with handmade lace and artificial flowers. Nor can I remember seeing a VCR, an item one occasionally encountered in Antananarivo or Diégo-Suarez, for example, although generally only in households that had children work-ing or studying abroad.

Furthermore, the infrastructure at times seemed nonexistent. Telegraph ser-vice to the capital was slower than mail; and although Ambanja was wired for tele-phones, I only saw the system function properly one day out of an entire year, when a friend received an experimental call from a house a stone's throw away. When she attempted to return the call a few minutes later, the system had once again failed. Ambanja certainly had one of the best networks of roads on the island, but those that truly had all-weather surfaces only extended a few kilometers out of town, built long ago and subsequently maintained to service the needs of the local plan-tations. Only the boldest of long-distance travelers would venture to this town via the southern route during the rainy season, and they would arrive bursting with elaborate tales of lengthy sojourns along the national highway, their transports reg-ularly unable to free themselves from knee-deep muddy pits. Ambanja's full-time inhabitants nevertheless enjoyed this season, for although it heralded cyclones, it also ensured the growth of crops and a sleepier urban existence, because the an-nual surge of migrants temporarily ceased. During the dry season, these strangers would reappear, emerging from transports with faces, clothes, and personal be-longings covered in a thick layer of fine dust.

It was in the realm of health care that the valley's residents suffered most, since all were forced to rely on a nearly nonexistent state medical system. Overworked doctors, nurses, midwives, and health auxiliaries attempted to deliver care in a nation where one scrambled to locate bandages, analgesics, anesthetics, and even the most basic of medications. For this reason, a small private workers clinic was established by a conglomerate of the valley's state-run plantations and other large businesses, but this eventually entered rapid decline when its skilled physician married and moved away in 1988. The shelves of pharmacies—like those of the neighboring boutiques—were dusty and bare, and patients would linger there looking bewildered, holding orders for prescriptions that could never be filled. Even worse, those medications had often expired, their potency transformed by the tropical heat and an unforeseen shelf life (cf. Silverman et al. 1982, 1990). Throughout my first year, two children whom I adored died, one of malaria, the other of diphtheria, and a third wasted away slowly from an unidentified form of cancer.[4] Numerous young adult friends were debilitated by childhood polio; and many a man was regularly incapacitated by high blood pressure or prostatitis. Two women I knew survived emergency reproductive surgeries only because they had been out of town and within range of two of the country's few exceptional hospitals.

By 1993, much of this had changed, and I barely recognized the Ambanja I had known in 1987. State employees were beginning to reap the profits of Ratsiraka's promises to increase wages: for some, this meant that their monthly salaries doubled or tripled, from FMG 30,000–50,000 to as much as 100,000–150,000. Boutiques were full of foreign goods, a trend that only increased in the next two years: refrigerators, television sets, and VCRs abounded (most bought on credit). Spurred on by the installation of a local satellite antenna, several of my friends purchased television sets in 1994, and throughout late June and into July, we would huddle together in single-roomed homes gleefully watching the World Cup soccer tournament. The town itself experienced several major improvements as well. The main street had been repaved, and, by late 1995, so had the highway to the provincial capital of Diégo-Suarez, so that the more daring traveler might actually make what had been an arduous day's trip in a matter of a few hours, sometimes even returning home late that same evening. Modest and mostly foreign-owned "luxury" tourist hotels had sprung up on nearby beaches. The ferry service to Nosy Be had improved, and more migrants had clearly moved in, arriving by land, sea, and air. The presence of new settlers was most evident in the expansion of the town's borders, particularly toward the north and east, as well as in the networks of a new sewage system on the town's northern end. The Catholic Mission had also delivered on its promise to construct an efficient, economical, and well-stocked hospital, complete with a sterile operating room, so that patients with serious emergencies no longer had to travel to (and, ultimately, die in) the larger state-run one on Nosy Be.

Following President Zafy's election in 1993, Ambanja's residents also suddenly felt the weight of newly introduced forms of foreign hegemony. Together the twin forces of the International Monetary Fund (IMF) and the World Bank had mandated an accelerated structural readjustment of the nation's economy. Ambanja experienced these policies and their accompanying development strategies as a mixed blessing. Significant funds were poured into the town for educational purposes, and buildings that had stood abandoned in 1987 suddenly received fresh coats of paint in anticipation of the town becoming a provincial center for teacher retraining. One of the island's new Peace Corps volunteers also eventually took up residence in Ambanja, where he focused on training English teachers. Within a year, yet another volunteer was placed to the north in Antankaraña territory to work on a health-related project. But everyone in town also suffered enormously under wave upon wave of currency devaluations, making it impossible for most people to buy even basic foodstuffs from one day to the next, as market prices literally doubled and tripled overnight.

Amid these changes, class differences in the Sambirano expanded, becoming more rawly evident than they had been a decade before. Among the most significant factors that drove this was the sudden reprivatization of the state-owned plantations. The most financially astute of their directors managed to pull together funds (sometimes illicitly) that enabled them to purchase the valley's largest farms and collection centers, which they had run as state employees only a year before. Since the majority of these directors were of Merina or Betsileo origin, highland-coastal differences were further exacerbated by the deeper entrenchment of class disparities in the valley. I watched some of these directors evolve into a substantially richer town elite, and several suddenly became immensely wealthy. "Nationalization is theft," Tsiranana had declared in 1969 (Paillard 1979, 350, n. 38), underscoring his desire to protect foreign interests. Twenty-four years later, Zafy's IMF-driven reforms quickly dismantled Ratsiraka's state capitalism, enabling several former directors of state-run businesses to increase their personal holdings a hundredfold, often literally bulldozing the soil and residences occupied by the powerless poor without a second thought as they seized even more land for their private use. Along with a few merchant families (some Sakalava, others of Indo-Pakistani, Chinese, or Yemeni origin), they began to build enormous, well-equipped mansions, some of which stood so tall as to defy gravity. It was not unusual to encounter manual laborers huddled together performing the back-breaking task of splitting rocks by hand to create gravel or decorative stone, a sight that awoke uncomfortable memories of enforced labor during the colonial era (see chapter 6). The town's older villas now seemed measly and ramshackle by comparison. Such developments only increased the awareness among Ambanja's students that local capitalist ventures indeed defined a significant impetus behind social and economic disparity.

An Experiment's Demise

The classroom also became an important target for Third Republic reforms. Zafy and his supporters regarded official Malagasy as being without question an educational quagmire. All were aware that throughout the Second Republic, children from elite families had been shuttled off to private institutions (often referred to as "French" or "European" schools, regardless of whether their location was domestic or abroad) in order to escape the isolating effects of Ratsiraka's educational policies. These children soon became fluent in French, often speaking it as their first language, not only in the classroom but at home as well. Unable to read and write official Malagasy with ease (or sometimes even speak their parents' dialects fluently), they nevertheless emerged at the beginning of Zafy's Third Republic eager to assume the new and coveted high-paying jobs that required French and even English fluency in such expanding sectors as finance, tourism, and foreign affairs. In this sense, they stood apart from students educated in state-run schools, especially those from coastal regions, who were linguistically at ease in neither official Malagasy nor French. Those few who had excelled still lacked the contacts and financial support necessary to go on to the university and eventually excel in Antananarivo. As a result, Zafy and his educational advisors brought malagasization to an abrupt halt, reintroducing French in the schools as the primary language of instruction. To facilitate the smooth success of this transition, Zafy brought in many new technical advisors from abroad—particularly from France—to restructure state schooling and generate new curricular materials. Malagasy schooling had, thus, in a sense, come full circle.[5] The remainder of this chapter outlines the complexity of education in Madagascar, exposing, too, the flexibility that is possible in as comprehensive a setting as Ambanja.

AN AMBANJA EDUCATION
Schooling in Madagascar: An Overview

The structure of primary and secondary education that characterizes Madagascar's history is deeply entrenched in the French model. Students pass through three levels of schooling (table 2), consisting of elementary, or primary, school *(primaire)*; middle school *(collège*, or, more formally, *collège d'enseignement général,* or CEG), and high school *(lycée)*. Each levels is further divided into grades *(classes)*. Thus, in primary school, one begins in the eleventh class and moves up to the seventh *(onz-ième–septième)*, years that correspond to the first through fifth grades in the United States. In middle school one progresses from the sixth through the third class *(six-ième–troisième)*; these correspond to the sixth through ninth grades in the United States. In high school, or lycée, one moves through "second," "first," and then "final" years *(seconde, première,* and *terminale)*; their rough equivalents in the U.S. system are the tenth, eleventh, and twelfth grades.[6]

This is, of course, an oversimplified as well as idealized portrait of the system, for very few students ever complete all three levels, let alone go on to university. A significant series of barriers is defined by three qualifying exams. These funnel an increasingly smaller number of students through the scholastic ranks. These exams are the CEPE *(certificat d'études primaires élémentaires)*, which one takes at the end of primary school; the BEPC *(brévet d'études du premier cycle)*, which falls at the end of the final year of collège; and the bac (baccalauréat), an exam that becomes a near obsession for many students in their final, or terminale, year at lycée.[7]

A lycée education, and, thus, the bac examinations, are divided into three tracks. Beginning in their second-to-last (première) year at lycée, students enter a specialized track of study that will then determine the focus of their bac. In theory too, all curricula shift to French exclusively at the beginning of this year in anticipation of university study. Throughout the course of my research, however, I never audited a lycée-level class at any of Ambanja's schools that was conducted exclusively in French; instead, they always involved a combination of French, official Malagasy, and Sakalava. The lycée-level tracks are terminale *série A,* which is structured around a humanities and social science core,[8] terminale *série D,* a natural science core appropriate for those who hope to study medicine, for example, and terminale *série C,* an advanced science core with a strong emphasis on mathematics and physics. Many students consider *série* D to be more difficult than *série* A, and few attempt the rigorous *série* C. Because of the lack of laboratory facilities, qualified teachers, and, in turn, interested students at its schools, the terminale C track was short-lived in Ambanja and, so, beginning with the 1991–92 academic year, no *série* C exams were offered.

A failure in any of these exams requires students to reenroll in the previous year of schooling in order to prepare, yet again, for their qualifying exams. That is, they must redo their septième class at the primary level, troisième in middle school, and terminale at lycée. Students who fail the CEPE or BEPC (and thus their septième or troisième class) a second time are forced to drop out. Only the regulations for the bac allow a student to reenroll in terminale and take the associated bac exam an unlimited number of times—as Mme. Vezo tells her students, "It's all bound by your courage!" In fact, when, in 1994, I first encountered the cohort of students from Ambanja's state-run Lycée Tsiaraso I, two were on their third try. Few lycée level students do so more than twice, however, because such preparation requires that young and healthy near-adults remain out of the workforce for yet another year, meaning that they and their kin must jointly make significant sacrifices to allow them time for serious study.[9]

Several strategies are used to facilitate success following an initial or even second failure. At the lycée level, students often make their first attempt at *série* D, only to switch to the humanities/social science curriculum of *série* A when they fail the bac the first time around. (Students cannot move from *série* A to *série* D, however, because they lack the necessary advanced science background, which begins prior to the terminale year; *série* D students have already studied philosophy and history/geography in addition to science, and so the switch is easier for them.) This trend is not unique to the Sambirano, but is characteristic of student behavior throughout the island, and it is hardly surprising given the often low quality of schooling available in mathematics and the sciences (Clignet and Ernst 1995). In Ambanja, it was a wonder that students acquired the necessary scientific knowledge for the bac, given that only a few years after the imposing state-run Lycée Tsiaraso I had been built, the laboratory facilities no longer functioned for lack of running water and other essential yet basic supplies. More generally, students at all levels in Ambanja frequently switch back and forth between the state-run schools and the private Catholic Academy, depending on their academic success the previous year, as well as their parents' financial situations. This pattern becomes especially pronounced at the lycée level. As a result, it is often difficult to determine the status of students enrolled at these two schools from one year to the next. Some parents, in order to bypass regulations, enroll their younger children in one of the town's three private unlicensed remedial schools, which offer classes at the primary and middle school levels. This allows students to make numerous attempts at the CEPE or BEPC exams beyond the officially mandated limit of two. As of late 1995, there was no such remedial program available at the lycée level.

From an American perspective, one might argue that schooling in Madagascar is unjust, because its design ensures failure more often than success (an argument that of course can similarly be made for much of rural Africa [Kirkaldy 1996] and poorer regions of the United States [Kozol 1991]). Certainly, the three qualifying exams are extraordinarily difficult (this is especially true of the bac), a problem only further exacerbated by the paucity of curricular materials, particularly outside the high plateaux. Furthermore, inability to acquire a passing grade on any of these exams guarantees that a student's education will come to an abrupt and permanent halt. In the Sambirano, this means that a child will inevitably return to work for parents or other older kin. Children from rural areas will begin to farm full-time; if their kin are town-based, they will be expected to hone their skills as seamstresses and tailors, merchants, fruit vendors, and so on (Sharp 1996). School success requires perseverance, because most students must repeat at least one year in their educational careers (this is true in France as well). Thus, students who are enrolled at the lycée level are often several years older than their American counterparts, as is evident in this study, where informants drawn from the state-run lycée fall between the ages of fifteen and twenty-four.

Nevertheless, Malagasy students stand above many of their American contemporaries in several respects: in Madagascar, there are essentially two levels at which one may complete a high school education. The first involves achieving passing grades in the terminale year. The more highly coveted baccalauréat certificate creates an elite group of students who excel at this extraordinarily difficult task. As a result, the studious lycée student's knowledge in such areas as world history, political and economic theory, and philosophy can easily rival that of many college students in the United States. The fact that such knowledge is acquired in communities bereft of books, maps, study guides, and libraries is truly astonishing; their knowledge is culled instead from class lectures and discussions with well-schooled elders.

Education and National Sacrifice

To complete this general summary of a successful student's career in Madagascar requires a return to the theme of sacrifice, this time as defined on a national scale in the context of education. A central plank of Ratsiraka's platform, as outlined in

TABLE 2 The French Model of Schooling Used in the Sambirano Valley

School level	U.S. equivalent	Classes	U.S. grade equivalent	Qualifying exam for next level of schooling	Schools in Ambanja proper			Additional regional schools		Totals
					State-run	Private licensed	Private unlic.	State-run	Private licensed	
primaire	primary or elementary	*11ème–7ème**	1st–5th	CEPE**	6	2	1	4	1	14
collège (CEG)	middle school	*6ème–3ème*	6th–9th	BEPC**	1	1	3	6	1	12
lycée	high school	*seconde, première, terminale*	10th–12th	bac**	2	1	0	0	1	4

NOTE: This table does not include part-time Islamic schools.

*The two private primary schools in town—the Catholic Mission Academy and the French Elementary School—also offer kindergarten (FR: *maternelle*).

**The three qualifying examinations are:

—the CEPE (*certificat d'études primaires élémentaires*), taken at the end of primary school; a passing mark qualifies the student for study at the *collège* level.

—the BEPC (*brevet d'études du premier cycle*), taken at the end of *collège*; a passing mark qualifies the student for study at the *lycée* level.

—the bac (*baccalauréat*), taken at the end of the *terminale* year of *lycée*; students have chosen different tracks that determine which exam (*série* A, B, or C) they will take. A passing score qualifies the student for a university education.

the *Boky Mena,* was the creation of a program known as the National Service (Service National Révolutionnaire, or SN) (Ratsiraka 1975, 111–15). During the Second Republic, all students who completed their schooling through the lycée level and who had passed their bac exams were entitled to a free university education. In addition to the central campus in Antananarivo, a number of newly constructed regional universities stood waiting to accommodate them, each with its own areas of specialization.[10] Before students could enroll, however, they were required to acknowledge their debt to the nation by serving for eighteen to twenty-four months in the national youth corps. Holders of bac certificates were first trained in how to handle artillery, so that they could be called upon to defend their country if necessary, and then they spent much of the remainder of their time serving the current needs of the country. Many were sent to villages whose schools were horribly understaffed, where they taught the sciences, mathematics, history, and geography, for example. Others served on literacy campaigns based on the Chinese model, where many of their pupils were the same age as their parents and grandparents (see fig. 5). Still others provided manual labor for road works and other construction projects. As the years progressed, however, far too many youth sat idle in the offices and even homes of upper administrators, where they were forbidden by their immediate supervisors to touch a phone or file, for fear that they might put underworked yet established lower-level bureaucrats out of jobs in a nation suffering from a failing economy. In response to public pressure and a shrunken national treasury, the National Service requirement was eliminated by the 1991–92 academic year (corresponding to the first year of the 1991–93 transitional period). New restrictions, too, placed even greater impediments in the way of successful bac candidates: the state began to charge tuition for a university education, which by the 1994–95 academic year had risen to FMG 35,000 a year, up from 25,000 in 1992–93 and 10,000 in 1990–91. Furthermore, only a few openings now existed at the nation's numerous campuses, and housing was often unavailable, which simply added yet another significant expense to students' limited budgets. Finally, by the early 1990s, university admission required that a student pass an additional set of qualifying exams, which also determined a student's course of study and scholarship eligibility.[11] In response, student strikes occurred every year between 1990 and 1996, either slowing study considerably or, as happened in 1990–91, shutting down the university system completely for the year.

Ambanja: An Exceptional Educational Domain

Historical Overview.   When set again national policies that seem to ensure failure, today Ambanja emerges without question as an impressive educational center for northern Madagascar (again, see appendix 4), whether viewed in contemporary or historic terms. Following French conquest of the island in 1895–96, the town quickly grew around a military post, expanding in response to the needs of newly established foreign-owned plantations. By 1908, the first colonial primary school had opened in the valley to serve Malagasy children (a separate school was maintained for children of European descent), soon staffed by Malagasy instructors trained for this purpose in Madagascar. In 1938, the Catholic Mission opened a second primary school for Malagasy children, run by French Franciscan nuns, and in 1953, the mission expanded its offerings to include a middle school curriculum as well. Throughout much of the century, the mission maintained separate schools for girls and boys. These merged in 1978, and in the following year, the newly formed Catholic Mission Academy offered classes through the terminale year of lycée. By the 1960s, the majority of the mission's educational staff was Malagasy, and in 1977, its directorship shifted from the control of French nuns to Sakalava priests. The academy's development is linked closely to another smaller institution, the Catholic School of the Upper Sambirano (CSUS), which is located in a small town approximately twenty-five kilometers southeast of Ambanja.

Quite a few of the children schooled in Ambanja during the colonial era excelled in their studies and emerged fluent in French, which remained the dominant language of instruction, especially beyond the primary school level (Covell 1995, 86). The majority of Ambanja's current older class of male and female intellectuals received their initial schooling at local institutions, where they were carefully selected for advanced training at outstanding schools such as that in Joffreville (located in the far north outside the provincial capital of Diégo-Suarez) and the École Le Myre de Vilers in Antananarivo, both of which trained civil servants and teachers. A few also acquired advanced training abroad, as exemplified by the story of Mr. Pascal in chapter 1. Other educated Sakalava elite of Ambanja include the late king Tsiaraso Victor III (Andriamanaitriarivo,[12] r. 1966–93), nearly all of the town's current school administrators, lawyers, and many royalty, including one of Madagascar's first women to hold a high post in the nation's independent government. The Catholic Church has provided yet another avenue for advanced study: many of the young women and men who joined the Catholic clergy later continued their studies in theology at the masters or doctoral levels, usually in Strasbourg, France. They now hold high administrative positions at the mission or at sister institutions located throughout the island.

Primary and Middle Schools: State-run and Catholic Opportunities.   The town of Ambanja, with an estimated population today of approximately 30,000,[13] has six state-run neighborhood primary schools. An additional four are scattered throughout the valley (the total regional population, including Ambanja, was estimated at 93,792 in 1986, and over 110,000 in 1995) (see appendix 3). All four of these rural schools were built for the children of plantation workers. There are approximately 12,500 children enrolled in the valley's ten state-run primary schools (a handful of others have since closed for lack of funding); during the 1994–95 academic year, the largest and best-staffed primary school, located in central Ambanja, had an enrollment of 807 (see appendix 5).

Unlike the island's larger provincial capitals, such as Diégo-Suarez and Maha-janga, Ambanja experienced no significant change beyond the primary level in the first decade of the First Republic. In the 1970s, however, a network of nine state-run middle schools were built; two of these have since closed down for lack of state support. The valley's largest and, again, best-staffed state-run CEG opened in 1971. It, too, is located in central in Ambanja. During the 1993–94 academic year, it had a total enrollment of 405 pupils, a large proportion of the valley's total estimated CEG enrollment of 1,450 (see appendix 5). Ambanja's CEG is an exemplary insti-tution, and its director, like that of the town's largest primary school, was born and raised here and is well known throughout the province for his high academic standards. The remaining CEGs of the Sambirano are typically located twenty to thirty kilometers apart, so that many rural children must either walk long distances to school each day or move if they wish to continue their studies beyond primary school. The latter trend is especially prominent in Ambanja, where a large pro-portion of CEG students are not from town. There are no dormitory facilities avail-able (save for the building reserved for the Catholic Academy's seminary students), and townsfolk are wary of strangers, even if they are children. As a result, many of these school migrants—who may be as young as ten years old—live alone, with a sibling, or with a few schoolmates in small rented rooms or houses scattered throughout the town. As will become clear in chapter 3, these school migrants are saddled with a staggering array of responsibilities, far exceeding those of their town-based peers who have adult kin to look after them.

Schooling opportunities, including primary, middle school, and lycée levels, are also provided through the Catholic Academy and CSUS, its rural sister institu-tion. These two schools provide an education of relatively high quality, and together they define a middle range between state-run and private elite schooling at a price that is affordable for many middle- and even low-income households.[14] (The acad-emy and CSUS share much of their staff; given that CSUS caters almost exclu-sively to the needs of children in a relatively isolated rural region, it will remain peripheral to this discussion of schooling in Ambanja.) Specifically, Ambanja's Catholic Academy differs from state-run schools in several important respects: first, although it, too, suffers from a lack of curricular materials, its problems are hardly as desperate. For one, the mission itself has a print shop, so that its more ambi-tious instructors sometimes produce handouts and other materials. Second, as a Catholic institution, it is linked to a much larger national and international net-work of educators who can provide some pedagogical support. As a private insti-tution, it is able to recruit its own staff, rather than having to rely on appointments made by state officials based in Antananarivo. The academy's teaching staff are well educated (as noted earlier, several hold the equivalent of masters' and doctoral degrees from France), and they speak French with ease. Also, the majority are of Sakalava descent and were born and raised in the Sambirano. They often em-pathize with their students on a level that highland-born state schoolteachers find difficult to achieve, and they may place a higher value on exploring the dialectic of local versus national histories than do, again, their highland peers. The academy's instructors encounter less linguistic resistance from their students, because the Sakalava dialect is often their first tongue.

Preferences regarding how best to make use of a private Catholic education vary among parents. Some choose to send their children to this academy for their first few years only, switching them to the state-run CEG if they pass the CEPE qualifying exam. For most, the reason is financial: the monthly tuition, which rises from FMG 4,000 at the primary level to 6,000 and 9,000 in middle school and lycée respectively, simply becomes too heavy a burden. Typically at this point, too, parents have the educational needs of other younger children to consider. Thus, the schoolteacher Mme. Vezo and her husband, for example, shifted three of their four children to the state-run CEG after they passed their CEPE exams; only the fourth, who had impressively high marks, was allowed to remain at the Catholic Academy. In other households, children who showed little interest in schooling would no longer seem worth the financial investment and would be transferred at various stages by their parents to local state-run schools. This is in fact what happened in the household of my friend Salima, a petty merchant who worked not one but two market stalls with her husband Abdul so that their two boys could attend the Catholic Academy. Their sons showed little interest in schooling, however, so Salima and Abdul reluctantly removed them from the Catholic Academy and placed them in the town's CEG. A year later, one had already dropped out of school. A widespread preference for academy schooling at these lower levels is evident in the school's enrollment figures: there are approximately 1,300 students in the academy's primary school, 550 in the middle school, and fewer than 200 at the lycée level. Class sections for younger children are relatively small, unlike at the lycée level, when classrooms may swell well beyond their capacity.

Remedial Schooling.   Because advanced schooling is highly valued by many of the Sambirano's inhabitants, three unlicensed remedial schools have cropped up in recent years, capitalizing on the desperation felt by parents and students alike when faced with school failure. (Similar institutions were relatively widespread elsewhere on the island during the First Republic; see Covell 1987, 36–37). These are Salvation School, the School of Courage, and The Helping Hand of Hope, institutions that concentrate on the final two years of primary and middle school education. Their tuitions are relatively high and their returns low; nevertheless, they suffer no shortage of pupils, many of whom are on their third, fourth, or even fifth try at the CEPE and BEPC exams. Salvation provides an apt example. This school opened in 1986–87 as a shoestring operation, primarily, as its director explained, "to solve my own sudden unemployment problems." In subsequent years, he has consistently hired other teachers who face predicaments similar to his own: that is, dismissal from a local licensed institution for general incompetence (and, in at least one case, severe alcoholism). The quality of Salvation's schooling is therefore suspect, although by 1993, the director had added to his part-time staff two highly respected state school instructors who chose to moonlight at Salvation in order to make a little extra income. Within six years, the school had grown considerably, so that classes were eventually moved from a pair of lean-tos made of palm fronds to a newly constructed, airy four-room concrete structure that they rented from a neighbor. By the 1992–93 school term, Salvation had an enrollment of 150 students, and had started to expand its existing middle school activities to include a few primary school classes as well. Two years later, it had swelled to 362.

After attending numerous Salvation classes over the course of three years, I have concluded that one could excel under the tutelage of its two French teachers; in contrast, one history/geography instructor's knowledge was frightening abysmal, and English instruction was essentially nonexistent under a part-time teacher whose response to my basic question, "Where did you learn to speak English?" was "Yes." The school nevertheless succeeded with some students: in the 1993–94 school term, nine out of thirty-five students, or 26 percent, passed the BEPC and thus qualified for study at the lycée level, a rate that corresponds to that for the valley as a whole in that same year (see appendix 6). Yet a handful of boys among their peers remained illiterate at the close of the school term, barely able to write even their own names. For such schooling, parents paid tuition fees only slightly lower than those charged by the Catholic Academy. The situation at the town's two other unlicensed remedial schools was similar, although two informants reported that the majority of the students at Helping Hand had previously failed at Salvation (and might thus be on their fourth or even fifth attempt at a single year of schooling). Regardless of the chances that Ambanja's remedial schools truly offer their students, their existence underscores the striking inadequacy of state schooling: enrollment figures alone reflect the fact that for every student enrolled at Ambanja's state-run CEG, there is another who has failed not once but at least twice and who now sits in an unlicensed classroom.

Elite Primary Education.   At the other end of the spectrum at the primary level is the French Elementary School. This small and exclusive institution was established in the mid 1980s in response to the educational needs that well-to-do highland and French parents identified as essential for their own children. It is truly an elite school, as shown most obviously by its tuition rates, which make it prohibitively expensive save for a very small number of households scattered throughout the valley. Beginning in the 1994–95 academic year, tuition was FMG 37,500 a month (compared to FMG 4,000 a month charged at the primary level by the Catholic Academy). Malagasy households carried the heaviest burden, because only those children with a parent who could document French citizenship could receive a substantial discount. Unlike Ambanja's other schools, the French Elementary School has adequate curricular supplies, so that its pupils travel regularly between home and school with workbooks and readers. This school was considered an eyesore by some of the town's more embittered inhabitants, who saw it as a reminder that a deep chasm lay between the educational possibilities available to their own children versus those from wealthy families. My friend Mélanie, who has her bac and who works hard to put her three children through the Catholic Academy, expressed her sentiments as follows: "It's already more expensive for those of us who are poor [*olo madiniky*, 'the little people'] to send our kids to the state-run school [with its new, albeit minimal charges][15] than it is for the rich [*mpañarivo*, literally, 'those who have thousands'] to send their kids to the French school. Just think of it—what's [FMG] 37,000 to them? They'll easily spend that during one night in a disco." The repercussions of these educational disparities between schooling and the opportunities open to the olo madiniky and mpañarivo are discussed in the final section of this chapter.

Instruction at this elite school is conducted strictly in French, and the majority of its young students speak French at home as their first language. Once they complete their first five years of primary schooling, they are inevitably sent away to one of several exclusive boarding schools located in the island's larger cities or, if their parents are wealthy enough, to private schools in Europe. These children are encouraged to assume foreign personae at school, where they are generally addressed by their "French" names (these may be baptism or confirmation names if they are Catholic, and thus inevitably saints' names), whereas the Malagasy names given to them when younger might still be used exclusively at home. Linguistic barriers are established at a very early age, for just as all languages other than French are forbidden within the confines of the school, at home these students are highly discouraged from using any words or expressions drawn from the local Sakalava dialect. As a result, many of these children grow up unable to speak any dialect of Malagasy fluently, even the one spoken by their own parents. As Noël Gueunier (1993; cf. Ramamonjisoa 1984) has argued, they, along with other children in the highest echelons of Malagasy society, inevitably grow up "talking white" (FR: *parler blanc*). After a few years at this small school, their facility with French is impressive, for although their vocabularies are certainly smaller, they often speak French with greater ease than do the most dedicated of students from the state-run lycée.

Lycée Opportunities

The Sambirano Valley stands in stark contrast to much of the rest of the island in that it has four secondary institutions: two that are state-run (one of these is a small, specialized Technical School), and two private Catholic schools. In contrast, one must travel a considerable distance outside the valley to encounter another state-run lycée: the closest requires a ferry ride across open ocean to the offshore island of Nosy Be; another educational center is Ambilobe, located 102 kilometers north of Ambanja; and a third is Antsohihy, which is 217 kilometers to the south. All of these centers, like Ambanja, have both state-run and private Catholic institutions.

In 1980, the town of Ambanja acquired state support to construct a small lycée and, then, in 1986, enough funding to build a more modern two-story structure, complete with science laboratories, at the edge of town on land donated by one of the larger state-owned plantations. After much debate, this structure was proudly named the Lycée Tsiaraso I, after the Bemazava-Sakalava ruler who reigned at the time of French conquest (see chapter 4). During the 1980s, an agricultural school was also in operation, located a half-hour's drive north of Ambanja, but it had closed down by 1993. The other remaining specialized state-run lycée, the Technical School, lies on the outskirts of town and caters to the specialized needs of approximately eighty students, the majority of whom are boys.

Today, the state-run Lycée Tsiaraso I and the private Catholic Academy are the valley's most important secondary institutions, and they compete for students, many of whom shift back and forth between the two, depending each year on their personal financial and/or academic status. Enrollments at the Lycée Tsiaraso I dwindled from 300 in the late 1980s to 145 during the 1993–94 academic year. In contrast, the Catholic Academy's enrollment climbed, so that by 1993–94, its lycée had 184 pupils (see appendix 5). As a result, the academy experiences periodic overcrowding at this level. I audited several classes where numerous students were forced to stand outside and look in through the doorways or windows because there were not enough seats to hold them all. This overcrowding places an extraordinary burden on academy teachers, for whom discipline, rather than the curriculum, may become a daily preoccupation. Classrooms at the state-run lycée, however, are often half empty.

The Catholic Academy's lycée incorporates a seminary program, in which a few dozen gifted boys handpicked by teachers at other northern Catholic schools for scholarships simultaneously receive theological training in anticipation of their joining the priesthood. Few of these students, however, actually choose to do so in the end. Seminarists stand apart from the majority of their classmates in that they are exceptionally talented students who have consistently excelled in their studies, and thus they are typically younger than their peers at the Catholic Academy or state-run lycée, because they have rarely been required to repeat a grade.[16] As mentioned earlier, school migration is a significant trend in Ambanja, characterized by the resettlement of students in town in unsupervised housing. Seminarists, however, enjoy the luxury of being housed by the mission in a dormitory bordering the priests' quarters, where a simple dining room, a television room, and a small library are reserved exclusively for their use.

Schooling and Success: The Potential for Advancement and Failure

An analysis of enrollment figures and exam success rates reveals a number of trends that characterize schooling in the Sambirano, which clearly funnels an increasingly smaller (and thus more select) group of students into institutions of higher education. Although primary schooling is considered a universal right of children in Madagascar (Ratsiraka 1975, 79 ff.; cf. United Nations 1995, 34, Article 28), there are, in fact, far more children scattered throughout the Sambirano than there are enrolled in its schools. A comprehensive census conducted in 1986, which registered ages for local residents (see appendix 3), recorded that the total number of youth between the ages of six and seventeen years living in the valley was 31,322 (15,697 boys and 15,625 girls), of which 11,682 (5,769 boys and 5,913 girls) were in the town of Ambanja. When analyzed in reference to 1990s trends, these figures operate as conservative population estimates for valley children, because they exclude similarly comprehensive information for those who were foreign nationals, and they do not allow for the fact that many students remain in school well into their twenties. These figures stand in stark contrast to the valley's current school enrollments even for a decade later, because census figures for 1993 and 1995 clearly reveal an even larger valley population (unfortunately, no breakdown by age was available). During the 1994–95 school term, figures for all schools (including state-run, private licensed, and remedial unlicensed) were as follows: there were approximately 13,700 primary school students, 2,250 enrolled in middle schools, and fewer than 490 students studying at the lycée level. Together these three levels of schooling account for only an estimated 16,440 of school youth—that is, a bit more than half of the valley's juvenile population. When compared to the nation as a whole, the valley proves no exception: in 1975, at the beginning of the Second Republic, 50 percent of Madagascar's children were not in school (Ratsiraka 1975, 80). Furthermore, those who currently are officially enrolled may, in fact, be receiving no education at all. This is a problem that plagues rural schools in the Sambirano, where one or a handful of teachers, when left without supervision or guidance, may fail to attend class and may even abandon their rural posts for prolonged periods of time (William Lambert, personal communication, 1998).[17]

Second, as noted earlier, a characteristic of Madagascar's French-based system is the tendency for the majority of students to experience at least one failure in their school careers, so that they are forced to redo a grade if they wish to continue their schooling. The effects of this trend are evident as early as the primary level. As enrollments figures from Ambanja's largest primary school show, a third or more of students in any given year may be repeating their class. As a result, as many as a third to nearly a half may be fifteen or older when they complete primary school (see appendix 5). In this respect, Ambanja is representative of much of the nation as a whole, given that at its largest primary school, the average age of students in septième is over thirteen years of age, and the national average is twelve and three-quarters years (Clignet and Ernst 1995, 103). This trend only increases at the middle school and lycée levels, so that by the time successful students sit for their bac, they might easily be over twenty years old, as were lycée informants Dalia (21), Foringa Josef (23), Hazaly (24), Lucien (20), Pauline (20), and Sidy (20). A similar lag in student age also characterizes enrollment figures at the Catholic Academy, although it is not quite as pronounced as it is at state-run schools. Also, as noted earlier, seminary students are far less likely to have repeated grades, and their ages thus correspond more closely to ranges that typify private schools in the highlands, for example (or, for that matter, expectations at adequate schools in the United States).

A third clear trend revealed by these figures is the sudden and drastic drop in enrollments as students advance through school. As current figures stand, only an estimated 16 percent of students from ten of the Sambirano's state-run primary schools will continue on to those at the middle school level, of whom only approximately 22 percent in turn will study at the lycée level. When the primary and lycée levels are compared, the discrepancy becomes even more striking: currently, lycée students account for only about 3.5 percent of all primary schoolchildren in terms of sheer numbers. The Sambirano thus approximates (although it slightly exceeds) a larger national trend, as described in prophetic fashion in the epigraph to this chapter: "If 100 students enter kindergarten together in Madagascar, only 10 percent from the same class will ever take the bac, and only 1 percent will pass it." It must also be understood that only a small percentage of terminale students sit for the bac in any given year (Madagascar, Service des Statistiques de l'Éducation, *Annuaire statistique*, 1987–90, 1990–91), and very few indeed will go on to university, a trend determined more often by financial limitations than school of origin.

As stated earlier, the French-based examination system ensures that a large number of children will fail their qualifying exams and thus be forced to end their schooling at an early age. Examination success and failure rates are difficult to pin down in Ambanja, because the few bits of data that exist show that scores fluctuate greatly from year to year (often as a result of student strikes generated by local and/or national concerns). Another barrier is that they are recorded sporadically by school administrators. This is especially true for the CEPE examination taken at the end of primary school for which no systematic figures are available for Ambanja; Clignet and Ernst (1995, 101) do, however, report that the national average success rate for the academic years spanning 1988–91 hovered around 32–35 percent. A quick look at enrollment figures for representative schools makes it all too clear that in Ambanja, there are more students enrolled in their final year of primary and middle school than there are of their successors in the following initial years of middle school or lycée.

Enrollment figures for the academic years spanning 1993–95 reveal more specific trends (again, see appendix 5).[18] In 1993–94, for example, 127 students were enrolled in the final, or septième, class in Ambanja's largest primary school. In this same year a seemingly impressive 133 students were enrolled in sixième, or their first year at the town's largest CEG or middle school, but closer examination reveals that this number included 34 boys and 37 girls who had failed the year before. As a result, only 62 new students entered this class. The leap up to the lycée level bears even fewer chances for success. At the end of the 1992–93 academic year, 546 students drawn from all of the valley's middle schools sat for the BEPC exam; of these, only 26 percent passed, or approximately 142 students, of whom under 40 entered the state-run lycée. A trend that typifies examination patterns at all levels is that students enrolled at the Catholic Academy fare much better. According to academy records, at the end of the 1992–93 academic year, 38 percent of their students passed the CEPE exam, and 40 percent the BEPC. The year before, an impressive 70 percent and 50 percent, respectively, passed. The fact that, in contrast, such a low number of the state-run lycée's students pass their bac only intensifies the collective sense of inadequacy among its instructors, who prefer to send their own children to the Catholic Academy, if they can afford it.

Bac scores fluctuated wildly during the period under study, making it difficult to predict outcomes during any given year. Success rates among students from the state-run lycée moved from 14 percent to 7 percent to 1 percent and then up to 23 percent between the academic years of 1990–91 and 1993–94 (see appendix 6). Again, scores are considerably higher at the Catholic Academy. At the end of 1992–93, the academy boasted a bac success rate as high as 50 percent; although acknowledged as unusually impressive, it has subsequently set a standard for what Ambanja's pupils can achieve. The school employed an unorthodox strategy to achieve this success rate. Wary of reports of corruption among northern examiners, its administrators hoped that their students would fare better if they sat the exam alongside their peers at another private Catholic school in Antananarivo and, thus, a few academy staff members traveled with twenty terminale students to the capital city to sit their bac exams.

Another striking development is that whereas enrollment levels at the valley's two Catholic schools have gradually increased since 1987, those for both the state-run lycée and the Technical School have dropped considerably. During the 1987–88 and 1988–89 school terms, the lycée's enrollments were around 340; in the following four years, they dropped to 277, 260, 235, and then 202. By the beginning of the 1993–94 school term, only 145 students enrolled, and by the end of this academic year 15 of these had dropped out, the majority without a trace. The figures for the Technical School reveal a similar trend: in 1987–88, 128 students enrolled, but by 1990–91 the figure had dropped below 100, and in 1993–94 the school had only about 80 students (Madagascar, Service des statistiques de l'éducation, *Annuaire statistique,* 1987–90, 1990–91).

Gender Discrepancies

Regardless of the institution or ethnic or regional affiliations, students who complete their schooling at the lycée level and who pass the bac in Madagascar are exceptional. The differing experiences of male and female students only further complicate the portrait of education in Madagascar. Fewer girls than boys ever reach the terminale year of lycée, although they consistently outnumber boys in their early years at primary school. As long as girls remain in school, however, they typically fare better in terms of academic standing, at least until they reach their teens. Furthermore, the small cohort of girls who sit for their bac exam are often at the top of their class.

In order to understand fully the experiences of girls and boys near the end of their secondary school careers, we need to return yet again to their early years (see appendix 5). As enrollment figures for Ambanja's largest primary school reveal, girls outnumber boys in all classes. Teachers from smaller neighborhood and rural schools report that girls may even outnumber boys by as much as two or three to one. If considered in reference to the population figures for the town and the valley, girls do appear to outnumber boys for particular age ranges, but not to such an extent as to explain these school discrepancies (in 1986, their respective overall population numbers were especially close for the 0–5 age rank, and it is this group that would later enroll in primary school in the 1990s). At the town's CEG, the gender gap appears to decrease, because girls hold the numerical advantage in some years, boys in others; in 1993–94, for example, girls outnumbered boys in the last two years of middle school, although the numbers of both boys and girls simultaneously dropped substantially.

At the state-run lycée, however, girls have clearly lost their numerical advantage. Boys now consistently outnumber girls, sometimes two or even three to one. Girls do outnumber boys in three respects at this level, however: first, they appear to be more likely to choose the terminale *série* A humanities and social sciences track (as the case of Dalia in chapter 7 shows, this may be a reflection of a girl's perseverance, or, as Mme. Vezo says, "courage," as she shifts to *série* A after failing the *série* D bac exam). Second, girls appear more likely to succeed in their studies throughout lycée, because their repeat rates are far lower than they are for boys. Third, girls and boys fluctuate in terms of holding the lower average class age at the lycée as represented by the figures recorded for the 1993–94 academic year. The Catholic Academy appears to exhibit similar trends (my own impression was confirmed by its director and two teachers), although representative figures are far more difficult to predict because of the tendency of students to shift to the state-run lycée if they fail the first time around at the Catholic Academy (for comparative data at the lycée and other levels, see appendix 5).

Girls also appear far less likely to repeat grades from the primary through middle school years than are boys (exceptions are evident in the sixième and troisième years at the CEG). School dropout should also be considered as a potential cause for lower repeat rates. Teachers and students from all schools consistently described girls as "more serious" (FR: *elles sont très* or *plus sérieuses;* also SAK: *miasa mafy izy,* "they work hard") in reference to their studies than boys.[19] A visit to any classroom provides anecdotal data: girls are far more likely to sit up front and volunteer answers, whereas a small group of boys invariably congregates at the back, sleeping or clowning around and sometimes creating serious disturbances. (Needless to say, however, most pupils, boys and girls alike, belong to the sea of those in the center.) Also, throughout my research I rarely encountered parents who voiced a strong desire to educate sons in preference to daughters. In their study of primary schooling, Clignet and Ernst similarly found no significant favoritism regarding Malagasy parents' preferences to send sons or daughters to private schools. More generally, they were struck by the dedication parents exhibited toward schooling both boys and girls, unlike their comparative data from studies based elsewhere in francophone West Africa. They found, for example, that 85 percent of all Malagasy primary students surveyed reported that a special place was set aside even in the most modest of homes for studying activities (Clignet and Ernst 1995, 105–6).

There are, however, more subtle social and economic forces that account at least in part for differences in dropout (and thus failure) rates among boys and girls. As I have argued elsewhere for Ambanja (Sharp 1996, 2002), although both sons and daughters are taught at a very early age how to help out in the home, greater labor demands are placed on young daughters. Thus, although girls may in fact strive harder than boys to succeed in school, they are more quickly called away from their studies to perform domestic and other household-related tasks. Older schoolboys often describe mothers and younger sisters (who may or may not be in school) rising early to clean the house and courtyard and prepare breakfast before school starts. After school hours, girls are less likely to be allowed to sit idly (or be left to play) than are their brothers when their elders require assistance.[20] As chapter 3 will show, however, school migrants provide an important exception to these gender-based rules. Where students live alone or only with one another, both girls and boys must attend to domestic chores on a daily basis, working together to keep their own homes and yards clean and tidy, and to ensure that they have enough food to eat each day.

Yet another significant factor involves a girl's age in school and her reproductive capacity. By the time many students begin middle school, they are already reproductively fertile. Many girls are forced out of school because they become pregnant. Lydia, a woman in her late twenties, summarized the school girl's dilemma in these terms: "A girl has more to lose . . . her parents make more sacrifices to send her to school, because they need her labor, but they also live in constant fear that she'll fail them because she'll fall pregnant." Lydia understood this all too clearly, because the year she passed her bac, she became pregnant with her first child and so was forced to abandon her desire to go on to university. Other girls are even less fortunate, finding themselves in a similar predicament but at a much earlier age. Typically, they are expelled from school, whereas their male partners escape punishment by school officials. The significance of such reproductive dilemmas is the focus of chapter 7.

Ny olo ambony sy ny olo ambañy (The people above and the people below)

Throughout the course of my fieldwork in 1987, which focused on Sakalava religious experience, adult informants especially were preoccupied—even obsessed—with marking distinctions along regional and cultural lines. Contrasts were constantly drawn between (we) côtiers versus highlanders; indigenous tera-tany Sakalava versus migrant vahiny; as well as many more carefully defined regional and ethnic categories: northern Sakalava, Makoa, Tsimihety, and Antankaraña; highland Merina, Betsileo, and Vakinankaratra; southern Antandroy, Antaisaka, and Antaimoro; and foreign vazaha (European), Silamo (Comoreans), Arabe (Yemenis), Sinoa (Chinese), and Karana (Indo-Pakistanis), all of whom also generated a host of métis categories through intermarriage with Malagasy speakers. These categories worked to define insider and outsider statuses, which, in turn, were reflective of the many overlapping circles of power that characterized the social world of the Sambirano.

When I returned in the mid 1990s, these remained just as deeply entrenched. There was, however, yet another, previously dormant layer of categorization that suddenly had become more pronounced in the wave of impending free market reforms that characterized the transitional period. Inhabitants of the Sambirano were now more concerned with disparities of wealth than they had been during the socialist era, so that a new hierarchy of sorts (based on an old and thus existing vocabulary) was now being laid upon other dominant categories that differentiated between the *olo ambony* and the *olo ambañy* (the "people above" and the "people below"). At the top sat the *mpañarivo* ("those who have thousands"), that is, the rich, sometimes also referred to as *snob-be* ("big snobs") when they exhibited their displeasure at contact with others less fortunate than they. Beneath the rich sat the *olo madiniky* ("little people"), or undifferentiated mass of common folk, who struggled to make a living as best they could. Further below these were the *laklasy mandry* ("the [servant] class that sleeps [in the house]"), wage earners who had no privacy as they lived under the suspicious gaze of their employers. This was a role truly abhorred by Sakalava, because of the total absence of independence, and thus the majority of house servants were from the poorest areas of the high plateaux, often shipped to Ambanja's elite Merina and Betsileo households by relatives back home. Beneath them lay the *tsy an'asa* ("unemployed") and, thus, potentially, the valley's poor, and, finally, the town's handful of *mpangataka* ("beggars") (Sharp 2001b). All of these categories were most relevant in the urban environment of Ambanja. In contrast, the valley's many landed peasants *(mpitsabo)* lived very simply, yet they were nevertheless considered rich because of their access to highly fertile soil and because they were economically independent.

These are by no means all the social categories that were at work in the Sambirano; it must also be stressed that they reflect predominantly nonelite Sakalava tera-tany sentiments toward intruders. The relevance of this small collection of ethnocentric terms lies in its ability to flesh out the economic tensions that currently characterize the valley. As such, their use marks a drastic shift in social orientation that is now significant to localized understandings of economic power. As the following section will show, distinctions between the mpañarivo and olo madiniky have become highly relevant to educational access and praxis.

STATE IDEOLOGY AND PEDAGOGICAL PRAXIS

All of the factors outlined in the preceding section reveal the hidden underbelly of schooling in one of the more affluent coastal areas of Madagascar. Over the past decade, the malaise that now characterizes the pedagogical spirit in Ambanja has intensified, coming to a head in the final years of Ratsiraka's Second Republic. Stu-

dents schooled during the later years of this regime quickly grasped the hopelessness of their predicament, an understanding that intensified as the paradoxes of
educational access worsened. This is because even those students who managed to
pass their bac exams knew they would most likely be denied access to the university, with new hurdles created by the limited number of available places, the instatement of yet another tier of entrance exams, and climbing tuition rates. Teachers, too, have suffered enormously from the malaise and apathy that plague their
students. They are now saddled with the new burden of yet another set of curricular requirements when they are still denied educational instructional materials, a
shortage that remains especially pronounced at the lycée level. Even worse, they
may not be able to speak French well enough to teach their students. By 1995, educational reformists had targeted the primary school years, because young students
were believed to embody the nation's new hope for the future. For the first time in
two decades, the valley's primary schools were beginning to be flooded with curricular materials. Students enrolled at the CEG were to come next, because they
might actually be salvageable. Lycée students, however, had clearly been sacrificed.

A Curricular Revolution

When I returned to Ambanja at the end of the 1992–93 academic term, there was
talk of abandoning official Malagasy. A year later, I found that curricular materials generated by newly formed Franco-Malagasy partnerships had begun to trickle
in. By 1994–95, the majority of Ambanja's educators felt they were solidly entrenched in the transition back to using French as the primary language of instruction. But what was proclaimed as fact in interviews and on paper diverged
from what I witnessed in the town's classrooms, and varied radically according to
the school level. Materials intended for lycée students were limited to a few comic
books with educational messages, some in official Malagasy, with stories and settings reminiscent of island life, and others, such as *Kouakou*, that are produced in
France for distribution throughout francophone Africa. Whereas lycée level students were, essentially, written off and ignored by the state, the campaign to rein-
troduce French and other curricular materials at the primary level was serious and
aggressive. Among the most effective of these early strategies involved the creation
of *La Plume* ("The Pen"), a trimester periodical produced during the 1993–94 school
term for distribution almost exclusively to all primary schoolteachers through their
local administrators. Attempts were also being made to design a similar regular
publication for the CEG level.[21] *La Plume* included standardized lessons plans, educational posters (on, for example, photosynthesis or wildlife conservation), and ge-
ographical information (one early volume included an insert with maps of the world
and Madagascar on reverse sides).[22]

The initial success of *La Plume* was, nevertheless, limited, for without teacher
(re)training, few instructors could make use of these materials. Mr. Léon, the principal of Ambanja's largest primary school explained:

My teachers come in regularly asking anxiously if the latest copy has arrived—they are hungry for lesson plans. So things are moving along. But the problem is that most of my teachers don't understand what's written here, and they [easily become discouraged because they] don't have the courage to study it [carefully] because it is in French. They tell me they're having trouble with something and I tell them, "Well, that's in [volume] 2—you should have a look at it," and then they say, "Oh, really? Where?" because they can't read it. Or else they say, "But I haven't even finished [volume] 1." But this is a *trimester* publication! . . . My youngest son, he often comes home and asks me to explain lessons to him, because his own teachers can't explain them correctly. When teachers make mistakes on my childrens' lessons, I have to go back and correct them, helping them to redo their assignments.

At the lycée level, such limitations were even greater, for instructors still had to rely on their own course notes to prepare students for their bac exams amid this radical transition. Under such circumstances, the success of lycée students has depended heavily on their teachers' "pedagogical dynamism" *(dynamisme pédagogique)* (Clignet and Ernst 1995, 39). Also, the linguistic requirements remained the same: students continued to be thrust suddenly into studying in French only in their final years of lycée, as had always been true throughout Ratsiraka's Second Republic, in anticipation of full-time study in French at the university level. Nevertheless, nearly all the lycée level students I encountered in Ambanja in 1993, 1994, and 1995 had chosen to take their bac exams in official Malagasy, certain they would fail in French. A more subtle change—this one ideological—made it even more difficult to prepare terminale students for the bac. Questions, regardless of the field—be it history, economics, philosophy, or English—suddenly stressed the values of supply-side economics, capitalist agendas over socialist concerns, and a greater interest in (and far less critical stance toward) the historical relevance of the United States and other Western powers, thus rejecting the Malagasy-centric approach that had characterized their entire formal education. It is no wonder, then, that already low bac success rates at the state-run lycée plummeted to 7 percent and then 1 percent in the first two years of the transitional period, as both students and their teachers were blindsided by this ideological shift (see appendix 6). The students I knew who passed at the end of the 1993–94 academic year—when the success rate jumped to 23 percent—were inevitably on their second try, and thus they and their teachers seemed better informed of the ideological concerns of examination questions.

Educational Visions

A deeper understanding of Madagascar's pedagogical crisis necessitates delving into a political economy of education. As has been demonstrated, schooling throughout the island has been shaped to a considerable extent by forces associated with European contact, conquest, and colonialism. In the Sambirano more specifically, the economic needs of the state have continued to define a pedagogical trajectory. Today, Ambanja is a center of not one but numerous hegemonies, the most significant being the state (most strongly represented by the county government, or *fivondronana*); the Bemazava-Sakalava kingdom (embodied in the living ruler, or *ampanjakabe*, and his spiritual advisors, including the greatest of the tromba mediums); and, finally, the plantations (Sharp 1993, 1999). These are not nested rings of power but, rather, three discrete yet overlapping and competing spheres of influence. Each in its own way has played a decisive role in shaping local education.

When viewed historically and in bureaucratic terms, Ambanja as an educational center assumes several guises. In colonial archival materials, it rarely appears as a noteworthy town, always being viewed under the shadow of the much larger administrative centers of Nosy Be, Majunga (now Mahajanga), and Diégo-Suarez (now Antsiranana), which at different times during this century have encompassed the valley as part of their respective domains. Throughout the colonial period—and especially during the first half of this century—district inspectors would make regular rounds of their territories, yet they often chose to bypass Ambanja, either because the roads were impassable, or because their greatest concerns lay with developments at the plantations lying to the west, north, or south.[23] Ambanja nevertheless soon lay at an important crossroads and thus could not be completely overlooked. Today, it is the point of intersection for the north-south national highway that leads from Antananarivo and Mahajanga to Diégo-Suarez; the east-west routes that extend to the port of Antsahampano, the royal tombs at Nosy Faly, and up river past the CSUS mission school and on to the town of Marovato; and a smaller, yet complex, grid of tertiary roads and pathways that make their way through many small villages and plantation fields spread throughout the Upper and Lower Sambirano.

Colonial presence in the earliest years necessitated schooling, because this was the primary means through which the "indigenous mentality" (FR: *la mentalité indigène*) could be redirected and molded at an early age. Within a region such as the Sambirano, this agenda had several goals: the co-optation of royal authority and power; the modernization (that is, the Europeanization) of agricultural techniques; and the promotion of a French morality (at times saddled upon a Catholic one) that would transform the colonized into obedient subjects who would embrace a French worldview without ever being allowed to touch many of its associated luxuries. Several examples illustrate the strategies employed to achieve these goals. First, as was true in Imerina, along the northwest coast, the French sought out royal children as pupils. Second, the teaching of agricultural skills was a priority by mid-century, and the school garden became an important aspect of the school curriculum (eventually it was mandated as a means for rural schools to become more financially self-sufficient).[24] As Fanny Colonna observes, the school is "the perfect vehicle for material innovation in housing, agriculture, hygiene, and health, both because of the knowledge it bestows and because of the attitudes and expectations it develops."[25] Third, opportunities in advanced education made possible yet another means to serve the colony, so that successful students later joined a colonial corps of petty civil servants and primary school instructors.

Such priorities inevitably create new hierarchies, particularly when shaped by racist understandings of ethnic and regional difference across the island. As has been well documented in the literature on the European occupation of Africa, colonial policies inevitably favored certain groups over others, which in turn generated a burgeoning educated elite that stood poised to assume control in the postindependence period (Clignet and Ernst 1995, 21; Fallers 1965; Sklar 1965; Vincent 1971). One of the most profound chasms to develop was that between highlanders and côtiers (discussed in chapter 1), and three successive presidents with coastal roots have found it necessary to entrench themselves in highland networks that are assumed to control bureaucratic and other structures based in Antananarivo.

The Isolating Effects of an Elite Education

Royal Failures.   One need only review the histories of Ambanja's oldest educational facilities to realize that although royalty were widely represented, they were not necessarily privileged in the educational sphere. They were, however, more systematically targeted than any other group, because local hierarchies could potentially be toppled or crippled through European schooling. Both boys and girls of royal descent were recruited as pupils, and many attended the Catholic Mission School, receiving, in turn, advanced training elsewhere on the island. Colonna notes how closely French colonization and schooling were paired in the analogous case of Algeria. Citing Jules Ferry, the architect of French schooling in Algeria in the 1880s, she describes this agenda as follows: "[B]ecause colonization is a right, it implies duties for the stronger nations; one of those duties is to bring education. . . . [As Ferry stressed,] the colonial enterprise involved an economic aspect, a civilizing aspect, and a political aspect." In this light, French colonial schooling was viewed simultaneously as a colonial *right* and a *duty*. In essence, then, the school had a "conquering function" (1997, 351–52; cf. Domatob 1996, 28).

In Madagascar, royal children offered the French a means to co-opt the local power base, because they could conceivably be transformed in their early years so as to embrace an array of sentiments that characterized both French and Catholic moralities. The occasional conversions of royalty to Catholicism, which served to undermine indigenous religious practices loosely connected with Islam, were among the greatest colonial coups in the north. Tsiaraso Victor III, whose nearly thirty-year reign ended with his death in 1993, was in fact schooled at the mission school and, as a boy, converted to Catholicism (Sharp 1997).

There is no denying the transformative character of French morality, for it often had a profound effect on royal power and stature. Mme. Fatima, a royal woman in her late sixties who attended a Catholic girls' boarding school in Antananarivo during the colonial era, makes this abundantly clear in describing her own experiences: "In addition to our basic studies, all of which were in French—mathematics, literature, geography, history—we were taught to assume the comportment and manners of proper Frenchwomen, that is, to sew, cook, eat, talk, and move like the French" (for a fuller account of her experiences, see Sharp 1996, 36). Her older cousin Said Achimo was similarly schooled by the French and, like Mme. Fatima and others who followed, he climbed slowly to the top ranks of the colony's indigenous hierarchy. His financial and administrative successes were ultimately his downfall, though, because they prevented him from attaining royal power, which was what he coveted most. In 1935, when he was the assistant governor of the region surrounding Ambanja, Said contested the selection of Rachidy (Andriamamefiarivo, r. 1935–45) as the next Bemazava-Sakalava ruler (ampanjakabe). Said sought and acquired the support of the colonial administration, requesting that its officers intervene on his behalf (CAOM DS 0526 [1935]). The most influential among his own people, however, would have nothing of it. In essence, Said lost any chance at local power because he embraced the colonial regime. As a result, his investment in the upkeep of the royal tombs remains his most important indigenous legacy, yet his status remains liminal: he is remembered as a royal of high stature, albeit one who never ruled. Fluctuations in royal prestige remain central to current reflections on an indigenous past, where colonial, royal, and state authority are often at odds with one another.

A New Elite.   Following independence, colonial structures remained fairly deeply entrenched in the Sambirano. Until the 1970s, the Catholic Mission's upper administration was still staffed by European priests and nuns, and the valley's imposing plantations remained in the hands of foreign interests established much earlier in this century. Much of this came to an end under Ratsiraka's socialist reforms. In the mid 1970s, all but one of the valley's privately owned plantations were nationalized, and directors of Malagasy origin came to dominate the local economic sphere. These new appointments reflected a national bias that favored educated highlanders and, thus, the upward mobility of an elite group despised by indigenous Sakalava. In 1987, the majority of these directors were Betsileo and not Merina, reflecting a concerted effort by the state to make appointments that would not undermine to such a great extent the social and political fabric of the valley.

This trend toward assigning highlanders to positions of economic power in the Sambirano persisted in the 1990s. With the transition from state capitalism to privatization, and as their own material wealth has expanded, the influence of the growing educated highland elite has become far more pronounced. One of their greatest difficulties is deciding what they should do with their children. Homesick for their kin in the cooler highlands, they fear that their offspring will become, as Sakalava would say, *tsaiky ny Sambirano* ("children of the Sambirano"), unaware of their own origins, unable to speak their parents' dialect, and embracing Sakalava customs more than highland ones. Elite schooling offers a partial answer to this dilemma, and so Betsileo parents, for example, typically enroll their young children in the French Elementary School. They later and very reluctantly send them far from home so that they may attend prestigious private schools in the high plateaux. In the process, however, these children are transformed not so much into Betsileo youth as into a Malagasy-French hybrid elite. Such educational decisions only widen the gap between the mpañarivo and the olo madiniky. They also bear significant ideological consequences for each successive generation of children.

The experiences of one young Betsileo student provide an example of these consequences. Vonjy was born in the provincial capital of Fianarantsoa in the southern high plateaux, a city that lies in the heart of Betsileo territory. When she was very young, her father, a banker, was posted to Toamasina on the east coast, where Vonjy's parents enrolled her in an exclusive private school. Her two younger brothers were eventually enrolled there as well. By the time Vonjy had nearly finished middle school, however, her father was transferred to Ambanja, where he had been stationed for two years. When I met Vonjy in 1993, she had just turned fifteen. Her mother had not been particularly impressed with any of the private Catholic schools scattered throughout Antsiranana Province, and so she decided to remain in Toamasina with her children until Vonjy could finish middle school there. At that point, she sent her two younger children to the city of Antsirabe, located south of Antananarivo, where they could attend school while living with their maternal grandmother. Vonjy, a stellar student, was then enrolled in an expensive Catholic boarding school in Antananarivo. As her mother explained: "[I]t wasn't just the quality of education [in and near Ambanja] that worried me. It's also important that [my children] go to school with others who are studious like them. I really miss my children—but you know, we've never felt we belonged here [in Ambanja], and I want them to be where they do belong." This final comment was laced with great sadness and communicated the full complexity of highland elite status in Ambanja. Vonjy's mother considered local schooling to be inferior, because it could never meet the pedagogical standards set by the island's finest private schools; she also feared that through social contact with local children, her own might very well become "tsaiky ny Sambirano," speaking a dialect she considered not only incomprehensible but far inferior to Betsileo. This point was driven home to me one afternoon in another Betsileo household, where a six-year-old was scolded harshly when she proudly explained that her new art pencil collection enabled her to color her school workbook with *kolora jiaby* ("all colors"). Her embarrassed mother, realizing I was in the room, quickly retreated to the kitchen, leaving me to explain to a confused little girl that she had just spoken in Sakalava.

Vonjy's experiences define a trajectory that this little girl's life is also expected to follow, for Vonjy was slowly being transformed into an odd hybrid that lay somewhere between elite Betsileo and partially assimilated French statuses. Vonjy is extremely bright and inquisitive, and quick to assist others in need. Her dilemma is that her life epitomizes that of Ambanja's mpañarivo, of whom Sakalava informants often speak so bitterly. Vonjy certainly enjoys the privileges that characterize her life, but she also periodically struggles with a sense that she rests upon unstable ground. One afternoon, she described her predicament as follows:

> I like it where I live in Tana [Antananarivo]—it's a small rooming house run by nuns, where it's quiet and secure—[although unfortunately] it is very expensive. I'm free to devote my time to my studies, because I don't have to do housework or laundry. . . . It's confusing, though—I hear you talking all the time about malagasization, and official Malagasy. But these ideas don't mean much to me—I've grown up speaking French, I've done all my studies in French, and I know I'll therefore take my bac in French. I know I'm Betsileo but, you know, I really can't speak it properly, and I have little understanding of how to write it. When I come home during vacations, my parents usually speak to me exclusively in French—except when they're mad at me, and then it's in Betsileo! But when I see my grandparents, oh, then, I know how limited my knowledge is [of Betsileo], because I often have a difficult time understanding them. Sometimes I wonder what my language is? At least I know that my origins are Betsileo, and so no matter what, I'll always be Betsileo.

This final sentiment was voiced even more strongly in another discussion we had one afternoon, when I posed a question I asked all young informants—that is, where her tanindrazana lay. To this Vonjy responded without hesitation, "Oh, that would be my parents' village near Fianarantsoa!" Amid her personal confusion, Vonjy nevertheless cared deeply about her nation. One evening, a visiting aunt made derogatory remarks about the Merina, attributing her personal hatred to the wars of over a century ago, when, as she explained, terrified Betsileo mothers fled to the forest with their infants in their arms. Vonjy suddenly exclaimed, "What difference does all this make? Aren't we *all* Malagasy?" and then, in atypical fashion, she stormed out of the family parlor and into her room.[26]

Envisioning History

As Marc Ferro (1984) has so succinctly and forcefully argued, French colonial education and its legacy imposed upon youth in the former French colonies a vision of the world in which their own lives are so inconsequential that they exist simply to serve the needs of more powerful nations. Nowhere is this message more clearly communicated than in the history lesson. On their first day of school, children in Algeria, Madagascar, Mali, Vietnam, and even Haiti, would inevitably be taught about "nos ancêtres les Gaulois" ("our ancestors the Gauls"). Thus, as Fanon (1963 [1961], 51) sarcastically observed, "the settler makes history; his life is an epoch, an Odyssey. His is the absolute beginning. . . . The settler makes history and is conscious of making it." Through this warped vision of identity, children colonized by the French quickly learned that their own pasts were of little value and hardly qualified as history at all.

In the wake of postcolonial agendas, Malagasy schoolteachers have since been forced to cope with the effects of these glaring inequalities. Although they receive some cursory guidance from the state, under Ratsiraka they were required, in a sense, to rewrite history so as to refashion and thus reenvision the essence of what it means to be Malagasy in a way that ran contrary to their own training. The nature of this struggle was made especially clear in an interview with Mme. Honorine, who is a headmistress at the state-run lycée (a rotating job that she shares with a man). She also teaches history and geography. Her husband is a teacher at the lycée level in Ambilobe, a town 102 kilometers to the north. As a result, Mme. Honorine lives full-time in their roomy house with their children, while he commutes between the two towns. They are both active board members of Ambanja's Alliance Française, and they take every opportunity to hone their scholarly skills. Their house is a whirlwind, with five unruly children running about, but it is also spotless, everything well polished and neat, so that one feels as if one is resting in the eye of a storm whenever the children retreat outdoors. When I asked her what she taught in her history classes, Mme. Honorine responded as follows:

> *Mme. Honorine:* Madagascar first. To know the history of others you must first understand your own. Then I turn to world history—I look at the United States, Japan, and other developed countries, and I ask, what is their evolution? How did they get to be the way they are? What lessons—for better or worse—can we in our country learn from them in terms of their social, political, and economic histories?
>
> *LS:* And what about Africa and Asia, for example?
>
> *Mme. Honorine:* Naturally they, too, are central to the discussion, for their history is [central to] the history of the world.

Mme. Honorine's house is also unusual in that nearly an entire wall is covered by a large bookshelf. When I first saw this, I stood before it in awe and asked her how she had acquired such an imposing collection. She replied:

> Books are truly rare objects here in Madagascar! But it is a teacher's job to find books. When we were at school in [Toliara], there were Indians who left for Réunion and other places, and so they sold us their books. You do the best you can, you manage as best you can. But I really have no books at all—it's all here, up in my head! Even with these books on the shelves, there's really not much to be found there. What's going on [in our lives] doesn't correspond with the reality of what I can find in these books here. In the university, we studied seventeenth- and eighteenth-century theory and history, we learned one thing, but now in school we often have to speak of something different. And why? Because we don't have the resources, we don't have the materials, and we're supposed to teach one thing, but we don't have the documents! I try to learn what I can, but the television is always down, the radio is rarely clear, and I can't get books or journals that tell me what's happening. I've seen books in lycées that were written for primary school students! Sure, there are books in Tana [Antananarivo], but they're too expensive. They're worth their weight in gold. So [here] we do what we can—we teach or talk about something else!

State Ideology and the Bac

The trials faced by teachers as committed as Mme. Honorine are exacerbated by the fickleness of the political agendas that govern pedagogy. As Mme. Honorine

confesses so honestly, in the face of limited knowledge, she and her peers have little choice but to "teach or talk about something else." Even attempts to determine
the proper tenor of a lesson's content thrusts an instructor into a political quagmire. "[T]here are always many histories," as Jean and John Comaroff put it (1991,
38). This dilemma is clearly evident in the shifting nature and content of Madagascar's bac exams.

A cursory review of sample bac questions reveals the centrality of state ideology in the context of education (cf. Willis 1977). That is, these questions expose
not only what students are expected to know but how they are expected to understand and interpret world events. I was unable to obtain sample exams from Tsiranana's First Republic, yet I was repeatedly assured by school officials that these
focused on the same larger debates and issues that characterized education in
France. In other words, Madagascar itself remained peripheral to any discussions
in history or geography. Maureen Covell's description of the curriculum at the University of Madagascar in Antananarivo during the Tsiranana era illustrates the
specific nature of this chauvinism: "[T]he regional geography course used the Paris
basin for its illustrations and the journal of the Faculty of Literature, *Lettres Malgaches,* published articles on Provençal poetry. . . . [T]he point was clear: it was
through learning about France, not Madagascar, that one had to pass to aspire to
even the subordinate position in the system for which Malagasies were destined"
(Covell 1987, 37). Madagascar was important only in that it allowed students to
address the theme of economic development, where a pervasive understanding was
that great potential lay in a newly independent nation's evolution toward agricultural self-sufficiency and industrialization.[27]

Under Ratsiraka's Second Republic, bac questions reveal a radical shift in orientation, with early questions from the 1970s challenging previous assumptions
about proper models of civil society and the dangers of socialism and communism.
These themes run throughout the disciplines, extending beyond history and geography and into philosophy. For example, in 1975, two philosophy questions asked
of students enrolled in the terminale *série* A track were:

It is said that an effective democracy cannot exist in a socialist society. What do
        you think of this?[28]
Can one speak of liberty without social equality?[29]

Students were then asked to comment on a passage from Jean Lacroix's *Panorama
de la philosophie française contemporaine,* in which he argues that philosophy encourages youth to develop a critical stance toward traditional opinions and to embrace
nonconformism.[30] Clearly, Madagascar's youth were now being encouraged to
question authority and its interests. Two years later, other sample questions, again
drawn from terminale *série* A exams, reflect the state's socialist leanings. In one, students were asked to comment on the themes of inequality and injustice as out-

lined in an excerpt from the writings of Mao Tse-tung; another focused on a text generated by an 1894 Conference of Socialist Students, where students first emerge as credible political reformers concerned with justice, nonconformity, and enslavement and a threat to those who passively accept subordination. Similar preoccupations characterized exams well into the late 1980s, when the writings of Marx and other socialist French and Russian philosophers, political theorists, and statesmen figure prominently.

Questions asked in *série* D examinations in history and geography likewise exhibit a preoccupation with socialist and communist economic models. As early as 1974, students were asked to write on one of the following:

The respective relevance of rich versus Third World nations for principles of
      world production. How so?[31]
The social, economic and political consequences of World War II in Africa.[32]

By this point, bac exams clearly took more of an Afrocentric approach than under Tsiranana. Students were also encouraged to be critical of the American political system and its economy, as reflected in this 1987 exam question:

Discuss the evolution of the American economy from World War II to the
      present, and what are its current problems?[33]

A question that followed asked students to comment on the Soviet economic system in reference to their own nation, with passages supplied from Madagascar's new 1977 constitution as relevant text. In 1988, students considered the Japanese economy, again following World War II, and then they were asked to discuss a passage describing the problems of postcolonial economic reconstruction in agricultural nations.[34] In this mode, Japan does not emerge so much as a world power, but as a vanquished nation whose experiences paralleled those of the colonized (see Raison-Jourde 1997, 32–34, on Malagasy interest in Japan). Yet another question underscored the shortfalls of American society and the relevance of its economic system as culpable in this downfall.[35] A final example, taken from a 1989 exam, asked:

Compare the importance, organization, and performance of agriculture in the
      USSR and the United States.[36]

One can easily imagine how schoolchildren in the United States and Madagascar might be expected to answer this last question. Those in the former would stress the dismal failure of communism in Russia, whereas their Malagasy counterparts might portray the collective movement as a just model of production, offering more promise for Madagascar than large-scale private ownership. Each answer does in fact contain its own kernel of truth, where a correct answer in this and any other era reflects the sanctioned ideology of the state. As these examples illustrate, "history lies in its representations" (Comaroff and Comaroff 1991, 35–36).

Since the 1991–93 transitional period, bac exams have exhibited yet another radical ideological shift. A 1991 *série* D exam in history reveals a new preoccupation with the centrality of the United States in the arena of foreign policy. Students were asked to discuss a quotation from the *Memoirs* of Harry Truman focusing on the significance of the Marshall plan for promoting the central role of the United States in establishing world peace.[37] Another in geography stated:

> The former Soviet Union has always been considered a world power. One nevertheless encounters widespread shortage there, even though it possesses all the resources to avoid this.[38]

This new preoccupation with the virtues of capitalism and the American model of democracy now dominated the Malagasy examination system. A question from 1994 asked students to discuss a passage from the French newspaper *Le Monde* (November 3, 1985) that correlated a new all-time low employment rate in the United States with the expansion of its economy.

To summarize, since the advent of the transitional period in the early 1990s, at least two central themes have begun to dominate Madagascar's bac exams. The first is that the United States has reemerged as a respected world power with a strong and impressive economy. Both are viewed as honorable characteristics. Second, this powerful nation now clearly overshadows Soviet political and economic models, which have ultimately failed. In essence, capitalism and privatization have triumphed over the Russian collective model as they are now understood in Madagascar. This ideological shift might indeed be viewed as evidence of the "bankruptcy of modernization rhetoric" (*faillite de la rhétorique de la modernisation)* following the collapse of Ratsiraka's Second Republic to which Clignet and Ernst refer (1995, 16).

The Moral Depravity of the West

For all their political power and economic robustness, Western nations do not, however, emerge as models of moral behavior, a theme that will resurface in this study, especially in chapters 3 and 7. In the context of the bac, the United States epitomizes the degenerate society, because its cultural values endanger the lives of vulnerable children and the poor, and can even destroy members of the privileged middle class. These themes are embedded in questions that characterized those posed on the English sections of the bac exam during the Second Republic and even beyond. Such questions provide a powerful venue for promoting moral lessons intended for a nation's youth preparing to enter the adult phase of their lives. Two examples drawn from the 1980s offer extraordinary illustrations of this.

The first is a text taken from the 1981 bac, adapted from an essay that originally appeared in *Newsweek* (April 30, 1973, 42). In this context, the American press provides poignant information that ultimately undermines any preconceived romantic vision of the United States that Malagasy youth might have. The essay is entitled "The Chickenhawks," and the full text reads as follows:

> A poor runaway boy emerges into the city streets and[,]lost and lonely, is only too quick to return the friendly overtures of a lad not too much older than himself. His new companion buys him a fine meal and promises to initiate the runaway boy into his own highly profitable, low-skill trade. Intrigued, the boy accompanies his patron to a nearby hiding-place and is quickly given some instruction about his new occupation. This boy has become not a pickpocket but a male prostitute. From now on he will sell himself to middle-aged men who eagerly pay up to $100 for sex with a young boy. In the parlance of his profession, he will be known as a "chicken." His customers are called "chickenhawks."
>
> As odious as it seems, the flesh market in young males is flourishing—both openly and clandestinely—in big cities such as Philadelphia, San Francisco, New York. Surprisingly, a percentage of the chickens are the products of fairly well-to-do but broken families.
>
> Pimps who cannot find their own boys have taken to haunting the bus and train terminals in search of teen-age newcomers to rape and then force into prostitution.
>
> Some pimps are cruel and even brutal. "I remember one pimp calling me to say that he had a nice thirteen-year-old he had just broken in," one chickenhawk said. "I go over and I find the most beautiful kid I've ever known. But he was handcuffed to the bed, crying desperately. The pimp had raped him and burned his initials into his buttocks with a cigarette."

Oddly, the brief list of questions that follow this disturbing passage focus almost exclusively on testing a student's understanding of grammar and vocabulary, a disjunction that renders the passage more powerful because the student who fully understands its content must be left in a state of wonder and horror. The messages imbedded within this passage are numerous and complex when viewed through Malagasy eyes: whereas Antananarivo's street children, who are organized into rings of petty thieves, threaten the safety of individuals (and, if well organized, potentially, the state), the United States is emblematic of the West, and its major cities offer a far more terrifying picture of (un)civil society, where children are raped and brutalized by adult pimps and clients. As we shall see in chapter 7, Malagasy are quite familiar with female prostitutes, whose prime targets are foreigners. The boy-child prostitute, however, is generally an unknown category (cf. Ebron 1997). As described in this passage, boys and adult men are reduced to "chickens" and "chickenhawks." Both have lost their humanity, reduced to animals through the medium of street slang and bound tightly together in a cycle of economic (and capitalist) exploitation. Even more terrifying is the fact that such children are not cared for but preyed on by adults. The fact that these boys usually come from elite rather than destitute homes only further underscores the dangers of capitalism and its more frightening forms of exploitation.

A far more common theme that is communicated through the bac English exams is the danger of drugs and their association with the West. A 1982 *série* A essay entitled "The Middle Class High" (taken from *Reader's Digest*, March 1981), de-scribes cocaine as the "drug of choice" for "millions of conventional citizens." As it explains, "a blizzard of white powder is blowing through the American middle class." Although it leaves no scars on the body like heroin or lung cancer, the user nevertheless crashes into states of depression and paranoia; furthermore, the trade itself is responsible for the upsweep in crime in America's cities, rendering the man in a business suit as dangerous as the burglar on the street. This theme appears in yet another essay from the same year, entitled "Why a Few People Never Stop Tak-ing Drugs." This essay listed causes for drug abuse, ranging from depression and overanxiousness to social isolation. Drugs offer solace and escape for complex prob-lems for which there are no simple solutions.

In addition to offering a disturbing portrait of American society, these two es-says reflect current concerns for students who live in isolation on Madagascar's uni-versity campuses. I have encountered numerous frantic and distraught parents who relate heart-breaking tales of children brought home from their desolate university lives. Their sons and daughters were once lively students, yet as soon as they en-tered the university far from home, they fell into states of deep depression or were plagued by madness spurred on by malicious possessing spirits. Both conditions often proved impervious to even the most intensive of cures, be it hospitalization in a provincial asylum or lengthy treatments by powerful spirit mediums (Sharp 1994; cf. Fisher 1985 on the dangers of "studiation" in Barbados). These dangers of schooling will be explored in detail in chapter 8.

YOUTH AND THE POLITICS OF SCHOOLING

As this chapter has shown, Ambanja and the surrounding Sambirano Valley si-multaneously offer typical and exceptional examples of schooling in Madagascar. First, they are representative of the limitations of coastal and rural life. A wide chasm separates this region from Antananarivo, because students in the Sambirano have suffered from chronic shortages of supplies, ranging from such basic materi-als as paper, pens, rulers, and slates, to other greater and even rarer luxuries, in-cluding dictionaries, textbooks, maps, and libraries. The Sambirano is, neverthe-less, exceptional in that it is a relatively affluent region of Madagascar, where schooling has been available to Malagasy children throughout this century as a re-sult of colonial, mission, and, later, state activities. Today, Ambanja stands apart as an important educational center for the north, offering an impressive array of state-run and private schools from the primary up through the lycée level. The in-dividual histories of these institutions are linked to demands and needs that are si-multaneously both foreign and local, and both elite and commoner in origin.

Ambanja, as a migrant town, is a microcosm of Madagascar as a whole (Sharp 1993); in turn, it should also be considered a microcosm of schooling, because it demonstrates without question the pronounced level of poverty that characterizes the island's schools as a whole (Clignet and Ernst 1995). At one extreme is the French Elementary School, an institution driven by the elitist agenda of a truly small minority; at the other lie three unlicensed remedial schools that offer alternatives to desperate parents whose children continue to fail in school. In the middle are the state-run schools scattered throughout the valley and two Catholic institutions. The manner in which members of each category have access to quality curricular materials and well-trained (as well as prepared) teachers bears much weight in determining the success of their students. As an earlier discussion in this chapter reveals, however, one's age and school level will ultimately determine how one's life is shaped by the significant ideological shifts that have characterized this nation since 1960.

The rhetoric of schooling and, ultimately, examinations reveal the fickleness of state agendas regarding the proper pedagogical trajectory to follow. Students enrolled in elite private schools have the best chance at success year-to-year, because they do not suffer nearly as much as do those in state-run schools from the nation's paucity of curricular materials. They do, nevertheless, suffer in other ways: whereas youth enrolled in Ambanja's state-run lycée profoundly understand their nation's current pedagogical quagmire, astute elite students such as Vonjy struggle to construct their identities and, thus, find their place in the context of daily social life. Students' responses to the questions hinge on their social station, which inevitably shapes their readings of exploitation, justice, equality, and sacrifice.

Against this, who truly falls into this nation's sacrificed generation? An early example would be those students who were schooled at the very end of the First Republic, and who completed their schooling in French but were then thrust into positions where official Malagasy suddenly emerged as the obligatory lingua franca. Teachers such as Mr. Victor (chapter 1) and Mme. Honorine, for example, truly struggled to make sense of this sudden and drastic shift in the classroom. In retrospect, however, it is their own students who have suffered the most, because malagasization's most destructive result is linguistic isolation, an isolation that has serious geographic, economic, political, and social consequences. Those few students who actually completed lycée and passed their bac exams found no reward awaiting them at the end of their school careers. In contrast, the offspring of wealthy households are assumed to have escaped unscathed, because their parents could afford to place them in elite, often European-run institutions, where they remained relatively untouched by radical change.

In conclusion, among the great paradoxes of malagasization is that it paved the way for increased disparity between the mpañarivo and the olo madiniky, as elite parents guarded their children from state schooling. We must also therefore consider Vonjy and her peers among those who have suffered from the educational reforms of the socialist era, given that many of these privileged children remain aloof from and uninformed about the problems that plague their nation. Their schooling generates a naïveté about the forces tearing their nation asunder, although, ironically, it is they who ultimately will possess the power to transform its most powerful—and oppressive—institutions. As such, it is the blindness that springs from their own elite education that marks them, too, as members of Madagascar's sacrificed youth.

CHAPTER 3

The Life and Hard Times
of the School Migrant

PORTRAITS OF DAILY SURVIVAL

June 20, 1993. It's 5:00 in the morning and the neighborhood roosters have begun to crow. When I open the wooden shutters that have barricaded my room throughout the night I notice the white glow of a fluorescent ceiling light emanating from the small room of my young neighbor, Olive. Now nineteen years old, she has come from Antananarivo to Ambanja to stay with her country auntie (and my landlady) in preparation for her second try at the bac. After tidying my room a bit, I step out and make my way in the pre-dawn light to the washroom we share. I pause to say hello, but she is so deeply involved with her studying that she does not hear or see me. Her thick, ill-fitting glasses ride low on her button nose, and her hair has been pulled back hastily into a top knot. Sitting on her hard wooden chair, she still wears the loose-fitting and faded *lambahoany* body wrap that serves as her favorite nightdress. The wrap itself is reminiscent of more festive and carefree times: although it is now late June, it is decorated with last year's calendar, flanked by Christmas poinsettias, flowers referred to locally as *Madagasikara*, because their petals resemble the island's outline.

I, too, am only half-dressed as I step out into the street in the early morning light, beat-up flip-flops on my feet and a lambahoany wrapped about my torso, my hair unbrushed but braided. Like many others I pass, I am in search of fresh bread for my early morning meal. I am tired of eating baguettes, and so I pass a nearby bakery in search of my old neighbor Maman'i'Fabrice, hoping to find her selling her delicious hot rice cakes of *mofo gasy.* I take a favorite short cut through town, passing nineteen-year-old Antoine, who is carefully sweeping his large courtyard. The broom leaves a pattern of neat arches upon the bare earth in front of his house, which is flanked by an array of beautiful flowers. His younger brother, Jacques,

squats in a far corner, making tea and reheating last night's rice over a simple bra-
zier. We exchange greetings as I make my way to Maman'i'Fabrice's a few doors
away.

Antoine has lived here by himself since he was fifteen, joined this year by
Jacques, who is two years younger. Whereas Antoine attends the state-run Technical Lycée, Jacques is enrolled in the private Catholic Academy. Their large, airy
house sits on land purchased by their Sakalava parents in 1974. Their mother, a
seamstress, and father, a mechanic, have subsequently settled in the countryside in
separate villages, which lie approximately five and thirty kilometers away respectively. Their parents also tend fields of rice and other crops on land inherited from
their own elder kin. This is a prosperous family, for this mother and father have
been blessed with a number of children considered ideal by Malagasy standards—
they have had seven sons and seven daughters, all of whom are in good health, and
who now range in age from seventeen to thirty-six. Of these, Antoine and Jacques
are the youngest.

These two boys are also among the best educated of their close kin. Their parents, who are in their late fifties, were the first among their own relatives to attend
primary school. Antoine is one of three sons who has made it to lycée: two of his
older brothers, who are now twenty-four and twenty-six years old, completed their
terminale year at the Technical Lycée. Neither of these brothers were able to find
jobs related to their training, and so they, like their parents, have returned to the
land to subsist as peasants. Their oldest brother, aged thirty-six, completed troisième
and now specializes in refrigerator repair in Diégo-Suarez. Two sisters also did exceptionally well in school: the youngest, age twenty-two, completed troisième, or
the final year of middle school, and yet another, aged twenty-seven, completed
her terminale. Both have since married men of foreign origin who were once stationed near Ambanja. These two sisters now live in France, where they are house-
wives and mothers. The five remaining sisters dropped out of school because they
became pregnant, and the two remaining brothers similarly abandoned their studies because they became fathers at an early age. All seven did so while enrolled in
middle school, and the majority were in troisième at the time. Their professions
include hotel chambermaid, plantation foreman, and mechanic; the remainder are
peasants. All have children and have settled in various locations scattered throughout the northern province of Antsiranana.

THE TRIALS OF SCHOOL MIGRATION

School migration is an experience that dominates the lives of many of Ambanja's
students. As much as 50 percent of a class may consist of "school migrant" students from the countryside.[1] Such students have received much encouragement
from teachers and elder kin to continue their studies far from home at the middle
school and lycée levels. The success of such a move necessitates long-term, regu-

lar support from adult kin. Nevertheless, many are forced to settle alone or with other students their age, because they lack local social ties and townspeople are wary of assisting strangers, even if they are children. The following case studies, beginning with an account from Antoine, expose the nature of the school migrant's life.

The Daily Responsibilities of Two Migrant Brothers

Antoine's day typifies that of many of Ambanja's school migrants, and he described it to me as follows:

> *Antoine:* My brother and I wake up around 6:00 [A.M.] and we clean the house— quickly, that is [he says this with an impish grin: clearly much care is taken to keep the house in order—the house is always tidy, as is the yard, and the floor has a waxy red shine]. We also sweep the yard every morning. Around 6:30 I go to market to buy our food for the day, and then around 7:00 I leave for school—classes start at 7:30. We both get home around 11:30. The first one home prepares [the noonday meal], and then the other cleans up. We always share the cooking, but usually I'm the one who goes to the market and who cleans the house, and Jacques does the dishes and the laundry. I go back to school around [2:00 P.M.], and I stay there until [4:30]. We then make dinner together, clean up, and then we study until we are tired. This is usually until [9:00] or so. If we have a lot of homework to do, one or both of us might get up early—say around 4:00 [A.M.]—to study before school.
>
> ... Each weekend we go to the country for food. [We have about] three hectares [of land] located three kilometers from here ... [that] belongs to our father.... No one lives there, so my brother and I work it together on the weekends. We grow manioc, bananas, maize, mangos, and some coffee and cocoa. We go each Saturday—we walk there early in the morning and then we walk back again in the late afternoon [because there is no house there where we can sleep]. We go to the fields, get what we need, and then we come back here [the same evening].... The rice we eat we get from my mother's fields ... and our parents send us a lit- tle money each month [for other supplies, such as soap, matches, charcoal and kerosene]. Sometimes our sisters in France send us a little money, too. [My father and mother separated about six years ago, and so] during vacations we sometimes go to my father's, sometimes to my mother's, or sometimes we stay with our sis- ter who lives on Nosy Be. Otherwise, we're pretty much on our own during the school year.... We have no regular visitors except my mother. She comes and [stops by] each Thursday, on market day. She stays for about three hours and vis- its, and then she goes back home....
>
> *LS:* ... What happens if you fall ill?
>
> *Antoine:* We try to go to the Catholic Hospital [if we can afford it]....
>
> *LS:* ... When you complete school here, what will you do? Do you plan to attend uni- versity?

Antoine: Ahh, no. There are no places [available for new students], and there's no work to be found afterward [anyway]. But if you repair automobiles, you can make money. And then I could always work the land like my parents.

LS: What do you do for amusement? Do you ever go to the disco or cinema, etc.?

Antoine: Sometimes we go to the cinema, and once we went to a disco. But we don't have a lot of [pocket] money, and so most of the time we just mill around *[mit-sangantsangana]* with our friends.

Throughout two subsequent seasons of research, I often encountered Antoine in the street late in the afternoon or on Sundays, sometimes riding a beat-up bicycle. By 1995, he had failed on his first attempt at the bac, and so he was seeking an apprenticeship with a man who repaired radios and other electrical appliances. As he explained, one of the main reasons he stayed in Ambanja was to look after his younger brother Jacques, who was still in school. Both enjoyed living in Ambanja and hoped to remain in the spacious house their parents had built.

Ketsy's Life Alone

When I met Ketsy in 1994, she had just turned eighteen, and had completed quatrième at the Catholic Academy middle school. Born in a small village approximately sixty kilometers southwest of Ambanja on the Ampasindava Peninsula, she had excelled at her local primary school. Her widowed Sakalava mother then decided to send her to live with a younger single aunt in Ambanja so that Ketsy could attend the academy. Both Ketsy's mother and aunt had completed their first year of middle school and then dropped out, the mother because of her weak health, the sister because her grades were unimpressive. Their parents were also in great need of their labor at home. An older brother had initially accompanied Ketsy to Ambanja, but he later dropped out of school, and by the age of twenty, he had married and settled in Ambilobe, a town just over 100 kilometers north of Ambanja. He helps his mother with the cost of Ketsy's tuition, working as a low-level bookkeeper for a transport company. Ketsy's maternal aunt, or *mamahely* (lit. "little mother"), is a single woman. Mamahely works as a housemaid for a stingy European woman who refuses to provide her with a ride home at the end of the day, even though their respective homes are several kilometers apart. As a result, Mamahely, exhausted, often prefers to sleep over with a friend who lives much closer to the Frenchwoman's villa, and so Ketsy usually has the house to herself.

Whenever I visit Ketsy's house, it is always in mild disarray. Although the floors are well swept, this simple, cramped two-roomed *falafa* (palm fiber) house is dusty and dingy, for which Ketsy's Mamahely pays an inflated rent of FMG 15,000 a month. Ketsy's room is well decorated, the walls plastered with photos taken mostly from faded teen magazines. There are several voluptuous, well-tanned European models posing beside expensive cars and swimming pools; one also finds a few soccer players; a wedding photo of the emperor and empress of Japan; and, smack in the middle, an isolated photo of the Pope, taken during his visit to Madagascar a few years before. Ketsy's room stands in stark contrast to the homes of so many other friends and informants. The room where Tsarahita, my research assistant, lives, for example, is decorated with a few carefully placed pictures, her bed is always made up with clean linens tucked tightly at the corners, and the floors inevitably glisten with polish. In contrast, Ketsy and I are kindred spirits in housekeeping, although she always has more dust and I more scorpions. A striking difference can be found outside Ketsy's house, however. As with Antoine's, the outside of Ketsy's is banked by a lovely flower garden, and caring for this is how Ketsy begins each day:

> *Ketsy:* I get up around 5:00 [A.M.] and I straighten up the house. And then I water the flowers. Since we've had so little rain, I have to go to a neighborhood well for water [which I haul back here in a bucket]. I then sweep the yard. I'm responsible for cooking my own meals, so I then go to the market. I do all of this before school. If [Mamahely] is here, I prepare breakfast for her, since we both leave the house early in the morning. If she's here, she'll have the midday meal ready for me; if not, I cook it myself. Regardless of who's here, it is always my job to clean the dishes.... I go to school around 7:00 and then I stay until noon. I later return to school where I stay from [2:30 until 5:00 P.M.].

> *LS:* What do you do when you get home in the evening?

> *Ketsy:* I go to the market [again] and then I cook another meal.

> *LS:* How do you pay for your food?

> *Ketsy:* Mamahely does this, but sometimes my mother will send us a little extra money, too.

> *LS:* What are your biggest problems or worries?

> *Ketsy:* [With sadness:] I worry a lot about my mother. She is ill much of the time with asthma. I don't think she thinks about me very much and this makes me very sad....

> *LS:* ... And what about in school?

> *Ketsy:* I love math, but it's very hard. I hate English. It's too hard. And I hate Malagasy. It's so exhausting....

> *LS:* ... What do you like to do for amusement? [Ketsy was puzzled by this question, and so I had to rephrase it several times before she could answer.] ... What do you do when you're not in school?

> *Ketsy:* During vacations I usually work at one of the local plantations, starting there around 7:00 [A.M.]—to get there on time I get up at 5:00. What I do depends on what sort of work is available, and what they need done. When that work ends, I go to another [company]. I do this all [summer].... Most often I sort coffee beans [seven to nine hours a day].

During this interview, I learned that Ketsy, like so many of her peers, is split in her professional aspirations. At times, she dreams of being a doctor, at others, she hopes to follow in the footsteps of a well-known Malagasy pop singer reminiscent of Madonna, whose songs consist of fatuous bubblegum pop. My own impression is that Ketsy has little chance of excelling at either. A major obstacle to Ketsy's academic aspirations is that she can hardly speak a word of French.

LS: What do you like to do?

Ketsy: I like to sing in Malagasy. And I wish I could speak French *[teny frantzay]*! It's so hard, but I wish I could speak French *[teny vazaha]*.

LS: What happens in school? Aren't you now studying in French?

Ketsy: Our teachers first say everything in French and then they explain it in Malagasy [i.e., in Sakalava]. . . .

LS: . . . What do you hope to do or to be? What are your aspirations?

Ketsy: I'd like to go to the university. I'd like to be a doctor and make lots of money. [She then reaches under her bed and pulls out a dusty teen star magazine. On the cover is a French model who looks even more emaciated than Kate Moss]. This is what I want to be like, but not a foreigner *[vazaha]*—I want to be a Malagasy version of this. I want to be a pop singer. I really like to sing in Malagasy. . . .

LS: . . . [Once the formal interview has been completed, I then ask]: Do you have any questions for me?

Ketsy: Yes, many. Why do you ask me so many questions?

Economic Survival

The extent to which kin are present on a daily basis—and able to finance their children's education—varies widely from one student to another. Key determinants include social class, localized networks, and access to such resources as food and shelter. Olive's parents, for example, are civil servants in Antananarivo and have sought the assistance of an aunt who is a member of Ambanja's highland elite. They have assumed correctly that Olive will find few distractions in Ambanja, so that she will be more inclined to focus on her studies the second time around. In Ambanja, Olive is housed and fed by her aunt; in return, she is asked to assist at mealtimes by setting and clearing the table and going to the kitchen for more food when it is needed. Other household chores are handled by two servants, so that Olive is able to devote herself almost entirely to her studies, which she does with great seriousness and passion.

It must be understood, however, that Olive's situation is truly extraordinary, made possible only because she has wealthy, caring kin living in Ambanja. Throughout Olive's stay, her aunt has taken her responsibilities seriously, seeking out scholastic assistance for her niece with a vengeance, investing her own time and money in hiring a string of private tutors for the doltish yet diligent Olive. She even attempted at one point to bribe an examiner, but this effort failed miserably, which embarrassed her deeply. Nevertheless, their combined efforts paid off, for Olive did, in fact, pass her bac in 1993. Olive then entered the university at Antananarivo in 1994, where she was admitted to a program in agricultural science (her bac scores were too low for her to study medicine as she had hoped).

Clearly, few students experience the luxury of such full-time care. Antoine, Jacques, and Ketsy are far more typical of their migrant peers. For one thing, each has connections to local tera-tany: Antoine and Jacques's parents lived in Ambanja for over a decade before returning to their natal villages to farm land inherited from parents and grandparents, and thus these two boys need not worry about finding housing or paying rent, because they now inhabit the house in which they spent the majority of their younger years. Their current lives are, however, devoid of reg-ular adult supervision, save for a brief weekly visit from their mother, who only stays a few hours. Antoine, having proved to be a serious student, is now entrusted with the care of his younger brother, Jacques, who also excels in his studies.

Ketsy, too, has come to Ambanja as a result of family connections, although she lives a far more isolated life, experiencing little adult supervision. She lives in the house of an older kinswoman, but her Mamahely is rarely home. Furthermore, the two share the financial burden of their monthly rent. Ketsy and her Mamahely must seek out physically taxing jobs if they are to survive in Ambanja, for neither has specialized skills. Ketsy's single mother is too ill to generate much income, so Ketsy's Mamahely has turned to the backbreaking work of housekeeping under a demanding foreign employer. Ketsy must generate enough vacation income to help keep them afloat, hopping from one temporary job to another, sorting export pro-duce in the warehouses of the Sambirano's numerous plantations.

The amenities that characterize school migrants' homes vary widely from one household to another and, thus, some experiences are more typical than others. Olive is housed in one of Ambanja's larger villas, where house servants are on call to wash her clothes and cook her meals for her. She is exempt from most forms of housework, and she occupies a private room where electricity functions through-out the year—if the town's system fails, her uncle simply turns on his generator. She can thus study late into the night without straining her eyesight, and she even has an electric fan, which she runs during the hottest hours of the day. A European-style bathroom is only a few steps away, and so she is never required to haul water from a well to wash each morning; nor is it necessary to make the fifteen-minute trek to the nearby forests to defecate, as remains true for the majority of Ambanja's inhabitants, who live without plumbing or latrines, but who maintain simple (and often pristine) lean-tos in which to shower and urinate.

Antoine, Jacques, and Ketsy, on the other hand, are all saddled with the triple burden of attending to the demands of schoolwork, housekeeping, and food sup-ply and preparation. None of their kin could ever afford a refrigerator, and so these students typically visit the market once or even twice a day, shopping for their mid-day and evening meals. Antoine, Jacques, and Ketsy also must rely on the faint light generated by weak oil lamps if they wish to study after sunset or before dawn, for although Antoine and Jacques's house is rigged with electricity, they find it far too expensive to rely on even a single electric bulb to illuminate it. Ketsy's home is much simpler and has never been linked to the town's power supply. School administrators recognize the lack of electricity as a serious problem for students entering their terminale year; in response to persistent urging from Dalia, in particular (see chapter 7), the Lycée Tsiaraso I now remains open until midnight during the end-of-year exam period so that students have a spacious and well-lit place in which to study.

Among the most arduous tasks that school migrants face is the constant search for food. Shopping in one of the town's two local markets is both time-consuming and expensive. Prices can fluctuate wildly during any given year, depending on the seasonal availability of produce and the effects of radical devaluation policies. No where is this felt as keenly as in the price of rice, the local staple, which is eaten at nearly every meal by many. Rice, in fact, is equated with food, and thus a meal without it is no meal at all. Antoine and Jacques are fortunate to have access to domestic rice from their mother's fields, which supply much of what they require throughout the year. It is only in the leanest months that they, like the majority of their neighbors, must turn to the town's markets to purchase what they need (at the highest prices) as they await the new harvest. They are also fortunate in that they have access to fields only a few kilometers away. Like many of their migrant schoolmates, they must travel each weekend to till the soil and take what they need for the following week. Although Ketsy is Sakalava, she hails from a village approximately sixty kilometers away, and so she faces the greatest economic hardships of all, because neither she nor her Mamahely have access to local farmland. Although they are much poorer than Antoine and his kin, they must expend more to survive, since they must purchase all of their food.

As should now be clear, the wealth of one's kin is an important factor in determining the daily rituals in a school migrant's life. Olive certainly represents an extreme of this: her aunt's housekeeper cooks every meal on a gas stove and can store several days worth of food in the refrigerator. Should Olive's aunt wish to go to the market herself, she can do so with ease in the family car (which is usually driven for her by a chauffeur). In contrast, the experiences of Antoine, Jacques, and Ketsy are far more typical, their daily lives paralleling those of other school migrants whose stories appear below and in subsequent chapters. As these experiences reveal, the well-being of the school migrant hinges largely on the strength of kin networks and, especially, the ties that such kin have to the land. A student will truly struggle to be productive and successful at school if he or she has little support from older kin—not simply in terms of financial resources, but also through access to inexpensive housing and, perhaps even more important, productive farm land. In essence, both indigenous Sakalava tera-tany and migrant vahiny youth from rural locales experience many of the same daily problems associated with social isolation and the lack of adult supervision. What distinguishes them, however, is that locally rooted Sakalava tera-tany students such as Antoine and Jacques inevitably fare better because they have land nearby that can supply them with nourishment.

Thus, sacrifice constantly resurfaces as a dominant theme that frames the daily survival of school migrants—both in and out of the classroom—where their worries must focus simultaneously on scholastic success and on the source of their next meal. In addition, parents and other elder kin who encourage children to continue schooling alone in Ambanja must invest time, energy, and financial resources to ensure their well-being. Given that many of these older kin are landed peasants, they may suffer economic hardship themselves during the prime agricultural seasons when their children are away in school. For this reason, students often leave school temporarily to assist older kin with their rice harvests—a time that may overlap with final exams. Parental faith in a child is evident in a willingness to let a student live alone. Such children must establish themselves at an early age in independent households, assuming all of the chores that otherwise would be shared by kin under a single roof, within a compound, or in the same neighborhood or village.

Some solitary children assume these domestic responsibilities at ages much younger than those of Antoine, Jacques, and Ketsy. I knew students as young as ten who did so. In fact, my first encounter with a school migrant involved a twelve-year-old boy who rented a small house (virtually a lean-to) in a friend's backyard in 1987. As a school migrant from a distant village, he was doubly an outsider, and my friend knew very little about him except whether or not he had paid his rent on time. This boy cooked his own meals, cleaned his dwelling, and washed all of his clothes and linens without any adult supervision. On weekends, he, like Antoine and Jacques, journeyed to the countryside, where he assisted an elderly grandmother who kept chickens and goats, and who had a small garden and some rice fields. He would then walk the fifteen kilometers back to town carrying a basket of food with which to sustain himself throughout the week. When he failed in his studies at the end of that school year, he promptly paid what rent he owed and went home to his parents' village seventy kilometers away.

When I expressed sadness over his predicament and assumed loneliness, my friend (and his landlady) quickly retorted, "I can't worry about some stranger's child—I already have three of my own to watch over!" As she and so many other inhabitants of Ambanja taught me that year, town-based tera-tany can hardly be expected to be responsible—or held accountable—for the woes experienced by strangers who enter their territory. Without local kin, a migrant will most certainly remain an outsider (Sharp 1993), and this rule holds true not only for adult migrants from distant regions of Madagascar, but for unsupervised children, regardless of whether they are of Sakalava or migrant vahiny origin.

The Seminarist's Sheltered Path

As described in chapter 2, there is yet another category of privileged school migrants who inhabit this town, whose experiences stand in stark contrast to those of Ketsy, Antoine and Jacques, and my friend's young male tenant, all of whom live relatively independent lives. This category consists of several dozen seminary students, whose experiences typify boarding school life. As part of a program established by the Catholic Academy in the early 1980s, these boys are housed in a two-story dormitory overseen by priests, and each is either given a private room or shares one with only one other student. Three priests sleep in the dormitory, and the rest live across a large yard in a separate building. Seminarists assist in the general daily cleaning of their private and common rooms (sweeping floors, for example) but otherwise they, like Olive, are exempt from the more time-consuming chores that dominate the daily lives of migrant youth. Their meals are prepared for them three times a day, seven days a week, and so it is unnecessary for them to visit the market once or twice a day, to haul water, or to journey each weekend to the countryside to collect produce for their own consumption. The majority of these students are on full scholarships, awarded such financial support with the understanding that they will seriously consider the priesthood as a vocation when they complete their studies (the annual cost of their tuition, room, and board is approximately FMG 150,000). As a result, their adult kin are relieved of much of the financial burden that troubles parents of other independent school migrants. Needless to say, there is no parallel housing and tuition program available for schoolgirls who aspire to the Catholic sisterhood, although there are several at the Academy who follow a similar academic path as the seminarists.[2]

Seminarists live under the watchful eye of adult priests, who are responsible for their safety and well-being. Strict rules are designed with care to curtail their movements. As part of this intense surveillance, these boys must respect an evening curfew, which dictates that they return to the dorm by 5:30 P.M., and they are not permitted to leave it until 7:00 A.M. the following morning, and then only in order to be in class by 7:30. One such student is Ignace, a nineteen-year-old seminarist enrolled in his première year. He comes from a village approximately 120 kilometers north of Ambanja. He described a typical day as follows, his account revealing a more regimented quality of life than is true for students such as Antoine or Ketsy who live on their own:

> *Ignace:* We get up at 5:00 [A.M.], and for the next thirty minutes we go to work on individual chores—we clean our rooms, and then we study a bit. At 5:30, we then go to mass—we have a small chapel for this purpose. At 5:45, we study a bit more, and this continues until 6:30. At 6:30, we eat breakfast [in the common hall].
>
> *LS:* What, typically, do you eat?
>
> *Ignace:* We [always drink] tea, and two to three times a week we have bread. On other days we might have *tsonjo* [a starchy root crop that is popular in the region]. Then we get ready for school.
>
> *LS:* Do you go together as a group?
>
> *Ignace:* No, we go as we need to. From 7:30 until 11:30 we're in classes. At 11:45, we have prayer back here, then lunch, followed by a siesta.... From [2:10 to 5:30 P.M.] we're back at school. Seminarists and students in terminale stay another hour for study hall. At [6:30] we go to chapel again. At [7:00] we have supper, and then we might watch television—we do this until [8:00]. We then study from [8:00 until 9:30], and then there's lights out, when we go to sleep.

Even the seminarists' spare time is regulated by adult overseers. Visiting discos in town is strictly prohibited,[3] but they have access to other luxuries that lie far beyond the reach of other students: there are free weekly video showings in the seminary dormitory (with many of the same films shown in town), and, as Ignace makes clear, there is a television in their common hall where they can watch the national news and broadcasts from France. They also have access to a modest library. As another seminarist stated cheerfully: "I spend most of my days between school and the dormitory. The mission provides for all of my needs."

Christian is yet another seminarist. At seventeen, he is much younger than many of his classmates enrolled in première. He has had to redo only one class since he began school at the age of six. "I've only repeated septième," he explained. "It was the teachers' fault. They didn't get their salaries [that year], so they didn't teach us anything." Christian is articulate and thoughtful. He is also among the most curious students I encountered, always available for interviews and discussions because of a strong desire to understand the purpose of social science and the focus of my research. He would often ask me to discuss "the sacrificed generation," a concept both novel and fascinating to him. He is from a small village just south of the town of Bealanana, where he attended a private Catholic school through the primary and middle grades. Bealanana lies nearly 350 kilometers from Ambanja on roads that zigzag south and then jut northeast again. Identified early on as an accomplished student, he was recommended for a scholarship at Ambanja's Catholic Academy. He has lived in the seminary dormitory for three years.

Christian comes from a family with a strong educational history. Three of his seven siblings had attended lycée, including a much older brother who acquired advanced technical training in agricultural science in Antananarivo, and a sister, three year's Christian's senior, who had passed her bac, but whom family financial problems prevented from pursuing a university degree. His parents also have impressive educational histories: his mother passed her post–middle school BEPC exam, and his father, who died very suddenly five years ago, finished his schooling through première. As is true of the majority of seminarists, many of Christian's kin are landed peasants: during a group discussion with ten seminarists, half reported that during their lengthy school vacation they would work in fields back home.

Christian is a bright student whose knowledge of French is impressive, yet he often struggles to do well in lycée. Since his arrival in Ambanja, his grades have fluctuated wildly from extremely high marks to failures. One of his teachers described him as intelligent yet "sporadic" in his successes and thought he seemed depressed. As Christian himself explained, sometimes he is, indeed, overcome with great sadness *(mampalahelo be)*, because he misses his dead father very much. A paternal uncle has taken Christian under his wing, and during his vacations, Christian looks forward to joining him as a photographer's assistant. He worries, though, about his two younger siblings and mother back home, wondering if they are managing to make ends meet. In his own words, "the territory around Bealanana isn't fertile like it is here—there aren't plantations and bountiful harvests like you find in the Sambirano. But rice does grow well in our fields." He also feels the pressure of the expectation that he become a priest, an aspiration that he says does not suit his temperament. When asked what he hoped to do in the future, he responded carefully, as if he had rehearsed the statement with care, "After I've completed my studies I wish to be a director of a tourist agency." This is, in fact, the same phrase he wrote on a questionnaire I distributed during one of his classes.

School migration also takes its toll. As Christian explained to me one afternoon:

> Coming here [to Ambanja] requires a great adjustment. Many of the seminarists are from [towns and villages to the] south, and so when we arrive here we are suddenly faced with learning a completely new dialect. You see, my mother is Tsimihety, and so is my father. I grew up [in Tsimihety territory] speaking that language. It takes at least three months to get used to the language here, and all the while your teachers are speaking to you in Sakalava in the classroom. As a result, we seminarists, we tend to stick together, because so many of us are Tsimihety. It helps to ease the feeling of isolation that comes from being only a guest *[vahiny]* in someone else's territory.
>
> ... I look forward to the long school vacation [at this point Christian becomes more animated]. . . . I join my uncle, who is a photographer, and I help him—well, I try to help him, anyway! We travel on foot from one village to another, because there are no roads that go to many of them. We take photographs of people, and then we send the film back to Antananarivo to be developed. Last year, we charged FMG 4,000 per pose. Maybe this year, we'll charge 5,000. . . . I like the work, and my uncle is a kind man.

Once I had completed the formal interview, I asked him, as I did Ketsy and all other young informants, whether he had any questions for me. Christian responded with a resounding "Yes!" He then reached into his pocket and pulled out a list of questions given out by one of his instructors in preparation for the bac exam. I tried my best to supply any knowledge I might have on such subjects as "the economic conflict between the United States and Japan," "the primary agricultural product of the United States," and "the major problems of agricultural production for a crop such as wheat" in, yet again, my own country. Unable to provide more than cursory remarks, I soon felt ashamed of the limits of my own knowledge.

Town-Based Students and Their Experiences at Home

The experiences of town-based youth fall somewhere between those of independent migrants, such as Ketsy and Antoine, and students who are housed and otherwise cared for by adults, such as Olive and the seminarists. Within town-based households, one often finds discrepancies along gender lines, for although adult kin generally place equal value on the schooling of sons and daughters (cf. Clignet and Ernst 1995, 105), girls are inevitably saddled with more domestic chores than are their brothers (Sharp 1996, 2002; cf. Bledsoe et al. 1993). Pauline is a case in point: a buoyant, bright young student whom I often found difficult to pin down for interviews, because she was inevitably running errands after school for older kin.

When we finally spoke near the end of my stay in 1994, she was enrolled in her terminale year at the Catholic Academy. She lives with her parents and two younger siblings, a sister, aged fifteen, and brother, aged twelve. Pauline is twenty years old, although she looks as though she is no older than about fourteen. Her mother works as a postal clerk, and on most days she comes home for lunch. Her father works for a merchant whose business is located just off the central market; when there is much to do, he eats lunch there with other employees, cooking rice in a common pot, and then he rests before the business opens again in the afternoon. Pauline bears much of the domestic work of her household, and so she typically rises earlier and goes to bed later than the majority of her peers. She rarely has time for a midday rest. Pauline described a typical day as follows:

> *Pauline:* I get up around 4:00 [A.M.] to do my schoolwork until about 5:00. I then make tea for everyone, I clean the house, I bathe. My [younger] sister usually goes to market to buy our food. Oh, and it's my job to haul the water. We then go to school. I usually get back around 11:45, and then I cook lunch for everyone. I wash the dishes with my sister's help, and I bathe again. Then I go back to school from about [2:00 until 4:30 P.M.]. I'm always home by [5:30]. I cook dinner in the evening, and I wash the dishes again. I do my school work until about [10 or 10:30], and then I go to sleep!

> *LS:* And your brother? What does he do?

> *Pauline:* He sweeps the courtyard in the morning, and then he studies before breakfast. In the afternoon, he's usually with his friends.

> *LS:* And what about the weekends? What do you do then?

> *Pauline:* I work! I wash all the clothes, and I do my homework. On Sunday I go to the FJKM [Protestant church], and then I go home to cook.

Another serious lycée student enrolled in his terminale year in 1994 was nineteen-year-old Jaona. He reported a daily schedule that at times approximated Pauline's, whereas at others it more closely resembles that of her carefree brother.

> *Jaona:* My brothers and sisters and I, we all live together in this cozy house with my mother. She's a midwife, and she works very hard, and because of her profession we're not always sure when she'll be home. Because of this we all have responsibilities that help her. We rely on my two sisters to run to the market, and to cook our meals, for example. Since we live near the lycée, I get home before everyone else. [As a result], I'm usually in charge of making sure the rice is ready by the time we all come home at midday. Or I might start cooking the rest of the meal, too, although that's usually not necessary. When I was younger, and [my siblings] were just babies, I helped my mother with a lot of the cooking.

> *LS:* What about morning responsibilities? What do you do then?

> *Jaona:* You know [my schoolmate] Foringa Josef, don't you? Each morning he gets up very early to help his brother-in-law take the cattle out to pasture before he goes to school. [They have three big young bulls. As for me, well, I don't do anything as important as that—when I get up in the morning, I go out and I feed our two

chickens! . . . My younger brother's the one who sweeps the house and porch and our tiny yard, and my sisters make the breakfast.

LS: And then who does the dishes after each meal?

Jaona: Again, that's the responsibility of my sisters. Because we live so close to the Sambirano [River], they prefer to take the dishes there, especially after the noon-day meal, when there's a lot to do. That way they don't have to haul the water. If our water [supply] is low and they need help, then I'll go with them to help carry water back home. They usually do the laundry at the Sambirano on weekends as well.

LS: What about the afternoons, what do you do then when you get back from school?

Jaona: My mother might send me on errands, especially if she needs to tell something to [one of her clients]. I can run fast, so I make a good messenger! But I usually do what I can to play soccer every day. Since I have a ball, I'm usually invited to play, too. Now that we're all studying for the bac, though, I have less time to play in the afternoons. If I can, I skip my siesta and play at midday instead.

The Domestication of Children: A Gendered Burden

As all of these students' narratives make clear, the daily expectations placed on them involve a pairing of responsibilities that include attention to schoolwork as well as domestic chores. None of the households described above, save Olive's, have servants that relieve students from domestic duties at home. Only a few households in Ambanja have running water, so it has to be hauled each or every other day from spigots and wells located throughout town. One is fortunate indeed if such a sup-ply of water is in close proximity to where one lives (as is true of one household I frequent, where a neighborhood well is located smack in the middle of its open compound). Electricity is an even greater luxury, which few can afford, as are energy-saving appliances such as gas stoves and refrigerators. As a result, two clocks simultaneously dictate the course of a student's daily life:[4] one is scholastic, the other domestic. A student's success hinges on his or her ability to reach school on time, to remain there throughout much of the day, and to complete assignments successfully and as required. The domestic axis focuses on the material needs of survival—especially on mealtimes and household maintenance. Such survival ne-cessitates access to productive fields, markets, and small privately owned stores and produce stands if one is to have rice, tubers of various sorts, tomatoes, onions, beans, greens, bananas, and other fruit, and perhaps an occasional bit of meat to eat, as well as a reliable supply of cooking oil, kerosene, matches, and charcoal for their preparation. In a household of only one or two children, domestic duties can be terribly time-consuming. Thus, solitary migrant youth clearly shoulder greater domestic demands than do many of their town-based peers. School migrants are truly at an advantage if they can divide these duties with a roommate.

Town-based youth such as Pauline and Jaona nevertheless expose other dimen-sions of daily survival. Both live under the watchful eye of kin, and thus experience an element of guidance that does not characterize the lives of Antoine or Ketsy. Throughout Madagascar, bonds between siblings are typically close (Feeley-Harnik 1991, 186 ff.), and since Pauline and Jaona are the oldest siblings living within their respective households, they (like Antoine) are also responsible for the care and well-being of their younger siblings. Larger households also require more work, because there are more mouths to feed. The effect of town-based household life on students varies, needless to say, by gender. As the oldest boy in his mother's home, Jaona certainly assists in all sorts of ways, but he often remains free throughout much of the afternoon. Pauline, however, is saddled with many domestic chores and has little leisure time at all.

The complexity of this double burden is well illustrated by the compound where I was a guest throughout much of 1987. Within a few months of my arrival, my landlords, a Lutheran pastor and his wife, who both grew up in the highlands, hired an eight-year-old girl named Tata to assist with part-time care of their new baby. This couple's ability to maintain her as a household servant hinged upon striking a clear balance between Tata's domestic and academic responsibilities.

Little Tata's Urban Duties

Tata's family is of Tsimihety origin, both of her parents hailing from a small village near Antsohihy, 217 kilometers south of Ambanja over rough roads. Tata's father had originally come to the Sambirano as a seasonal laborer during a coffee harvest in 1984. In 1985, he decided to return with his entire family in order to settle here long-term. The following year, however, Tata's mother died from post-partum complications, leaving her father with a newborn baby (who soon died) and two other young children to feed. Tata's father was a devoted member of the pastor's congregation, and he and the pastor soon grew close as a result of counseling sessions that focused on his terrible misfortunes. In early 1987, the pastor decided to approach Tata's father to ask if his eight-year-old daughter might help his wife with the part-time care of their new baby. Tata's father agreed without hesitation. Tata quickly became so attached to the pastor's family that she often preferred to sleep there at night; soon she took three meals a day there as part of her payment. Her domestic chores also increased: I often encountered her in the early morning making breakfast for the pastor's family before she left for school, and although she seemed very young to me, she was often my best teacher, for she taught me how to light charcoal, use a coffee sock, and polish my drab old concrete floors.

In mid 1987, the pastor learned that he had been appointed to a prestigious post in the provincial capital of Diégo-Suarez. He therefore approached Tata's father to ask if she could accompany them when they moved. After several days of deliberating, Tata's father gave his consent, but on one condition: that Tata be permitted to continue her schooling in Diégo. Should her studies suffer, he assured the pastor, he would insist that she return to Ambanja. When I visited the pastor's family near the end of Tata's first school term in Diégo, I found a thriving family and a healthy young girl whose school marks were high, thanks in part to the careful and regular supervision of both the pastor and his wife.

Tata's story is truly exceptional in ways that cannot be ignored. In 1987, she was, after all, a young child, and when she started to work for the pastor and his wife, she was still in primary school. Although it is not unusual for children as young as she to be employed as domestic servants in Madagascar, such a practice is not typical of Ambanja households. Furthermore, when children are employed, they often define a class of essentially indentured servants with few or no rights. The highly exploitative nature of such relationships most certainly excludes schooling. The value of Tata's tale is that it illustrates the manner in which a delicate balance must be maintained between domestic and scholastic duties if such a girl is to succeed in school.[5]

In spite of this household's reliance on Tata's labor, it would be ethnocentric to assume that the domestic sphere is exclusively a female domain in any of the households described above. Nearly all boys and men I have encountered over the course of a decade of research are not only capable of cooking but truly gifted at this art. In many urban households in Ambanja, wife and husband will often take turns cooking meals, or each may specialize in particular dishes, so that the availability of certain foods will then determine who cooks. Work schedules also play a part. Should a man's wife or partner leave him either temporarily or permanently, he will, without hesitation, generally take over all of her domestic chores himself, rather than look to female kin for help (although if he has a mistress, she may quickly move in and fill this role, thus forcefully asserting her new position vis-à-vis her lover; cf. Sharp 1993, 218 ff.). One only need compare Antoine's home with Ketsy's to see how well boys can care for a house and yard. The example set by Antoine and his brother Jacques is neither unusual nor striking in a northern urban Malagasy context. What is true, however, is that although all boys learn to perform all domestic chores, once their sisters are old enough to learn such tasks, these girls will inevitably be expected to assume them nearly full-time. In other words, boys are exempt from many of these tasks if there is a sister available to perform them. As Pauline's story reveals, a girl will assume these domestic responsibilities beginning in her early youth. Her responsibilities at home often cease only when she moves out and establishes her own independent household, or, after her marriage, she may eventually transfer such duties to her own children as they grow. This gendered pattern sheds light on the domestic organization inherent in a radically different context as well: the Catholic Academy's seminary program ensures that a select group of boys can devote their efforts full-time to their studies without the added demands of heavy domestic requirements. Their female peers currently are provided no similar opportunity by the academy, even though, ironically, this school was originally established to satisfy the educational needs of young northern girls.

Social Status and Schooling: What, Ultimately, Is a Child?

"In Madagascar, parents will take care of their children up to the age of thirty—they watch over you. If you are still a student then they pay all your expenses. This is the Malagasy way," Félix, an eighteen-year-old lycée student, told me in 1994, during a discussion of our respective experiences with schooling. Félix (as well as Tsarahita, who was also present) looked aghast when I explained that when I reached the age of eighteen, my divorced parents had expected me to be relatively financially independent. Fortunately, they had continued to bear the burden of my hefty college tuition expenses, but I was not permitted to live with either of them for long periods of time; rather, I was soon required to bear the full burden of room and board elsewhere throughout my lengthy vacation breaks. By the time I had graduated from college at the age of twenty-one, I was living independently from both parents. The same requirements were imposed on my younger siblings, even in the face of financial hardships and illness. These were expectations I took for granted; they do not, however, resonate with Malagasy understandings of familial structure and obligations toward children.

Although Félix proposes his model as normative Malagasy behavior, it in fact does not typify the experiences of many young people I have met in Ambanja. It seems truer of households in Antananarivo, where rentals are scarce and prohibitively expensive even for well-educated, salaried professionals, so that one often encounters people in their twenties and thirties who live in their parents' or grandparents' homes, sometimes with spouses and/or children of their own. If their older kin own these homes, these younger inhabitants stand to inherit them.

In Ambanja, a variety of models of household organization typify settlement patterns, ranging from communal dwellings shared by single male entrepreneurs, to the homesteads of adult sisters and their offspring, to nuclear units, to single mothers and occasionally fathers with children, to elderly grandmothers who care for their daughters' offspring (see Sharp 1993, 2002), in addition to those consisting of independent school migrants. The value of Félix's statement is that it underscores the commitment of parents to their children. A child who does not return home regularly, even in the advanced stages of adulthood, is perceived as having abandoned kin, home, and hearth. The imposition of such responsibilities ensures that children will remain rooted to the land, both materially (as peasant farmers, for example) and symbolically (by maintaining ties to the tanindrazaña or ancestral land). Félix's statement is important in yet another way, too, because it underscores the absence of boundaries distinguishing young from old. This is particularly important if we are to understand the social relevance of the school migrant, especially in reference to such troubling categories as "child," "youth," "adolescent," and "adult." These are highly fluid categories of experience in the urban community of Ambanja.

As noted earlier, the concept of "adolescence" is problematic, especially given the highly flawed assumptions that characterize academic writings on this subject.

Although teenage schoolchildren in Ambanja are occasionally referred to as "adolescents" (FR: *adolescents*) by educated adults, the lives of such students as Antoine and Ketsy clearly illustrate that their experiences range far beyond the liminal and often assumed carefree (or troubled) status that characterizes Western constructions of the term. In fact, the phenomenon of school migration in northern Madagascar calls into question even the categories of "child" and "adult."

Independent Malagasy school migrants of rural origin cannot be packed together neatly in any single social group. When Ketsy's and Antoine's experiences are compared to those of the temporary elite houseguest Olive, the seminarists Ignace and Christian, and town-based Pauline and Jaona, it becomes clear that childhood as a social category is highly variable in Ambanja. There is no single label that either adequately describes all of them. None, however, would be considered full-fledged adults: they are not yet fully productive economically, because they must continue to rely heavily on a host of adult kin for food, shelter, and additional cash with which to pay for tuition and/or school supplies. It is not so much the amount of financial support they receive as, rather, their inability to reciprocate *equally,* as would adults of similar status. In other words, a child who works for her parents in their fields is not the social equivalent (and thus of the same social standing) as two adult sisters with children who regularly exchange goods or favors. Second, none of these students have entered adulthood by way of their reproductive capacities, a fact that is reflected symbolically in the names they use—at times, names they have borne since their infancy (as with Ketsy) or acquired as a mark of their having been baptized or confirmed in the Catholic Church (as with Ignace and Christian). A radical shift in status is proclaimed through teknonyms upon the birth of a first child, or, in professional contexts, by such titles as "Monsieur" or "Madame" (regardless of whether one is truly married).

Nevertheless, several of these students lie closer to adult status than others by virtue of their domestic responsibilities *and* abilities. From a Sakalava (and, more generally, pan-Malagasy) point of view, Antoine and Jacques, as well as Ketsy, approximate the responsibilities of adulthood, because they maintain independent households. In this sense, they can be considered much wiser (*hendry;* "clever," "prudent," or possessing social intelligence) and more capable (*mahay*) than Jaona or, to an even greater extreme, Ignace and Olive, both of whom have far more time to devote to their studies by virtue of the fact that they are supported by full-fledged adults (and, in Olive's case, servants). Furthermore, the amount of time invested in domestic responsibilities is also highly variable and hinges on multiple factors, including socioeconomic status, landedness, the density of locally based kin groups, and gender. Olive experiences the luxuries associated with an elite household, which enable her to immerse herself in full-time study in preparation for the bac. In time, her shift to adulthood will diverge sharply from, say, the experiences of Ketsy or Pauline, for in establishing her own household Olive will most likely have a servant herself.

Other forms of wealth are illustrated by the case of Antoine and his brother Jacques; these reveal a variety of responsibilities that ultimately may affect school success. They are clearly at a far greater advantage financially than Ketsy, because they have supportive kin scattered throughout northern Madagascar, as well as two siblings who live in France. Furthermore, they pay no rent, since their parents own the house in which they live, and they have access to productive fields. It is by virtue of these two forms of wealth—housing and land—that they are able to subsist on their own without regular attention from adult kin. Ketsy, on the other hand, is often alone, and she and her Mamahely must struggle to make ends meet throughout the school term and during her school vacations. As a result, Ketsy has entered the labor market at an early age; if she fails in her studies, she may very well be destined to work nearly full-time at one of the local plantations, assuming she does not return to her mother's rural homestead. Finally, Pauline and Jaona face the highly divergent domestic expectations of eldest children in town-based households. Pauline's experiences in particular approximate those of youth who are not in school: she already bears a considerable domestic burden, which in the end will prepare her for running a household of her own.

In contrast to these examples, the seminarists seem suspended in a prolonged state of childhood, in ways that parallel those described by Philippe Ariès (1960), because they assume only minimal responsibilities beyond the demands imposed by schooling and are thus sheltered from the sorts of daily worries experienced by independent students. School migrants who live alone or share their accommodation with student roommates are thrust more quickly into adult roles. Finally, there are the town-based students who live with their adult kin. Among these, girls more quickly assume a wider assortment of domestic responsibilities than their brothers, and one cannot help but wonder how such girls manage to succeed in school at all, much less excel, as some ultimately do.

THE TENUOUSNESS OF SCHOOL SUCCESS

Mme. Chantal, a thirty-one-year-old part-time French teacher at the Catholic Academy, complained to me in 1994:

> One of my greatest frustrations as a teacher is that my students simply are not motivated. They work for money, and that's it. If they have [fields of] coffee [or other crops] then that's all they want. Here you study for work to get money. But in Ambositra [in Fianarantsoa Province, where my father comes from], it's different—there they work really hard because life is so difficult. They know that they have to do well in their studies if they are to survive. They [don't have the same] resources. Look, in Ambositra, apart from their rice fields, they have nothing. There, manioc takes two years to grow. Here it takes six to eight months and then it is ready to be harvested and eaten! For rice [you break your back] but here it just grows and grows and grows.

Mme. Chantal's background is an unusual one, giving her a unique perspective: her mother is Sakalava, her father *métis* (his mother was Betsileo, and his father was a Frenchman in the foreign service). Although Mme. Chantal's father had been raised in Ambositra, he traveled through much of the island during the late colonial period as an engineer's assistant. On Nosy Be, he met Mme. Chantal's mother and married her; he then left his colonial post and established a lucrative trading business on the island. He sent his two daughters to private Catholic schools and then to the university in Antananarivo. As a result of their education and the father's personal efforts, Mme. Chantal and her sister are fluent in French and Sakalava, and also comfortable speaking Betsileo. Mme. Chantal arrived in Ambanja in the early 1990s, when her husband, Mr. Prosper, then aged thirty-four, acquired a job teaching philosophy at the state-run lycée. She teaches at both the middle school and lycée levels at the Catholic Academy and hopes to master English one day, although the opportunities for doing so in Ambanja are limited.

Mme. Chantal's criticism of her students echoes those of other adult inhabitants of Ambanja, ranging from other schoolteachers and administrators to parents. Many expressed such sentiments with greater disdain and frustration—after all, several teachers of highland origins have had to face the sharp words of students who express open disdain for the teacher's craft, and who refuse to converse directly with an instructor as long as the language spoken is official Malagasy. As one student put it, "Why should I [strive] to be a teacher? They aren't paid enough to support their families, and so they live in [relative] poverty. I can make more money during the coffee season than they can in an entire year. I'm better off being a peasant." In contrast, Mme. Chantal is popular among her students in part because of her empathy. As a young woman from Nosy Be, she identifies herself as Sakalava (although some consider her *métisse,* because her father was half French). Throughout her stay in Antananarivo, she longed to return to her tanindrazaña in northern Madagascar, and she was thrilled when her husband received a post in Ambanja, even though she knew she had few prospects of employment there. "It is here in the north where I belong," she explained.

Mme. Chantal completed lycée during the Second Republic, and her final year was truly difficult. Her best friend's father was transferred suddenly to the east coast, and he requested that young Chantal be allowed to accompany his daughter so that she would not be alone in a new place. Mme. Chantal's parents consented, even though it meant that their own daughter would spend her final year of lycée at an inferior state-run school. "[We had] no teachers of Malagasy, of French, or of English," Mme. Chantal told me. "And there was only a little philosophy and history. How could [we] pass the bac under such conditions? What I knew I knew from seconde and première in Nosy Be." Both girls managed to pass their bac exams, however, and they entered the university together the following year. It was there that Mme. Chantal met her husband, Mr. Prosper, a Betsileo man who, like Mme. Chantal's father, hailed from Ambositra in the high plateaux. Mr. Prosper was several years ahead of Mme. Chantal in his schooling. Unlike the majority of his peers of highland origin, he longed for a coastal post. "I've never supported the cold weather of the highlands; and my happiest years as a child were spent in Morondava [in the far southwest], where my parents worked for a few years," he said.

When Mr. Prosper received news of his appointment in Ambanja, Mme. Chantal abandoned her studies to follow him. She was, however, determined to pursue a career as a teacher.

Much of my research with adults involved understanding how they identified students who had the greatest problems, and some of the more thoughtful answers to my questions came from Mme. Chantal and Mr. Prosper:

> *Mme. Chantal:* Who has the greatest problems? Those [children who come] from the countryside. Imagine—each weekend they have to go home! This is really hard. They have no time to study. [Instead,] they have to pound rice, getting so many [servings] for the week. The thing is, they really want to study. But they have no time.

> *Mr. Prosper:* And look at the [barriers] they face. People here live in obscurity, they don't even . . . leave their villages, their biggest town is Ambanja. They don't travel [so they know little] of the world. . . . As for studying, well, they must [cope with] teachers [who are unprepared], and strikes. Even their parents don't or can't help them financially. Look at [a student we all knew]—Well, he has to find money for his studies. Every month, this is a serious problem for him. . . . If you go walk in front of the pharmacy at the central market, there, in front, you'll see a boy who sells bread and other things. [He and] two others, and a girl, every morning they get up at 5:00 A.M., they buy their bread at the bakery, and then they sell it in the market at a higher price. They're always there—two brothers and their two friends.[6] The brothers, they only make enough for one of them to go to the Catholic Academy, so the other goes to the [state-run] lycée. He's one of my students. These are the ones who really want to study. To do well they have to sit and read, but how can they do that when they must support themselves, too? . . . The kids from the country[side], they're the most serious of all. Think of it—to come here from the country—they [must] really [be] motivated. But they might sleep in class, simply because they're so tired. This is the paradox—the ones who want to work the most, who care the most, may in fact be the ones most likely to fail.
>
> I'd say, too, there are three categories of [migrant] students. First, there are those from the villages who are really serious, but they have significant problems [to face]—food and finances. Second, there are those [from the villages] who really like life here in town, who are not serious at all. [They fail and] they go back home. Third are the children whose [parents come from areas of the high plateaux where schooling is strong] and they know the value of education. Their parents have really studied hard. [They also live with their parents in town so they can] oversee their studies. They are typically the ones who excel.

> *LS:* Is their success a result of where they come from, or the fact that they live with their parents here in town?

> *Mme. Chantal:* It's complicated, isn't it? We debate this all the time here at home, Prosper and I. Look at my best student—she's younger than everyone else in her class. Her father's a doctor at the hospital—he's educated, and expects the same of her. But it's true, he's also there to oversee her studies and make sure she takes her schoolwork seriously. So she has an advantage over many of her classmates. . . . But overall, the most serious students are the seminary students—they are the best.

They are *very* serious about their studies. And overall, they choose French as the language for their exams. They even ask to borrow books in French from us, and we lend them to them. They're very capable in French.

LS: What of town-based children who are from this area?

Mme. Chantal: People will tell you they are the best students. But, you know, it's the migrant *[vahiny]* children—in all the categories that Prosper mentioned, who really work the hardest of all. Because they know how serious they must be if they are going to do well in school. But so much is working against them that their chances of succeeding are minimal. *That* is the paradox of schooling in Ambanja.

There's one other thing: [we, too, are to blame]. You know, it's very sad what has happened. Before, [during the First Republic], the teachers were conscientious. Teachers worked with their hearts. But now it's "I work to get my pay." That's it. Look at the level of students, and the teachers. [All of us—] we know nothing! We are poorly cultivated. Look at the teachers who can't speak French, but who teach it anyway. . . . They . . . tell [us] to teach, but they don't tell [us] *how* to teach.

LS: Madagascar has now reverted back to French as central to the curriculum. You yourself teach French. What do you think of this?

Mme. Chantal: This defines the essence of the "sacrificed generation." What it means [to revert back to French]—it means that for these students, they are sacrificing their culture. This makes me very, very sad. You know, I always wear my hair like this [she holds up a pony tail of braids]. This is how I know Maman'i'Clarice [a mutual Sakalava friend]. I go to her house every Sunday and she plaits my hair for me. And this is the reason why: when I was first married, I went to live with [my husband's kin] in Ambositra. And my mother-in-law, she said, "Whatever you do, don't ever cut your hair. Wear it long. Always. Short hair, that's the European style. But to have long hair, that's the mark of the Malagasy." And so I've never cut it. And I'll always wear it long for that reason. Because I am Malagasy. And so it is with our language—Prosper and I, we are teaching our own children Malagasy first—to speak, read, and write it. When they're older, then we'll teach them French. But now, it's so important that they know and love their own language.

Later, with these words echoing in my mind, I could not help but pause for a moment on my way out their door, for there, on the porch, sat their eight-year-old daughter reading a story in official Malagasy to her illiterate Sakalava grandmother.

Miscreant Migrants

In spite of the evidence offered by teachers with firsthand experience with students, other adults in town overwhelmingly express the opinion that it is solitary migrant children of village origins who do worst in school. This springs largely from urban constructions of "the bush" (FR: *la brousse*) or "the countryside" (FR: *de la campagne,* SAK: *an-banvolo,* literally, from "near the forest") as opposed to "in town" (FR: *en ville,* SAK: *an-tanambe*). In contrast to French connotations, these expressions are not used to convey backwardness nearly so much as to stress an assumed innocence of rural people and, therefore, their susceptibility to urban dangers. By drawing upon these expressions, adult inhabitants in Ambanja underscore the pervasiveness of the threats of town life to the social and intellectual well-being of youth. All children require protection from such forces, but it is those of rural origins who live without supervision who are perceived as the easiest prey, because their previous lives were devoid of many of the pernicious forces associated with cosmopolitanism. A subtext at work here is the idea that rural youth are incapable of *ever* adjusting to town life, as though innocence were inherent in their characters by virtue of their births and early socialization.[7]

In Ambanja, town life is often described as rife with *diversions* ("distractions"). The fact that a French term is used is important here, since it underscores the recurrent belief that the majority of urban dangers originate abroad (FR: *de l'extérieur,* SAK: *an-dafy*). Such critiques, however, are often blind to the economic realities of the lives of migrant students such as Antoine and Jacques, Ketsy, and a host of others whom Mme. Chantal and Mr. Prosper encounter in their classrooms. Ironically, the seminarists and town-based elite youth such as Olive have far more opportunities made available to them to experience town life. An understanding of these contradictions necessitates an analysis of those factors considered the most menacing to students' well-being.

For over a decade, the movie theater (or, now, the public video cinema), discotheque, and television have surfaced repeatedly in my interviews and less formal conversations with urban adults whenever the topic shifts to the problems of schooling and parenting. (Other people's) children are often imagined as flocking to cinemas and bars in droves. Such fears are reminiscent of parental concerns cross-culturally; yet it must be stressed that the tenor of concerns as voiced in Ambanja reflects *localized* understandings of social decorum and the proper socialization of children. Television, videos, and dance halls are not considered dangerous simply because they are sexually charged, for example.[8] And although concerns about drug consumption (especially marijuana; SAK: *jamal*) are sometimes voiced, such comments do not figure prominently. Instead, the danger lies in their perceived threat to a student's scholastic productivity. This is articulated in several ways.

First, students who regularly go to discos and video cinemas will be left with insufficient funds to purchase essential school supplies or even food. Second, videos are said to endanger students because they offer examples of superficial concerns: kung-fu heroes consumed by their desire to perfect their kick-boxing skills do not focus steadily and seriously on their schoolwork. Such well-known stars as Arnold Schwarzenegger, Sylvester Stallone, and a host of Italian-produced cowboys and American soldiers (who inevitably remain lost in Vietnam long after the war) are similarly considered inappropriate social models. They are passionate for revenge and, as such, are loners adrift in worlds often bereft of social relations. Also, they, too, do not go to school.

At the heart of such fears is a concern that students may acquire social personas remote from current adult understandings of social worth (understandings that are often conflated, as if no variation could exist across class, ethnic, or regional lines). Of particular note is that it is educated parents and school administrators who are the most concerned, and their comments often quickly take on a paternalistic tone. Mr. Jaozara, a popular history teacher from the state-run lycée, expressed his sentiments in these terms:

> *Mr. Jaozara:* I believe that [exposure to these things ultimately] transforms the mentality [FR: *la mentalité*] . . . [of our] students—they don't respect their [adult kin]— *this* is the crisis of our youth today. . . . They understand only the very [rudimentary aspects] of Malagasy culture. . . . The films, with Stallone and others—oh, I don't know, I can't keep up with them!—but what I see is this: they see a film and it affects them *internally*—I see a change in their comportment, in their self-understanding. They have no desire to acquire knowledge—they don't want to understand, to comprehend, or to work at the things that affect their [immediate] lives.

It would be naïve to say that exposure to media of foreign origin has no impact at all on the psyches of Ambanja's youth: after all, such exposure lies at the very heart of schooling in Ambanja and beyond. That is, it is knowledge that reaches beyond one's immediate experience that has proved so transformative to many of the students who speak throughout this book. Yet adults assume that town life by itself will ultimately transform students' dreams and desires such that they will most certainly oppose those values embraced by a previous generation of adults. A further underlying assumption is that transformation is uniquely a threat to the *current* generation. Such critiques are fairly easy to embrace, especially if one finds comfort in romanticizing the past (taloha) and local traditions (ny fomba). This vision of contemporary life is, however, bereft of subtlety, for it presents a static view of culture and identity. Furthermore, it is based on false preconceptions of who frequents video cinemas and discos and what it is they take away with them.

Who is it who is most likely to frequent these venues in Ambanja? What is it that happens in these contexts, as opposed to what adults imagine? As my own data reveal, interestingly it is not migrant children of rural origins but relatively well off town-based youth. Material concerns figure prominently in determining such trends. Students such as Antoine and Jacques, Ketsy, Pauline, and Jaona consider a video entrance fee of FMG 500 to be prohibitively expensive; and discos, which typically cost twice or much more than this, are even farther out of reach. Spending one's money in this way means going hungry, because FMG 500 can equal rice for several days. The few students I know who have stepped into a disco have been able to do so only because a much wealthier (and, inevitably, town-based) classmate paid their entrance fee. When I asked Antoine, who enjoys the cinema, whether he could afford the showings at the Alliance Française, which sometimes cost as little as FMG 100, he responded: "Even that price is high if you consider what you may need to spend on kerosene or charcoal the next day."

As a result, I actually found it difficult to identify any school migrants who had ever visited a video cinema or disco. Like other townsfolk, students had the use of the public television set mounted outside the town hall, but when they did, it was typically with a small group of friends, and watching television would eventually give way to lively conversation on other topics, because the set itself was small and difficult to view from the ground. Also, the majority of broadcasts were of sports matches, the pronounced preference of the agent who controlled the town's satellite connection.

As I argue in more detail in chapter 7, it is town-based youth who come from homes of at least moderate (and more likely, elite) incomes who have greater access to broadcasts of foreign origin. This is so for any of the following reasons: they have pocket money to spend; they may have televisions and VCRs in their homes, so that they can view one of the many videos that make their way about town; and they have more spare time on their hands, because most household duties are shouldered by younger siblings or even servants, who bear the brunt of domestic labor. The seminarists, who lead relatively sheltered lives, also have access to these media. They are forbidden to leave the dormitory for these public spaces, yet the Catholic priests who supervise them do not condemn all dancing and video viewing. For example, the Catholic Academy hosts an annual disco night that is popular among Ambanja's inhabitants of all ages. It is organized in large part as a fundraising event by students themselves, and current or former students from Ambanja may very well be the musicians in a popular band hired for the occasion. Furthermore, mission priests regularly borrow videos for in-house dormitory showings for seminarists. These might be romance stories, or kung-fu, western, or Vietnam commando films. The priests argue that viewing foreign films helps seminarists perfect their French; furthermore, by controlling seminarists' access to these materials, the priests can also guide or monitor related discussions. In contrast, independent school migrants who might have the pocket money for cinemas or discos generally lack the free time to participate, because their weekdays are consumed by domestic chores and they generally spend each weekend in the countryside. Overall, I have found that neither discos nor video cinemas are heavily frequently by school youth, regardless of their backgrounds. Instead, on any given night at one of the town's many bars and cinemas, the vast majority present are not school youth at all, but slightly older adults, ranging in age from their mid twenties to late thirties. In Ambanja, these public venues are frequented by members of the urban proletariat and professionals, such as teachers and civil servants.

The imagined threat of these venues is driven in part by their political potential, a fear that is hinted at above in the language used by the history teacher Mr. Jaozara, who fears that video viewing might warp the *mentalité* of Ambanja's youth, using a term that is especially loaded in the Malagasy context. Mr. Jaozara's concerns are rooted in realities that are historically based, for during the colonial era, cinema and theater productions were regularly scrutinized for subversive material, and Malagasy community leaders and elders often sat on town censorship boards.[9] Later, during the Second Republic, a few daring opponents of President Ratsiraka's regime used film as a means to raise the consciousness of the nation's peasantry, touring small villages in trucks loaded with generators and film equipment. These films and the discussions that followed operated as powerful forms of subversive propaganda designed to persuade small-scale farmers to vote against Ratsiraka.

Thus, on the one hand, Mr. Jaozara's comment appears to champion the cause of youth, since on the surface, its tone seems protective of their needs. On the other, it smacks of condescension, because he assumes that school-age youth are unable to filter out messages and images of foreign origin. As this study reveals, however, these very same students whom he and other adults consider so vulnerable have in fact grown up during a period of radical political and economic transformation. As a result of the powerful lectures that Mr. Jaozara himself delivers, his students hunger for knowledge of what lies beyond their own boundaries. They long to explore other possibilities not so much because of an intense need to dismiss the past as, rather, in order to seize upon their origins as a means to forge a stronger sense of collective destiny. It is not, as Mr. Jaozara would lead us to believe, that video viewing in and of itself is radically and dangerously transformative. Instead, students' burgeoning political consciousness is fostered in school and at home. It is their consciousness that in large part determines how, in turn, they will interpret visual media, and, even more important, how they will draw from what they see in order to make sense of the disparities of life.

ENVISIONING A FUTURE
Three Women Dream

On a lazy Saturday afternoon in early July 1993, I lay on a floor mat with two of my dearest friends, Mme. Vezo (whom I and her kin refer to as affectionately as Mama Vé when she is at home) and Mariamo, both of whom are in their thirties. We had spent much of the morning preparing and, then, subsequently, devouring an impressive lunch of chicken stew over rice, cucumber salad, fluffy *pako-pako* bread, and cardamom pudding. With our bellies full from this delicious meal, we soon grew lethargic and lay down to take a siesta. We were all unable to sleep, though, and so we chatted away for the next few hours. As sisters-in-law, Mama Vé and Mariamo are especially close, often taking each others' sides in domestic quarrels, even though Mama Vé is married to Mariamo's beloved older brother, Saidy, and in spite of the fact that Mama Vé is not of northern Sakalava origin but, rather, grew up in the distant south, moving to Ambanja with her husband a little less than fifteen years ago. Both women live modestly in relatively large yet sparsely furnished houses at either end of town, a style that belies their level of education and respective professional successes. Mama Vé is a dedicated schoolteacher at the lycée level who specializes in both official Malagasy and history/geography. She has traveled a fair amount within Madagascar, for she was born in the southwest and attended university in Antananarivo, where she met her husband. Their first teaching assignments were in a state-run lycée on the northeast coast; two years later, her husband was transferred to his home town of Ambanja, where he now teaches math at the town's CEG. Although Mama Vé regretted leaving her first job, with perseverance she acquired lucrative part-time work at two of Ambanja's schools.

Mariamo is an accomplished merchant, and she and her husband Tantely maintain not one, but two small grocery stands: the first is based in one of the town's two large markets, the other on the front porch of their house, which they rent from the mother of a close in-law. Mariamo is determined to save enough money so that one day they can own their own home. This year she invested a portion of their savings to construct a brick oven, which now sits in the front yard. Within four months, she was conducting a lively bakery business, and her regular clients included two tourist hotels on Nosy Be. Juggling her market and bakery activities quickly exhausted her, however, and so she decided to hire a team of four boys to help her prepare the dough, mind the oven, and make deliveries. Mariamo's father, a Yemeni merchant who immigrated to Ambanja earlier in the century, felt strongly about educating all of his children. Thus, Mariamo completed her studies up to the end of lycée (she was among the first students to attend the Catholic Academy's terminale class, although she did not take the bac exam). She, like her sister-in-law Mama Vé, speaks French with ease. Although Mama Vé herself specializes in language instruction, Mariamo struck me early on as a skilled teacher, and so she has long been my primary Sakalava tutor. Since 1987, Mama Vé's and Mariamo's homes have been havens for me and, over time, their kin have become my kin as well.

Like many of the parents I have come to know, these two women invest much of their own earnings in their children's futures; furthermore, they rarely speak of their own desires or personal concerns. As we lay on the mat inside Mariamo's airy house that day, I decided to ask them about their dreams:

LS: If you had [a million dollars]—if you won the lottery, what would you do with it?

Mama Vé: I'd buy nice furniture for my house, I guess.

LS: No, but you have [a million dollars]. Then what else would you do?

Mama Vé: OK, let's see. I would have a really *nice* home. Beautiful furniture, everything really nice [giggling]. I guess I'd buy a house—it would be good if we could own our own, and then I would put the remaining money into my children's education—I would want them to go to the best schools, and to be able to study at the university, or even abroad. Isn't that what every mother wants, the best for her children? Yes, that's what I'd do.

Mariamo: Hmm. I don't know, I guess I'd want a really nice, big home, too, yes, with all sorts of conveniences [she laughs]. And a big store of my own, one made of *durable* materials [that is, of concrete and not corrugated tin], and then I'd pay someone or several people to work there for me so I could just stay home all day and admire and enjoy my new home.

Mama Vé: And I would want to travel! [Very seriously:] I would want to go visit anglophone countries, because English has become a universal language—I would want to go to England, or Canada, or the United States so I could perfect my English and learn what it's like in those countries. Yes, that's what I'd do.

LS: [To Mariamo:] What about you—

Mama Vé: —Tana [Antananarivo]! [Laughing] She wants to go to Tana!

Mariamo: Yes! [Laughing, too]—Tana!

Mama Vé: What about outside of Madagascar? Would you want to go anywhere?

Mariamo: [pensive]—

Mama Vé: —[interrupting] I know, Nosy Be! [laughing as she teases her sister-in-law]. She wants to go to Nosy Be!

Mariamo: [Laughing too]: Yes, I want to go to Nosy Be!

Mama Vé: That's the exterior for her! It's not the same island as Madagascar, ha ha!

LS: But what if you really could go abroad—where would you go?

Mariamo: Let's see—I think I'd want to go to Paris. To the Côte d'Azur. Yes, the Côte d'Azur, oooh! [On a wall in another room is a magazine advertisement that reads "Va à Paris!"("Go to Paris!")].

Mama Vé: And what about you?

LS: I guess I'd want to buy my mother a home, because it makes her sad that she doesn't own her own. And I'd pay off my debts.

Mama Vé: And where would you travel? [Teasing:] Besides Madagascar, *drakô* [my friend]?

LS: Australia, I suppose. Because it's so vast and the animals are so unusual.

Mama Vé: Yes, that would be interesting, and it's anglophone, too.

Mariamo: Is that where the animals live that keep their little babies in their pockets?

Mama Vé: Yes.

Mariamo: Huh, that could be interesting, too.

I have chosen to open this chapter's final section by focusing on the hopes of adult women for several reasons. First, as will become clear below, Mama Vé's and Mariamo's desires are not that different from those expressed by many younger informants, who also hope some day to be well-trained professionals, prosperous, and free to travel within Madagascar and beyond. Second, as mothers (Mama Vé has four children between the ages of seven and fifteen, and Mariamo has two teenage sons), their children are foremost in their thoughts. Although it is Mama Vé and not Mariamo who speaks of investing in her children, Mariamo is in fact deeply committed to assisting younger kin. In addition to raising her own two boys, she has also taken under her care a niece in response to the financial negligence of the child's father (who is Mariamo's younger brother); a year later she also took in his infant son. (The significance of these relationships will be shown later, in chapter 8.) Third, these are two women who, by their mid-thirties, have become successful professionals. Although both often struggle day to day with serious financial worries, each is competent and confident of her abilities in her respective spheres of influence. My own presence underscores the interplay between the local and the foreign, a dynamic deeply rooted historically in especially urban forms of self-representation in northwest Madagascar.

Schooling also figures prominently in the lives of these two women. Mama Vé and Mariamo completed their educations in French just as Madagascar was embracing malagasization, and their academic achievements have proved essential to their respective professional successes. This is most strongly reflected in the fact that they both speak French well, and that Mama Vé is also fluent in official Malagasy, since it emerged as essential to her university studies. Mama Vé's linguistic abilities set her apart from many of her professional colleagues who never mastered this bureaucratic language, or who now struggle to teach the new curriculum in French. Mariamo, following her father, is an impressive businesswoman who has been able to put her linguistic abilities to good use: her ability to speak French has enabled her to cultivate lucrative clients at nearby tourist hotels. In short, this pair of sisters-in-law has succeeded where many others will inevitably struggle and fail.

The Dreams and Desires of Youth

This discussion at Mariamo's motivated me to look further into students' hopes and professional aspirations. The following year, Tsarahita and I decided to draw up a simple, one-page questionnaire, consisting of eleven questions, which I then distributed to 254 students at the primary, middle, and lycée levels. The majority of these questionnaires were given to students who knew me and understood my purpose for being in Ambanja, because I had audited their classes at various schools. Schoolteachers were especially helpful in explaining the significance of the project and easing the concerns of students who initially perceived the questionnaire as, for example, an examination of some sort. Students also understood that their participation was strictly voluntary, and that neither their teachers nor school officials would be reading their responses. Only two students whom I encountered at the middle school level chose not to participate, bringing the total number of completed questionnaires down to 252.[10] Questions were phrased in both French and official Malagasy, and students were free to give brief answers in either language (now that French was the primary language of schooling, French appeared first, followed immediately by a rephrasing in official Malagasy). To summarize, the questionnaire was completed by students at the following levels (their responses are tallied in appendix 7):

- Sixty-three students at the lycée level, of whom 25 were enrolled at the state-run lycée and 38 at the Catholic Academy. Of these, 28 were girls and 35 were boys. Fifty-three questionnaires were distributed in classes I attended; the remaining 10 were completed during one-on-one interviews.

- One hundred sixty-seven students at the middle school level, consisting of 24 from state-run CEGs (6 were drawn from rural schools in the Sambirano Valley, the remainder were from the larger central school in Ambanja), 77 from the Catholic Academy, and 66 from two remedial schools. Of these, 98 were girls and 69 were boys. The majority were distributed in classes I myself attended, although 33 were handed out and collected by the testing director immediately following the BEPE exam.
- Although I had not originally intended to target primary school students, I included a small sample at the suggestion of the principal of the town's largest primary school, who distributed them to 22 of his own students. A few children found this assignment difficult to complete; in such cases, the principal posed the questions orally and then completed the form as they instructed him to. Here 7 girls and 15 boys were surveyed.

The questionnaire consisted of eleven questions. The first ten requested the following basic information, where answers required a word or two or, at most, a one-phrase answer. First, it asked students of their origins: that is, where they were born, where they currently lived and with whom, and the geographic and ethnic origins of their parents. These questions were designed to distinguish Sakalava from other groups, town-based students from school migrants, and to identify specific students who were solitary migrants living without regular adult supervision. Students were also asked to state their age, so that I could then compare this to their class standing; and I later separated them along gender lines in order to identify any patterns that might typify girls' versus boys' desires. The final question (# 11) required the most detailed answer and asked, "What do you hope [to be] when you are an adult?" [FR: "Qu'est-ce que c'est tes aspirations quand tu seras adulte?" / OM: "Inona no zavatra tianao hatao rehefa lehibe ianao?"]. In addition to supplying general information on their aspirations, students' answers gave me a rough sense of their preferences for—and facility in—writing in French or official Malagasy.

Clearly, these questionnaires can only provide rough estimates of the aspirations of a small proportion of Ambanja's school-age youth; nevertheless, the responses echo trends that also emerged during one-on-one interviews. It must be understood, too, that their statements reflect *idealized* aspirations. What such students might in fact accomplish is determined by their abilities to overcome a series of substantial hurdles, as detailed earlier. To review, these hurdles include their success in school over time; the financial ability or willingness of adult kin to allow them to attend school at the lycée and, subsequently, university levels; the actual availability of places and scholarships at appropriate university campuses should they pass their bac; their ability to enroll in a university curriculum of their choice (since this is determined in large part by how well they do on entrance exams in a variety of subjects); and the realities of the job market, should they succeed in their studies. Coastal youth are well aware of the fact that existing barriers will most likely prohibit them from ever satisfying their desires. They do, nevertheless, dream of many possibilities.

Students' responses have been separated into four categories, determined by the level of education needed to realize the ambition. These four categories are:

1. *Advanced education,* the minimum requirement being a lycée degree, but often a passing score on the bac exam and advanced university or seminary education are also required;
2. *Mid-range education,* requiring specialized skills and high literacy;
3. *Low-level education,* where specialized skills again come into play, but little formal education and minimal literacy are required; and, finally,
4. *No formal education,* involving specialized skills in the service and subsistence sectors, but where literacy is not essential.

As I tallied these data I was struck by how insignificant the type of school (state-run, Catholic, or remedial) was in determining students' answers. For example, although two students from remedial schools chose "peasant" and "fisherman" as their answers, another offered "president of Madagascar" as a response. Also, whereas seven students chose "Catholic nun/priest" as a profession, they were not necessarily enrolled at the Catholic Academy. Furthermore, the responses provided by school migrants did not stand out (although it is true that only those of rural origins familiar with peasant farming and fishing chose these two professions.) Far more significant were gender and school level. In light of this, several distinct trends emerge.

First, education emerged as highly valued by full-time students at all levels, for the vast majority of answers (265 provided by 169 girls and 96 boys) fell within the first category, "advanced education." Professions identified included health care, scientific research and support, engineering, journalism, the Catholic clergy, law and government, tourism (including work and travel abroad), domestic business, and teaching.[11] Girls consistently outnumbered boys in their professional choices in all subfields in this first category, with the exception of scientific research and support (1 girl to 2 boys), engineering (2 girls to 4 boys), and law and government (0 girls to 8 boys). The most popular professions (with two-digit totals) among girls were midwife (57), doctor and teacher (22 each), flight attendant (19),[12] and secretary/office staff (10). Among boys, they were doctor (36) and teacher (17). It should be understood that girls do not necessarily experience significant barriers in terms of the legitimacy of the choice to pursue advanced training in many of these professions. What is far more important is the manner in which domestic responsibilities may work against their ability to pursue professions that require advanced schooling, a situation that is only further complicated by regional and class disparities, as Olive's story illustrates so clearly.

Boys outnumbered girls in the remaining three categories: under mid-range education, 1 girl versus 11 boys chose commerce, supervisory military, police, and (lay) marine roles, and electrician and mechanic/technician. None of the boys' answers reached the two-digit range, although mechanic/technician was the most popular (4), followed by electrician (3 answers). The one girl said she hoped to be an independent merchant (like my friend Mariamo). Under low-level education, 8 girls and 17 boys supplied answers that have been grouped as follows: nonsupervisory roles in the military and (lay) marine, and trades that require specialized training or apprenticeships, such as furniture maker, tailor/seamstress, driver, and artist. Boys chose soldier (4 answers), sailor (3), and tailor (3) the most often; whereas girls showed a strong preference for seamstress (5). Under the final category, involving specialized skills that require no formal education, 3 girls and 10 boys provided responses. They identified the following professions: peasant/farmer, fisherman, factory worker, and cook. Boys showed a strong preference for peasant/farmer (7 answers), whereas the 3 girls chose factory worker, cook, and peasant/farmer.

Although the sample sizes for primary (22 students), middle (167), and lycée level (63) students are hardly comparable, the data nevertheless suggest some potential patterns that warrant further study. Girls, for example, appear to become more aware of teaching as a profession once they reach middle school. More generally, many of the other professions listed under "advanced education" were not supplied by either girls or boys in primary school. In other words, the manner in which children of this age envision their professional futures is limited. Both girls and boys of this age selected health professions as possibilities, although girls gave a wider variety of answers (doctor, midwife, nurse, healthcare/unspecified) than boys, who only chose doctor.

The majority of middle school students chose advanced education professions; their choices, nevertheless, also dominate the "mid-range," and "no formal education" categories; and they are also strongly represented under "low-level education." A significant number of middle school students in this sample were enrolled in remedial schools and/or had just taken the pre-lycée BEPE entrance exam. In light of this, their answers suggest that they still considered advanced education as a possibility in their lives, even though they might be on the brink of dropping out of school altogether. When they are compared to primary school students, they also appear aware of a wider spectrum of professional choices.

Other patterns emerge from the responses supplied by lycée-level students. First, they overwhelmingly preferred professions requiring an advanced education. There were more responses than there were students completing the questionnaire, because students sometimes provided several answers to Question # 11. Girls provided 30 and boys 38 responses out of a total of 68 answers from 63 lycée-level students. Their answers fell off significantly in all other categories: 1 response (provided by a boy) under "mid-range," 10 under "low-level" (from 3 girls and 7 boys), and 2 under "no formal education" (from 1 girl and 1 boy).

Why do some fields appear more popular than others? One of the most obvious reasons is the fact that they pay better. This was made clear by the responses of two lycée-level boys (one from the Catholic Academy, the other from the state-run lycée): "[I want to] learn accounting and make money," and, "I am poor. My goal is to get money, to become a doctor or [work in] management. If you choose these [professions] it is easy to find a job." Girls' responses, too, reflect financial concerns. A local schoolteacher who helped me with unfamiliar (and, inevitably, poorly spelled) terms, or where the student's gender was unclear, was struck by how often schoolgirls of all ages chose the profession of midwife. Many saw this as a high-paying profession, with a constant stream of clients, he emphasized. More-over, midwives in Madagascar are government employees, so they are guaranteed annual salaries, even though raises are infrequent. The same is true for many teachers I knew in Ambanja who did not, in fact, work full-time, yet who were guaran-teed a full-time salary because they were on the state payroll. It must be understood, however, that financial success does not correlate completely with students' pro-fessional preferences. A peasant with productive fields of cocoa and coffee may very well make much more than a full-time lycée teacher, and an independent merchant far more than a nurse at a state hospital. Yet the lower status associated with these professions renders them less desirable than teaching. To survive financially as a teacher often requires great ingenuity; teachers with children complain bitterly that their pay is insufficient to cover all their monthly costs, and so many hold other jobs to help make ends meet. Mama Vé, for example, is a gifted seamstress with many clients, and she also tutors students on the side; and Mr. Jaozara both moonlights at a remedial school and sharecrops. Nevertheless, with teaching as their primary profession, they experience greater job security than do those in many other fields. Finally, although plantation directorships are among the most lucrative jobs in the Sambirano, none of the students surveyed selected this (or any other high-level managerial job in these settings) as a profession of choice. This is most certainly because the students surveyed identify strongly with coastal concerns and view plan-tations as having disrupted the integrity of the local *tanindrazaña* (a theme to which I shall return in subsequent chapters).

The decision to supply more than one answer enabled students to express a range of possibilities. For example, three girls enrolled at the CEG level at the Catholic Academy offered these answers: "midwife, doctor, dressmaker," "teacher, midwife, marriage, secretary," and "a flight attendant, but if I'm not beautiful then I'll be a doctor." A girl from a remedial middle school answered as follows: "When I'm older I'd like to be a midwife, but if I can't do that, then something I'd like to do is be a hairdresser or a dressmaker." Such answers often give high-level profes-sions as the first choice and entrepreneurial ones second. "[I want to be a] doctor, business[woman] or math teacher," another student from the state-run lycée said. Finally, Jaona wrote this lighthearted answer: "Doctor, but I also really like soccer. I'd love to play abroad. I know it is hard to integrate the two—[but perhaps I can be] a doctor-player!"

Whereas the responses reported in appendix 7 reflect idealized professional vi-sions, the experiences of Olive and Antoine reflect grounded realities. Olive, de-spite her hard work in 1993, did not achieve her goal: although she was set on be-coming a doctor, her bac scores were too low to qualify her for the medical school track at the university in Antananarivo, and so she accepted another course, which was chosen for her. In studying agricultural science, she will ultimately make use of much of her science training; furthermore, she has been allotted a place in a field of high value in a country whose economy is dominated by the agricultural sector and burgeoning conservation projects. She may, ironically, have more opportunities for employment than will those emerging from medical school. I often encounter young doctors who are unable to find posts anywhere on the island. Antoine's predicament, on the other hand, is more typical of the experiences of coastal youth in Ambanja. Unlike Olive, he has no kin with whom to live in Antananarivo or elsewhere near other campuses, nor do his parents have the financial means to support him were he to attend university. He himself acknowledges that there are few places available at any of these campuses, and there is little work to be found afterward. As a result, he now searches for employment that requires a mid-range education, where he can apprentice himself to a skilled technician and master a trade. This path parallels that of several older siblings who did well in school but who later fell back on technical skills they could practice locally and independently.

Ketsy's answer—that she'd like to be a doctor, or perhaps a singer who specializes in Malagasy music—is a far more complicated one. Her idealized aspirations echo Olive's experience in part, simply by virtue of her awareness that few can ever hope to enter medical school. At first glance, her desire to be a Malagasy singer may seem driven simply by an infatuation with pop culture; it must be understood, however, that her exposure to this distant world is extremely limited. She does not attend disco parties, nor can she afford to go to video cinemas (where an hour of foreign rock videos generally precedes the feature). Instead, her knowledge is drawn from print media, in the form of discarded teen magazines and, more regularly, from radio broadcasts of Malagasy songs that move her. This love of music is similarly reflected in the light-hearted response from yet another CEG student: "I want to sing on a plane as an airline flight attendant. I want to sing and travel." Perhaps more so than this student, however, Ketsy's dream is driven by her deep love of Madagascar and Malagasy culture.

The responses of other lycée students (and students at lower levels as well) exhibit a hunger for knowledge of what lies beyond their experience. Many are taken with the well-paid professions related to the island's small yet growing tourist trade, and girls are especially interested in being airline flight attendants (the most successful of whom travel regularly to Paris and beyond). Not all their aspirations thus depend on financial reward, which may be overridden by other considerations. Christian, who is a serious and inquisitive student, hopes, for example, that directorship of a tourist agency might answer his curiosity about foreign lands and offer contrasts to a life bounded by the Indian Ocean.

A significant number of students felt compelled to explain their answers; inevitably this reflected a strong sense of familial or, more often, national duty. "[I want] to help my mother . . . and to be polite and kind," a girl in primary school explained, and a boy from the town's state-run CEG wrote: "Since my childhood I've wanted to be a soldier because I care about my country." Others proclaimed a sense of duty to help those in need. One girl from a middle school class at the Catholic Academy stated: "I want to be a peasant because we [Malagasy] don't have enough food to eat." Yet another female classmate of hers wrote: "I want to be a responsible [person] who will claim the rights of the Malagasy."

Lycée students who were preparing for their bac exams almost without exception wrote detailed answers. This may have sprung from their familiarity with my research interests, but I believe it was also a result of their schooling, and thus of their consciousness of their potential as they prepared for exams that might qualify them for university study. For example, a male school migrant, who lived in town with an older brother, was the only lycée student who chose "peasant" as a potential profession. His dream was to study agricultural science. "I want to breed animals and plants—my parents are still peasants and I want to be like them," he explained. "I really want things to be better for them. I used to live in the country so [the life of a] peasant is the only possibility for me if [I want to] remain in the country[side]." Another male classmate of his responded as follows: "I want to do something important in science to help the human race, [conducting] research on illnesses for example that [hurt] people and the environment. [I want to be] a pharmacist perhaps or else a researcher." Another female student echoed these concerns, saying: "I want to be a doctor so I can save others as well as members of my own family who lack medicine." Among the most compelling was this final response from a male student, because it reflected a change of heart, based on what he had learned in school: "Since I was young I've wanted to be a pilot and a doctor, but now I know I want to cure others because of all the sorts of [illnesses] that we can't cure."

These findings seem to suggest that students' professional aspirations are little more than idealized, unattainable dreams. The quality of coastal schooling, paired with significant financial constraints, apparently undermine any possibility of attending university. This is true of many of Ambanja's most gifted students. Tsarahita, with whom I have worked so closely for over a decade, is a compelling reminder of this possibility . She passed her bac in the mid 1980s, but her father, a transport driver, and her mother, a peasant and occasional part-time merchant, could ill afford to send her to university. Only her eldest brother (of a total of eight siblings) accomplished this goal; he is now a school administrator in a large town to the north. Tsarahita has spent little time outside of Ambanja, and now, as a single mother with three young children, she has abandoned any hope of a university degree. Through great perseverance, she has, however, acquired a part-time post at the Catholic Academy, because her skills in French and official Malagasy are strong. Coastal origins impose significant constraints upon success: in this chapter it is, after all, Olive, and not Antoine, who enters the university in Antananarivo. For students at all levels, however, the answers they supplied on my questionnaire were not mere fantasies, but envisioned as possibilities, albeit perhaps remote ones. In desperation, many of them, in fact, wrote questions at the bottom of the questionnaire such as: "How can you help us achieve our goals?" This study is a partial response.

The experiences of adult professionals such as Mariamo, Mama Vé, and Mme. Chantal underscore that some students succeed against enormous odds, although they often struggle to make ends meet financially. Schoolteachers are especially sensitive to the problems that plague their students' lives but impotent to help them. Amid the pedagogical transition from official Malagasy back to French, teachers are deeply troubled by what may lie ahead for Ambanja's youth. New educational policies bear promises of comprehensive teacher retraining, an influx of schoolbooks and other essential supplies, and, ultimately, exposure to new forms of foreign knowledge. Against such developments, many adults, including experienced teachers like Mr. Jaozara, worry that exposure to new ideas has already undermined students' respect for indigenous institutions. As we shall see in part 3, however, school youth are in fact critically aware of the dilemmas that confound easy understanding of selfhood, community, and nation. In response, they revere the past, drawing on their teachers' inspiring lectures to make sense of their nation's predicament. In the end, the tales they tell privilege indigenous knowledge and experience. Furthermore, they underscore the centrality of youth in their island's history, where young royalty, nationalists, foot soldiers, and laborers all emerge as crucial actors in the colonial period and beyond, all inevitably reordering their world.

PART THREE

Freedom, Labor, and Loyalty

Figure 6. Ampanjakabe Tsiaraso I (Andriamandilatrarivo, r. 1887–1919). Reprinted with permission; from the personal photographic collection of Françoise Raison-Jourde, Fonds privé. Raison-Jourde 1983, pl. 4.

Freedom, labor, and loyalty: these themes are central to part 3. As Ambanja's school youth struggle to make sense of their current predicament and tenuous future, they ultimately rely on often highly localized reconstructions of the past. The tales they tell generate a history of a particular sort, one that consistently underscores the devastating effects of foreign encroachment on the tanindrazaña and its precolonial royal splendor. Thus, chapter 4 focuses on the contemporary significance of royal authority, where a new young ruler—himself a member of the sacrificed generation—fashions highly eclectic and unorthodox interpretations of the past as he strives to reawaken a dormant kingdom. Against such developments, school youth must consider the significance of past and contemporary royalty in their lives. One figure looms especially large in their collective consciousness: this is Tsiaraso I, whose reign coincided with French conquest and for whom the town's state-run lycée is named. This king is deeply revered as a heroic figure who, although ultimately overrun by the French, nevertheless inspired many Sakalava to serve royalty as a sign of their devotion. Among the Sakalava, it is rulers who make history, and, thus, Tsiaraso I's tale inspires school youth to ponder the historical and contemporary significance of loyalty, enslavement, and freedom.

These concepts undergo radical transformations during the colonial era: as described in chapters 5 and 6, among the more devastating effects of colonial rule was the subsequent exploitation of Malagasy—and of boys and young men in particular—as conscripted soldiers (chapter 5) and peacetime corvée laborers (chapter 6). Ambanja's school youth consider such policies poorly disguised forms of enslavement, their understandings embittered by the knowledge that prior to French conquest, the Sakalava possessed the power to enslave others. Throughout the colonial era, the French insisted upon willingness, loyalty, and even patriotism from their workforce. Sakalava, however, emerge as consistently resistant to French hegemony in ways that often confounded their colonizers. As school youth reconstruct the past, they draw heavily on their elders' firsthand accounts, melding these with school lessons; the tales they tell are in turn complemented by data culled from archival sources. As we shall see, the interwoven themes of freedom, labor, and loyalty are central to students' readings of conquest, colonial hegemony, and nationalism. In the end, it is their historical knowledge that shapes their political consciousness.

CHAPTER 4

The Resurgence of Royal Power

Tromba [spirit possession] and royal rituals—you know about these? . . . But these are on the decline. . . . Young people today don't participate in them. Possession, no, you don't see this in school anymore. . . . Why? Because we are modern. Young people today are serious about their schooling—we don't care about these things. Royalty—they're asleep. They're not part of the modern age.

ANTOINE *(1993)*

THE REAWAKENING OF A DORMANT KINGDOM

The New Prince

Friday A.M., June 24, 1994. It is just past dawn and I am slowly waking up on one of my first mornings back in Ambanja after a year's absence. As I reach consciousness, I realize I can hear drums and, soon after, women ululating. I struggle to identify the purpose: it cannot be a tromba possession ceremony, for mid June marks the beginning of a taboo *(fady)* period for many of these spirits, and, besides, drumming would be out of place; nor does it sound like a Comorean wedding celebration nor even a lively Tandroy funeral procession. It is a bit too early in the day for a royal *rebiky* dance and, furthermore, the beat is unrecognizable. I dress quickly and step out onto the street. As soon as I round the corner, I am confronted by an animated procession of young Sakalava women dressed in new and brightly colored body wraps and bedecked with gold jewelry. This joyous band chants and sings in unison as it makes its way toward me. Poised nearby on a bicycle and watching the procession is a schoolteacher I know who is of royal descent. Seeing my puzzled expression, he yells excitedly across the road: "Fananganana ny Ampanjakabe Bemazava!" ("[We are] instating the [new] Bemazava king [today]!").[1] I immediately fall in behind these women as they shuffle quickly and in step to a lively beat down the main road of my dusty quarter.

Within minutes, we are in an open courtyard crowded with women of all ages dressed in smart body wraps and much gold jewelry. Several take turns dancing animated celebratory steps. The beating drums are hard to resist, and so I, too, jump in and kick up some earth, at which point two Sambarivo women, or royal retainers, approach and ask who I am. I am then led forward by two other newfound acquaintances, and together we remove our shoes and step onto the porch of a small, modest two-roomed palm fiber house. Just before I enter the doorway, however, a teenage girl grasps my arm and asks me, "Misy lio? ("Are you menstruating?"), to which I promptly respond in the negative. She then releases me and another aged Sambarivo woman approaches and wraps me snugly in a fresh *salovaña* body wrap and pushes me through the door.

Once inside, I am offered a chair, but I insist on kneeling respectfully upon the floor at the prince's feet, as do my two companions. I immediately recognize a few of the men within—several are middle-aged royalty whom I have known for years. They are huddled together on wobbly chairs, and on the floor beside us sits another man who is perhaps in his seventies, his eyes glazed with cataracts, one hand gripping a weathered silver-tipped staff. As the primary official royal advisor *(manan-tany)*, he mediates discussions and serves as interpreter for visitors who, like us, have come to honor the young prince. Before us all, sitting quietly in an armchair, is twenty-four-year-old Andriatahiry Parfait, a slender young man, the second oldest son of the previous king, whom I had known so well. It is the first I have seen of him, and I am struck immediately by how much he resembles his handsome father, who passed away only six months before.

June 24, 1994, was most certainly a festive day, since it fell near the end of a series of complex rituals that would establish Parfait as the subsequent monarch of the Bemazava-Sakalava of the Sambirano (figs. 7a and b). After I had paid my respects, I scurried home, bolted down my breakfast, bathed, and rushed to a friend's house to borrow a matching set of body and head wraps; and then off I went to find Tsarahita, who arranged to meet me later at the royal residence *(zomba)*. Shortly afterward, I returned to the simple, temporary thatched falafa dwelling and watched Parfait's departure. He was carried like a small child in the arms of an older man to the car that would transport him the short distance to the residence of his predecessors. I then joined a tremendous crowd of loyal subjects who followed on foot to the zomba, where Parfait was greeted by his mother, siblings, royal advisors, retainers, and two animated drummers, as well as by a British film crew that happened to be passing through town on its way to the Antankaraña kingdom farther north.

Many people I knew would appear at the zomba: mediums who had been key informants during my research in 1987, royal family members, loyal adult Bemazava-Sakalava citizens,[2] and a multitude of curious children of all ages. I was informed, however, that I would not glimpse a dear former acquaintance, the third and final wife of Tsiaraso Victor III, for she and her children had been banished from the zomba when Parfait, the second son of his father's first estranged wife, was proclaimed the successor. Although the third wife still lived in town, she and her children would avoid the royal compound today.

Throughout the day, the zomba was alive with activity. The new king, his mother, and his retainers made several appearances within the large airy courtyard, retreating afterward to the interior of the zomba. In order to document these events, a few British cameramen were perched precariously in the delicate branches of trees, a ceaselessly comic site for those of us who passed hesitantly beneath their bulky figures. The zomba's courtyard swarmed with visitors, and children were pervasive. Midday was marked by a generous feast, offered to all who chose to drop by to greet the prince or simply watch the activities, and by afternoon several men and women were drunk on palm wine supplied freely within the royal compound. Two skilled drummers also worked enthusiastically to encourage participants to perform *rebiky* dances, which occurred with rarely a break. Subjects and royalty alike assembled in turns to form competing pairs of costumed warriors of old who would make their way slowly and gracefully to the seated prince (fig. 7b). A host of tromba spirits also arrived spontaneously that day, seizing even the bodies of royal women in mid dance, the occasion being far too joyous to keep these ancestors at bay. As dusk approached, the large crowd suddenly dispersed, marking the completion of this significant phase of Parfait's instatement.

A Prince's Rebirth

Although this was indeed a momentous day, one marked by great celebration and glee, at fleeting moments, I found myself fighting back waves of sadness, for I kept remembering a letter I had received from Tsarahita in early 1994, when she wrote "Nihilaña ny ampanjakabe" ("The king is dead").[3] The news of the passing of Parfait's father, Tsiaraso Victor III (r. 1966–93), had come as a terrible shock to me, as it had to many inhabitants of the Sambirano. Loyal Bemazava expressed their grief profoundly, appearing publicly in town unwashed, their hair unkempt, and dressed in disheveled clothes throughout the month of December 1993. At the completion of his mortuary rituals on Christmas Day, the late king was granted the praise name Andriamanaitriarivo, for he was most certainly "The Ruler Who Surprised Many" when he died suddenly following a heart attack.[4] After much debate and intrigue, Parfait was declared his successor.[5] Following initial celebrations before the royal tombs on the sacred island of Nosy Faly, the royal retinue made its way back to the main island, where it formed an impressive procession, weaving its way through the kingdom so that Parfait could be presented formally to his subjects. The instatement ceremony I witnessed in June 1994 was among the more significant events that would mark the transition of this young prince toward the status of a newly established ruler, or *ampanjakabe*.

The path to kingship is a gradual one, and in Sakalava territory, this necessitates body purification, the investment of ritual power, and a slow and deliberate education reserved for royalty. As such, a newly declared ruler is persistently treated and handled as a child who is innocent or lacking in wisdom *(tsy hendry)*. Throughout the instatement stages that spanned 1994, Parfait was consistently referred to as being "like an infant" or "child" *(mira-mira zaza/tsaiky)* or a liminal boy or "man-child" *(tsaiky lahy)*. A series of events also heralded his gradual return to his kingdom and a rebirth of sorts within it. For this ruler, in particular, acts of purification were paramount, because he had spent much of his life outside the kingdom and, most recently, in Merina territory, where he spoke that highland dialect.

Figure 7a. The instatement of Tsiaraso Rachidy IV, June 24, 1994.
The young king is seated next to his mother.

Thus, earlier in April, just prior to the arrival of a new moon,[6] Parfait was led
down to the Sambirano River, where, before all subjects who cared to watch, he
stood unclothed, as would a little boy, vainly trying to hide his nakedness as old
women bathed and purified him. They washed him with silver and sacred river water, both of which harbor ancestral power. First they cleansed his royal body of
the filth (*maloto*) associated with his highland-based military life, and then his mouth,
since it had been defiled by speaking Merina, a dialect that is taboo in Bemazava
ritual contexts. By late August, his instatement was complete, so that he now assumed the full official royal title of Tsiaraso Rachidy Parfait IV, one he will bear
for the remainder of his life or as long as he rules. No longer a prince but a full-
fledged Bemazava ampanjakabe, he toured the Sambirano Valley yet again to greet
his many subjects, this time as their true king. At the sacrificial (joro) feasts and

Figure 7b. A pair of performers at a *rebiky* dance staged in honor of Tsiaraso Rachidy IV.

other celebrations that coincided with these events, his subjects in turn declared their love for him, their loyalty expressed through eating when, their bellies full, all bad thoughts disperse.

These final ceremonies also marked the official beginning of this young ruler's sacred education, through which he would learn slowly and carefully how to be a respected—and respectful—ruler. As we shall see, this sacred education depends heavily upon a knowledge of local history and understanding one's place in it. In a broader sense, these principles apply not simply to rulers but to their subjects as well.

The Education of an Exiled Royal Son

No ruler assumes command lightly. This was all too clear to the young and shy Parfait, who was only twenty-three when declared his father's successor at the end of 1993. As a young child, he had been exiled with his mother and siblings to distant southern Sakalava territory when his parents' marriage failed, growing up in Toliara, a city in the far southwest, approximately 1,000 kilometers from Ambanja. In terms of his secular education, Parfait progressed slowly and methodically in school, but he did not excel. A university education seemed unattainable, and, so, when he reached his midteens, he chose the army as a career. Soon thereafter, he was stationed in the central highlands.

When telegrams were dispatched announcing the death of Tsiaraso Victor III, it was Parfait, and not his older brother, who came to Ambanja to honor his father, a response that proved central to his eventual appointment as royal successor. After much heated debate among competing factions, on the morning of December 24,

1993, the most powerful of the Bemazava ancestral spirits *(dady* or *razambe)* declared Andriatahiry Parfait the next ruler. "I was stunned and giddy from the announcement," Parfait later said. "I was confused, but of course I was overjoyed." The spirits' decree struck some as oddly unconventional, for although other Bemazava rulers had assumed command at even earlier ages, Parfait was, nevertheless, a stranger in a strange land.[7] He could not speak the local dialect, the majority of people who surrounded him were unknown to him, and customs and knowledge that he had taken for granted were in many ways foreign to the territory he now ruled. He was young, unmarried, and, furthermore, now unemployed. What, then, was this young king to do? Some quietly presumed that this naïve young man would inevitably become a puppet of established royalty and other elder advisors.

Within only a year of assuming command, however, Tsiaraso Rachidy IV emerged as a creative and enigmatic ruler. He is both a renegade and a vanguard figure, qualities typical of the sacrificed generation, of which he is a member. In stark contrast to his father's understated style, this new young king quickly adopted a highly unorthodox approach to royal power, one that is, to borrow Antoine's words, fully *modern*. Under the leadership of Tsiaraso Rachidy IV, whose attempts to reinvigorate bygone sentiments of loyalty and love challenge established understandings of the royal past, the meaning of the Bemazava tanindrazaña is being reshaped and this once dormant kingdom is being radically transformed.

One of his most stunning acts has involved the refurbishment of his father's seaside Palais Royal and its conversion into a disco hall. This action is simultaneously controversial—for it defies a host of important royal taboos (fady)—and a highly innovative application of a ruler's authority. To understand its full significance necessitates a detailed review of entrenched understandings of royal power and the weight of local history. More specifically, Tsiaraso Rachidy IV stands as the inheritor of a line of rulers named Tsiaraso, a fact that is significant for several reasons. First, his actions undo the apathy generated under his father Tsiaraso Victor III, a shy ruler who assumed power soon after independence and during President Tsiranana's neocolonial administration. Second, he instead draws upon the legacy of a greatly admired ruler from the Bemazava past, Tsiaraso I, whose reign coincided with French conquest at the end of the nineteenth century. Third, he adds his own eclectic mix of the modern to forge a highly personal style of rule, rejuvenating his kingdom. To comprehend the full power of Tsiaraso Rachidy IV's approach necessitates that we consider both young and old Bemazava subjects' perceptions of this transition; the shortfalls of his father's reign; and the prominence of Tsiaraso I in shaping contemporary collective memories of the Sakalava past.

Youth and the Royal Question

By mid 1994, the question of royal authority occupied the thoughts of many Bemazava. During interviews, royalty, for example, were quick to offer me detailed descriptions of proper ritual decorum, pondering in turn the ancestral decision to appoint a man as young and inexperienced as Parfait. With their statements in mind, I then sought to explore the sentiments of school youth. Thus, a few days following the June instatement ceremony, I raised questions about royal authority during a group discussion with several lycée students. I was struck first, by the depth of their knowledge, second, by their collective skepticism of the relevance of royalty in their lives, and third, by their underlying fear of the dormant powers of bygone rulers.

LS: Did any of you attend the instatement ceremony? [A few stifled laughs, then:]

Hasina: No. None of us.... We're not interested in those things.

LS: Why not?

Hasina: Because the rulers today, they have no power!

Hazaly [of royal descent on mother's side]: Yes, you see [writing on the ground in chalk], we here, we are very *scientific*! These sorts of things don't interest us now.

Jaona [boisterously]: But if you go to the lower Sambirano *[Sambirano anbañy]* . . . there you'll find plenty of people who are scared of the ampanjaka. At New Year they go to the king and they give him cattle, money, rice. It doesn't matter how poor they are. They come to him and they say, "Here, this is for you, because you are the king." So the king never has to go out and get these things! People just bring them to him.... And ... when the last king died ... you know, it takes a long time to [entomb] a king! A month! They took three weeks when the king died. And people like this, they don't do anything for a long time—for a whole month they don't work, if they really respect the king. But most of us, we don't do this—imagine, you can't work for a month? How are you supposed to live? You need money to live, and if you don't work, you don't have money!

LS: Then what is the meaning of being Sakalava now?

Foringa Josef: The people here who say, "I'm Sakalava"? They're the ones who really love the ampanjaka. But they're really like slaves.

In response, however, Pauline's quickly offered these cautionary words:

Pauline [nervously]: But then there's the *tsiñy* . . . the invisible forces, like phantoms, that live in the air, everywhere.

Jaona [assuming a more serious and quieter tone]: If you do something bad against them, against the ampanjaka, it is the tsiñy who see to it that you pay for it.

Dalia [in a hushed tone]: They can be found in the woods. They are the spirits of dead ampanjaka. They are the ones who make sure that the rules of the ampanjaka are followed.[8]

As these final cautionary words reveal, although the power of living royalty may seem inconsequential, their dormant power is potentially intensely potent. These interlocking themes will reemerge throughout this chapter as Bemazava and, especially school youth, consider the historical significance of royalty in shaping their contemporary concerns.

The Reluctant King

The collective skepticism of Ambanja's youth was shaped by the long reign of Tsiaraso Rachidy IV's father, Tsiaraso Victor III (Andriamanaitriarivo, r. 1966–93), the only ruler they had hitherto known. An intensely shy man, Tsiaraso Victor III assumed power after his father died when he was in his twenties and only six years after independence. Throughout his reign, he was uncomfortable being ruler.

His personal history offers some explanation for this unease. Born in the middle of this century, Tsiaraso Victor III was among a select group of young royalty schooled at the Catholic Academy, at which time he abandoned Islam—the faith that typically marks Bemazava royal status—and converted to Catholicism, making him the first local Bemazava ruler to do so. He was trained during the colonial era for a lifetime of civil service work, and under the independent government of Madagascar, he eked out a very modest living as a county tax collector, indicative of his weak status. Tsiaraso Victor III was visibly repulsed and embarrassed by subjects who would insist on sitting at his feet when they came to see him at his office; in response, he would gently but firmly send them away, unwilling to assert any authority except in the privacy of his home at the zomba. He lived a frugal life, often struggling to feed his many children: although rulers are entitled to collect gifts from their subjects, they are also expected to care for them in need, something he did willingly throughout his reign.

Although Tsiaraso Victor III's directives would be quickly followed by the most loyal of his subjects, he rarely issued orders of any import. In fact, the only decree I ever knew of was a call for royal service in 1987 to repair potholes on a street adjacent to the seat of the county government; a handful of subjects responded, but they quit after a few hours without completing the task. Although he occasionally hosted ceremonies at the royal tombs on the island of Nosy Faly, he did not initiate these ritual events, instead awaiting occasional suggestions from his official advisors. As a result, Tsiaraso Victor III reigned over a dormant kingdom. Bemazava subjects spoke of him affectionately yet sadly as a "simple" and "timid" man. More outspoken and active neighboring Bemihisatra royalty located to the west on Nosy Be and the Antankaraña who lie to the north viewed him with puzzled dismay. To them, his kingdom appeared sleepy and uninvigorated, especially when contrasted to the Antankaraña, whose ruler, Tsimiaro III, had begun to revive and embellish a host of ceremonies. One, the Tsangantsaiñy, drew an estimated crowd of 7,000 subjects when I was there in 1987, attracting the attention of the news media, national scholars, and even the provincial governor (cf. Lambek and Walsh 1997).

It is with little surprise, then, that in 1994 Ambanja's school youth expressed little interest in the deeds of living royalty, given that, until very recently, they had never witnessed any massive collective expressions of devotion. Instead, their knowledge remained limited to their understandings of the royal past, for which they expressed great pride and nostalgia as they spoke of older generations of kin who were involved in unfaltering devotional forms of royal service (*fanompoaña*). Many of these tales were bedtime stories they had heard as children from their now aged grandparents. Tsarahita herself described such devotion among her elders, drawing upon the language associated specifically with royal work to underscore its centrality in their lives:

My [maternal] grandmother was pure Sakalava, and she was intensely devoted to the ampanjak[be]. She told us many stories about royalty when we were children—they were beautiful and moving tales. My grandmother was one who worked for royalty *[ampanompo]*, performing many difficult tasks *[raha sarotra]* as a subject [of the kingdom], even when it took her away from her rice fields. *She was Sakalava.* My mother knows a bit about these things, but she can't remember the specific duties very well, nor even what our clan accomplished. But this much I know—my grandmother always spoke of doing it out of love *[fitiavaña].* This was what true Sakalava did, without hesitation and without question. And the rulers looked after their subjects in turn.

In contrast, in school lessons—that is, in contemporary bureaucratized historical accounts—the fate of royalty emerges as emblematic of a debased past, as the French sought actively to undermine royal power. This is most evident in published accounts of the fall of Imerina, whose highland monarchy came to an official end in the 1890s. In the northwest, however, the Sakalava and Antankaraña royal houses have remained intact and, as noted above, in some cases they exert tremendous sway among their subjects. Within the Sambirano, Bemazava recount tales of their collective past that underscore the difficulty of love for and devotion to royalty. Many, like Jaona above, speak of their emotional or economic inability to respond to the demands of royal service, sometimes even shamefully (Sharp 1997).

I therefore wondered if in fact any students had any experience with royal service. I posed this question to two of royal descent, who offered contrasting responses to its significance in their daily lives:

Hazaly: Do *I* follow the royal customs *[fomba ny ampanjaka]*? Ah, no, absolutely not. The royal taboos *[fady]* are too involved, too difficult. I'm Silamo [Muslim-Comorean] like my father. My mother [who is Sakalava ampanjaka] attends royal ceremonies, but I never do. This would not be Silamo.

Lucien: What does it mean to be Sakalava? To follow the customs of the ampanjaka. Tuesday is a taboo day. [In our household,] we never work our fields on Tuesdays. Instead, we rest here at home.

Whereas Hazaly's reaction is marked by defiance, Lucien expresses no difficulty in outlining the expectations associated with the royal taboos of quotidian life. Yet as Foringa's earlier comment underscores, royal devotion is inevitably akin to enslavement. Enslavement not only shapes understandings of royal-commoner relations; in the postindependence era, it also emerges as a potent idiom through which school youth articulate understandings of local history. As we shall see in this chapter and the two that follow, loyalty and devotion to royalty on the one hand and attitudes to the French on the other inspire intensely different emotional responses among students. Whereas they currently express a disinterest in contemporary royal affairs, they nevertheless honor and respect the power of past royalty. They consistently view the French, on the other hand, as oppressive invaders who sought unsuccessfully to squelch Sakalava unity, fierceness, and pride.

Royal Love, Devotion, and the Weight of the Past

During the instatement of Tsiaraso Rachidy IV, nearly forgotten questions of loyalty and devotion suddenly weighed heavily upon this kingdom's citizenry. It is, after all, one's willingness to work for—and, thus, in Foringa's words, to *enslave* oneself to—a ruler that is the mark of true devotion. Yet when Bemazava such as Tsarahita, above, speak of "sacred things" *(raha masina)*, especially royal practices, they typically rely on expressions such as "Sarotra, sarotrabe ny fomba ny ampanjaka," that is, "Royal customs are difficult, very difficult." Today, this conveys two meanings. First, it reflects local concern that many of the customs have been "forgotten" *(nanadino)* or "lost" *(very)*, a development arising in response to complex historical factors associated with conquest and the subsequent displacement of royalty by the French colonial state. To follow royal customs today, even as an adult, may very well mean studying or "learning" *(mianatra)* them with care. Such forgetting has unquestionably characterized daily life in Ambanja. Sakalava under forty years of age frequently explain in private and in a hushed tone that they do not follow the ampanjakabe because the associated customs are far too difficult to understand or master, yet the majority also offer detailed descriptions of the very customs of which they claim ignorance. An underlying tension here is a reluctance to enslave oneself to royalty, laced simultaneously with a sadness that one lacks the strength to overcome a highly individual desire to remain independent or free. In turn, such concerns also underscore that this localized understanding of "difficulty" is paired with the inevitable force of forgetting the past. As such, one's reluctance to enslave oneself to the ampanjakabe endangers the future of Bemazava culture.

This notion of "difficulty" encompasses older meanings as well, for it stresses the complexity of royal rituals, whereby observance is the outward manifestation of one's respect for and unwavering devotion to royalty. As Gillian Feeley-Harnik's comprehensive work from the Analalava region illustrates, Sakalava royal ancestors are described as "difficult things" *(raha sarotra)*, whose demanding nature is, indeed, akin to enslavement (1991, 56ff, 74 ff.; 1982). Jean-François Baré likewise translates *raha sarotro* as objects and actions whose very "difficulty" renders them "precious," "dear," "dangerous," and "forbidden" (1980, 241, 289). As Tsarahita underscores above, the quintessential expression of "love" *(fitiavaña)*—and, thus, devotion—is manifested through the actions of those "who work for royalty" *(ampanompo)* or who perform "royal service" *(fanompoaña)*. This social category includes commoners, royal retainers, and servants or former slaves. Thus, when faced with the sudden death of their ruler, Bemazava were required to remember their past and to learn how to express their allegiance to him. Those who did so inevitably declared their loyalty to a highly localized royal state, one where the Sambirano Valley was reasserted as their true tanindrazaña.

Against these developments, Ambanja's school youth seem to emerge as uninterested in contemporary royal affairs. Yet a quick survey of events that have characterized their own lives exposes their respect for the power of dead royal *ancestors* as a means to reassert their own claims on the tanindrazaña. At the height of malagasization in the early 1980s, destructive, angry spirits seized the bodies of a multitude of schoolgirls during classroom hours, and, in the end, only tromba mediums and other spiritual authorities were able to still their frantic and unpredictable actions. These healers located spiritual danger within the confines of the schoolyard, where the French had defiled sacred ancestral ground by building schools and administrative complexes upon Sakalava tombs (Sharp 1990). Under President Ratsiraka, local and state authorities subsequently sought ancestral approval before a single spade of earth was overturned at future construction sites. As we shall see, among the most significant of these projects was the construction of the local state-run lycée, which is named for none other than the ruler Tsiaraso I.

In contrast, the living ruler inspires a host of other responses among school youth. Although the instatement ceremony I witnessed was marked by a high turnout of younger children, I did not encounter a single town-based lycée-age school informant there that day. Instead, these students consistently viewed the power of contemporary royalty as eclipsed, impotent, and, at times, impractical, illogical, and even, as Hazaly implies above, unscientific. In a word, for them, the splendor of Bemazava royal power lies in the past. This sentiment was expressed with candor by Pauline, whose house lies in the same quarter as, and equidistant from, the zomba and the imposing Lycée Tsiaraso I:

> *Pauline:* Who is the new king? [His name is] Tsiaraso Parfait. But I don't know him—he didn't grow up here. Who follows royal customs anyway? . . . If you want to understand royalty, you must look to the past. You should ask people about Tsiaraso *I*—he was ampanjaka[be] when the French arrived in our territory. Yes, ask about Tsiaraso I.

CONQUEST AND ROYAL RESISTANCE

Pauline suggested I ask Sidy, who is of royal parentage, whether he ever thought of Tsiaraso I in reference to his own history. He responded:

> Tsiaraso I—of course, he would mean nothing to your students [in the United States], but to us he is very important. He reigned during a tragic time in our history—he witnessed the arrival of the French, and he watched them try to dismantle his kingdom. In the face of this—the French, you know, they had guns, and cannons—he was very brave. If you go to Hellville on Nosy Be, you can see some of these old cannons. But how could he stop them? . . . Look at this Valley—it is fully occupied by plantations. . . . And these [plantations] go back to the early days of the French occupation. . . . Tsiaraso I? We [students] think about him a lot, we think of him every day. We think

TABLE 3 The Northern Bemazava-Sakalava Dynasty of the Sambirano Valley

Name during Reign	Praise Name	Years of Reign
▲ Boanamaka*	Andriantompoeniarivo	approx. 1820–21
▲ Tsimandro	Andriamanotranarivo	1821–32
▲ Matandrabo [Malandiabo?]	Andriamandriambiniarivo II	1832–37
● Irana?	Andriamamelonarivo II	?
● Tsiresy I	Andriamanomponarivo	1837(?)–52
▲ Monja	Andriamamahoñarivo	1852–57
▲ Tsiaraso I*	Andriamandilatrarivo	1887–1919
[French conquest; Madagascar declared a colony of France		1895–96]
● Tsiresy II*	Nenimoana	1919–1935
▲ Rachidy*	Andriamamefiarivo	1935–1945
[By 1940s, if not earlier, Bemazava rulers had relocated from the seaside palace (doany) at Ankify to the residence (zomba) in the town of Ambanja.]		
▲ Tsiaraso II*	Andriamandefitriarivo	1945–1966
▲ Tsiaraso Victor III*	Andriamanaitriarivo	1966–1993
▲ Tsiaraso Rachidy IV*	—	1993–present

SOURCE: After Sharp 1997, 307.

NOTE: Asterisks designate rulers mentioned in this chapter; ▲ = male ruler, ● = female ruler; question marks indicate cases where royal tomb guardians were uncertain of the names these rulers bore in their lifetimes and of exact dates of their reigns.

of him each time we walk through the doors of our school. You know that it's named for him, don't you? The lycée, it's proper name is Tsiaraso I *Mixte* [i.e., coed]. That's where we go to school, and each day it reminds us of our past—of a spoiled [one], but be certain, it's not a forgotten [one].

In subsequent conversations, I found that other students, too, were reminded of a "spoiled" past by Tsiaraso I, because his reign marked the sudden rupture between precolonial splendor and the inception of colonial hegemony both in the Sambirano Valley and in Madagascar as a whole. These students expressed an intense desire to communicate this historical narrative to my own students abroad. At their urging, I therefore offer the following reconstruction of Tsiaraso I's reign.[9] I begin by venturing to the beach at Ankify, about fifteen kilometers from Ambanja, a site that became central to Tsiaraso Rachidy IV's radical reforms nearly a century later.

A Past Royal Splendor

Throughout my fieldwork in Ambanja in 1987, I ventured to Ankify on several occasions, accompanying friends on vacation for a day of rest at its placid seashore.[10] Although it was said to be a royal village, there was little evidence of this, given that the ampanjakabe rarely visited this site and hosted no royal ceremonies there that year. A stark yet barely visible reminder of its past splendor were the ruins of Tsiaraso I's old *doany* (royal palace), marked only by the traces of a foundation and a few crumbling walls. Local people gathered here only to gossip, and although taboo to this spot, dogs frequently sunned themselves here, while goats and chickens wandered freely beside tethered, grazing zebu cattle.

Tsiaraso I (Andriamandilatrarivo, r. 1887–1919) was the sixth inheritor of a dynasty established in 1820 by the founding ancestor, Andriantompoeniarivo (r. 1820–21), who had left his original ancestral land and moved north following a dispute over royal succession. Andriantompoeniarivo became ruler of the large expanse of territory that encompasses the upper and lower Sambirano, extending approximately seventy kilometers from the sea, and including the island of Nosy Faly as well, where he and all subsequent Bemazava royal dead are entombed.[11]

Tsiaraso I began his own reign in the late 1870s, around the age of sixteen, building his doany by the shore at Ankify. Although the French had been active in the region since the 1820s, they had hitherto been based primarily on Nosy Be, which had been formally annexed by France in 1840 (Baré 1986, 383 ff.; Dalmond 1840; Gueunier 1991–92; Paillard 1983–84), and rarely ventured into the Sambirano, fearful of Bemazava warriors. In 1895, however, when Tsiaraso I was approximately twenty-four, French forces under General Gallieni swept through the Sambirano, and a year later, the valley became French colonial territory.

What ensued was what Jean-François Baré has aptly termed "an atmosphere of truly inconceivable violence,"[12] involving the conversion of meaning and rights to ancestral land (tanindrazaña) that, within a decade, reduced this royal kingdom to a patchwork of large agricultural concessions. Initially, French soldiers were given plots of land as rewards for military service; when they failed at farming, foreign planters from Réunion and elsewhere quickly moved in and bought up their fields. In the words of Yvan-Georges Paillard, "the Sambirano Valley was the region most menaced by the intrusion of colonial agriculture,"[13] for it was the site of the greatest expropriations in northern Madagascar. From 1894 to 1904, over 600,000 hectares[14] of land were alienated from the Bemazava (Koerner 1968, 168, as cited in Baré 1980, 72).

One can only imagine the thoughts of Tsiaraso I as he faced the frustrations and defeats that characterized his reign. From contemporary descriptions, he appears to have been circumspect and difficult to read. In 1897, Gallieni described him as "apathetic" (Paillard 1983–84, 366), a term that conveys, on the one hand, the frustrations of this French colonizer and, on the other, the seemingly passive yet firm resistance of a reticent ruler. Throughout the north, small units of French soldiers were stationed next to or overlooking royal compounds, and Ankify was no exception. Within a year, the Sambirano was in turmoil, as was much of the island. Colonial records say that Tsiaraso I assisted the French by supplying their army with porters to penetrate more isolated areas of the kingdom, yet this ruler was simultaneously suspected of clandestine relations with rebel forces. The Bemazava raided military posts, and at least a dozen French guards and colonists were killed in October and November 1898. Tsiaraso I and other local rulers quickly became immediate suspects in these insurrections. When a neighboring ruler, Tsialana of the Antankarāña, was imprisoned for fifteen days, Tsiaraso I refused to follow any orders issued to him by the local French commander, who in response mounted charges against him as well. He managed, however, to escape the harsher sanctions imposed on other rulers, some of whom were exiled (Baré 1980, 73–74; Paillard 1983–84, 366–67).

Eventually, additional military power was needed in the Sambirano. Fresh troops were brought in under Lieutenant Colonel Prud'homme, who policed the Bemazava and neighboring kingdoms, sought out the leaders of local insurrections, and arrested and imprisoned suspected rebels. French troops included warriors drawn from elsewhere in Madagascar as well as Senegalese soldiers, who were deeply feared by the Sakalava (cf. Fanon 1963, 269). As Foringa Josef explained: "They were so cruel our ancestors believed they were cannibals. There is a place on the road to Nosy Faly [the island of the royal tombs] where Senegalese soldiers were ordered to kill a number of villagers. These things are hard to forget. . . . But we must remember that they did this because they were ordered to do so by the French. It's the French, after all, who seized the kingdom. The Senegalese—they were [simply] obeying orders."[15]

Under the yoke of colonialism, Tsiaraso I was granted the hollow honorary title of *gouverneur,* which he held until 1915 (see Raison-Jourde 1983, pl. 4). This marked the onset of Bemazava royalty serving as indigenous civil servants *(fonctionnaires indigènes)* to the colonial regime, a system initiated by Gallieni as a means to rein in rulers and thus undermine local political hierarchies (Baré 1980, 70–73). Paillard refers to such rulers as *roitelets,* or "petty kings," to whom the French delegated only such mundane tasks as taxation and the forced recruitment of soldiers and laborers for the colony (Paillard 1983–84, 344, 345), themes certainly echoed much later in the career of the ineffective Tsiaraso Victor III.

Upon his death in 1919, the Bemazava abandoned Tsiaraso I's palace, as dictated by royal custom."[T]he fact that 'the earth is filthy' or 'the earth is hot' because a ruler has died is the recurrent reason [given] for moving the royal capital to a new location," Feeley-Harnik explains (1991, 73; for specific examples, see 134–43). To defy such sacred rules is to incite royal wrath *(tsiñy)* (Baré 1980, 289 ff.). Thus, his palace's ruins marked not an abandonment in faith in royalty but, rather, quite the contrary. New Sakalava rulers assert their power by building new palaces.[16] Thus, near this site, others were subsequently built by Tsiaraso's sister and successor, Tsiresy II (Nenimoana, r. 1919–35), and, later, by her nephew, Rachidy (Andriamamefiarivo, r. 1935–45), after whom the current ruler, Tsiaraso Rachidy IV, is named. By the 1920s, however, Andoany village at Ankify beach, which is separated from the rest of the Sambirano by a long stretch of mangrove swamps that floods regularly at high tide, had been eclipsed by Ambanja, the newly established seat of French power in the region. Under subsequent rulers, Ankify eventually ceased to be a site of royal activity altogether. By the 1940s, young

Sakalava men who had served as laborers and soldiers in World War II returned from Europe with the awakened consciousness of the politically oppressed (among these was the young ruler Rachidy). In response to this development, and to subsequent uprisings elsewhere in 1947, the French stepped up their surveillance efforts in the Sambirano. Fearful of the power of royalty to inspire local rage, the French forced Tsiaraso II (Andriamandefitriarivo, r. 1945–66) to abandon his doany at Ankify and relocate to the royal residence, or zomba, in Ambanja, where he would be under the watchful eye of the colonial authorities on the hillside just above.[17] Surprisingly, when Tsiaraso II died, his zomba was not abandoned: although tainted by the death of the former ruler, it was nevertheless occupied in turn by his son Tsiaraso Victor IV.[18] As the town of Ambanja grew, so did the zomba. Today, it is a modest yet well-built one-story concrete structure located at the heart of town and near the central market. The doany at Ankify, however, had long been reduced to a small, two-roomed thatched house, typical of those inhabited by the poorest of commoners in Ambanja.

In contemporary imagination, Tsiaraso I emerges as a brave ruler and part-time insurgent who was nevertheless overpowered by the superior firepower and military might of the French. As such, he is frequently described by students in terms that approximate their own predicament: he is not a weak victim, but, rather, a local hero of bygone days who sought to preserve his kingdom even as his sacred territory was rapidly being partitioned by foreign invaders. His stature is underscored by his *filahiaña,* or "praise name," Andriamandilatrarivo, "The Ruler Who Was Honored by Many." This stands in stark contrast to that of Tsiaraso II, or Andriamandefitriarivo, "The Ruler Who Was Tolerated by Many." Today, Tsiaraso I occupies an especially important position in local collective memory, his stature rendered all the more obvious through recent creative uses of public space.

ROYAL MODERN

When I returned to the Sambirano in 1994, after a seven-year absence, I was surprised to find an imposing two-story building standing starkly upon a shoulder-high concrete platform in the center of Andoany village at Ankify beach. This was no ordinary structure: although several wealthy families had built private villas near Ankify, no one would have dared erect one in the center of this royal village. Furthermore, its architectural style was too impersonal and bureaucratic in appearance for it to be much of a home. It lacked a shaded veranda, something favored by the owners of even the most modest dwellings, the second story had no a porch of any sort, and it was devoid of flowers or shady fruit trees.

Its design was also odd for this location: it was reminiscent of the government buildings one encounters in Hellville on Nosy Be, but it nevertheless stood alone at the beach. Although somewhat dilapidated, it was painted a brilliant white, with light blue shutters, and its new peaked roof was a handsome, deep brick red. Furthermore, it stood smack in the center of the road, so that occasional *taxi-brousses*

Figure 8. The Palais Royal at Ankify Beach.

had to work their way around it in order to reach the seashore or turn around for the return trip to Ambanja. Its three front entrances, which were rounded at the top and fitted with iron gates, faced northeast, simultaneously in the sacred direction of the ancestors and toward the sea. It was as if the building were standing guard over this sleepy village, and I half expected to see cannons inside it. A quick look revealed, however, that the building was empty. A few steps below it, there was a free-standing arch painted in the royal colors of white and red, bearing a small red star nestled within a crescent moon, an Islamic symbol that stands for the local Bemazava-Sakalava dynasty. The archway bore a red inscription in French, which read: PALAIS ROYAL (fig. 8).

The Palais Royal defies a host of rules or "customs" (*fomba*) and "taboos" (*fady*) that guide royal action in Sakalava territory throughout western Madagascar. As noted earlier, strong prohibitions prevent a ruler from reconstructing, inhabiting, and even entering a predecessor's residence, for it is considered tainted by death and thus "dirty" (*maloto*) or polluting to the royal body. As I soon learned, Tsiaraso Victor III built the Palais Royal in 1989 on the abandoned site of Tsiaraso I's original doany, with funds provided by President Ratsiraka, who offered this as one of several rewards to local royal elite in exchange for ensuring support in the national elections. For the town as a whole, Ratsiraka erected a satellite antenna, freeing the region from the grip of an archaic and inoperative communications infrastructure. He also promised the ampankajabe funds for the reconstruction of a royal palace at Ankify. Although Ratsiraka failed to secure the necessary votes nationwide to recapture his presidency,[19] he did, nevertheless, remain true to his word, paying for supplies and skilled masons. The Palais Royal now stands as an imposing legacy of the otherwise unremarkable reign of Tsiaraso Victor III.

Once built, however, the Palais Royal remained a neglected, hollow structure. Tsiaraso Victor III left it unfurnished and never set foot inside it, preferring his older doany, a simple thatched dwelling, smaller than many of the neighboring village houses. Nor during his reign did any other royalty ever attempt to sleep in the Palais Royal, fearful of royal wrath (*tsiñy*) or of the displaced spirits of generic dead (*lolo*) who might lurk within.

Within a year of his instatement, however, Tsiaraso Rachidy IV and other royalty decided to use the Palais Royal as a beachside vacation house. By 1994, it had received a fresh coat of paint, and it now frequently bursts with new energy. When Tsiaraso Rachidy IV visits Ankify, drummers stand by the palace beating out the polyrhythms of the sacred royal drums (*hazolahy*); even more remarkably, the Palais Royal is rented out as a dance hall for seasonal discos.

At issue here are questions of the legitimacy of such actions: should the newly constructed Palais Royal stand upon the foundations of a bygone doany? Does such an act defile sacred ground and threaten the well-being of the ruler and his kingdom? How might this development differ from the actions of the French, who built schools and other colonial structures upon sacred Sakalava land? Furthermore, how can a doany operate as a disco hall and yet still remain a sacred palace? As I have argued extensively elsewhere, the value of such questions is limited, for they rely heavily on romanticized notions of the traditional (Sharp 1997). In short, they assign a static rather than dynamic nature to culture and ignore the resiliency and even playfulness of religious practice and belief. As such, they deny the possibility of deliberate, collective acts of innovation. More dangerously, such myopic visions render royalty passive victims, for whom the impact of change wrought by foreign cultures is far too great to resist, alter, or overcome.

The actions of the Bemazava and of Tsiaraso Rachidy IV more particularly demand alternative readings, especially in reference to contemporary, localized understandings of modernity (cf. Comaroff and Comaroff 1993b; Pred and Watts 1992). As Gillian Feeley-Harnik (1984) has argued, historically, the Sakalava have long resorted to ritually innovative approaches in response to French encroachment on their royal domains. In the case of the Palais Royal, creative innovation arises from careful reflections on the past. An unraveling of this process thus necessitates a close analysis of a new enigmatic ruler and his place within highly localized royal history.

The Innovations of a Young Urban King

Tsiaraso Rachidy IV is without question a vanguardist, for whom creative acts of royal authority are consistently marked by a playful intertwining of the archaic past with contemporary meanings of the modern. This playfulness is evident even in his appearance: with his striking profile, dominated by high cheekbones and an imposing nose, he is the spitting image of his father, so that one does a double take in his presence, and he deliberately encourages the comparison by wearing his father's fedora whenever he appears in public. Yet there the similarities end. When I returned to Ambanja in mid 1995, I was struck by the shift from the shy and serious young man I had first encountered a year before. His authority now sanctioned by royal ritual, he had shed his father's demeanor, emerging instead as quick-witted and possessing a strong sense of humor, so that even taciturn old men laugh heartily at his lively stories.

Under the careful grooming of several of his father's own advisors, Tsiaraso Rachidy IV now appears at ease as a new young ruler, his confident manner standing in stark contrast to his father's nervous reluctance. His success is facilitated by the fact that he has quickly mastered the northern Sakalava dialect. In bureaucratic spheres, he encounters greater obstacles, for, like other members of the sacrificed generation, he struggles to comprehend French; nevertheless, he speaks highland Merina and thus can converse loosely in official Malagasy. As a result, little escapes his notice, and, far from what many expected, he is not easily manipulated by older, established Bemazava advisors. By mid 1995, Tsiaraso Rachidy IV had begun to settle in as the new ruler of the Bemazava, showing signs of mastering—that is, of *learning*—Bemazava customs. He remains, nevertheless, a royal anomaly, his actions bearing evidence of a young king set on breaking with the immediate past as a means to define his own unique style of reign.

The Palais Royal is of paramount importance to this process, heralding a radically eclectic approach to reconstructing royal power in the Sambirano. In response, local royalty rarely describe this building in sacred terms, as would normally befit a doany. As noted earlier, fears about the curse of angered tsiñy or lolo who may haunt the site seem to have dissipated. As one senior royal explained, "as long as no one lives there, it's fine . . . it doesn't matter if the ampanjakabe goes in or uses it *temporarily*." At work here too is the manner in which Bemazava negotiate meanings of the modern in ritual contexts. Whereas royalty in neighboring kingdoms describe the Bemazava as "vulgar" or "bastardized" in their approach to the sacred, Bemazava speak freely and with pride of their ability to be ritually flexible. When sacred performances stray from orthodox forms (as when royalty were possessed by tromba spirits at Parfait's instatement), a typical response is that "anything is possible" where capricious and independently minded royalty are concerned. More generally, royalty—like school youth in reference to their own lives—often speak of their ritual practices and outlook as "contemporary" and "modern."[20]

Bemazava usually describe the Palais Royal as a "royal Hôtel de Ville," or city hall *(firaisana)*. This comparison is telling, because the Firaisana in Ambanja is the seat of civic power and a magnet for public discourse on and displays of local identity, housing the office of the mayor and other important officials, several of whom are also prominent members of the Bemazava royal lineage. One man in particular has now informally assumed the role of Tsiaraso Rachidy IV's primary town-based advisor, so that he frequently displaces the official *manantany*, who lives in a rural village elsewhere in the Sambirano. This new advisor has held the much-coveted position of director of public works for several decades. He approves all local construction projects, orchestrates parades and all other important public events, and can assert control over public television broadcasts. This servant of the king also has the ear of the mayor and the president of the county government *(fivondronana)*. His pivotal roles allow in the end for a merging of royal power and civic authority. This new style of rule stands in stark contrast to that of Tsiaraso Rachidy IV's father, who served the Fivondronana as a tax collector.

Against such developments, the Palais Royal directly challenges a boundary that has long divided the sacred from the secular. Through this structure, Tsiaraso Rachidy IV is actively engaged in transforming staid, older meanings associated with royal power. As such, his doany serves a dual purpose: at times, one might encounter the polyrhythmic drumming so central to sacred rebiky dances here; at others, it serves as a discotheque, blaring out foreign pop tunes such as "Tarzan Boy," "All That She Wants Is Another Baby," and "La femme de mon patron" ("My Boss's Wife"), or the songs of Malagasy singers such as Jao Joby and Rossy, who sing of unrequited love and the trials of HIV infection. As such, the Palais Royal is a truly enigmatic edifice, one that commemorates sacred historic space while simultaneously charging it with the newfound contemporary energy of modern life.

Sacred Secularism

The Palais Royal is not the only structure in which the sacred and secular converge in such eclectic fashion. Rather, the unorthodox use of local public space has its origins in, of all things, the state-run lycée (fig. 9). The lycée was completed in 1987, set on a patch of land donated by one of the valley's oldest and largest plantations. This reversed colonial practice, for this expanse of sacred ground was originally alienated from the Bemazava by the French nearly a century before. Today, the lycée stands at the edge of town on the road leading to the lush plantation zone of the upper Sambirano, and it is also less than a stone's throw from the zomba. More significant, however, is the name it bears: whereas Ambanja's other state-run schools are named for their neighborhoods, this is the Lycée Tsiaraso I.

The fact that the school bears an ancient ruler's name is peculiar, because this defies several serious royal taboos. The most significant involves employing the name of a deceased king, for when Sakalava rulers die, "the name is buried with the person" (Feeley-Harnik 1991, 39). Instead, only praise names should be used when speaking aloud of past rulers. When the lycée was built, townsfolk nevertheless sought out the approval of the royal ancestral tromba spirits on Nosy Faly, who in the end sanctioned this decision (Sharp 1999). At the building's official dedication, the lycée was treated simultaneously as secular and sacred space: in addition to serving as a platform for speeches delivered by local elected state officials, the lycée grounds also provided a setting for rebiky dances that honored the power and memory of bygone royalty.

Figure 9. The Lycée Tsiaraso I, Ambanja.

As noted earlier by Sidy, the lycée currently stands as a daily reminder for students—and, I would add, for adult royalty and townsfolk, too—of a troubled colonial past. The name, inscribed clearly on its façade, inspires students to reflect daily on local royal history, where Tsiaraso I emerges as a heroic example of Bemazava resistance in the face of inevitable conquest. Because the lycée is banked on two sides by lush cocoa fields, it is difficult to forget that it stands almost defiantly upon land once confiscated from the Bemazava by the French and reappropriated during Ratsiraka's socialist era for local collective use. Like the Palais Royal, the lycée reclaims the past by seizing upon meanings associated first with royal power and, second, indigenous rights to the tanindrazaña.

In this light, the Palais Royal and the lycée stand together as monuments of sorts, and Tsiaraso I emerges in students' minds as a local martyr of colonial violence. As David Graeber notes, "no postindependence Malagasy government has, to my knowledge, ever erected a statue in the European sense—that is, one bearing some kind of likeness. Public monuments always take the form of standing stones" (1995, 277, n. 23). These "standing stones," or *tsangam-bato,* can be found throughout the island, serving as individual markers for lost bodies or as collective monuments raised to honor wartime dead. (As we shall see in the following chapters, it is the spirits of dead lost through the brutal actions of the French that are more likely to haunt the thoughts of the living than do those displaced through royal actions.) When viewed as monuments to the dead, the lycée and Palais Royal assume additional significance, honoring, first, Tsiaraso I himself, a ruler who now looms large as a hero in the collective memory of the Bemazava, and, second, Bemazava resistance to colonial penetration, conquest, and occupation.

As I have shown, it was the sudden and unexpected death of a Bemazava ruler that jarred local collective memory. Suddenly, nearly forgotten royal rituals of mourning and instatement were revived in this dormant kingdom by royal and commoner Sakalava alike. All were forced to reconsider the relevance of kingship in their lives. Many asserted their identities as devoted Sakalava by choosing actively to "learn" *(mianatra)* local customs through embodied acts of mourning and, later, celebration. As they did so, they became *ampanompo,* or "those who work for royalty," willingly enslaving themselves to their ruler. Such actions affected even the most reticent of lycée-age students, who bore witness to these collective displays of loyalty. School youth nevertheless remain skeptical of the significance of living royalty in their lives, asserting they are too "modern" to devote themselves to the ampanjakabe. Yet they in fact bear much in common with the new ruler himself, who likewise is a member of the sacrificed generation. His instatement behind him, the youthful Tsiaraso Rachidy IV now faces the difficult task of mastering royal customs and rebuilding a base of power. If he is to succeed, he must strike a delicate balance between honoring the past and reinvigorating a neglected kingdom. One must not forget, too, that by virtue of his status as a ruler, this young man will inevitably make history.

It remains to be seen whether this modern king can capture the hearts and minds of Ambanja's school youth. His initial responses, offered so early in his reign, already draw heavily upon the symbols of the modern. The attention he has given to the Palais Royal underscores his deliberate attempts to transform his kingdom. As with the slightly older lycée, this royal edifice draws on the memory of a heroic bygone ruler as a means to reinstill local devotion and pride. The daily reminder of Tsiaraso I's legacy inspires great nostalgia for the past among Ambanja's school youth, who understand that the kingdom's stability relies on unwavering devotion and willing enslavement to royalty. This theme of enslavement resurfaces in their critiques of colonial wartime conscription and peacetime corvée labor, on which the next two chapters focus. In precolonial and colonial contexts, loyalty and freedom ultimately assume radically different meanings. The manner in which students understand these competing epochs of local history inevitably bears heavily on their collective political consciousness.

CHAPTER 5

Our Grandfathers Went to War

"I want to tell you about war," said Foringa Josef. "The great wars, the wars of the world." He paused for a moment to collect himself. Tsarahita and I were sitting together with Foringa and his girlfriend, Dalia, inside Dalia's tiny house. When he spoke again he was trembling. "You really should meet my grandfather. He's an old man, and he has seen many things. He could tell you stories! But he'd *never* talk to you. At night before I go to sleep he lights a little oil lantern and he talks to me. . . . And what he says to me is this—'The vazaha, the whites! Keep them out! If we let the vazaha in here, it will only lead to World War III. We'll be the same as them, we'll lose all our fomba, our customs, our ways.' And he says, 'don't even talk to any vazaha, because they'll kill everyone in your family!' "

"So, you see, he'd never talk to you. And it would anger him to know that I am talking to you right now. But here is a story you should know. . . . "

"My grandfather is an old man—he was born in 1900 on the east coast. He came here to the north when he was sixteen to find work. And he came on his own. He's [Betsimisaraka] royalty—his name is Andrianambinina. He has never gone back home. He has seen the century! Many things. And he was in France during World War I. He fought for the French in Europe."

"How did he become a soldier?" I asked.

"They just came and took him." Foringa then fell silent once again.

Dalia interjected, "Go ahead. You should tell her the story."

So Foringa continued. "This is what happened: they just took him. The army would just come to the door. They would drive up in these big trucks—just like the ones today, the ones that drive workers to the plantations every morning. The big ones, the flatbed trucks.[1] The army—the soldiers—they stood there in front of my grandparents' house with chains in their hands. They threatened to take him as a prisoner. But he was no where to be found. It was my grandmother who stood there on the porch. And they looked at my grandmother and they said, 'If he won't come, we'll put him in jail!' "

Dalia explained: "They did this everywhere. They would drive up to the houses of Malagasy and summon the women. They would look at the wives, the mothers, the grandmothers of men and they would say, 'You can *help* them. You can find the men for us and bring them here. And they can get on the truck. Or we will find them ourselves. And then we will put these chains on them.' " She lifted her hands as if holding heavy shackles.

Foringa then continued his story: "So, my grandmother, and other women like her, they would cry out, 'please, take them, take the men, but please don't put them in chains.' And so my grandmother went and found her husband, and she led him to the truck. He drove away in that truck. That's what they did with the men. He was a soldier for twelve years."

"For twelve years? Where?" I asked.

"Four years in France. And then another eight here in Madagascar. It was twelve years before he was able to return here."

To this Dalia added, "War? It was [nothing but] slavery."

The political consciousness of young Malagasy of the sacrificed generation was shaped by *Les guerres mondiales*—the world wars, or, in Foringa's words, the wars of the world.[2] In Foringa's story, they loom as powerful specters of colonialism, framing the islandwide subjugation of the Malagasy. World War I fell within the first two decades of conquest, and World War II followed barely twenty years before independence. Colonialism demanded the abandonment of beloved royalty for the foreign invaders, who unceasingly required labor, and in turn, expected loyalty from their subjects. In the Sambirano Valley, which was radically transformed by expansive, foreign-owned plantations, wartime only rendered more obvious this exploitative relationship imposed upon indigenous inhabitants whose ancestral land had already been alienated. Thus, not surprisingly, the two world wars were favored topics of discussion among Ambanja's school youth, providing significant points of reference for a "still evolving, reevaluation" of "decolonized history" (Ferro 1984, 14). This chapter is the second of three that focuses on the oppressive policies of French colonialism: the previous chapter examined the destructive effects on royal power; this one now explores the brutality of wartime conscription during World War I;[3] that which follows analyzes the unrelenting quality of domestic corvée labor during peacetime as yet another form of enslavement. Together these chapters uncover the troubling interconnectedness of freedom, labor, and loyalty in the colony.

THE COLONIAL HUNGER FOR AFRICAN LABOR

The colonization of the Sambirano Valley was marked from its inception by a pronounced military presence. The initial "pacification" (Gallieni 1900, 1908) of the region, as described in chapter 4, relied heavily on military know-how, because soldiers were not only essential to squelching armed resistance but met the economic needs of France as well. Military men conducted careful surveys of the region, where intelligence operations focused on geography and local culture, their records highlighting the potential for agricultural exploitation. Recognizing the fertility of this alluvial plain, they rapidly displaced sparsely settled villages of indigenous Sakalava onto inferior lands. The Sambirano was unusual in this regard, being one of the few regions where the French created reserves for indigenous people. Within a decade the valley was transformed into fields of manioc and sugarcane, farmed by foreign planters and soldiers paid for their service with alienated land.

Soldiers could thus be found throughout the valley. In what is now Ambanja, an obtrusive military post was established, noted on early survey documents as a flagpole perched high on top of the hill that today overlooks the zomba. Around this post, the town eventually grew. When trouble was afoot, soldiers and gendarmes could respond immediately from their respective posts nearby, and others were stationed on the road to Nosy Faly and at the beach at Ankify. There was also a garrison house at Ambanja, which today serves as a prison stockade. In this light, the early town of Ambanja emerges as a French military settlement.

As Foringa's narrative underscores, the military placed oppressive demands upon the colonized, where his account of events in 1916 underscores the fear, psychological violence, and the beginnings of a larger pattern of forced labor. In his account, the conscription of soldiers emerges as an early form of colonial enslavement. World War I suddenly transformed this colonial territory into a pool of exploitable workers, where colonized men were ultimately sacrificed to the demands of an empire to which they felt no loyalty.

The Wartime Conscription of African Men

When Andrianambinana (whose name means "The Prince Who is Favored") was conscripted by force to serve France during World War I, he was several years younger than Foringa was when he told me his grandfather's story. Like other young men from the east coast, he crossed the threshold of manhood as a migrant, traveling alone on foot for several hundred kilometers "to seek his fortune" *(hitady harena)* and find wage labor in the Sambirano. By the end of his sixteenth year he had settled in the region and his new wife—Foringa's now deceased grandmother—was pregnant with their first child.

Foringa's grandfather was no an ordinary man, for as his name testifies, he was of royal origin. His fate did not match the name given to him, however, because he was one of an estimated 450,000 African soldiers who participated in France's military operations, in addition to yet another 135,000 wartime laborers put to work in French factories (Andrew and Kanya-Forstner 1978, 14–16; see also Balesi 1976, 269–70; Clarke 1986, 5; Michel 1974).[4] A total of 45,863 Malagasy soldiers were enrolled in the French army, of whom 41,355 fought in battle, some as young as fifteen (Labatut and Raharinarivonirina 1969, 154, 157; see also Gontard n.d. a., 1,

11). In 1911, the population of Madagascar was estimated to be 3,154,000 (1,501,000 male and 1,652,000 female) (Mitchell 1982, 39), so the French conscripted approximately 3 percent of the island's total male population. Perhaps Andrianambinana's true good fortune lay in the fact that he survived this terrible war.

France, unlike other European powers, had established a pattern of relying heavily on its *force noire* (Mangin 1911), having already used African troops over half a century earlier in the Crimean and Franco-Prussian wars (Andrew and Kanya-Forstner 1978, 14). With the outbreak of World War I, foreign soldiers were quickly transferred from North Africa to Europe, giving France by far the largest force of African soldiers in Europe. This army consisted of North African troops, Malgache (Malagasy) battalions, and Senegalese tirailleurs, all valued as fierce warriors capable of standing up to German forces. As a result, these men participated in every major battle along the western front (Andrew and Kanya-Forstner 1978; Balesi 1976, 269–70; Clarke 1986, 9; Page 1987, 4–9). In the words of one French witness who protested their high casualty rates, Africans were often regarded as nothing but "black human cannon fodder" (Page 1987, 9, citing Barbusse 1920 and 1974). The number of Malagasy killed in action is officially around 4,000, but "an unknown number of thousands more died of wounds and illnesses suffered in France" (Thompson and Adloff 1965, 21, citing Dandouau and Chapus 1952, 279). More broadly speaking, many Malagasy soldiers never returned to Madagascar after the War (Thompson and Adloff 1965, 444). When French troops mutinied in 1917, they were patrolled by and replaced with African reserves. Foringa's grandfather Andrianambinina survived the dangers of European warfare only to remain in Europe: he and other Africans then policed towns in France and occupied German territory. Held captive by a colonial army, Andrianambinana did not set foot on Malagasy soil for four years, at which time he then remained a soldier in his own land for another eight.[5]

Madagascar made other significant contributions to the war effort. Domestic labor efforts responded to wartime needs in the island's factories, fields, and graphite mines, and skilled laborers, such as butchers, tailors, and nurses, were deemed especially valuable at home and abroad to feed, supply, and assist soldiers in France. The highlands paid by far the heaviest toll in terms of sheer military manpower, supplying four-fifths of the colony's conscripted soldiers, thus sparing the north from a more significant burden. Tales such as that told by Foringa, however, reveal that the number of soldiers matters less than the fact that they were taken by force, and that their kin were threatened if they did not cooperate. Diégo-Suarez was a favorite military port, so that soldiers from elsewhere on the island passed regularly through the north. Individual Malagasy households and communities also supported the war through significant forms of direct taxation, "contributions" (totaling five million gold francs by the end of the war), and payments of cattle and rice. In all arenas, Malagasy participation often amounted to nothing more than "forced voluntarism":[6] in the highlands, through military recruitment, and in coastal areas, through domestic labor and economic hardship. Such demands were imposed regardless of hunger, inflation, and ravaging cyclones (Gontard n.d. a and b; Thompson and Adloff 1965, 21–22).

Captive Warriors or Willing Compatriots?

The question of colonial patriotism is complex and extends beyond the focus of this chapter, but it warrants brief attention, because it shaped students' understandings of loyalty and freedom. Maurice Gontard's primarily economic surveys of World War I (Gontard n.d. a and b) assume a higher level of Malagasy loyalty than I have encountered in the Sambirano, whose inhabitants speak of this era only with bitterness and sorrow. Nevertheless, Gontard reports that when the first 40 or so of an initial 650 Malagasy foot soldiers departed from Antananarivo in October 1915, they were greeted by "a great patriotic demonstration in the capital. Thirty thousand people assembled on the Avenue de France to cheer for the foot soldiers and to distribute among them flowers and delicacies."[7] Local newspapers had expressed dismay that other colonies were sending soldiers—why not Madagascar? (Gontard n.d. a, 9). Gontard's account may thus in fact reveal important regional differences.

We, of course, do not know what thoughts passed through the minds of those lining the streets of Antananarivo or of the soldiers themselves. Yet I find Gontard's portrayal of Malagasy patriotism troubling. Gontard himself questions a "characteristic anecdote" delivered by Governor-General Hubert Garbit at a conference in Paris in 1919, where he argued that a high level of patriotism existed among even rural Malagasy women:

> Following the death of a young Malagasy [soldier] in France, he [Garbit] sent to the provincial *chef* the bad news to the family along with his personal belongings. The provincial *chef* met with the lost man's mother, wife, and brother. [Garbit said:] "The wife of the indigenous soldier burst into tears. But then the mother said to her: 'You must not cry for your husband. He died a glorious death.' And she then turned towards the administrator and added 'I have another son who is here; I give him to you so that he may go to France and replace the one who is no more.' And the young man immediately volunteered."[8]

Again, one obviously can not know what this mother was in fact thinking (or even if she existed). This tale is nevertheless compelling, because it uncovers the complexity of French (mis)readings of Malagasy responses to wartime conscription. On the one hand, it uncovers a deep-seated desire to portray colonial subjects as loyal and willing, where the importance of wartime demands was evident even to an old peasant woman when confronted with the death of a son. As wartime propaganda, it promotes the power of colonial authority to a French audience back home while also exposing a weakness among colonial officials who needed to justify their exploitative practices.

After all, Foringa's girlfriend Dalia contended that wartime service was perceived by Malagasy as nothing more than glorified slavery.[9] Characterized by capture and forced conscription for unspecified lengths of time, military service frequently terminated only with the death of a soldier. From the point of view of the French, soldiers were expected to serve the colony willingly, driven by a patriotic loyalty to the war effort abroad. A closer examination of students' narratives on the war, however, uncovers a radically different reading of this history, where the theme of enslavement emerges regularly as a strident critique of oppressive wartime policies. As students underscore, the Sakalava enslaved others, a fact that only further intensified the horrors associated with wartime conscription. Deciphering the significance of slavery to school youth of the sacrificed generation necessitates a brief discussion of its relevance in the Sakalava past.

CONQUEST, CAPTURE, AND ENSLAVEMENT

A Lucrative Trade

Well before the eighteenth century, when legislation against the slave trade was passed in Europe, Malagasy of diverse origins enslaved others.[10] From the tenth century onward, Arab accounts describe a flourishing Indian Ocean slave trade, in which the Sakalava played a significant role from the fifteenth to the late nineteenth century.[11] Slaves came not simply from the African continent but from within Madagascar as well, since warring groups were known to enslave captives, especially as they expanded their kingdoms. European presence in the Indian Ocean only increased the demand beyond the island's borders. In the seventeenth century, the Dutch, for example, attempted to capture Malagasy slaves and take them to what is now Mauritius; when their efforts failed (Malagasy slaves were considered difficult to control), they turned to Kilwa, Zanzibar, and other ports along the East African coast. Sakalava coastal towns also became important stopovers for ships bound, for example, for India and Southeast Asia.

As the British and French subsequently developed sugarcane plantations on the neighboring Mascarene Islands of Mauritius and Réunion, they created a large-scale and regular demand for slaves, so that by the eighteenth century Sakalava were among the region's most important traders. Sakalava raided East African ports and the Comoro Islands for captives, although most were brought to Madagascar by Arabs sailing from Kilwa, Zanzibar, and Mozambique. Lyons McLeod, a former British consul to Mozambique, says that Malagasy on the northwest coast raided one of the largest Portuguese slave posts; they also captured ships, seizing slaves and dismantling these vessels for their iron and copper (McLeod 1969, 251 ff., citing Guillain 1856, 160).[12] S. A. Slipchenko (1989, 322–23) likewise reports that "so entrenched in the trade were the Sakalava . . . that they sent a fleet to attack Kilwa between 1817 and 1818. After an initial success, the invasion was repulsed." The Sakalava reaped continuous benefits as they became increasingly involved in regional and global trade networks. They exchanged captives for cattle and rice, which they would then trade again to merchants who supplied these goods to feed the inhabitants of the Mascarenes. Slaves were also resold for guns, ammunition, or rum. Whereas many slaves traveled as far as the Americas, others remained in Madagascar to serve indigenous elites.

Sakalava slavers, like others of the Indian Ocean, defied a host of local and international decrees that outlawed the trade in the nineteenth century.[13] Following the British Abolition Act of 1807, for example, the Sakalava were middlemen who facilitated the refashioning of slaves' identities and origins, their coastal communities providing important stopovers for French-acquired slaves bound for plantations elsewhere. Many who passed through Madagascar had been acquired in Mozambique; they were then taken to the Seychelles, where they were dressed as old (previously owned) slaves, given rudimentary training in Creole, and then "reimported" to neighboring islands. Réunion alone required as many as 10,000 slaves per year; between 1670 and 1810 approximately 160,000 slaves were taken to the Mascarenes, of whom approximately 45 percent came from Madagascar. Sakalava also cooperated with Arab and British traders in other illegal slaving activities.

Slavery likewise continued to flourish on the island itself: although the 1817 Anglo-Malagasy treaty outlawed the trade to Madagascar, it nevertheless persisted. As one British sea captain, Fairfax Moresby, described to a parliamentary select committee in England, as late as the 1850s, slaves were brought to the west coast of Madagascar, marched across the island, and reexported from the east coast to Mauritius. The fact that the region's slave trade was not carefully policed enabled it to persist well into the 1870s, at which time the Merina, under European pressure, waged expeditions against the Sakalava ostensibly to stop the very traders who previously had supplied them with slaves. Along the northwest coast, slave trading nevertheless continued as late as 1900, the year that Foringa's grandfather, Andrianambinina, was born.

Upon abolition, many slaves remained in Madagascar. Once "indigenized," they labored, for example, in the royal rice fields of Merina rulers (Aderibigbe 1989). In the highlands and elsewhere, one still encounters Malagasy of slave origins. In Merina territory, for example, *andevo* ("slave") and *mainty* ("black") are highly derogatory terms that are applied to stigmatized members of society, many of whom today comprise the urban poor (Bloch 1971, 3–4, 68–71; Gow 1979, 31; Molet 1974). In the capital city of Antananarivo, one encounters a spectrum of Merina who claim commoner, noble, or royal origins, many of whom may speak with loathing of those they assume to be andevo (although they will nevertheless tolerate them as house servants). Sakalava also kept slaves of their own to work in the royal rice fields. The name Makoa (derived from Makua, an ethnic category in Mozambique) has been preserved as a label for lower-status coastal peoples assumed to be of relatively recent African origins. By the mid twentieth century (and, thus, on the eve of independence), it had been transformed to define a subgroup of Malagasy speakers, appearing, for example, on historical and cultural maps of the island (see the 1958 map in Deschamps 1972, 300–301; cf. Thompson and Adloff's ethnic survey 1965, 265). Today, in the north, Makoa are more often conceived of as a subcategory of Sakalava. Throughout this region one encounters villages whose inhabitants are primarily Makoa and who may continue to work for royalty as their ancestors once did (cf. Feeley-Harnik 1982).

Sakalava Enslavement

When members of the sacrificed generation in the Sambirano Valley spoke of slavery, they were thus thinking of older Sakalava institutions, based on a collective sense of local history that links nostalgia for a powerful kingdom with a lucrative trade that spanned several centuries. In light of their history as former slave traders, northern Sakalava specifically speak with deep bitterness and anger of moments in the past when they themselves were threatened with enslavement by others. Two former enemies loom especially large in such accounts: the Merina and the French, each of whom sought to impose their specific style of hegemony. These chapters of their history are familiar to both schooled and unschooled youth of the Sambirano.

The Merina wars of the late eighteenth and early nineteenth centuries are particularly important to Sakalava as they seek to reconstruct their past, because highland encroachment on the west coast led to the subsequent displacement of numerous Sakalava communities. Although the Sambirano and immediate surrounding territory were never conquered by the Merina, the northern Sakalava nevertheless identify strongly with the suffering of other communities and dynasties located further south. In 1837, the Merina established their northernmost post just south of the Ampasindava Peninsula, or roughly 130 kilometers south of present-day Ambanja. For several years afterward, Sakalava from this region sought shelter on Nosy Be and Nosy Faly (see McLeod 1969, 246–47). As noted earlier, the Sakalava on Nosy Be sought assistance against the Merina from the French, after failing to obtain it from the sultan of Zanzibar; as a result, Nosy Be was declared a French protectorate in 1841. Although Nosy Be was already inhabited by foreign planters, traders, and missionaries by the early nineteenth century, the formal transfer of this royal domain to France is considered a significant, fateful step that ultimately paved the way for future French expansion and conquest.

The French are now often equated with former incursions into Sakalava territory by the Merina, among whom the conquest of territory was inevitably followed by attempts to enslave local inhabitants, either directly or in the form of royal service. The Sakalava struggled successfully against Merina hegemony and subsequent enslavement, using strategies that included isolation, escape, warfare, and even suicide, the latter commemorated in the tales associated with members of the Zafin'i'fotsy royal dynasty who drowned themselves in the Loza River when confronted with Merina colonization. The bodies of these ampanjaka are described as forever lost, and today their mediums observe strict taboos associated with a wide array of fish who are said to have devoured their corpses (Sharp 1993, 120–22; see also Verin 1986, ch. 11). Such strategies proved futile, however, with the French.

THE ABANDONED BODIES OF LOST ANCESTORS

On the edge of the Lycée Tsiaraso I's playing field stands a small monument to Ramanandafy, a twin who died overseas while serving as a conscripted soldier during

World War I. Although similar in shape to grave markers just down the road in the local cemetery, it is, in fact, a *tsangam-bato,* or "standing stone," erected to the memory of someone whose body remains eternally lost. This tsangam-bato (text reproduced below) marks the spot where Ramanandafy's house once stood, and, like the lycée itself, it offers students a daily reminder of the violence done to the local tanindrazaña and its people by colonial oppressors: before the war, Ramanandafy was forced to surrender his land to the foreign owner of a newly established plantation, which has since grown into one of the valley's largest agricultural concessions. Every few years, this monument is lovingly repainted by his descendants, who live elsewhere in a remote, rural village of the Sambirano. As noted in chapter 4, spirits, or lolo, displaced by the Palais Royal seem to inspire little distress among Sakalava today. Rather, as the subsequent narrative reveals, it is the dead who were lost and displaced through colonial violence who remain dear to them.

FAHATSIAROVANA
———

HAMBALAHY
RAMANANDAFY

maty—ANDAFY
ADY—1914–1918
V   V

* * * * * * * *

IN REMEMBRANCE
———

THE MALE TWIN
RAMANANDAFY

died—OVERSEAS
[during] THE WAR—1914–1918
V   V

Wartime's Middle Passage

One afternoon, I asked Jaona, one of Foringa's classmates, what moments in Madagascar's history he felt needed to be told. He, too, focused on the Great War in Europe: "I think it would be the First World War. . . . Why? Because there were *so many* dead. Many Malagasy died then. . . . The French came and took Malagasy away and made them serve in the army. And, you see, their bodies stayed there. We don't know where they are! They died in foreign lands, they died at sea. When they died on the boats on the way to Europe, they just threw their bodies overboard.

And so we don't know where they are. They sank to the bottom. They were eaten by fish and sharks." He quickly looked away, with a pained expression. He then looked directly at me again and said, "They just threw away the bodies of the dead like they were garbage. They are out there, but they are lost. Unclaimed. Forever."

Jaona's tale is deeply nuanced with multiple readings of injustices that run through recent reconstructions of the Sakalava past. A striking motif is that of bodies abandoned at sea, an image reminiscent of the transatlantic slave trade. As A. B. Aderibigbe stresses, the Indian Ocean "had its own horrors of a middle passage" (1989, 325). One eyewitness described slaves being transported in the holds of small Arab dhows stacked in tiers, with children placed on top of them. With little air, food, or water, as few as a dozen might survive out of several hundred after ten days at sea. The bodies of these dead were regularly cast overboard.[14]

Although certainly far more survived the middle passage during World War I, captured African men nevertheless feared the fates of slaves from a century before. Joe Harris Lunn's research among former West African soldiers exposes the raw emotions of wartime sea voyages during World War II: one man spoke vividly half a century later of soldiers' fears during their journey to Bordeaux, for many could not swim and did not trust their ship's seaworthiness. Confined to quarters throughout the voyage, they fell ill, and all feared they had been taken as slaves, not soldiers. If they were indeed to be soldiers, they did not grasp the purpose of fighting. When they landed in France, ironically all were relieved when they were greeted by other African soldiers already in training for warfare (Lunn 1987, 35).

In Madagascar, the image of the lost bodies of ancestors is a terrifying one, for the dead must be placed carefully and lovingly in tombs if they are to be remembered as ancestors (OM: *razana;* SAK: *razaña*). If displaced they become lolo, joining instead an obscure category of unnamed, lonely, and vindictive dead. Thus, "placing the dead" (to borrow a phrase from Maurice Bloch) is an essential component of identity in life and after, shaping in profound ways personal and collective histories (Bloch 1971; see also Mannoni 1990, 49–88). All Malagasy place great emphasis on the elaborate rituals surrounding the care for and placement of corpses; among the Sakalava, this is particularly true of rulers, whose bodies undergo radical and elaborate transformations before they are entombed (Feeley-Harnik 1991; Sharp 1997).

Jaona's narrative reiterates these fears and associated anger, reminiscent, too, of the tales of the ubiquitous Zafin'i'fotsy tromba spirits of the Sambirano, which likewise speak of drowning and being devoured by carnivorous fish.[15] It is the bodies of those lost at sea—be they slaves, ancestors, or soldiers—that underscore self-sacrifice on the one hand and recall, on the other, the brutality of conquest. In Jaona's tale, as a result of crimes committed against the dead by the French, the ocean now seems littered with lolo, or the displaced spirits of Malagasy dead; others who died in battle are now lost on foreign soil. In this light, the anecdote recorded above, as recounted by Garbit in Paris in 1919, is truly remote from Malagasy understandings of the proper handling of wartime dead. Although displaced from their homeland long ago, the spirits of conscripted soldiers continue to haunt the memories of successive generations of Sakalava.

French Dead on Foreign Soil

The colonial archives offer little information on the disposal of the bodies of Malagasy men who may have died away from home. They are, however, spotted with fairly elaborate accounts of how the French handled the bodies of their own people when they died in Madagascar. Records spanning 1938–48, for example, offer accounts of the exhumation of the bodies of several colonists who died on the island. One, for example, focuses on the death of Lieutenant Aviateur Rossigneu in the city of Diégo-Suarez in May 1942. His remains were later transferred to France in 1948 in response to a request made by his father. Since he had been in the military, it was the colony itself which shouldered the cost, as decreed in April 1925. Other accounts describe the immediate or subsequent (following exhumation) transportation abroad of the bodies of other colonial employees, as well as those of settlers' wives and children who died in the colonial provinces of Diégo-Suarez (now Antsiranana)—including one case from Ambanja—and Majunga (Mahajanga). Some were men who had spent their entire adult careers in Madagascar; even after two decades, however, the island still was not considered a proper resting place for their bodies. By the late 1930s, records offer highly detailed accounts of the proper preparation of bodies for transport and coffin construction, as well as elaborate instructions on how to prepare the necessary paperwork.[16] At times, little remained of the dead, so that arrangements had to be made for the transfer, not of entire bodies, but simply what could be unearthed. Thus, the French, like the Sakalava, were compelled to guard the relics of their own dead with tremendous care.

This colonial obsession with the remains of the deceased exposes elements of a French mentalité concerning the bodies of colonized subjects. With such evidence in hand, it is difficult to defend the French as simply naïve about Malagasy customs—that is, that they could not imagine the severe angst experienced by Sakalava who witnessed the apparently heedless disposal of Malagasy bodies. Yet the French administration acknowledged the anguish of compatriots who sought to retrieve the bodies of kin. From a Sakalava perspective, their response to the handling of bodies of colonized men was truly brutal, regardless of whether or not they were, as seems more likely, interred (and not simply abandoned) in France. The fact that Malagasy soldiers were sent to the front only further underscores how French racism informed the lack of military compassion for conscripted colonized dead.

COLONIAL RESISTANCE

The brutality of colonial oppression rarely goes unanswered, although indigenous responses may certainly be downplayed, hidden, or denied in colonial discourse (Scott 1985; Stoler 1985). A fear many Europeans shared was that the participation of Africans in World War I would forever alter colonial relations, because veterans who had witnessed Europeans slaying one another would inevitably return with ideas that would undermine French superiority and the power of the empire (Page 1987, 3; cf. Thompson and Adloff 1965, 20). Soldiers' experiences abroad could help shape a collective African political consciousness, where violence against Europeans emerged as an immediate threat.[17] The First World War did indeed prove pivotal to the rise of early nationalism in Madagascar.

Wartime Labor and Political Unrest

Within Madagascar, such fears are reflected in a flurry of correspondence generated by interim Governor-General Martial Merlin, who came from French Equatorial Africa in late 1918 and remained on the island until mid 1919. The majority of wartime recruiting had already been carried out under his predecessor, Garbit, who in 1917 left Madagascar for three years to supervise Malagasy troops and laborers in France. Merlin wrote repeatedly to the minister of colonies in France, his tone eventually reaching a level of exasperation as he was called upon constantly to supply more soldiers for the war effort. He felt that Malagasy men saw through the propaganda (his word) of French conscription and realized that that which was labeled "voluntary" was in fact obligatory,[18] which ultimately threatened the stability of the colony. Yet his concerns were ignored, and battalions of hundreds and even thousands of soldiers were shipped from Madagascar's ports; thousands more were steadily recruited well into 1920, approximately two years *after* World War I had officially ended, providing inexpensive laborers to rebuild wartorn France. Merlin linked activities of a newly exposed secret society, the Vy Vato Sakelika (generally translated in English as "Iron Stone Network") or VVS, to wartime conscription: the power of the VVS to recruit members seemed to increase with the relentless demand for soldiers (CAOM, SG c. 316, d. 822, 8/1919; Gontard n.d. a, 20; Thompson and Adloff 1965, 21, 24).

Colonial Violence and Early Nationalism

In response to conquest, colonization, and conscription, Malagasy waged their own war on the French, and World War I became a catalyst for early nationalism. As Maureen Covell (1987, 22 ff.) and other scholars make clear, and young informants in Ambanja confirmed, the first few decades of colonial occupation saw a host of small-scale revolts and other forms of resistance. Numerous battles, uprisings, secret organizations, and early political parties are now regularly analyzed as important early nationalist movements in scholarly writings, school textbooks, and classroom lectures in Madagascar.

Three movements in particular emerge as emblematic of early nationalism: the Menalamba of the late 1890s; the VVS, established in 1913; and the insurrection of 1947.[19] In Ambanja, students regularly make reference to all three, and they are important subjects for teachers' lectures. Yet students' discussions of the Menalamba and events of 1947 are brief and lack the fervor that characterizes those of the VVS. This stems in part from how they perceive the first two. Students understand the Menalamba as an important chapter of highland history, because it arose in response to the French invasion of Imerina. A key concern was the reassertion of the Merina monarchy, a purpose that fails to capture the imaginations of coastal Sakalava. Furthermore, it relied upon older religious institutions as it asserted royal power, a response considered dated by modern school youth.[20] The 1947 insurrection is problematic in other ways: although it spread throughout the island, it was most strongly based on the east coast. Moreover, it is very much a part of living memory, and students' elders are reluctant to speak of local events for fear of future reprisal by unspecified parties.[21] In contrast, the VVS occupies a privileged position in their reconstructions of history, and it was a favored topic of discussion. For contemporary school youth, its significance lies in their perceptions of the VVS as being the first nationalist movement led by educated and politicized young students like themselves.

Félix communicated its centrality one day during a one-on-one interview. I had just posed a question that I asked of all school informants: "If you were to address a group of my students in the United States, what topic would you choose in order to teach them something about Madagascar?" Without hesitation, he replied: "I'd talk about the period of... the VVS.... This is really when the Malagasy started to work for independence." An important source for Félix is the classroom history lesson. I thus turn to the lectures of one gifted teacher to illustrate how political history is communicated in Ambanja to Félix and his peers.

Schoolroom Nationalism

Sister Estelle is a history and geography teacher at the lycée level at the Catholic Academy. A woman proud of her highland origins, she nevertheless has adopted an eclectic style that, when paired with the intelligence and sheer power of her lectures, inspires great admiration in many of her students. The content and focus of Sister Estelle's lectures are representative of those of other teachers here and at the state-run lycée. She is, however, the most charismatic and organized teacher I encountered, so I have chosen to quote her here and in the following chapter. This and subsequent passages are drawn from a review lecture delivered in anticipation of end-of-the-year examinations in history. Sister Estelle spoke primarily in French, periodically clarifying her remarks in official Malagasy.

Thus, one morning in June 1995, I sat as a guest in one of her classes. She entered the room wearing a white cotton *lamba* draped about her shoulders in characteristic Merina style, but she is also known to prefer Sakalava hairstyles, which remain hidden under her wimple. She removed the lamba and placed it ceremoniously upon her desktop before she began to speak. She then guided us with great mastery through a hundred years of political history. She began with what she con-

sidered to be early, localized revolts, including the Menalamba of Imerina, the Bemazava revolt of the Sambirano under Tsiaraso I, and brief references to southern uprisings. These topics then led to subsequent discussions of, first, the VVS,
followed by a critique of oppressive domestic labor policies, the development of
significant political parties following World War II, and then the insurrection of
1947. In this lecture, she was quick to distinguish between a revolt and nationalism: "A revolt involves violent action. Nationalism in this context was defined as a
pacifist movement. The leaders [of the latter] used the press to express their ideas.
And they used political parties [as an important vehicle for political change]." She
then turned to a discussion of the VVS:

> *Vy Vato Sakelika:* "Iron Stone *Solidarity*"—the message here was solidarity. This was
> their purpose. The VVS was active here [in our region]—in fact, Father Venance
> [a priest who figures prominently in the history of the Catholic Academy] was a
> member of VVS, although few people here realize this. He was a priest from Nosy
> Be who was very interested in nationalism. . . . VVS gave rise to the solidarity of
> the Malagasy. It expressed the spirit of solidarity. The object of VVS was to re-
> claim our solidarity—that is, our "fraternity" or our fihavanana.[22]

Whereas Sister Estelle deemphasized the potential or actual violence that characterized nationalist sentiment and action during the colonial period, Hasina, a
state lycée student, offered a different interpretation with a contemporary twist
that underscores parallels between events at the turn of the century and the socialist revolution seventy years later, under which Hasina himself was raised and
schooled:

> *Hasina [laughing slyly]:* We [students] have a way of remembering VVS —we use an
> expression that means "Kill the vazaha [European]." VVS —you know, of course,
> what it stands for—Vy Vato Sakelika. Why "Iron" and "Stone"? Because these
> are both durable things—things that last. The message was to carry yourself like
> those things that endure, that last—[in other words,] be strong. But the expression
> we use to remember VVS is "Vonoa Vazaha Sisa tavela": *vonoa* means "to kill," or,
> as Sakalava say, *mamoño; sisa* and *tavela* both means "those that remain"; for exam-
> ple, *sisa* is the rice that is left over after the meal is finished. So the joke among stu-
> dents is "Kill all the vazaha who remain," because many—but not all—left during
> the [socialist] revolution in the 1970s. In the end, we are the ones who endured.

As Sister Estelle also explained, young nationalists communicated their ideas
through an indigenous press and in their own language, which was not unlike official Malagasy of half a century later. Maureen Covell notes as well that "the resistance of the educated elite was harder to control [than armed revolts]. A written national language freed them from the need to communicate in the language
of the colonizer." In response, the French imposed prepublication censorship
(known as the *indigénat*) upon all non-French newspapers and banned "meetings
other than family and traditional gatherings. In general, any activity likely to have
a 'disturbing' effect on public opinion was forbidden" (Covell 1987, 23).

The VVS, a literary society founded in 1912 by educated Malagasy youth, was among the first of these nationalist movements.[23] Its more prominent members were students enrolled at the newly established medical school in Befeletanana as well as the secondary school Le Myre de Vilers in Antananarivo (the latter trained many of the older school teachers and other educated elite of Ambanja). The VVS subsequently attracted other educated youth from the metropole and elsewhere. Inspired in part by Japan's victory over Russia seven years before, members of the VVS sought to preserve indigenous (albeit primarily) Merina culture. As schooled elite, they simultaneously admired and resented Western technology; of primary concern to its 300 or so members, however, was that they pledged to fight to restore the homeland. In 1915, the French accused the VVS of plotting to overthrow the colonial government by poisoning all Europeans in Madagascar. Although no arms or poison were found, approximately 200 students were arrested, many of whom were imprisoned on Nosy Lava, an offshore island located in Sakalava territory near Analalava. Some were required to reside in Antananarivo, where they could be observed by French authorities; still others were exiled completely from the island and imprisoned elsewhere.[24]

A Nationalist Poet

Among such exiles was the poet Ny Avana Ramanantoanina, who emerges as the movement's most celebrated hero in accounts offered by Ambanja's school youth. For them, his life epitomizes the highest values associated with early Malagasy nationalism: through his example students choose to emphasize a strong nostalgia for the lost homeland, rather than the potential for physical acts of violence against colonial oppressors. These themes are embodied in the melancholy tone of his poetry. As Pauline explained one day:

> *Pauline:* Do you know the poetry of Ny Avana? It is very moving; it truly expresses the heart and soul of what it means to be Malagasy. This is a man who was exiled from his own island—one he loved dearly—by the French. When he was away from home, he wrote such beautiful poetry!

Another classmate expressed similar affection for Ny Avana. This was Clement, an eighteen-year-old who had just completed his first year (seconde) at the state-run lycée. Like other students I encountered not only in Ambanja but also in Antananarivo, he identified one poem in particular as among those he knew and loved most:

> *Clement:* Ny Avana Ramanantoanina? So, you've heard of him? I wish I could recite his poetry, but it is very difficult. Among my favorites is "Izay Sambo Izay."

Thus, I include it, along with its translation, here.[25]

IZAY SAMBO IZAY

Mba sambatra, ho'aho, iry sambo iry
fa lalan'ny mody mankany aminay!
fa reraka kosa ity tenako ity
fa voro-mifatotra latsaka an-kay!

Ny lohan'ny manina mamelovelo,
ny kibon'ny lavitra be sentosento;
ka, hono, ry Sambo, ity fo malahelo
hanafatra kely ka indro mba ento:

Ry Sambo tsy tana, fa maila-pisosa
mamaky ny onja tsy lany lanina,
manaraka anao ny velomako kosa;
veloma malefaka sady mangina!

Veloma mivalona tsara fifono,
tsy hain'olon-kafa borahina foana;
veloma manitsy ny "Mahandrihono",
dia ireo mahatsiahy sady tsaroana!

Veloma, ry Sambo, am'ilay niaviako,
d'ilay Nosin-tany tsy tazako maso!
Raha toa manantsafa ny fianakaviako,
tontalin'ny foko ny hoe: *"Mba andraso!"*

Handeha, ry Sambo, veloma masina,
tongava any soa, tongava any tsara!
ny dia ho tomombana sy hotahina,
ambonin'ny lalina tsy hita fara!

Tsaroako, Rasambo, fa ... "Mamy ny mody",
izany no anaovako kopa-mosara!
Ka dia miverena ho faingam-pitody
hitondra ny valiny ao afara!

THAT PARTICULAR SHIP

So fortunate, I say, is that distant ship
for it is on its way back to our homeland!
oh, but this body of mine in contrast is weary
like a bound bird fallen from a cliff!

Its head is weighed down by homesickness,
its far away belly full of sobs;
so, Dear Ship, this broken heart
will send a little message, so please transmit it:

Dear, unheld Ship that floats by so fast,
breaking waves of endless depth,
my farewell follows you,
a soft and silent goodbye!

A folded farewell, packaged with care,
which no other person can carelessly unwrap;
For, as they say, a simple farewell "Makes wise,"
both those who remember and who are remembered!

Farewell, Dear Ship, bound for that place from whence I came,
The Island [Home]land that I cannot glimpse!
If my loved ones talk about me,
with all my heart I say: *"Please wait!"*

You are leaving, Dear Ship, blessed farewell,
may your homecoming be sweet, may it be safe!
May you complete your blessed journey,
above the deep and expansive sea!

I remember, Dearest Ship, that . . . "Sweet is the homecoming,"
that is why I wave this handkerchief!
So hasten your voyage for a quick arrival
so you can later bring back an answer [for me]!
   17 August 1916

The life of early educated young Malagasy nationalists is exemplified by that of [Ny] Avana Ramanantoanina (1891–1940).[26] Born in Avaradrano in Imerina, he was well educated by colonial standards. In his youth, he attended a Quaker school in Antananarivo and later enrolled at the École Le Myre de Vilers, a celebrated metropolitan secondary school that trained Malagasy of diverse origins as civil servants and teachers. As a student, he was exposed to the works of such French writers as Alphonse de Lamartine, Alfred de Musset, Victor Hugo, and Charles Baudelaire, whose concerns and tone, certainly, are reflected in his own individual style. His first poems were published in a Malagasy journal under his pen name Ny Avana ("The Rainbow") when he was only sixteen years old.

By the early twentieth century, such elites, often educated by the French themselves, were already seen as posing a potential threat to the colonial state. As Covell (1987, 23) and others have argued, Malagasy elites were difficult to control, because written Malagasy freed them to communicate in a language other than that of the colonizer. In this regard, Madagascar was unlike many other French African colonies, for few indigenous languages existed elsewhere that were potentially comprehensible to all subjects within the boundaries of any given colonial territory. Even when Malagasy political writings were suppressed, literary journals still flourished on the island, because they allowed members of the Malagasy elite to print critiques of colonialism in veiled language (Adejunmobi 1994).[27] Among these writers was Ny Avana, who, although fluent in French, chose for political reasons to write exclusively in Malagasy. At the age of twenty-five, Ny Avana was arrested and deported to Mayotte in the Comoros archipelago, where he was imprisoned for five years with other exiles until 1921, and he wrote much of his poetry, which figures centrally in the literary movement known as Embona sy Hanina (HP: "Sighs and Longing," or melancholy) while in exile.

Following his release, he remained a staunch nationalist. Open political activism was impossible, but between 1931 and 1934, he nevertheless led yet another literary movement, known as Mitady ny Very ("Search [for] what is Lost"), whose purpose "was to rid the Malagasy language literature of the slavish imitation of foreign (in particular French) models and to urge a return to the traditional sources of Malagasy inspiration" (Adejunmobi 1994, 6). His poetry appeared widely in Malagasy journals, and he was an immensely popular poet throughout his lifetime. On March 5, 1940—barely a week after his fiftieth birthday—Ny Avana died in Antananarivo, where he held the modest post of a bookshop attendant.

Adejunmobi has argued that Ny Avana's writings easily reached all strata of Malagasy under colonialism, yet such popularity would inevitably have had to rely upon widespread literacy. His arguments do ring true, however, when applied specifically to contemporary educated school youth. As the comments of Pauline and Clement reveal, My Avana's poetry resonates with their own nostalgia for the past as they struggle with the meaning of nationalism. Adejunmobi has also argued that Ny Avana remained relatively obscure until an anthology was published in 1992 by the Ministry of Culture "as part of a programme of promoting the treasures of the Malagasy language" (1994, 7). My own interviews based in Ambanja and Antananarivo contradict this, however. Malagasy who were in their late thirties in the mid 1990s remembered reading Ny Avana two decades before, and school youth I encountered throughout the island reported that they had access to at least a handful of his works earlier than 1992, although I have been unable to identify their sources. My suspicion is that schoolteachers had copies of at least a few poems that they had acquired during the course of their university studies. His poetry may also have appeared in bac examinations, especially during the Second Republic under President Ratsiraka.

Within this contemporary framework, Ny Avana is cherished by students because he remained so steadfast in his refusal to serve—and, in the end, enslave himself to—the French, and because he was imprisoned and exiled for ideas he communicated through his heartfelt poetry. From his writings emerges a deep nostalgia and longing for his homeland, a great island that can only be reached by a lonely ship that sails upon the sea. Since he ended up as a petty clerk in a bookshop, his was a life with no economic future, paralleling the lives of the students who cherish his work today.

As I have illustrated throughout this chapter, the colonial hunger for African labor during World War I ravaged the Malagasy in innumerable ways: boys as young as fifteen were taken from the island and packed into the holds of ships bound for hostile territory. In France, their skills were honed in preparation for battle and hard manual labor, many dying in exile for a cause that meant nothing to them. Still others were held captive abroad for years before they could return home. France relied heavily on these colonial "child soldiers" (Furley 1995), and thus many from Madagascar lost their youth—or their lives—working, fighting, and dying in exile from their beloved tanindrazaña.

A significant consequence of this era of Madagascar's colonial history is rampant fear. Soldiers perceived supposed voluntary conscription for what it truly was: the exploitation of captured hostages. Later, as they awaited their fates on board ships, their collective voyage to an unknown France revived childhood memories of elders' tales about coastal enslavement, transforming their own shared experiences into a terrifying middle passage. The colonial archives reveal other fears among the French: they were distrustful of the very men they exploited, predicting that wartime service could awaken in them an awareness of their own subjugation. The insatiable demand for wartime labor did in fact fuel early nationalism, in the form of the VVS, whose leaders were not soldiers but educated young men.

These themes figure prominently in the historical narratives of Ambanja's lycée students, their politicized understandings of the past synthesizing lessons gleaned from elders' firsthand accounts and teachers' lectures. From this synthesis emerges their own subaltern critique of colonial domination. It is their selective tales, after all, that correlate conscription with slavery, humiliation with fear and anger, and political exile with nationalism. How Ambanja's school youth envision their past ultimately hinges on their ability to retell—and thus reformulate—events that shaped the lives of older Malagasy, who were foot soldiers, prisoners, and political activists during French occupation. What is significant, then, is *which* stories these students choose to tell, and what these tales reveal about their readings of colonial oppression.

CHAPTER 6

Laboring for the Colony

At nineteen, Hasina is in the terminale year at the state-run lycée. His age alone confirms he is an exceptional student, because his peers are typically a few years older than he.[1] Hasina consistently earns high marks in school but, as he explained to me once, he feels as though some teachers refuse to take him seriously and treat him as an outsider. His name suggests that he is of highland origins, and he was in fact born in a town outside Antananarivo. Yet Hasina considers himself to be *tsaiky ny Sambirano*—a "child of the Sambirano"—and his peers accept him as such, because he moved to the north when he was only five, and he has lived in Ambanja since he was eight. He has no memory of his Merina father, having been raised since infancy solely by his mother, who is Tsimihety. She herself is educated through the lycée level and has long served on the secretarial staff of Ambanja's county courthouse. By virtue of her civil service position, she was able to acquire subsidized housing for her family, which consists of Hasina and several younger siblings.

My initial interview with Hasina was a memorable one: although relatively shy in class, he is a bright, articulate young man and consistently offered detailed answers to my questions. These often strayed into complex philosophical musings on the meanings of indigenous Malagasy concepts, although he was most taken with discussions of inequality in Madagascar and beyond. In this sense, he soon became a teacher of sorts for me. In 1994, we lived within a stone's throw of each other's homes, and so we sometimes sat together on his veranda exploring his ideas more informally after school when he was left in charge of his younger siblings as they played in the yard.

Hasina was in fact the first to alert me to the historical significance of oppressive colonial labor practices. When I asked, "What would you like to talk about if you were to address a group of my students in the United States?" he replied: "As for me, I would like to teach others where Madagascar is, and who the Malagasy people are. I would talk about their lives. I would also tell them about the pride,

the dignity of the Malagasy people. And then I would talk about SMOTIG"—
that is, the Service de la Main d'Oeuvre des Travaux d'Intérêt Général (Manual
Labor Service for Works of General Interest). This emerged as a favored topic
during our subsequent meetings as well. Although three other young men—Jaona,
Félix, and Foringa Josef—also spoke of SMOTIG, Hasina communicated with
great force and passion the anger and humiliation associated with oppressive colonial labor policies. Thus, throughout this chapter, Hasina emerges as a principle
guide.

As Hasina made clear, wartime conscription was not the only form of labor
forced upon the Malagasy; they were also regularly exploited during peacetime.
In 1900, the French parliament passed a law requiring colonies to be economically self-sufficient in all areas except the military, and by 1901, to " 'liberate' a
work-force by creating a need for money" among the conquered (Covell 1987,
20), a head tax had been instituted in Madagascar (Thompson and Adloff 1965,
310). "Voluntary labor" *(travaux volontaires)*, "public works" *(travaux publics)*,[2]
"prestations" *(prestations)*,[3] "indigenous labor" *(travail indigène)*,[4] "national service,"[5]
"civilian conservation corps" and "civilian labor 'army' ":[6] these and other eu-
phemisms in colonial and postcolonial documents describe what was, in fact,
forced or corvée labor. Among the most dreaded forms were institutionalized under SMOTIG, a program started in the 1920s and abolished, at least on paper,
in 1946.[7]

For Hasina and his peers, SMOTIG epitomizes the degree of suffering endured
on a daily basis by Malagasy during sixty-four years of colonial occupation and
attempts by the French to transform the Malagasy into the willing subjects of the
empire. As we shall see, the French employed a host of strategies designed to colonize the minds of their subjects. Sakalava with few exceptions, however, remained
steadfast in their refusal to submit to colonial domination, especially in response
to its economic and ideological demands. SMOTIG nevertheless haunts the Sambirano's inhabitants as a specter of oppressive colonial hegemony.

A HISTORY OF FORCED LABOR
Colonial Beginnings

Even prior to conquest in 1895, French settlers in Madagascar relied on corvée labor: as early as the 1880s, Malagasy were impelled in some regions to provide manpower for early road construction, for example. Following conquest in 1895, Gallieni
(as military general, and, later, as the colony's first administrative governor-general
[1897–99, 1900–1905]) immediately passed legal decrees that institutionalized forced
labor practices throughout the island. Among the most significant measures was that
of October 1, 1896, which served as a foundation for many subsequent policies. In
terms of this, all men between sixteen and sixty were subject to compulsory public
labor for fifty (and later, thirty) days annually if they could not prove they were already employed.[8] Laws against vagrancy and vagabondage also allowed a series of

governor-generals to justify the seizure of men as laborers; in the early years of the colony, many of these men had in fact only just been freed following abolition of slavery on the island in 1897. Direct taxation in 1901 also ensured that many would now be in need of cash earnings. Only men who were infirm or who already worked on private plantations, for the military, or elsewhere in colonial service were exempt from these newly imposed labor demands. These measures were often accompanied by large-scale land seizures.[9]

In Ambanja, the complex sequence of events that paved the way for exploitative labor practices are well know to school youth living in one of the islands' most productive agricultural regions. The introduction of these programs was forcefully described in a lecture by Sister Estelle:

> Agriculture is central to our understanding of economic measures and policies [during the colonial period]. You mustn't forget profit and exploitation—these were key concerns for the colonizers. Now, what did Madagascar have at this time? Agriculture . . . an important theme here [in the Sambirano] is the plundering of local lands: Madagascar was at the periphery of colonization . . . here, the colonizers recognized this as a fertile region, and so they drew a perimeter around [the region], taking lands from local peasants, who were then forced to provide labor [on the very lands] alienated from them. . . . [To ensure control and ownership, the French] then instituted the Service de Domains [Office of Land Deeds], which regulated land ownership. [Since] Malagasy could not read, write, or speak French, they lost control of their lands to the French because they did not have written proof of ownership. This is yet another example of plundering. . . . Finally, laws were passed to make forced labor possible. Malagasy were told they would go to prison if they didn't cooperate. By the age of fifteen, Malagasy men were actively engaged in the colonial economy, because men between the ages of fifteen and sixty were required to pay taxes. . . . This is how the colony [was to become] self-sufficient.[10]

Corvée labor projects reveal a blurring of public and private sector demands. Although roadwork and telegraph lines, for example, initially served the needs of the military and, subsequently, a web of colonial administrators, these and other efforts soon enabled plantation and smaller concession owners as well to engage in islandwide trade networks and export produce overseas. Furthermore, the colonial government bore much of the responsibility for conscripting labor for the private sector. This was particularly important in the Sambirano, where the needs of local plantations and the colonial state were soon nearly inseparable (cf. Covell 1987, 19–20; Stratton 1964, 97).

SMOTIG's Rise and Fall

World War I inspired the colonial administration to rethink labor recruitment. By the mid 1920s, new approaches were institutionalized under SMOTIG, whose primary architect was Governor-General Marcel Olivier, who already had twenty years of colonial experience, especially in French West Africa. He was stationed in Madagascar from 1924 to 1930,[11] a time now described as marked by a prosperous economy and political stability. During his tenure in Madagascar, he introduced the first local bank note (used in Madagascar and the Comores), drafted land and survey laws (of particular significance were those that undermined Merina rights to their ancestral lands), and instituted widespread labor reforms designed to serve "the general interest" of the colony (Brown 1975, 261; Labatut and Raharinarivonirina 1969, 159; Thompson and Adloff 1965, 25–26, 286).

Historically and administratively speaking, SMOTIG was, from a colonial perspective, an ingenious economic reform, because it was designed to draw no funds from the colonial budget. Early SMOTIG projects focused primarily on the building of a railway from Fianarantsoa to the east coast and on roadworks for four major provincial centers: Tulear (now Toliara) in the southwest, Majunga (Mahajanga) in the west, Ihosy in the south, and Diégo-Suarez in the north. Roads were built in strategic locations around these towns so that their administrators could then employ substantial feats of engineering, building dams, railways, and even, in one case, a cathedral. French pride in these projects is evident in photos prepared by Olivier for the Brussels International Exposition of 1935, which feature suspension bridges, ports and harbors, tunnels, canals, and airport runways. By World War II, Madagascar's infrastructure included approximately 25,000 kilometers alone of passable tracks and roads.[12] The effects of such projects is readily evident in the Sambirano for, as Hasina explains, "the roads here wouldn't exist at all if it weren't for the needs of the plantations." Demands for Malagasy laborers to construct these, though, were high and reflected little concern for the enormous strain they placed on individuals, households, and communities.

To Gallieni, enforced labor had an ideological component as well. It would, he believed, create "a large group of indigenous people charged with the task of progressively transforming the [mind and] mentality of the native races."[13] Olivier's views echoed Gallieni's; "the freedom of the worker to choose his job should only become part of the laws of a country when the obligation to work has become a customary practice," he contended (trans. Heseltine 1971, 160–61). SMOTIG was thus not simply intended to build a colonial infrastructure but to transform the minds of the colonized. More specifically, it was envisioned as a program that would assist Malagasy in learning (that is, developing a consciousness of) the worth of their own productivity. Olivier and others were well aware of the exploitative nature of corvée labor; he himself acknowledged that salaries were unusually low, for although wages had doubled from 1914 to 1924, the cost of living for Malagasy had increased fivefold. Nevertheless, he saw SMOTIG as essential, since it both served the colony's commercial interests and might potentially alter the desires, economic interests, and even loyalty of Malagasy subjects (Heseltine 1971, 161–62).

From a Malagasy perspective, however, SMOTIG was simply another form of institutionalized slavery. French audacity is underscored in the bitter reminiscences of Andrianambinina, Foringa's ninety-four-year-old grandfather, who, in addition to serving as a soldier in World War I, subsequently provided many additional years of labor for public works. In words paraphrased by Foringa, this elderly man spoke of enforced labor as emblematic of colonial greed:

LS: What, then, do you think colonialism means to your grandfather?

Foringa: Ahh, it's something really serious. The French were like this, they'd say: "I'm your God. If you don't go to church, you can't have any work from me." And the Malagasy worked very hard. You know Betsiaka [on the northern road from Ambilobe]? They had a lot of gold—they still do. The French [vazaha] came to get gold with shovels and picks and they forced the Malagasy to work there [from the 1930s to 1950s]. These men found it hard to escape and they were worked like slaves.

Throughout the colonial period, men faced demands that ranged from 10 to 180 days of annual labor, and many were in fact captives of the colony. All Malagasy men potentially could be recruited for several years of military service, and Olivier seized upon this as a means to acquire a reliable labor force in peacetime as well (Thompson and Adloff 1965, 446). Initially, SMOTIG recruits were expected to serve for three years, and only after such lengthy service were they granted leave; in 1929, this policy was altered, so that workers were entitled to leave time after two years. The work was so despised that desertion was a chronic problem. In response, eventually, SMOTIG workers were housed in guarded camps so that their movements could be strictly controlled. Men deemed fit for service were first taken to assembly camps, where they were given clothing and then sent on to their actual work camps, where they were paid to labor forty-eight hours a week. The daily rations were meager, too: each man was to receive 750 grams of rice, 250 grams of beef or fish, 100 grams of "indigenous condiments" (such as greens), and 15 grams of salt; during especially taxing projects they might be given an additional 50 grams of beef and 50 grams of rice.[14] If wartime conscription was slavery, then SMOTIG was this as well as sanctioned imprisonment when no true crime had been committed.

SMOTIG was in fact based on a military model. In a draft document dated July 10, 1926, Olivier described his vision in detail. The heaviest burden was to fall upon single men, the youngest of whom were "around sixteen," the same age as many soldiers conscripted during World War I. They were to be stationed in camps composed of a minimum of 500 men, who were housed together in barracks. These laborers were dressed in military-style uniforms similar to those worn by the Moroccan and Senegalese tirailleurs, with headgear (the French African tarboosh) emblazoned with an "M" for Madagascar. In fact, Olivier hoped to "recruit" as many former Malagasy tirailleurs who had served in France as possible, since he believed that they would be able to impart French values to workers and thus help to redirect the "indigenous mentality" of their compatriots. SMOTIG's "voluntary workers" served under French commanders, acting through Malagasy sergeants and lieutenants, and their compounds were guarded by the colonial Garde indigène.[15] Another striking aspect of Olivier's vision is the near total absence of—and disregard for—women and children. The colonial authorities focused on women's value in the domestic sphere (and, as explored in chapter 7, their sexuality), rather than their labor power.[16]

As sources generated outside Madagascar make clear, this level of institutionalized exploitation was unusual for the colonial world. Madagascar soon attracted attention from within and outside France: the International Labour Organization (ILO) in Geneva, for example, accused the colony of practicing slavery, as did some members of the French parliament. Olivier nevertheless defended SMOTIG, stating that it differed little from military service, which went unquestioned by those same agencies. Nevertheless, by 1929 the ILO successfully imposed some restrictions on Madagascar's forced labor policies, and the following year France signed an official agreement to cooperate. By the 1930s the new Popular Front government (the first to legalize labor unions in Madagascar) expressed concern. Yet SMOTIG persisted in full force for over a decade longer. "As late as 1943 the official statistics of the Inspector of Labour give 3,810,000 man/days of forced labor for the year," Nigel Heseltine reports, stressing that this figure excluded the number of additional days laborers spent walking to work.[17] SMOTIG ended officially with the Law of April 11, 1946, which rendered it illegal to impose "forced or obligatory labor" in Madagascar. A significant impetus for this measure was a 1944 conference in Brazzaville, where leaders from francophone Africa drafted a charter of human rights and demanded widespread colonial reforms.[18]

When set against actual practices, the history of official decrees designed to eliminate corvée labor bear an uncanny resemblance to the ending of slavery a century before (see chapter 5); for instance, the colonial administration continued to recruit laborers against their will throughout the 1930s and even after 1946, when SMOTIG was officially abolished. New forms of "voluntary recruitment" (Brown 1978, 262) were regularly formulated to replace others. During World War II, for example, policies inspired by SMOTIG had already been expanded under the guise of wartime conscription, so that Malagasy men were forced to serve as soldiers and as workers for the war effort both abroad and at home. In other words, wartime needs justified the intensification of the very sorts of obligatory labor policies that had been rendered illegal during peacetime. As a result, throughout the colonial period, many men spent their lives in service to the colony. Foringa's grandfather, Andrianambinina, worked for five decades as a public works laborer in both war and peacetime, because, as Foringa explained, "he was big and robust—1 meter 96 cm tall—so they always wanted him."

SMOTIG's Demise and Colonial Fears

Following the official dismantling of SMOTIG in the mid 1940s, successive colonial administrations implemented other oppressive measures in their attempts to maintain a steady flow of labor within the colony. One innovative solution involved the creation of pass laws.[19] As Sister Estelle explained in class, these racist policies were yet another insidious form of social control that clearly marked one's inferior status. These raised vagrancy laws to a new level, so that now the undocumented could be seized and forced to labor for the colony:

> *Indigènes* were Malagasy who didn't have citizenship. Indigènes didn't have the same rights to circulate. They were required to have a motive for why they wanted to move. They had to carry passes, and if you were found without your pass you were imprisoned—you were then forced to do full time labor for the [public] works force. . . . As you can see, social programs were [often guided by] economic [needs] . . . it all comes back to the regulation and control of labor.

The regulation, control, and supply of labor in fact posed serious problems throughout the colonial era, even with such oppressive policies in place. By 1946, local *notables* (officials appointed by the colonial administration) in the northern provinces of Majunga and Diégo-Suarez (now Mahajanga and Antsiranana) regularly contested these policies. They argued that the burdens of taxation and labor recruitment fell squarely on their shoulders, and by this point the demands were too great. Several notables insisted that substantially larger salaries and other forms of compensation had to be offered if they were to succeed in their recruiting efforts. For example, Sondrota, the chief advisor to the Sakalava queen Soazara in Analalava, argued that "the worker must be: well paid, well fed, and well clothed" and compensations promised should include "[a fair] remuneration, an abundant ration, and distributions of cloth."[20] Yet such demands were consistently ignored by colonial officers. In this case, the regional administrator responded simply by demanding the continued guarantee of a substantial workforce in subsequent months.

Colonial documents also record a plethora of responses from foreign planters—ranging from frustration to outrage—over the unending problem of labor shortages. This became even more pronounced with the elimination of SMOTIG. By 1946, many local economies were in a state of crisis, and the north was no exception. A panicked letter from Marovoay (located near Mahajanga) detailed how rice and sugar production had plummeted because of the loss of hundreds of men. Another letter from the work inspector of Diégo-Suarez to the governor-general outlined the problems faced by a prominent planter who had encountered serious difficulties with local notables. He searched in vain for adequate labor to harvest fifty tons of paddy rice within twenty-five days, and he feared he would lose his entire harvest were he forced to wait another month. Nosy Be likewise desperately needed 1,500 to 2,000 supplementary workers, and thus local authorities requested permission to recruit labor for three months from further south in Analalava, Bealanana, Antsohihy, and Befandriana.[21] The director of the region of Majunga reported that in Marovoay "the public fields have been abandoned."[22] This region's local authorities reported a loss of 500–600 field hands. In addition, the Water Service was in an alarming state, lacking sufficient labor to irrigate fields, which in turn would make it impossible to harvest local rice. In response, many local employers preferred to rely on migrant labor from more depressed areas rather than offer greater remuneration to lo-

cal inhabitants as a solution to their economic woes. In Analalava, only the recruitment of local prisoners and others from distant Tulear (Toliara) could save the year's
harvest.[23] Similarly, the work inspector from Diégo reported that planters in his region were hiring workers from distant Yemen.[24] Yet another project proposed the
recruitment of Tonkinese men, women, and children from the newly formed northern territories of Vietnam. These laborers were to be hired on five-year contracts
and would help offset the loss of 8,000–10,000 Malagasy laborers on northern sugar
plantations. Ultimately, the proposal failed because the relevant administration
abroad refused to release any laborers bound for Madagascar.[25]

Yet another grave concern was that the elimination of SMOTIG would ultimately undermine the stability of the colonial government. Again, as the director
of the region of Majunga wrote in 1946, "I fear for [the region of] Port-Bergé—I
fear [that this] well reflects the sentiments of many Malagasy, even those who live
along the coast: 'the *Vazaha* [French] . . . can rule us no more. They can no longer
force us to work, nor can they imprison us. We are now free to do what we wish.'"
The increasing problems wrought by labor shortages in turn had serious political
implications. This director predicted imminent disaster, concluding "without a
doubt, we shall take it upon ourselves to fight against the expansion of this state of
mind."[26] According to him and to other colonial officials, the new public awareness (the Brazzaville conference declarations were attached to his letter), paired
with new labor policies generated in France, would inevitably "catapult" Madagascar toward independence. He was right, of course, and histories of Madagascar invariably link SMOTIG with resistance movements (see Brown 1978, 261 ff.;
Covell 1987, 22 ff.; and Labatut and Raharinarivonirina 1969).

Laboring for the Nation

President Tsiaranana's First Republic not only revived the dreaded pass system in
1962 but required all Malagasy with land to cultivate at least one hectare of rice or
corn to feed the nation. Tsiranana also sought to institute a form of civil service that
would rely heavily on the labor power of the nation's youth. The following year, 1963,
saw the opening of the École des Cadres du Service Civique (Civic Service Training
School), a program designed to prepare small groups of students in skills deemed necessary to the success of this new country: these included commerce, civics, and physical education. These plans all met with great resistance because of the painful memories of SMOTIG and coerced wartime service under the French. Furthermore,
organized resistance exposed regional and class divisions. University students in Antananarivo protested strongly and openly, arguing that they, as member's of the nation's elite (many of whom were Merina), should not be forced to abandon their studies for the needs of what they considered Tsiranana's côtier government. Also central
to this debate was whether the educated elite or unemployed urban youth should bear
the burden of public works projects (Thompson and Adloff 1965, 255, 447, 464).

Whereas the French and, subsequently, President Tsiranana, failed to acquire widespread support for their labor policies, President Ratsiraka was truly gifted at inspiring school youth to work for the nation. As discussed in depth in chapter 1, Ratsiraka offered potent critiques of colonial oppression, generating a new language of the state that was infused with indigenous meanings. (As we shall see below, this mirrored similar yet failed attempts by the French.) Ratsiraka successfully mobilized vast numbers of students to work in the public domain. As Hasina explained one afternoon, Ratsiraka transformed the language of "Tsiranana's neocolonial measures," instilling a new vigor and, ultimately, a strong collective sense of pride and dignity into youth, who willingly worked for the new and, as Ratsiraka argued, truly independent socialist nation.

The cornerstone of Ratsiraka's labor policies was National Service (Service National Révolutionnaire, or simply SN), as outlined in his *Boky Mena*. As he explained in the chapter entitled "The Popular Armed Forces, Youth and National Service,"[27] an immediate goal of the nation was to promote rapid reform through "democratization, decentralization, [a] revolution of the mind, etc."[28] Both the army and youth corps were recruited in service to the nation, and university-bound youth now bore special obligations, because as the "privileged citizens of a Nation for which the people have consented to a heavy sacrifice ([in the form of] scholarship, schools, the university [, etc.]), it is normal that they give eighteen months to two years of their lives in gratitude in service to the people."[29] In so doing, Madagascar's youth would also confront the realities of rural life as they came to the aid of the *fokon'olona* (OM: "community")—that is, people of all walks of life. It was through their labors that they would thus contribute to "the national unity of the Malagasy people."[30] Malagasy youth would be rewarded for their efforts with a university education, fully subsidized by the government, at one of the nation's campuses, trained to assume future leadership roles as educators, policy makers, political advisors, and so forth.

Thus, all lycée students who passed their bac exams were required to perform National Service before they could continue their studies. These students provided manpower in government office jobs, clinics, the forestry service, adult literacy programs (see fig. 5 in chapter 2), or they taught at one of the nation's many primary schools and CEGs. The majority of these positions were in poorly serviced rural areas. Transforming the island's infrastructure was also an important duty, as illustrated in the *Boky Mena* by a photograph that shows a group of youth dressed in National Service fatigues engaged in construction work (see fig. 10). As was true under the French, laboring for the nation and military service were merged: these paid "volunteers" also received several months of military training in order to prepare them, if necessary, to defend their country. A significant difference, however, is that National Service was an obligation of young men *and* women.

The National Service survived for fifteen years before it was openly questioned in political debates, and reasons for its demise are complex (see chapter 1). Objections raised by Ambanja's students clash with those who were educated in the 1970s

Figure 10. Malagasy youth engaged in road construction work as part of their National Service. From Ratsiraka 1975, 115.

and early 1980s, who typically express respect and awe for Ratsiraka's program. Mme Vezo (alias Mama Vé), a schoolteacher in her thirties, put it thus, underscoring the thrill of personal freedom and responsibility invested in youth, including young women, to forge a new nation:

> National Service? It was really interesting! I finished my high school studies in Morondava in 1977. I was already living away from home, because I went to boarding school, but we were carefully watched, especially since we were girls. When I did my National Service, now, that was very different. It was the first time I was on my own—I worked with a group of girls, and we were sent far from home to the north to teach. I didn't think I could do it! I worked at a junior high school where I taught geography and some history. Fortunately, these were my strong areas when I had been in lycée, and that's why I went on to study these subjects at the university, and why I teach them now, too. You felt so grown up—on your own, making a difference for the nation.

In contrast, the responses of younger informants drawn from the sacrificed generation reveal a new disillusionment with Ratsiraka's labor policies. A significant problem for them is simply passing the bac no longer guarantees university placement. As eighteen-year-old Clement from the state-run lycée explained:

> Today you don't even know if you will be able to go to the university in the end—there are already too many students there, and not enough places. I myself, I want to go to the university in Antananarivo, but I've been told that the dormitories are full of former students who refuse to leave, because they can't find affordable housing elsewhere. This means in my generation we will be forced to pay for our schooling, but who has the money? My parents are poor . . . they don't have money for that.

Faced with an exceptionally large number of graduates, by the late 1980s, the state began to place increasing numbers of National Service youth in jobs with little purpose. Doda, now a twenty-six-year-old university student from Antananarivo, explained that in the final years of Ratsiraka's Second Republic, he had the dubious honor of working in the vast headquarters of a prestigious government minister, only to find that he and other National Service cadets had nothing to do but sit and listen to the radio day after day in a room that had no furniture. In contrast, his sister Suzy, seven years Doda's senior, and her husband Rommy were proud of how hard they worked together as math and science teachers in a village fifty kilometers from the capital. They, like Mme. Vezo, embraced Ratsiraka's idea that working collectively was vital to the process of transforming—and truly liberating—the Malagasy as a people and a nation. They therefore accepted the end of National Service in the 1990s with regret, whereas Doda celebrated its demise, openly voicing his disillusionment, although he and his peers nevertheless recognize the power of Ratsiraka's early policies, still celebrating his challenges to a racist colonial ideology that insisted upon the inherent inferiority of Malagasy *indigènes*.

COLONIAL LOYALTIES:
LA MENTALITÉ COLONIALE, LA MENTALITÉ INDIGÈNE

Throughout the colonial literature—be it published works or private in-house correspondence now housed in national archives—French colonizers reveal an obsession for discovering, grasping, and outlining the nature of "the indigenous mind" *(la mentalité indigène)* and deciphering how, ultimately, it could be colonized. This becomes particularly significant in reference to domestic labor recruitment. Colonial officials and settlers were truly perplexed by what Maureen Covell has labeled "inertia as passive resistance" (1987, 22; cf. Thompson and Adloff 1965, 255; Scott 1985), a response exhibited by Malagasy subjects who showed little interest in improving themselves through bogus opportunities that only more deeply entrenched them in colonial servitude. A central concern within this section, then, is how little the French understood Malagasy resistance. In the end, their observations and strategies to transform the mentalité indigène are, in fact, more deeply revealing of a mentalité coloniale—of a colonial mentality.

Colonizing the Indigenous Mind

Throughout the colonial period, French administrators embraced a localized rendition of "the white man's burden," one introduced at the onset by Gallieni, who argued for a pairing of taxation and education, because together they would encourage—rather than force—the Malagasy to embrace French ideals of productivity. More specifically, Gallieni viewed taxation as an "indispensable stimulant to the energy of the native" (trans. Heseltine 1971,160–61).This process also necessitated an educational program that would in turn promote new skills—especially in agriculture and commerce—and ensure greater productivity (and, again, in a never-ending circle, increase tax revenues).[31] Gallieni and his successors imagined that through such efforts, the colony would soon thrive in response to the willing efforts of Malagasy subjects to promote prosperity through their own labors. Gallieni imagined this as a colonial duty, for to deny the colonized such opportunities excluded them from the right to progress. In short, it would be "immoral, impolitic, and futile" if the French simply forced them to work (Thompson and Adloff 1965, 247).

As Ann Stoler (1985) illustrates in her study of the colonization of Sumatra, colonial documents downplay the fact that relations between colonized and colonizer are frequently fraught with danger. As a result, they obscure evidence of hatred toward and violence against the colonizer as meted out by the colonized. In Madagascar, colonial officials regularly relied on bureaucratized forms of silencing, for new strategies designed to confront local resistance were often handled as secret documents, marked for "oral transmission" only.[32] Close inspection reveals that Malagasy were especially troubling subjects of the French empire. Among the most perplexing responses was their widespread and consistent refusal to work, so that, according to Covell, "more ordinances regulating labour were passed in Madagascar than in any other French colony" (1987, 20, citing Feeley-Harnik 1984; cf. Stratton 1964, 97).

Perhaps payments (albeit in the form of low wages and meager rations) blinded the French to the hardships imposed by colonial work requirements. In the end, the French generally interpreted Malagasy responses not as legitimate forms of resistance but, rather, as evidence of an indigenous weakness in character. Thus, in addition to imposing increasingly oppressive physical restrictions on Malagasy laborers, a succession of colonial officers relied heavily on propaganda designed to transform how the Malagasy understood colonial hegemony and its labor requirements. Of greatest concern to the French was an intense desire to impose a Euro-capitalist work ethic on their colonized subjects, who would then offer their labor voluntarily in service to the empire.

The "Problem" of Slothful Resistance

Among the most trying problems associated with labor recruitment was the high rate of desertion by Malagasy.[33] SMOTIG documents contain detailed accounts of the most common infractions: "negligence, laziness, unjustified absence and

[a] refusal to obey";[34] these were typically punished with social restraint or imprisonment. The harshness of French reprisals is reflected in indigenous terms for corvée labor in the Sambirano. As Mme. Lucie, a Sakalava women raised in the Sambirano who teaches at the Catholic Academy explained to me one day, colonial labor service was referred to locally as *sazin-gasy,* "the punishment [of the] Malagasy." This expression plays upon the term for fines or punishments imposed by royal retainers when Sakalava—and even royalty—break local sacred taboos. Hasina, too, underscored corvée labor as a punishment reserved solely for Malagasy, stressing as well its racist undertones:

> During the colonial period there were two categories of people, the *citoyens* and the *indigènes.* The indigènes had to do the SMOTIG work. They had to do work for free for the colonials—it was like a form of punishment. . . . They used the Malagasy to build up the infrastructure. You see, there were taxes that you had to pay; if you couldn't then you had to do SMOTIG work. There were all sorts of reasons why you might have to do this forced work, to build up the infrastructure—to *restructure* the infrastructure [laughing at the seemingly endless layering of tasks].

Interestingly, as they sought to enforce these oppressive policies, the French seemed less likely to interpret the actions (or lack thereof) of Malagasy as potent forms of resistance, but as an inherent flaw in their character, where some groups emerge as more capable and thus dependable than others. By the 1930s, the phrase "la mentalité indigène" permeated colonial documents. Malagasy character was thus the subject of several papers delivered at the Congrès International et Intercolonial de la Société Indigène as part of the Exposition Coloniale Internationale in Paris in 1931, where economic productivity was among the central concerns. Père Dubois (1931), for example, argued that it was difficult to describe Malagasy character because it was such a mix of cultures and types. Nevertheless, groups considered to be the most "African" (namely, the Bara[35] and Sakalava) in physical type were described as "more savage, [possessing a] more independent character, [and a] spirit less easily assimilated to our civilization."[36] In other words, their racial heritage and other assumed differences were barriers to their ability to embrace French ways, quite unlike the "Malaysian Merina" whose moral temperament made it possible for them to comprehend—and, perhaps more important, desire—commercial, political, and diplomatic skills and power in French terms. In a somewhat self-conscious moment, Dubois defended his assessment by arguing that Malagasy themselves had an elaborate vocabulary for describing the strengths and flaws of human character.

A far more elaborate critique was offered by Perrier de la Bathie (1931), who explained that workers and progress were not at odds with one another. Nevertheless, the Malagasy clearly required assistance from the French if they were to develop as a race, and thus here he echoes Gallieni's early philosophy of labor exploitation:

> The Great Island is vast and rather poor, and it is sparsely populated. Without work, without order, without labor, this country would remain or become what it was before we took charge of it, an immense land, ravaged and sterile, upon which live in-

dolent and weak peoples who are devastated from time to time by famines and who only set their indolence aside to massacre and pillage each other. French peace, that of Gallieni, has fortunately changed all of that. Yet that is not enough.[37]

Perrier de la Bathie separated Malagasy workers into three categories, and the Sakalava emerge as the most resistant and unreliable of all. These categories inform current understandings of laborers as voiced today by plantation directors in the Sambirano (cf. Sharp 2001b) and so they call for a brief discussion. He considered Antandroy and other laborers from the south to be the most capable and hardworking. He viewed highlanders, and especially the Betsileo, as efficient farmers because of their knowledge of irrigation; and although reluctant to perform wage labor, they worked effectively when allowed to do so independently. The Sakalava, however, "live under precarious conditions."[38] Furthermore, these are "indigenous people who rebel against all forms of work, who do not give themselves over [even] under the constraints or force of hunger or other causes, who are content to live, most miserably, when left to do [as they please], [upon] extensive yet risky agricultural crops."[39] He believed that no regularly cultivated fields could be found in their territory, or at least had not existed before conquest. He credited the military, Gallieni, and other administrators with startling improvements in their cultivation methods. As a result of the Sakalava's inherent slothfulness, however, he predicted that "this great tribe, that had formally conquered half of the island, today is, in effect, in obvious regression [and] on the road to extinction."[40]

When allowed to speak for themselves, Sakalava emerge not as passive and dullwitted creatures, but, rather, as rebelliously insolent (recall Gallieni's frustration with Tsiaraso I, as described earlier). From the inception of the colonial period to the present, Sakalava have staunchly refused to succumb to the demands of the local plantations that still occupy lands alienated from their *tanindrazaña*. This is a fact that frustrated not only colonial planters, but, now, contemporary plantation directors, the majority of whom are currently of highland origins. In the Sambirano, terms that describe local notions of slothfulness and laziness are common, with different ethnic groups often ranked according to their ability—or, perhaps more important, their willingness—to labor for someone else for cash wages. In other words, the conceptualization of "laziness" (FR: *la paresse,* SAK: *kamo*) is locally constructed and invoked differently by competing parties.[41] Much like their predecessors of the colonial era, the directors of the Sambirano's plantations frequently bewail Sakalava as insolent and lazy and, thus, they, too, prefer to hire Antandroy from the south, whom they consider hardworking, albeit fierce and savage (see Sharp 2001b). In contrast, Sakalava are frequently described as people who would rather remain on the edge of poverty (or, more euphemistically, "live simply"; FR: *vivre simplement*) than work for wages.

The words of Mr. Laurent, a thirty-five-year-old bank employee of highland origins, typify the opinions of many of the non-Sakalava elite living in Ambanja. In the following statement, he explains why he believes Sakalava show so little interest in (or, from a Sakalava point of view, have evaded) wage labor, unlike the migrants who flock here from other severely depressed regions:

> You see, here life is not hard enough. You need something to eat? You pull a mango or banana off a tree. What do you need money for? The people here, the Sakalava, they are lazy—they refuse to hold down jobs, and when they do, they quit as soon as they have what they need. And when they do take jobs, their families are angry and do not support them in their efforts. Only the most desperate come [to the Sambirano] to work. But the Antandroy, the Tsimihety, they are another matter. They come because they need work. And the Antandroy especially, they work very hard, because they have many mouths to feed back home. Without their wages, those people will not survive.

As illustrated earlier in this study, however, today students of rural origin may in fact perceive independent peasant farming as far more lucrative and stable than, say, their teachers' careers. As was true of their grandparents, Ambanja's educated youth may in fact embrace a simple rural life because it specifically guarantees a high level of economic freedom.

Legitimate and Illegitimate Labors

An understanding of the significance of Malagasy resistance to SMOTIG is further enhanced if we delve deeper into contemporary constructions of work. Hasina proved impressively articulate in this regard:

> *LS:* I have a question—today, visitors from abroad often complain of the lack of an efficient infrastructure in Madagascar, as well as evidence of a now decrepit one that perhaps worked more efficiently in an earlier era. . . . Can I propose a theory here? Is it possible that, perhaps, Malagasy would prefer to let things go rather than to do this sort of work? For example, every time I see that group of men up the road breaking rocks by hand [for a local rich man's villa], I wonder what makes their efforts any different from the forced labor of the colonial period?
>
> *Hasina:* Yes, I think that's certainly possible. You see, Malagasy don't like to do work that isn't *sitrapo* or "voluntary" [also: "willful" or of one's own desires]: this [on the other hand] is what we call *mitambitamby* ["coaxing," "bribery"]. When it's something that is obligated—that is, *mañery* or, as we also say, *miforcé* [from the French *forcé*, "forced"]—ah, well, no one is interested in doing this.

As I have described elsewhere (Sharp 1993, 49–51; 1996; cf. Feeley-Harnik 1984), the Sakalava concept of work is complex and competes with French constructions of *travail*. In daily life, the Malagasy terms *asa* ("work") and *miasa* ("to work") are applied to tasks that generally require skill or finesse to be accomplished properly. Such forms of work are conceived of as the willful occupation of the performer. *Asa* may also be viewed as a necessary activity, as with skills central to daily survival. For example, one may appear at a friend's house only to be told, "Miasanazy" (or "Miasa izy"): that is, "She is working," perhaps in her rice fields, or preparing a meal, or washing clothes at the river nearby. In performing such tasks, the actor, to borrow from Hasina words, takes pride in her work. Thus, in turn, a child who is described as *hendry* or *mahay* (wise or capable) is one who shows signs of mastering adult abilities. In an indigenous sense, it is in these settings that one speaks of the joy of learning to labor. In contrast to plantation lands where one must work for another, here one labors freely, independently, and for oneself and one's kin and, ultimately, with great mastery and pride. (I discuss this in greater detail in chapter 8, which explores children's labor experiences.)

These values stand in stark contrast to those the Malagasy associate with SMOTIG and other colonial labor programs. In these contexts, the French introduced a new form of work: that is, alienated wage labor, whereby taxation and other new impositions on life necessitated that men especially contract for work on local or distant plantations and factories, sometimes throughout their lives. Northerners found such labor especially loathsome. Fortunately, even limited land holdings often allowed Sakalava to avoid plantation labor, for the valley's fertile soil meant that the occupants of even the smallest of homesteads could still sell produce and animals to pay taxes. They nevertheless experienced the dreadful hardships of SMOTIG.

The Language of Exploitation

One of the most insidious moves by the French was not accomplished through legislation but involved appropriating sacred Sakalava language in order to justify their actions as conquerors. Among the Sakalava, in addition to everyday work *(asa, mi-asa)*, there is also the labor one performs in deference to and love for the ruler. As explained in chapter 4, Sakalava clothe the lives and actions of rulers in a specialized sacred language, setting royalty *(ampanjaka)* apart from commoners or the masses *(ny olo,* "the people," or, simply, the Sakalava). Royalty, for example, do not die *(maty)* but turn around *(mihilaña)*, nor do they inhabit houses *(trano)* but, instead, special residences *(zomba)* and palaces *(doany)*. Similarly, when one works for royalty, one does not labor as in daily life *(miasa)*; rather, one performs "royal service" *(fanompoaña)*, where the setting and circumstances dictate a strict set of practices. Among the most elaborate of these surround rulers' mortuary rites (Sharp 1997) and the subsequent honoring of their might through the periodic care of their tombs and the bathing of royal relics *(fitampoa)* (see Chazan-Gillic 1983; Nérine Botokeky 1983).

As the French sought to usurp Sakalava royal power, they also attempted to appropriate meanings associated with fanompoaña to their own advantage. Specifically, the French hoped, first, to put an end to an indigenous practice that *they* regarded as slavery, and, then, to redirect the devotion of commoners from their rulers to colonial needs through institutionalized wage labor. They falsely assumed that Sakalava would rather work for cash earnings and to further the prosperity of the island than enslave themselves to faltering rulers. Thus, early in the colonial period the French drew upon indigenous concepts of work and sought to incorporate them as part of an elaborate propaganda of labor. Evidence of their simplistic understandings of royal ritual and hierarchy are readily apparent in the early actions of Gallieni, who used the related Merina term *fanompoana* to describe corvée labor throughout the island (Heseltine 1971, 153). Similar language was later incorporated into the rhetoric of SMOTIG. The French also declared Sunday an islandwide Christian day of rest as an institutionalized colonial labor policy.[42] In the Sambirano, this undermined the local practice of honoring Tuesday *(Talata)* as the day when labor was prohibited *(fady ny asa)*, as decreed by local rulers for purposes of royal service. These audacious forms of linguistic and cultural appropriation marked attempts to transform royal institutions, driven in turn by the hope that Sakalava would, in time, offer themselves willingly to the colonial state's needs through modernized forms of fanompoaña.

Shifting Hierarchies

As they undermined royal authority, the French thus sought to transform local hierarchies of power. One ubiquitous example involved the use of the Merina term *fokon'olona* (one that Ratsiraka reappropriated during the socialist era.) Directly translated, it means "community," yet it is also heavily laden with a multiplicity of other meanings and associated sentiments. As a community, the fokon'olona implies institutionalized cooperation shaped primarily by kin-based loyalties (see Bloch 1971). In its application, the French drew on the previous actions of the great Merina unifier (or conqueror, depending on one's station, location, and thus point of view) Andrianampoinimerina (r. 1787–1810), who introduced it as an administrative institution throughout his highland kingdom (Grandidier 1960, 21 ff.; Rajemisa-Raolison 1966, 55–59). The myopia of French colonial practice is embodied in such a decision, for in applying the concept of the fokon'olona to their own methods of rule, they superimposed Merina institutions upon peoples who regarded this highland group as former conquerors. This action only further exacerbated highland and coastal animosities that persist today.

As outlined previously in chapter 4, local rulers such as Tsiaraso I were incorporated into the colonial structure and granted the dubious title of local *gouverneur.* The colonial administrative hierarchy also included local authorities referred to as *notables,* and the French appointed these and other leaders in locations where no equivalent had existed, creating, for example, such positions as *chef de canton* and *chef de village.* Particularly heavy burdens fell on these authorities, who were expected to recruit laborers during times of peace and war, as well as collect cash earnings, produce, and livestock as tax payments. As Maureen Covell stresses, their "privileges were not always great, but even being appointed to organize rather than being obliged to participate in a forced labour group had its rewards" (1987, 21). A patriarchal bias also characterized French rule, so that authority was traced through a hierarchy of male leadership, from the governor-general in Antananarivo all the way down to the male family household head; as a result, they regularly overlooked the authority of women (cf. Feeley-Harnik 1991, 95, on female royalty).

There was also a wide range of educated civil servants and other government employees *(fonctionnaires)* who were trained from an early age to be loyal first and foremost to the French. Within the colonial structure lay a parallel administration that consisted of indigenous authorities who were often called upon to do the dirty work of the colony. It is here that one encounters troubling evidence of a few loyal subjects. One young man, a locally raised Sakalava fonctionnaire named Victorien Tombo, offers a striking contrast to such honored heroes as Tsiaraso I and the nationalist poet Ny Avana, who were his contemporaries. Tombo's story offers a particularly poignant example of the successful colonial infiltration of the indigenous mind, where reformulated ideas of labor, loyalty, and love privileged, not indigenous rights but, rather, the desires of the French colonial empire.

Undermining Royal Authority: Victorien Tombo, a Sakalava Turncoat

Serious conflicts arose on Nosy Be in 1918 between colonial and royal authorities over the legitimacy of royal service. In August, Binao, the Bemihisatra-Sakalava queen and *gouverneur principal* of Nosy Be, decided to sponsor work activities (fanompoaña) at the royal tombs. Fanompoaña is among the most sacred of royal events, where Sakalava subjects honor their ancestral dead and reconfirm their loyalty to the living ruler. A detailed file entitled "Fanampona *[sic]* . . . corvée labor to repair the Royal tombs [in] August 1918"[43] reveals that a tumultuous series of events arose in response to her efforts, for Binao's actions were quickly perceived as an affront to colonial power. Although she was required to obtain permission from the French before proceeding, she appears to have attempted a clever subterfuge, having written an obsequious request designed to reach the local colonial authorities only after this sacred work had begun. Unfortunately, the plan backfired: the work was soon interrupted, and Binao and many of her subjects soon felt the heavy hand of colonial authority. As it happened, the party most involved in levying sanctions against the Sakalava was not the local French commander (who was away on business), but his assistant, a locally raised Sakalava fonctionnaire named Victorien Tombo. The actions of this Sakalava turncoat reveal a man whose life was rife with contradictions, molded by the foreign ideology of power.

Colonial personnel files reveal this about Tombo: he was born around 1880 to Sakalava parents in Antanabe on Nosy Be, and by 1914 he was married to a Sakalava woman named Moboty Mara, but had no children. He entered the colonial administration in December 1909, having been schooled in Antananarivo, where he was trained as a scribe and interpreter. After working in the south in Tulear (Toliara) from 1909 to 1911, he was transferred to Nosy Be, where he quickly advanced through several grades of chef de canton. In 1914, his superior praised him highly as "serious, active, intelligent, speaking and writing our language with great fluency."[44] Tombo proved to be particularly impressive as the chef de canton in Befotaka on northern Nosy Be, where he emerged as a ruthless tax collector. As his supervisor explained, no other Malagasy administrator came anywhere near Tombo's success rates in extracting tax payments in their districts. As a result, Tombo's superior soon recommended him for the position of *gouverneur adjoint;* by the time the events involving Binao occurred, Tombo had indeed been promoted to this position.

Throughout his tenure on Nosy Be, Tombo was regarded as a loyal subject of the French. During World War I, he voluntarily wrote an oath of extraordinary loyalty that set him apart from the majority of his Sakalava contemporaries:

> Dear Sir [Mr. Administrator],
> I have the honor of requesting your assistance in transmitting my request to be enrolled voluntarily in the war in France; I consent to give my life for France, and I would be quite content to be a lone Sakalava amid all these warring peoples.
> I request that you transmit my request with your full support.
>
> *Befotaka, December 2, 1915*
> The chef de canton, V. Tombo[45]

Tombo nevertheless remained on Nosy Be during the war, and he proved especially ruthless when faced with the most significant of sacred royal events in his district.

Word of the fanompoaña appears to have reached Tombo in the form of eyewitness reports from others who had spotted travelers making their way to the royal tombs *(mahabo)* on Nosy Be. Tombo's immediate response was to shut down the ceremony. He then ordered an extensive inquiry into the events (which in itself was an odd move, given that he was a Sakalava man from the region who should have been at least somewhat familiar with the significance of and events that typify a fanompoaña). In many cases, Tombo himself ran the interrogations. Anyone who had been seen on the road either bearing large quantities of food or herding cattle toward Nosy Be was subsequently questioned. The seriousness of Tombo's efforts are reflected in the voluminous paperwork this project generated: records exist for the interrogations of over 150 people. Tombo's efforts targeted local leaders in particular: these were *chefs de village,* royal counselors *(rañitry),* royal spirit mediums *(saha),* and a few royalty *(ampanjaka).* The interrogation of a spirit medium named Moana from the village of Ambatozavavy of Nosy Be serves as a typical example:

Q: What were you doing at the Royal Tombs?

A: I arrived at the Royal Tombs four months ago to work my fields and my harvest rice.

Q: Were there not many people at the Royal Tombs on the night of the 11th to the 12th of August? And what was the purpose of that gathering?

A: Yes: they were there to repair the roofing on the "Royal Fasina [Tombs]" but when a request for the authorization [to do so] was [not granted?], we all dispersed very early the next day.

Q: What did you do that that night?

A: We danced before the Royal Tombs until the next morning.

Q: What are you?[46]

A: I am the "saha" [royal spirit medium] for Andriamamalikarivo, [the overseer] of the Royal Tombs.

Q: What role do you play as a "saha"?

R: I carry out close to the same [sorts of] functions as those of the "rangitry ampanjaka" or the queen's counselors, and I enjoy endless privileges.[47]

[signed Monday, August 19, 1918, by the scribe-interpreter Giamny]

Other participants were asked point blank why they were escorting cattle, and then if they had realized that this was forbidden. Many were also asked to name others present, especially other *rañitry* and *saha*. In one case, the *manantany* (the queen's primary counselor) was pressured until he provided the names of sixty-one people.

Tombo's subsequent recommendations to the French administration were clear and direct: in a memo to his superior dated August 28, Tombo advised that any similar activities be suppressed. He argued that such action was justified because royal ceremonies countered the interests of both the French and the Sakalava. Tombo underscored that royalty were not to be trusted, citing as an example the revolt of 1898, a time when, as he explained, the rulers Tsiaraso I of the Sambirano, Binao of Nosy Be, and their advisors assisted local insurgents against France (see chapter 4). Although these rulers claimed they were innocent, their actions had in fact encouraged local subjects to hate France and the French government. Tombo explained that Tsiaraso I, for example, often held tromba possession ceremonies, and that he and other royalty were controlled by diviners *(mpisikidy)* and spirit mediums (he referred to them as tromba). He likened this to Binao's more recent actions as being similarly "against French civilization."[48] For these reasons the actions of the Sakalava of Nosy Be should be carefully scrutinized, and Binao and her followers should be punished for their actions.

The archival records reveals scant evident of immediate reprisals meted out by the French to the participants of this fanompoaña. Nevertheless, Binao was later pressured to abandon her doany and pass it on to her half-brother, the French forcing her to live in the town of Hellville (Feeley-Harnik 1991, 95).[49] For such an event to occur in a ruler's lifetime was unusual, shameful, and humiliating, serving as evidence of the power of French rule on this smaller offshore island. The devastation of this blow was enhanced by the fact that this triumph was spearheaded by a Sakalava man from the region.

It remains unclear why Tombo sought so aggressively to squelch Binao's efforts to host a fanompoaña and punish its participants. Gillian Feeley-Harnik (personal communication, 2000) postulates that perhaps Tombo came from a village connected with royal service and that his parents may have been former slaves; this could indeed account for his animosity toward the local queen. Unfortunately, the archival records remain silent on these details of his origins. More simply, Tombo had been groomed at an early age to serve the colony, and thus had been estranged as well from his own culture. As such, his story seems at least at first to emerge as a triumph of French schooling and the power of colonial propaganda. Yet subsequent developments reveal that Tombo later approached his mission with perhaps too much zeal even, in the end, for the French themselves.

Tombo resurfaces fourteen years later as the indigenous assistant governor in Majunga Province (now Mahajanga), where, with even greater virulence, he attempted to block a local fanompoaña at the Sakalava royal capital of Boeni.[50] Records show that here he ordered the Sakalava to destroy associated royal structures and desist from holding tromba ceremonies; he also forbade them to honor the local royal ancestor Andriamisara. Tombo also traveled throughout the district delivering a series of formal addresses (kabary) in local villages, threatening Sakalava with imprisonment if they failed to obey his orders. He also told them to go to church, and, further, embracing current French ideology, he even lectured villagers on the importance of agricultural production.

In rapid response, the French administrator for the province received a flurry of formal protests, not only from local village authorities, but from royalty on distant Nosy Be, including a formal and detailed letter from ampanjakabe Amada. Although Amada's letter was addressed to the French administrator in Majunga, he sent additional copies to the equivalent administrator in his own province of Diégo-Suarez, to the mayor of Nosy Be, and to the governor-general of the colony in Antananarivo. Amada underscored with force the destructive and dangerous nature of Tombo's past and present actions, stating explicitly that Tombo had originally been transferred out of Nosy Be because he was a political threat to local Franco-Sakalava relations. Furthermore, Amada also argued that Tombo's renewed hostility defied a long-term agreement, whereby the French had promised to respect local customs in exchange for the Sakalava having welcomed them originally into their territory. Copies of Binao's older request to host her own fanompoaña were are included with his correspondence.

The provincial administrator was compelled to conduct investigations into Tombo's actions. In order to restore local tranquility and avoid any more local conflicts, the Sakalava were, in the end, granted formal, written permission to host their ceremonies. As for Tombo, he then vanishes completely from the colonial records of Majunga and, perhaps from administrative service, too (whether demoted, transferred, banished, or retired is unclear). Tombo's efforts failed to destroy Sakalava royal power because they fueled the open expression of royal anger against the colonial government, upsetting the delicate balance of power that French officials strove to maintain in the colony. Although Tombo wrought irreversible damage on Nosy Be, in the end, royalty throughout Sakalava territory eventually had their own revenge on this indigenous turncoat.

Self-Loathing in Contemporary Discourse

Among the most troubling aspects of colonization is the collective internalization of self-hatred among colonized subjects (Fanon 1963; Fisher 1985; Mannoni 1990; Memmi 1965). An investigation of Tombo's career immediately raises the question of whether or not such developments are evidence of flaws in his own character. Yet another interpretation is that he was the victim of an overzealous colonial education, one designed to transform indigenous subjects like himself to serve colonial desires. Most likely, both are true. If we consider the initial goals of colonization as laid out by Gallieni, the colonial refashioning of the indigenous mind inevitably insisted that Malagasy embrace French ideals and, in so doing, come to loathe their own origins. Such is certainly the case of Tombo, who nevertheless in the end fell victim to the wrath of the very royalty he sought to destroy.

As argued throughout this study, Malagasy youth exhibit an astounding sense of pride in their nation even when they encounter on a daily basis the effects of long-term economic disparities. As a result of their schooling under malagasization, they readily assign blame to colonial practices that ultimately undermined indigenous hierarchies, household structures, and local economies. As Ratsiraka repeatedly stressed, true independence required that all Malagasy reject the ideological underpinnings of colonial oppression, an ideal embodied in his famous declaration "Tsy mandohalika": "We shall not go down on our knees" (1975, 117). At times, however, doubt creeps even into the minds of politicized school youth, who pause to question why, in fact, their nation remains so poor. During his own fleeting moments of self doubt, even Hasina was driven to say that "Madagascar is poor because Malagasy are lazy."

Today, during times of economic crisis in Madagascar, outsiders are typically targets for local rage. Most frequently these are merchants of foreign origin who are blamed for sudden increases in prices for essential items sold in their stores. In July 1994, however, I witnessed a surprising shift in Ambanja (a town that in the past had remained peaceful when elsewhere foreigners or their property were attacked). Instead, it was rural Sakalava who bore the brunt of urban anger. At this point in the year, Malagasy had experienced repeated currency devaluations that dug deep holes in their pockets. Throughout Ambanja, many rumors circulated about the wealth reaped by independent peasants who, until then, had always been celebrated as the backbone of Madagascar's economy.

My friend Antoinette's reactions were typical. Antoinette is thirty-four and the daughter of Tsimihety and Sakalava parents, and she was born and raised in Ambanja. As a landless petty merchant, she ekes out a living by selling such inexpensive yet indispensable items as matches, kerosene, tinned tomato paste, and a few baked goods and other prepared snacks from a stand she sets up each day in front of her small rented house. She also works from time to time sorting produce at a local concession to help make ends meet. As she declared angrily to me one afternoon, "Why, just the other day a man came in from a village and bought not one but *three* VCRs for his home—one for him, one for his wife, and one for his children! But does he work as hard as I do? Never! He only has to tend to his fields occasionally, while I must hold down several jobs to feed my five children."[51] When I asked how such a man could actually power three redundant video systems in a village that probably had no electricity, Antoinette blurted out, "He would have several generators, of course!" In reality, however, it is hard to imagine a peasant so rich, and, in 1994, no such man, even if he had the cash, would have been able find three VCRs, three generators (and three televisions) for sale at any one time in Ambanja.

With these themes in mind, let us return to Hasina's troubling words. Clearly, within his cohort of politicized youth, self-doubt and even self-hatred occasionally can surface in otherwise well informed critiques of colonialism. In a world of rich and poor, colonizers and colonized, First and Third worlds, it is those who resist who may still at times question their own motives or, more important, the weakness of their national character. Others experience the anger and frustration voiced so openly by Antoinette, who resents the successful efforts of a mythical peasant, one who ironically embodies the ideals of an agricultural nation that struggles to feed itself, and who even exemplifies the life led by her own grandparents. Her jealousy is fueled by the peasant's assumed independence, because in 1994, Antoinette, like other landless urban dwellers, found herself more vulnerable than ever to the precarious nature of national and international economies. Whereas Sister Estelle provides her students with critiques for understanding long-term colonial exploitation, Hasina at times expresses self-doubt, and Antoinette, at her worst moments, despises her own people.

As illustrated throughout part 3, young Malagasy men were significant targets of exploitative colonial practices, their labor power deemed essential to building and maintaining the island's economy. Men at least as young as sixteen were forced to serve as foot soldiers in war and corvée laborers in peacetime, and it was not unusual for such demands to dominate much of their adults lives. They bore the brunt of colonial success, for only through their labors could the French develop an impressive infrastructure of roads, bridges, communication systems, and waterworks. All of these were essential to the productivity of foreign-owned plantations and other industries, both of which occupied lands alienated from Malagasy. The demands of colonial service not only taxed the physical strength of men, but forced many to become salaried wage earners as well; furthermore, these imposed intense suffering on individuals, households and entire communities. Among such sanctioned forms of colonial enslavement, SMOTIG emerges as the most dreadful of all, robbing local communities of many of their most productive workers. The legacy of colonial labor policies has subsequently been a troubling obstacle for the nation's presidents, as Tsiranana and then Ratsiraka forged their own visions of independence. Under each, school youth emerge as a significant players in determining their ultimate failure or success.

Colonial oppression did not end here, however, for the French demanded loyalty from their subjects, too. From Gallieni on, labor legislation was driven by a duty to reshape and thus colonize the mentalité indigène. Labor practices were consistently framed by the ideological understanding that colonial subjects must be transformed into willing, productive laborers who wholeheartedly embrace capitalist colonial desires. The Sakalava emerge with rare exception in this context as among the most perplexing of colonized people, for they remained steadfast in their refusal to serve the colony.

As Tombo's career illustrates, however, the French did succeed in colonizing a few. The lesson here is that colonial exploitation can engender the internalization of self-doubt, and, in the end, a hatred for one's own people as well. Such possibilities are even possible in contemporary life, as exhibited by responses generated by Hasina and Antoinette. Hasina is a particularly perplexing example, since he speaks on the one hand of the pride of the Malagasy, yet doubts still linger in his mind as to why his country consistently occupies Third World status. As his words show, self-blame can overshadow his thoughtful critiques of colonial hegemony, as imparted by such gifted teachers as Sister Estelle. At times, Hasina wonders if, perhaps, "Madagascar is poor because Malagasy are lazy." Such a statement fully embodies the long-term destructiveness of the colonial legacy, which can poison even the thoughts of Ambanja's more enlightened youth. In the chapter that follows, Dalia offers a radically different reading: highly reminiscent of Ratsiraka's preachings, she insists that colonial practices have simply been reshaped to serve neocolonial agendas.

PART FOUR

Youth and the Nation: Schooling and Its Perils

The French occupation of Madagascar transformed myriad social categories, reducing rulers to petty royalty, sons and fathers to foot soldiers, and peasants to enslaved legions of peacetime laborers. Women's experiences differed because they were so frequently sexualized: not only did they harbor the ability to reproduce labor, but some also became the *deuxième bureaux*, or mistresses, of colonial men. As this slang expression implies, female sexuality was laced with danger, for the original Deuxième Bureau was the French office of state security. In contemporary discourse, the prostitute in particular has the ability to sabotage both household and national stability. Such fears also frame localized understandings of the vulnerability of schoolgirls, for whom video cinemas and discotheques define special urban perils that threaten their scholastic success. Girls are said to respond most readily to highly sexualized foreign values and practices, succumbing in the end to prostitution as a form of urban survival. Prostitutes more generally bear the blame for a new foreign invasion, their bodies harboring AIDS, which threatens this already fragile island nation. With these trends in mind, chapter 7 explores the gendered nature of urban danger and its relevance to school success.

If women's bodies harbor danger, then children embody the nation's future dreams. Yet childhood, too, is rife with perils. A host of diseases can end children's lives suddenly and tragically, and additional hazards lurk in the schoolyard. Whereas chapter 4 opened with the sudden death of a beloved ruler, chapter 8 focuses on the terrible passing of a successful student who, as a target of anonymous jealousy, falls victim to potent forms of magic *(fanafody raty)* that kill or maim students in the prime of youth. His tragic tale demands an assessment of the larger values assigned to children, who emerge as a precious form of wealth for their kin, community, and nation.

CHAPTER 7

Girls and Sex
and Other Urban Diversions

TOWN GIRLS

It is midafternoon in July 1994 and I am visiting with Dalia in the small and comfortable room she inhabits with her younger sister, Flora. At her prompting, we have been discussing problems specific to schoolgirls' lives: sexual encounters, unwanted pregnancies, and their effects on academic success. Suddenly she looks at me and says, "Are you interested in medicinal plants, in the *fanafody-gasy*?" Although puzzled by what seems to be an abrupt shift in topic, I say yes, certainly. We are then up and out the door, making our way down the road to a small house where her grandmother lives. We see her in the yard, a woman perhaps in her early sixties who is busy washing clothes at an outdoor spigot. Freshly washed sheets already hang from a line, being bleached by a midday sun that beats down so hard that they are certain to dry within half an hour.

This grandmother's garden is a truly wondrous place, exhibiting a copious array of plants. It is unlike any other I have ever seen: rather than being arranged in neat rows along a grid, hers consists of small trees and bushes scattered haphazardly throughout the yard. I immediately recognize imposing guava, mango, papaya, and coconut shade trees. Beneath them springs an assortment of *feliky*, or edible greens, as well as pineapple and manioc, a single small wild coffee plant, and some banana trees. Just over a little bend behind the house I also catch a glimpse of bright green rice paddies. Although the region's rich flood waters are ideal for wet rice production, I am astonished—after all, seven years ago I lived only a stone's throw from here, but oddly I had never noticed this patch of *matsabory*. A row of tree stumps provides a clue as to why this area previously remained hidden from my view.

Dalia begins her tour with the air of an expert. I first point to one tree whose bark has been stripped. Dalia says, smiling, "You see, people have been busy removing the bark for medicine *[aody, ody]*." I then ask about a tall papaya that has large gashes cut in its trunk, and ask if it, too, has been used for this purpose. "Ah, no, that's a Malagasy custom of sorts—if you have a tree that won't produce anything, you get a little angry at it and you hit it, over and over, yelling, 'Give me fruit! give me fruit!'—ha ha!—and, you know, it agrees and does it!" I then remember how my own grandmother used to "beat" her house plants to make them flower. I ask if this is a typical garden—is this what I would see if I went deep into the countryside? To this Dalia replies, "Oh, no. Here we usually plant trees of the same kind all together. Coffee with coffee, bananas with bananas. But this is the way my grandmother likes it. She has done it this way for a long time. Now, let me show you what she has."

And so we tour the garden. It is a lush array of many plants, each with medicinal properties: I recognize *mapaza, mahogo, avocaty, katra*—papaya, manioc, avocado, and the heavily-seeded *katra*. And then many others whose names are new to me, with medicinal effects that range from curing headaches, to stomach woes and malaria, to listlessness and insomnia. I soon realize, though, that Dalia has brought me here because several are known by schoolgirls to be powerful abortifacients.

Independent Rural Girls in Town

At twenty-one, Dalia is a feisty and popular student enrolled in her terminale year at the state-run lycée.[1] Her parents, both of whom are retired schoolteachers, currently live in a village just a few kilometers north of town where they sharecrop a quarter of a hectare of land.[2] They themselves are from Nosy Be and Ambanja; her father is Antankaraña, while her mother's parents are Sakalava and Tsimihety. Although Dalia was born in Antalaha on the northeast coast, she has lived in the Sambirano since 1979, and so her peers consider her to be tera-tany. Dalia is the oldest of eight living children, the youngest being three years old; a year ago a ninth boy died at age fifteen from heart failure. In 1990, Dalia and her sister Flora relocated to Ambanja in order to further their schooling.

These two schoolgirls currently share one side of a simple, two-room thatched falafa house that belongs to a maternal aunt, who, like their grandmother, lives nearby. Much of the land in this quiet neighborhood is in fact their aunt's. She inherited this property from her own father, who settled here in 1937, on what was then the outskirts of Ambanja, establishing the lush fields of matsabory just beyond. Dalia and Flora pay her no rent, instead regularly giving her gifts as informal payments including such luxury items as yogurt and soap, or fresh produce bought in the local markets. Over the course of any given month, these are worth approximately FMG 15,000–20,000, a high price to pay when viewed as rent for their single room. In so doing, however, they assist an aunt and an aged grandmother economically in exchange for other forms of care these elders provide them while they are in school. In other spheres, these two sisters carefully economize on their daily and schooling expenses. Each month they eat about one *daba* (a large kerosene can) of rice, which costs approximately FMG 38,000. As typifies the lives of many school migrants, Dalia and Flora go home on foot nearly every weekend to work their parents' fields, at which time they acquire additional food to eat.

Although small and dark, their room is airy, especially when the two large windows are open. They find it a peaceful place to live, especially because the tenant next door is frequently gone for long stretches of time. Their room is furnished with two single beds, two comfortable small tables, and a squat, unstable bookshelf, upon which they store some of their study materials. Other notebooks are stacked high on a large tin can with a touch of kerosene inside, an effort designed to prevent insects and rodents from devouring these precious items. Whenever I drop by, I find the house neat and tidy, the beds made up and covered with wrinkled but clean sheets, one embroidered with flowers, the other with the words "Danga maro tia" or "Many like *danga*" (a kind of rice that is popular in the region). Cooking pots are stacked neatly in the corner, and the front courtyard is carefully swept. They cannot afford electricity, and so at night they rely on feeble oil lamps when they work on their homework assignments. Each time I visit Dalia, I experience an intense nostalgia: I know this house well, for throughout 1987 I spent many hours there attending tromba ceremonies hosted by its former inhabitant, a spirit medium and gifted healer named Marie. The bulk of Marie's clientele consisted of schoolgirls who suffered from bouts of possession sickness or unwanted pregnancies, problems that inevitably brought their schooling to an abrupt end (Sharp 1993, 188–96). Marie has since relocated to a town further south, her dwelling now inhabited by two successful schoolgirls.

Like all homes in Ambanja, the walls are decorated with an array of colorful pictures. Unlike most I have visited, however, there are no international soccer stars, images of foreign seascapes or industrial parks, or even the ubiquitous shots of scantily clad Asian women torn from inexpensive calendars distributed by local merchants. Instead, I am surprised to see the faces of well-known American pop stars. In the room's darkest corner loom the large, imposing images of Michael Jackson and Michael J. Fox, a reclining Patrick Swayze, and Brandon from *Beverly Hills 90210,* along with Gérard Depardieu posing for the American film *Green Card* (fig. 11). Whenever I visit this house, I can't help but feel I am being scrutinized by these men, especially the pensive Mr. Swayze. On two other walls are mug shots of African students who, by writing to francophone teen magazines, advertise their interests to prospective pen pals. Their serious faces offer evidence of students' imaginings of a global network of peers whom they will never meet. There is also a faded world map sent by a Canadian who taught for a few months in Ambanja, and a calendar from a local hotel with the dates of July 25, 26, and 27 circled and marked *bac.*

Dalia is respected among her peers for her strong will, her clearly defined desires, and her wry sense of humor. She also strives regularly to help others. Her home is a popular gathering spot for her friends, especially Foringa (who is her boyfriend), Pauline, Jaona, Hasina, and Félix. In addition, this year she organized an evening study group for the end of the term at the state-run lycée, persuading

Figure 11. Inside a schoolgirl's home.

town officials to keep the building open and lit at night so that students from all local lycées would have a quiet place to prepare for the bac. Dalia is a formidable student who is at the top of her class. Her French is superb, so she has opted to take
the bac in that language and not official Malagasy. She nevertheless failed on her
first attempt in 1993, as did the majority of her classmates.

When I asked Dalia one day what she liked or did not like about school, she
looked at me with a puzzled expression. Tsarahita, in response, sought to help her
by rephrasing the question: "What makes you suffer *[mijaly]* and what gives you
pleasure *[mahafaly]*?" After much thought, Dalia responded as follows:

> No, no—I understand the question. But it's that I like practically everything . . . I love
> to learn. But you see, before I was in *terminale série* D [the science core]. I was getting
> these horrible headaches that would last for days. I finally went to see [Dr. B.], and
> he said I was working too hard—that science was too hard for me, so he said I should
> change to *terminale* A. I hated doing it, because I really love science, but it was mak-
> ing me ill. *[Terminale]* A is easier and, so, I'm now more satisfied with my studies and
> I suffer less than I used to.

This doctor's assessment was not an unusual one; as I knew all too well from
conversations with Dr. B. and the town's other health professionals, the presump-

tions that informed his advice are rooted in older colonial constructions of a mentalité indigène. Although at first glance it may seem that he judged science too difficult for a girl, he in fact views coastal students as less capable than highland ones.
In a sense, this is not far from the truth, not for the reasons he might suppose, but
rather because lycée lab facilities in Ambanja are useless, lacking crucial supplies
and even running water, and there are no trained science teachers on the staff.
Dalia's response, however, was not to drop out of school but, rather, to choose a
more realistic path. Driven by her thirst for knowledge, she followed the doctor's
advice and shifted to terminale A, and by mid 1994, she was preparing for her second attempt at the bac.

Dalia passionately wanted to attend university, where she now hoped to be
trained to teach philosophy, or perhaps history and geography. In so doing, she
would establish a tradition in her family, for both of her parents are retired primary
schoolteachers who attended the prestigious teacher academy in Joffreville outside
Diégo. As I learned later from a letter written by Tsarahita, Dalia did in fact pass
her exams, but she could not afford a university education. At her parents' urging,
she relocated to Diégo, where she now lives with and assists a paternal uncle who
runs a small but flourishing dry goods store. She now intends to apply specifically
to the local campus so that she can continue her studies while working.

When I returned to Ambanja in mid 1995, I was surprised to hear from a number of Dalia's teachers that the real reason she had ended her studies was that
she was pregnant. These proved to be false rumors, however, as Tsarahita and others close to her assured me. Although Foringa had been her serious boyfriend for
several years, Dalia was well versed in abortifacients drawn from the local phar-
macopoeia, and she often assisted other students with this knowledge, acquired
from her grandmother. I also knew that she made regular use of the local family
planning program at the state hospital, where she received monthly injections of
Depo-Provera. I soon began to realize that teachers assumed that so gifted a student must have fallen on hard times if she had indeed failed to continue her schooling at university to the south; Foringa, after all, had also passed the bac and was
now studying at Toamasina. But whereas his parents were able to pool resources
from a large extended family, Dalia's faced far greater economic hardships and
could ill afford to send her to university, even when her schooling would be subsidized by the state.

As such rumors reveal, a schoolgirl's life is assumed to be plagued with special
dangers, where her own sexual coming of age may inevitably undermine her ability to succeed in school. As underscored throughout part 2, many girls are deeply
committed to their schooling and, in fact, may be less likely than boys to fail. Yet
other pressures threaten their long-term success, and these are linked to their sexuality. Ultimately, many are forced to drop out of school because of unexpected
pregnancies. But other capable girls never even enter the upper grades, because
their parents are so fearful of their involvement in what is assumed to be a highly
sexualized urban world.

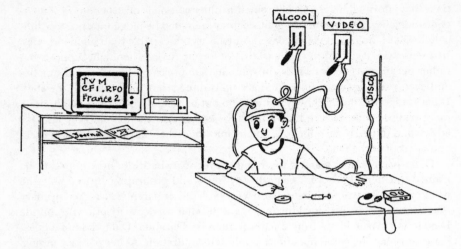

Figure 12. Town diversions and the corruption of youth. From *Akony ny Sambirano* 1994, 27. Reprinted with permission from the editor.

WORLDLY DIVERSIONS

Over the course of nearly a decade of research in Ambanja, I have found that the towns' school administrators, teachers, and parents have consistently reiterated the same themes when I ask them about problems in their children's lives. As described in chapter 3, video cinemas and discotheques are assumed to pose the greatest threats to students' social and psychic well-being. Adults argue that foreign music and films "destroy our children" and "their minds," "are responsible for school failure rates," "keep our children out of school," and "undermine their respect for local ancestral customs [*fomban-drazaña*]" and "for one's parents." (For a student's rendering of these themes, see fig. 12.) Another dominant assumption is that solitary school migrants are especially vulnerable: lacking adult supervision, they are most likely to succumb to their allure, wasting their precious study time and limited funds on such corrupting diversions. They choose instead to stay out late, carousing and drinking heavily, so that by midmonth they have no money left for food or essential school supplies. Then, as they struggle to make ends meet, boys turn to petty thievery and girls to prostitution. These factors contribute to the social corruption of students, who fall asleep in school, fail their studies, or altogether disappear from the classroom. Girls are assumed to be in greater danger, because they inevitably fall pregnant. With these concerns in mind, I turn to the imagined dangers versus the realities of girls' lives.

Cinemas and Disco Dangers

Urban adults identify as especially threatening the provocative messages embedded in media of foreign origin—as encountered through television, the cinema, and discotheques—that promote Western materialism, excessive violence, and licentiousness. These pose the greatest threats to rural innocents, especially to solitary school migrants. Yet, as I argue in chapter 3, town-based students are in fact more likely to be exposed to foreign visual media. School migrants lack the necessary pocket money and leisure, typically seeking out part-time work or establishing their own small businesses to help make ends meet. Many also travel home nearly every weekend to assist kin in their fields. As explained earlier in this study, cinemas and discos are in fact frequented by slightly older adults in their late twenties and thirties. If students do view videos, they usually do so at the Alliance Française, whose director is a school principal. Students flock here to perfect their French, watching popular westerns imported from India, Italian-made "commando" films, and martial arts extravaganzas from Hong Kong.[3] Nevertheless, a pervasive sentiment, voiced by Mr. Jaozara and others, is that foreign media threaten to transform students' mentalités, driving them in the end to embrace foreign values. In so arguing, such critics ignore the fact that teachers themselves make advances to students. By locating the origins of such dangers beyond their own community, they thus expose larger fears of foreign invasions now seen as threatening the tranquility of life in postsocialist Madagascar.

In order to understand more clearly the experiences and sentiments of migrant school youth, I asked all students I encountered, "What do you like to do for fun?" Dalia responded, "I love to listen to the radio." At first, because of the posters on her walls, I assumed this meant that she liked French and American pop music, but she surprised me by explaining, "Ahh, no, I love sentimental Malagasy music . . . and I like to *promenade,* that is, *mitsangantsangana* [SAK: 'walk about town with friends']."

"Do you go to discos or the cinema?" I asked.

"No, I hate discos," she replied. "I go to maybe one a year; [besides,] they're expensive, you know—they're regularly FMG 1,500 or 3,000 . . . and during holidays as much as FMG 7,500."

As I learned from other interviews and through observation, it is not poor, rural migrants who venture to discos but, rather, urban youth from prosperous middle-income households. The offspring of upper-level civil servants, successful merchants, and state health professionals, for example, have the greatest access to the town's public diversions; furthermore, it is a mark of social privilege to be able to attend them. In contrast, Dalia and her friends typically only promenade the streets at night, perhaps pausing briefly to view the televised broadcasts from the mediocre set mounted above the doorway of the Firaisana, or city hall. Similarly, younger children from the town's most modest homes rely almost exclusively on outdoor, inventive forms of social play. The youngest can be seen playing together energetically with whatever tools they might encounter on the street: sticks turned into swords, abandoned car chassis into percussion instruments, and a *bricolage* of plant material, wire, and twine that they fold, twist, and bend into elaborately fashioned miniature cars and other brilliantly made toys (cf. Cerney and Seriff 1996). In short, the poorer the child, the greater the demand placed on the imagination for daily distraction and play, and the more limited the exposure to foreign media.

Elite children define yet another extreme category of experience rarely being permitted to venture beyond one another's homes, where, cooped up and bored, they rely heavily on the distractions offered by television and VCRs. Such children may watch repeatedly bootleg music and film videos copied from French television and hand-carried to Madagascar, which slowly make their way about town, passing from one elite household to another. These also offer shows not readily available in the town's cinemas. Some are dubbed reruns of *Starsky and Hutch* or *Dallas;* many others feature films far more violent or sexually explicit in their dialogues, lyrics, and visual displays. The offspring of elite households also have the added ability of being able to understand what is being said. Like Vonjy in chapter 2, they are often fluent in French, a language they may speak not only in the classroom, but at home with their parents.[4] The lives of two young girls, Rova and Rachida, illustrate this range of experiences.

An Elite Housebound Child

Rova is the precocious oldest daughter of a town-based elite Betsileo household. In mid 1995, she had just turned seven. Her father is a powerful plantation director, her mother a housewife and part-time petty merchant. This family employs two full-time house servants, a private chauffeur, and a night watchman, and they inhabit a luxuriously furnished three-bedroom house that is partially air-conditioned and has two bathrooms with European plumbing, including bidets. Their most prestigious possessions include two cars, a large color television set, and a VCR. Little Rova attends the town's exclusive French Elementary School, where she speaks French exclusively (as she does at home with her parents), and where she is known only as "Rosalie." She never ventures out of doors unescorted by an adult, and she is allowed to travel the town's peaceful streets only when driven by the family chauffeur. Her playmates are hand-picked by her mother and are always the offspring of other elite Betsileo families, which also represent important business contacts for her father. Rova spends much of her time at home, her only regular companions being her younger brother and two family maids, to whom Rova feels little emotional attachment. In a word, Rova is bored: although she loves to read, she has no books, and her toys are typically so expensive that they spend much of their time on display in a tall glass case in the family parlor. When Rova has nothing else to do, she watches—often repeatedly—her parents' rotating collection of borrowed videos, many of which contain frightening images of brutal murders or lurid sex scenes that run drastically contrary to modest Malagasy conceptions of public displays of affection. On many an afternoon, I have encountered Rova sitting by herself on the sofa, her mouth agape as she stares in awe at the images displayed before her. Her strong, deep-seated identification, not with her ethnic origins, but with her parents' accumulation of expensive commodities of French origin, is shown by the fact that when I first met her and asked what her full name was, she replied "Rova Renault!"

It is, of course, difficult to predict Rova's future as a child of Ambanja's migrant highland elite. The snobbery that characterizes members of this small, exclusive class has, however, already begun to make its mark on her psyche. Rova fears contact with other children, and she reveals a keen sense of difference, especially when confronted with children of lower social status, at which point she will remark quietly on their tattered clothes, for example. As a Catholic, Rova attends only the French services at the town's imposing cathedral, and she assumes that those who go to Malagasy services are less devout than she. In 1993, when she was almost six, Rova refused to leave her family car and descend into the street to join me and other children parading with paper lanterns on the eve of the annual independence celebration. Surprised by the invitation, she responded coolly that she "had a headache," making a dramatic swooning gesture with her hand on her forehead to emphasize its debilitating effects. She preferred to stay in the car with her chauffeur. Later that evening, as a guest in her home, I watched Rova and her little brother run about on their second-floor veranda, creating their own private parade, until the two-year-old boy brought the celebration to an abrupt halt by dropping his lantern and setting a tablecloth on fire.

Ambanja's Little Lucifer

Rachida, who at eight is only a year older than Rova, stands in strong contrast to the latter. Unlike Rova, Rachida was born and raised in Ambanja. She is the oldest of three children whose father is Arab-*métis* (his mother is Sakalava), and whose mother grew up 300 kilometers to the south but settled in Ambanja nearly fifteen years ago. By Ambanja's standards, this is a fairly typical low-to-middle-income tera-tany household: Rachida lives in a somewhat dilapidated concrete house facing the central marketplace, built nearly fifty years before by her paternal grandfather, a Yemeni migrant and merchant. Rachida's mother Yvetty, her household's primary breadwinner, is an energetic woman who works hard as an itinerant merchant. Off and on, Rachida's parents own various luxury appliances: perhaps a modest portable stereo system, or a color television set, or a small refrigerator, each being an item that Yvetty has acquired in trade. These vanish, however, as soon as cash is needed to make ends meet. Each month, Yvetty makes the arduous two-to-three-day journey to Antananarivo to buy coveted imported goods, such as clothing, which she sells at a high markup in Ambanja and Nosy Be. Rachida's father occasionally makes money, too, primarily by selling contraband acquired from a brother-in-law who is a customs official. Usually, though, he lazes about the house; when Yvetty is gone, he tends only half-heartedly to his children and household.

Until the age of seven, Rachida was a local hellion, a rag-tag little girl who often refused to go to school and ran wild with other young children. She could often be seen playing outside, kicking up much dirt and dust as she darted about at high speed, perhaps waving a large stick over her head. She was never within earshot when someone needed her to run an errand. In response to her reputation as a wild child, a favorite uncle referred to her affectionately as his "little Lucifer." But by the middle of her seventh year, Rachida showed signs of transforming into a wise or clever *(hendry)* child. She started to devote herself to her studies, helping older kin with daily household tasks, and mastering rudimentary marketing skills. Throughout the week of independence festivities she rode herd on her two younger siblings, the three of them sitting in the shade on the main road selling party hats and other favors to child clients their own age (Sharp 1996; fig. 13). Her mother Yvetty and other female kin are now grooming her to be a merchant: soon Rachida will be trusted to help her favorite Auntie Mariamo in one of her two shops alongside two older female cousins, and perhaps, too, she will accompany her mother on her monthly excursions to Antananarivo. On the evening of Independence Day in 1994, Rova, again in her Renault, drove past barefoot Rachida, who marched proudly through the streets with her cousins of many ages, bearing examples of her finest wares. Rachida carried a paper lantern, balanced carefully to protect the lit candle inside, and, in her own extravagant style, she wore not one, but two colorful hats, one with "Commando" stenciled on it, the other facing backward in order to display the name "Zorro."

Wayward Daughters

As illustrated above, the more prosperous the urban-based household, the greater the potential exposure to foreign mass media. As illustrated by Rova's life thus far, children in elite households may be confined to their homes and left to amuse themselves with privately owned videos unavailable elsewhere in town. Rova may escape the assumed dangers of the disco or cinema simply because her parents will inevitably send her to a highland boarding school, where she, like Vonjy (chapter 2), will remain under lock and key. Nevertheless, at seven, Rova is more aware of things foreign than Rachida will be perhaps a decade later. Conversely, while Rova lies idle at home, Rachida is busy developing an array of sophisticated business skills, which, if fostered with care, may enable her to master a lucrative market trade like her mother (see chapter 8).

If we shift to the lives of older girls, clearly those from prosperous professional households are most likely to become involved in the town's night life. This is true because they have pocket money to spare as well as leisure time on their hands. The

Figure 13. A children's market stand.

latter is especially true if a part-time servant works in the house, freeing them from a range of domestic chores. Their ability to attend disco parties becomes socially important, marking their elevated economic status in public arenas. Yasmine is an example.

Yasmine is the daughter of Alida, a woman whose life I have followed closely since 1987 (Sharp 1993, 214 ff.),[5] and who is well known in Ambanja as a nurse, her name being practically a household word in town. Alida is now widowed, but her husband was a highly respected school principal, who provided well for his family, so that she now owns a large, five-room concrete house with an enormous fenced-in courtyard. Although the house lacks indoor plumbing, it has electricity and, for over fifteen years, it has been furnished stylishly with lovely armchairs, a color television set and VCR, a stereo, a gas stove, and a refrigerator.[6] A side room, where she receives clients as a skilled part-time seamstress, houses an Italian sewing machine. Alida must work long hours and at odd times, and so she employs a young girl to help her clean house, wash dishes, and do the laundry. This servant's assistance also gives Alida's children far more free time, ostensibly to devote to their schoolwork.

Yasmine is the second child and oldest daughter in this family of six children. In 1987, when Yasmine was sixteen, Alida was deeply concerned about her children's futures. She longed for her oldest son, Abel, to attend university and succeed in medicine, as had her own father, so she appealed repeatedly to a well-known tromba spirit medium named Marivola for powerful magic *(fanafody-gasy)* that would boost his chances for success. Meanwhile, Yasmine, who was often seen carousing with men her mother's age and older, had become a source of much frustration and worry. Alida openly expressed her fear that Yasmine would become pregnant before completing her studies, only to be thrown aside by a reckless philanderer. (I suspected in fact that Yasmine had already had one abortion, although confirming this proved difficult, since abortions were illegal in Madagascar in 1987. Alida, who had strong contacts in the town's medical community, certainly could have seen to it that Yasmine had a safe and secret one, as well as subsequent access to legal forms of birth control.) In her attempt to rein in her daughter, Alida took Yasmine for a personal consultation with Marivola, whose spirits threatened the girl with illness and other dangers if she did not obey her mother and take her studies seriously. For the next few months, Alida attempted to confine Yasmine to the house, but this proved impossible, because Yasmine not only had to go to school every day but also ran errands for her mother. Once school was out, I frequently encountered her sauntering around the town with classmates, and twice in the back of a bar with her two closest girlfriends.

When I returned to Ambanja in 1993, Yasmine was twenty-two, and her mother's fears had in part materialized. Yasmine had indeed failed in her studies at the private Catholic Academy and thus never completed lycée. Possessing few skills worthy of her station, she remained unemployed and spent much of her time idle at home. She had also become the mistress (deuxième bureau) of an older, wealthy married man, who picked her up each afternoon in his air-conditioned Peugeot. Although Alida knew the man would never marry her daughter, she was resigned to Yasmine's behavior. This situation was well known in town, since Alida and Yasmine's lover were both prominent citizens. Nonetheless, the sight of the couple barreling down main street each afternoon inevitably raised a few eyebrows.

Town opinion among adult professionals was divided on this affair, which cut across the categories of age and class. Schoolteachers who already knew Yasmine were especially vocal in their opinions. Mr. Saidy, a lycée instructor with three daughters of his own, argued that Yasmine was now, after all, capable of bearing the responsibilities of adult life and should not be condemned. In any case, it was clear that Alida appreciated the extra money provided by her daughter's lover. Yet many others—including Mme. Chantal, Mr. Prosper, and Mr. Jaozara—argued that Yasmine had sacrificed her virtue to become the deuxième bureau to a powerful married man. As this label implies, she posed a threat to his marriage and household, her actions likened to covert military operations (see Sharp 1993). Other critics were even more forceful in their comments, calling her a *makarely,*[7] or prostitute. Such critical sentiments could only be expressed in the slang of a foreign tongue, where Yasmine was perceived as following a path long ago established by other young northern beauties who had served as lovers to colonial officials. All parties agreed that Yasmine had sealed her fate, for in time her rich lover would inevitably abandon her. She would then drift among men in search of the wealth and prestige that inevitably accompanies such unbalanced relationships, trailed by a string of children fathered by men reluctant to assert paternity.

As Yasmine's example illustrates, town life offers numerous temptations for students with time on their hands. The greatest problems arise when a girl suddenly finds herself pregnant, because all of Ambanja's public and private schools impose strict sanctions on such girls, although not on their male partners, even if their identities are known. When a girl's pregnancy becomes obvious, she is immediately expelled from school and, typically, close kin are contacted by school officials so that they can care for her until she bears her child. Although in recent years, the state-run lycée (but not the Catholic Academy) has begun to readmit girls once their babies are born, few girls are able to juggle the demands of young motherhood while attending school unless their mothers or other older female kin are willing to assume virtually full-time responsibility for child care. Because nearly all mothers in Ambanja breastfeed exclusively, they must remain in constant proximity to their babies throughout the first year of life. As a former school director argued at an education conference in the mid 1980s, Madagascar could not hope to make strides in controlling adolescent pregnancy as long as boys went unpunished and were allowed to remain in school (Sharp 1990). His words fell on deaf ears, however, and the burden of pregnancy (expressed in Sakalava by the term *mavesatra* or, literally, "[to be] heavy") is thus the sole responsibility of girls themselves.

Ambanja's teachers argue that although the handful of girls who remain in school each year are often their best students, collectively girls show less interest than boys in completing their studies. The reasons that inform such impressions are complex. For one thing, many girls never even make it past primary school, because parents are generally reluctant to let their daughters advance, if this requires that they become school migrants. As a thirty-year-old engineer named Gérard explained in 1987,

> I completed my studies here at the Catholic Academy eight years ago, and then I went on to university. My parents live far from here, out in the countryside on the Ampasindava Peninsula. You see, I had a primary school teacher who was impressed with my school work, and so when I completed troisième and passed the qualifying exams for middle school, he went to my parents and persuaded them to let me come to Ambanja to continue my schooling. It took a lot of doing—my father needed me to help him in the fields, and both of my parents were afraid to let me go so far away. They finally consented only when the teacher agreed to accompany them here to help me find a safe place to live. My parents have never talked about it, but I think my teacher may even have helped pay part of my tuition that first year; in exchange, my parents gave him a little bit of land to farm. It was hard for me—I was very lonely those first few years. But now we are all happy I did it. Look at me—I have a good job as an engineer at one of the local plantations. But my sisters, no, my parents would *never* have let any of them go away alone to school. My father was certain they would have gotten into trouble and fallen pregnant in no time. It was only after I was established here that I myself persuaded my father to let my youngest sister come here to study. The others, they are all married now and have children, and nearly all live in my parents' village. Only one [of them] ever even completed primary school.

In other words, girls do not necessarily drop out of school but, rather, require special protection if parents are to let them leave home for advanced schooling. This may necessitate the intervention of older siblings, other relatives, or teachers who recognize their abilities. As I have argued elsewhere, many schoolgirls suffer from an extraordinary angst when they suddenly find themselves pregnant. Pregnancy signals school failure, and their suffering is compounded by their knowledge of their parents' great disappointment. This is a trend that characterizes the lives of school-girls throughout Africa; as Caroline Bledsoe and her colleagues stress, "having a child effectively terminates a girl's education" (Bledsoe et al. 1993, 10). In Ambanja, preg-nant schoolgirls are frequently struck by disturbing forms of possession sickness, through which they articulate their frustration, guilt, and sorrow (Sharp 1990).[8] Some seek spiritual intervention from skilled tromba mediums like Marie; others turn to a classmate like Dalia who is familiar with locally available abortifacients. Against these developments, the average age at marriage has climbed slowly for Malagasy boys over the past two to three generations; their female peers, on the other hand, must withstand pressure exerted on them at a younger age by older men, who may be local merchants, well-off travelers, or, frequently, their own schoolteachers.[9]

Controlling Pregnancy

It is late morning, and very hot outside. Dalia, her boyfriend Foringa Josef, their classmate Félix, Tsarahita, and I rest within the cool interior of Dalia's small room. Dalia and Foringa have chosen the topic of discussion for today: a comparison of our respective customs *(fomba)*. We discuss burial practices, tombs and cemeteries, Thanksgiving and Christmas, and the events that are important markers in our per-sonal lives: births, cutting teeth, circumcisions, and wedding anniversaries. Then Dalia asks suddenly, "What about abortions? Can you get them in the United States?" My response typifies my middle-class American academic feminist lean-ings: I begin by talking about *Roe v. Wade,* and the manner in which legal statutes define the beginning of life and personhood in my own society. I then ask, "When do Malagasy think a baby becomes a person *[olo]?*"

> *Foringa [right away]:* At birth, of course, just like you, or when it's still in the mother's belly. Abortions are illegal here because of this.

> *Dalia [after thinking a moment]:* No, now, wait, I think she means what's the Malagasy way of thinking about this. Think about the old people—they don't think this way, do they?

> *Foringa and Tsarahita [together]:* No, no, right. It's different. Now we say the baby in a mother's belly is a person, but the old way . . .

> *Tsarahita:* It's when a baby cuts its teeth . . .

> *Foringa:* Right, when it's a *zaza mena vava* [lit: "a child with a red mouth"].

> *Dalia:* Exactly. This is when it's a human being.

> *LS:* But how do you say "person" as opposed to something that's not yet one.

> *Félix:* You say *olo* instead of *tsaiky.*

LS: What happens if a baby that isn't yet a *zaza mena vava* dies? What do you do with it?

Félix: You bury it right away. You don't wait a few days like you would with an adult. You can bury it wherever.

Dalia: No, where [my father comes] from, on Nosy Be, you find a tomb that is especially for babies. You put them all there, or you put them directly in the ground.

LS: Can you put a baby in a tomb?

Tsarahita: No.

Dalia: No. At least not in the tomb that adults go in.

LS: So what about those other ceremonies? When do you give a baby its name? When do you cut its hair?

Tsarahita: Well, now you name it when it is born . . .

Dalia: Right, most people do this. But the old way was to wait until it cut its first tooth.

Tsarahita: This is still the moment when you cut the baby's hair for the first time. As we say, this is when it's a person because this is when it can eat rice: *mety mihinambary.*

Félix: Mety mihinam-akoho ["it can eat chicken"], ha ha!

Dalia: Akoho ["chicken"] !?

Félix: Sure!

Tsarahita: That's not the expression!

Félix: But it can eat it! You give it the thigh [so it will learn to walk].

Dalia: OK, right. . . . But we were talking about abortions.

LS: The plants [you showed me the other day], how do you use them? Do you eat them raw and as they are?

Dalia: No, no. You boil them really well and then you drink the water.

Tsarahita [with a touch of frustration]: Yeah, but none of them work—*mapaza, avocaty, katra.* None of them.

Dalia: Let me tell you what we use here for abortions.

LS: I understand *feliky mapaza, avocaty, katra.*

Dalia [laughing]: You can't say *"feliky"* for leaves you don't eat. *Feliky* means edible greens. Instead, you say for example *ravin-mapaza* [papaya leaves] for leaves you don't eat.

LS: What other plants are abortifacients?

Dalia: Oh, there are lots.

[Dalia, Foringa, and Tsarahita detail a wide assortment of medicinal plants and their uses.]

LS: With medical abortions, how does this work? It is surgical?

Dalia and Tsarahita together: No, no, it's an injection in your rear end.

Dalia: . . . plus antibiotics.

Tsarahita: . . . and a tetanus shot.

Dalia: Oh, right.

LS: Does anyone use anything else? I heard sometimes you can put a stick in the uterus.

All together: No, no. [A few minutes later, however, Dalia returns to this subject.]

Dalia: I think some put *feliky mahogo* [the leaf or twig of the manioc] in the uterus. It's a little stick. You leave it there for 48 hours.

LS: That's *very* dangerous.

Dalia: I know, but if you have no money, what else can you do?

LS: How do you say birth control in Madagascar? Or family planning?

Together: It's FISA, Fianakaviana Sambatra. It means "happy family" [or "wise" and thus "healthy family"].

Perhaps partly because I was older, because of the trust engendered by repeated visits, and especially because of the changed political climate, this discussion was much more candid than those I had had in 1987. Under President Ratsiraka in the 1980s, birth control was very hard to acquire, and although performed by a few doctors in private practice in the north, abortions were illegal. In 1987, I knew a handful of women who received Depo-Provera injections, but no other clinical form of birth control existed in town. By the early 1990s, however, the range of possibilities had changed radically. Injections of "Depo" were sometimes free, and the FISA office at the state hospital now dispensed spermicide in suppository form for FMG 400 each; the pill at FMG 300/month; and *kapoty anglais,* or condoms, for FMG 100–150 a piece. As far as I know, IUDs and Norplant were not available,[10] although in 1995, I assumed that at least the latter would arrive soon: the ease with which it can be dispensed to rural women is highly appealing to foreign population specialists, who regard Third World women as dangerously noncompliant. This is a theme that Dalia herself raises below.

THE IMMORALITY OF PLAY

Current town-based critiques of foreign media underscore their potential to corrupt Ambanja's youth and, more particularly, schoolgirls. Their danger lies in their assumed power to encourage immoral and sexualized forms of play, a reading conventionalized through long-term exposure to values of colonial origin now internalized by educated adults in Madagascar. Judgments levied against the imagined activities of migrant youth on the one hand and Yasmine's own experiences on the other expose a double standard. Social critics are quick to focus on the naïveté of rural girls, who are assumed to be more readily seduced by the allure of sexualized urban realms. This critique, however, skirts the historical relevance of the colonial encounter, thus ignoring the unequal and potentially predatory nature of foreign men who relied on the sexual favors of Malagasy women. As we shall see, school youth like Dalia are in fact deeply aware of this legacy.

Yet, adults' critiques are often laced with a prudishness that assumes that discotheques and video cinemas are dangerous milieux because they introduce exotic and newly eroticized forms of play, where the sexualization of public display sanctions promiscuity, machismo, and militarized violence. Within this framework, mass media evidence a new foreign invasion that followed the fall of Ratsiraka's isolationist regime. The long familiar sounds of upbeat horn orchestras from the Antilles, the intoxicating rhythm of African *kwassa,* and the repetitive, slow-paced reggae born in Jamaica have since been joined by the latest arrivals from the United States: erotic videos starring Madonna and the crotch-grabbing gyrations of Michael Jackson. Music videos that precede the main film also feature opulent displays of material wealth and consumption, where dark men escort light-skinned women in expensive cars, luxurious homes, or flashy boutiques, where the clothes are garish and the food consumed outlandish. Viewers inevitably wonder how they can hope to touch such luxuries when they remain unavailable in shops in town or even in distant Antananarivo. In the feature films themselves, one finds the inspiration for the ostentatious consumption in the musical shorts. Yet here clearly the greatest social and economic power rests with Anglo or Asian males who are strong, single, and virile: Stallone and Schwarzenegger, Eastwood and other cowboys, and Bruce Lee and other kick boxers and kung-fu masters from Hong Kong.

Objections to these media underscore, too, assumptions regarding the inherent vulnerability of minors, whose imitative and provocative gestures might perhaps signal some form of bravado or even effete resistance but certainly not cultural maturity. In short, children may periodically challenge the status quo, but they lack the social sophistication or deeper cultural knowledge that would enable them to levy sophisticated critiques or generate sustainable cultural forms (cf. Stephens 1995; Amit-Talai and Wulff 1995). Keeping in mind the renovation of the Palais Royal by Tsiaraso Rachidy IV, however, yet another interpretation emerges: school youth are in fact highly innovative in their reformulation of contemporary forms of play.

Ny Soma

Sharon Stephens (1995a) argues that the notion of play provides an especially provocative paradigm for challenging the assumed innocence and cultural immaturity of youth. She asserts instead that youth may in fact be creative social actors who, through cultural inversions, may generate imaginative and sustainable cultural forms. When viewed in this light, the discotheque is not a *degenerate* space but, rather, offers evidence of *generative* forces at work. When set within the framework of older culture forms, the disco and its associated behaviors no longer appear as radical departures from social norms. Rather, together they offer evidence of a highly embellished indigenous style of social expression as shaped by *les forces modernes.* The embodied gestures of the discotheque in fact share much in common with other festive ritualized events so familiar to the Sakalava of the Sambirano.

Nowhere is this more evident than during festivities hosted by local royalty. Within any large-scale royal ritual in the northwest—a royal child's first hair cutting, a prince's circumcision, a ruler's instatement ceremony, or the annual cleaning of royal tombs—much of the surrounding festivities are defined locally as valued moments of "play" *(misoma)*.[11] These involve, characteristically, dances (especially the graceful *ribiky)*, praise singing as well as bawdy songs, and possession ceremonies, during which time both living subjects and ancient spiritual ancestors arrive to participate in such "games" *(ny soma)*. Nighttime in particular is a liminal period of sexual intrigue, where adults *and* youth participate in group singing, dancing, and drinking, and also stroll about *(mitsangantsangana)* in search of erotic encounters. In anticipation, girls and women may spend a significant amount on new clothes. For large-scale royal events, their attire most often consists of matching body and head wraps fashioned from commemorative cotton cloth *(lambahoany)* that has specifically been designed and printed at the nation's textile mills for these ceremonies. Groups of young friends may travel long distances together unaccompanied by older kin; sticking close together throughout the event, promenading girls dressed in identical outfits merge to form moving masses of brilliant colors (fig. 14).

What, then, renders such events so significantly different from the discotheque? What are we to make of the organized party (FR: *bal* or *boum)* held in the lobby of City Hall, or perhaps in the same indoor market structure that, during the day, houses rice sellers, vegetable hawkers, and butchers, or even at the Palais Royal by the beach at Ankify? During bals or boums, the nighttime again provides a veil behind which one may seek out new sexual partners and participate in eroticized play, where the female body in particular is elaborately decorated with preordered and individually designed, flashy garb, this time consisting of tight and tailored dresses of bright satins or polyester silks. Men, too, pay close attention to their appearance, sporting brilliant white running shoes and T-shirts purchased at inflated prices from Ambanja's boutiques and itinerant street merchants. At these town events, a successful sexual encounter can involve pairing up with an anonymous single or married partner. In other words, the spirit with which one approaches the royal festival and the bal are similar; it is simply the milieu and attire that define where the most radical innovations occur.

The paradoxes that underlie judgments of such events are perhaps best exemplified by occasional celebrations and fund-raisers hosted by the Catholic Mission. Not only is the mission's congregation dominated by Sakalava parishioners, but most of the staff are also Sakalava, including the monsignor and a throng of lively and outspoken sisters, although a handful of priests are European. The mission hosts a celebrated annual disco night—complete with an electric *salegy* band—that begins in the late evening and runs until dawn, organized each year by the Catholic Academy's lycée students as a school fund-raiser. The majority who attend are the town's adult professionals, although the mission's students, priests, and nuns also join the dance floor. Disapproval is nevertheless voiced in some quarters, especially by the town's more observant Protestant vahiny. These critics claim to shun such

Figure 14. Young girls at the Royal Antankaraña Tsangantsaiñy festival, 1987.

events as mildly sacrilegious, perhaps stressing their disdain for one particularly animated nun who goes by the name of "Sister Disco." Yet even they may find it difficult to stay away from this lively event, especially since it attracts the town's most powerful elite. Their disapproval of the use of the animated body inevitably exposes a prudishness of foreign origin, one that collides with the joyfulness associated with indigenous forms of social play. In the end, once this patina is penetrated, it becomes difficult to distinguish the spirit with which one participates in such events, be they staged at a village ceremony or on an urban disco dance floor.

Ny Sida

Here the discussion could end, were it not for the current complications that link sexual intimacy and infection. Beginning in the 1990s, sex was now laced with physical danger in Ambanja, as AIDS, or *sida (syndrome d'immunodéficience acquise)*, as it is known in the francophone world, emerged as a public health concern. Madagascar, by virtue of its assumed doubly isolated status—as a socialist nation and a remote island—had until now been imagined by its inhabitants as having escaped this pandemic. In 1987, for example, AIDS was assumed to be only an impending threat in Ambanja, and local health officials would regularly cite as evidence a survey of coastal prostitutes, all of whom had tested negative for the virus.[12]

By 1994, however, the epidemiological picture had shifted (partly in response to the fact that President Zafy was a physician). AIDS was now openly recognized as a grave threat that had only recently invaded Madagascar's borders, brought from abroad not so much by Malagasy travelers or sailors as by thrill-seeking foreign tourists drawn to this island by dreams of sexual encounters with exotic African women.[13] In Ambanja, local clinics now displayed posters on AIDS, radio soap operas included stories of the infected, and relevant public health messages were integrated into the state curricula. At home, children and parents would debate the topic, with students usually being far more informed than their parents on the biological modes of transmission. A predominant assumption was that a new wave of foreign invaders was responsible for this impending threat. Whereas only a handful of foreigners appeared in Ambanja in 1987, by the mid 1990s, the town had emerged as an important site of activity for the World Bank and IMF, the Peace Corps, and new environmental initiatives. Ambanja was also experiencing a radical increase in the flow of itinerate tourists, for whom the town's hotels offered a comfortable overnight stopover. By 1993, the idiom of foreign invasion shaped local commentaries, informed by indigenous understandings of the colonial encounter. Such associations were foremost in the minds of politicized school youth.

Liza, the Girl with Sida

One of the most significant sources of AIDS education among Ambanja's lycée students is a comic book that chronicles the life of a Malagasy girl named Liza (fig. 15a and b). *Liza* was issued during the 1993–94 school term as a volume of *La Plume*, a quarterly school publication funded by and developed through a French-Malagasy partnership based in Antananarivo. *La Plume* was among the first curricular materials to reach Ambanja in nearly two decades, and enough copies were sent so that every teacher could have one. The lycée acquired a surplus and distributed the extra copies to students. A review of this story uncovers pervasive themes that link youth and sexual dangers.

Liza's tale is designed to be highly reminiscent of the lives of lycée students throughout Madagascar, even though the scenes depicted are unquestionably in Antananarivo. *Liza* thus emerges as a generic morality tale intended for all Malagasy school youth. As an elderly storyteller explains in the beginning, Liza was a village girl who dreamed of being a great singer. Although this is a nearly impossible aspiration for a rural girl, her drive and intelligence allowed her to succeed. Such aspirations, however, inevitably drew her into the fast-paced, highly sexualized world of foreign popular culture.

Liza's story resonates strongly with Ambanja's students, because she, too, is a school migrant. As the reader soon learns, when she is twelve, Liza's father takes her to Antananarivo to live with her loving Aunt Marthe so that she can continue school beyond the primary level, and Liza quickly excels in her studies. Here Liza is also exposed to the wonders of the city: historical monuments, imposing churches, and . . .

well-dressed prostitutes. As a lycée student, she is invited to her first boum in a class-mate's home; respectful of her elders, she first asks her aunt's permission to attend. Liza feels terribly out of place at the party, and so she decides to leave, at which point her hostess introduces her to Mike, who works in the music industry. He invites her to dance, and by the end of the scene, Liza agrees to sing publicly for the first time, inspiring an enthusiastic response from her classmates.

Mike soon becomes Liza's serious boyfriend, and she eventually decides to invite him home to meet her parents. Upon their arrival, however, she realizes that her parents await her with a prospective husband. At first, she vehemently objects, but in the end she honors their wishes and marries him, leading a serene life as a doting mother and active community member. Her marriage eventually fails when she discovers her husband in bed with another woman, and so she leaves him, obtains a divorce, and gains custody of their children. It is at this point that she pursues a career as a singer. She establishes a group called the Crazy Zebras, and they are an instant success in Antananarivo, Paris, London, and New York. Although she is courted by her dear friend André, she remains single. Mike cautions her to be prudent, but Liza takes many lovers (see fig. 15b): older and younger men, Malagasy and perhaps foreign (their relevance will be discussed below).

Eventually, Liza begins to show signs of fatigue and illness, and word of this soon hits the press. Mike accompanies her when she consults a doctor, who informs her that she has tested seropositive for AIDS. Liza, in shock, exclaims: "WHAT?! I have AIDS, me? . . . But I was never a drug addict! . . . I never had a transfusion!!! . . . Are you sure? . . . Redo the tests!!!"[14] Among her first fears is for her children, but later they and Mike, too, test negative, underscoring the idea that she contracted AIDS while on the road for her new career. That night Liza has terrible nightmares: she imagines herself as a demon, driven from her village by an angry mob; she is judged "guilty" by a court of law; monsters beckon her to hell; and she, too, becomes monstrous as she lies dying in a hospital bed. She later asks Mike to help her guard her secret. Distrustful of condoms, she decides to be celibate. She continues her career, while also remaining a good friend and mother to those she loves. In the end she is hospitalized; following a visit from her closest friends, all of whom are men from the music world, Liza dies alone and quietly in her sleep. André assumes the guardianship of Liza's children, and, posthumously, she gives a hefty donation to the national program responsible for combating AIDS in Madagascar. The comic book ends with a detailed question and answer section in French and official Malagasy that covers such topics as modes of transmission, medical terminology, and preventative measures. Here, as part of a campaign that advocates safe sex, abstinence, fidelity, and sex between virgins are all equally encouraged as partial solutions.

This comic book promotes several ideas relevant to this current study. The first is the strong contrast between rural and urban life, where, more than anything, wealth and urban diversions are portrayed as corrupting forces in Liza's life. This is evident in the appearance of the prostitutes on the street, and in the boum held at her class-mate's home, the latter being where Liza first truly participates in the fast-paced life

Figures 15a–b. *Liza* comic book cover and selected page. From Madagascar 1994.

of the capital. It also emerges in the character of her bourgeois husband and, finally, in the international whirlwind of the pop music world. All of the characters in this story (save, perhaps, Liza's husband) are portrayed as decent people who strive to do the right things even when the demands of a situation contradict expectations promoted throughout childhood. Liza, a rural girl at heart, is always kind and thoughtful: she honors the wishes of her elders by studying hard; she never stays out late; she marries a man chosen by her parents; and she funds community projects. Her only fault is that she naïvely falls into a fast-paced, sexualized cosmopolitan world as she pursues her career as a singer. In this elite urban world, her most intimate relationships are not with girlfriends or, as typifies village intimacy, siblings,[15] but, rather, with a string of anonymous lovers and male musicians like Mike. This transformation inevitably characterizes the social demands of the world of pop music. Most striking of all, though, is the fact that Liza alone contracts the disease, signifying yet again the special dangers associated with the assumed sexual promiscuity of schoolgirls.

Youth on Sex and AIDS

After I learned of *Liza*, I actively sought out students' reactions to this story. A significant factor that shaped their responses was the issue of private as opposed to public schooling. Whereas students at the state-run lycée have read and might even own a copy of this comic book, it is unknown to those at the Catholic Academy. The latter are, nevertheless, exposed to AIDS education through oblique references during general school lectures on health and hygiene, and more elaborately through radio plays and other broadcasts, and during discussions with peers. In June 1995, I organized a focus group with ten seminarists in order to talk about mass media images of foreign origin.[16] Unlike students from the state-run lycée, only one seminarist had even seen *Liza*. This is the discussion that followed:

Alphonse [Looking over the comic book and saying wistfully]: Liza.

Bert: What's this?

LS: Have you all seen this?

[Only one of ten are familiar with it; three remained silent throughout this discussion.]

Christian: What's it about?

Alphonse [paging through it]: She's a singer.

LS: It's about a girl who contracts AIDS.

David: [Takes it from Alphonse and opens it up.]

Edmond [Looking over David's shoulder with Bert, Edmond, and Ignace]: She's from the country.

David: When she was very *young* she was from the country. [David later passes the comic book around to others.]

LS: What do you think of AIDS?

Edmond: It is a mortal danger.

Florent: It's brought by foreigners.

Alphonse: Comoreans...

Florent: ...vazaha [European foreigners]...

Ignace: ...Africans.

LS: Africans? Which Africans?

Ignace: Comoreans then.

LS: Do you learn about it in school?

Alphonse: Ahh, no.

Christian: It's on TV, the radio.

Edmond: And at "Sanitary Central"—at the hospital they talk about it.

LS: How do you keep from getting it?

Ignace: They talk about the value of marriage. And condoms.

LS: Is there anyone here [in Ambanja] with AIDS?

Alphonse: Ahh, no, not yet, but its coming.

Bert: But there was a vazaha here who had it. Oh, it's just gossip, you know. He was dead from AIDS is what some people say.

LS: Tell me more about him.

Bert: He lived in [the neighborhood] behind the mission.

Christian: He was about 35.

LS: He was from Ambanja?

Bert: No, he was staying in a hotel.

Christian: No, no—I think he rented a home.

David: Me too, over by the Hotel W.

LS: He died at the Hotel W?

Bert: Oh no.

David: It's what people say happened. You know, its just talk.

Alphonse: A rumor, not official news.[17]

LS: So, how do you get AIDS?

Alphonse: Blood transfusions...

Ignace: ...and sexual contact.

Bert: But a lot of people don't believe it.

Alphonse: Or they're from villages and know nothing.

LS: Any other ideas that are false about transmission?

Christian: What are you taught in the United States?

LS: [I review three major categories: unprotected sexual intercourse, blood transfusions, and needle sharing for drug use.] But my father has this strange idea that it is transmitted by mosquitoes.

Alphonse: Yeah, some people here think that, too, because they are full of blood. But then I guess that means we all have it! [We all laugh—mosquitoes are ubiquitous in Ambanja, especially at night and throughout the rainy season.]

Christian: Others think you can get it when you get a shot with the same needle at the hospital.

LS: But that's true! that's really serious![18]

These seminarists' reactions to *Liza* were enlightening, particularly because this was the first time they had seen the comic book. A primary theme that caught their attention involved contrasts between a fast-paced urban life and village ignorance. As Alphonse describes the uninformed, "[T]hey're from villages and know nothing." A second idea I wish to pursue here is the imagining of AIDS as an invading force that has only now begun to threaten Madagascar. Alphonse, Florent, and Ignace state this explicitly, identifying Comoreans, vazaha, and Africans as lethal carriers. This sentiment is also embodied in tales of Ambanja's assumed first victim, a man with no local kin ties who is alone, white, and foreign.

These themes were also expressed by members of the cohort from the lycée, yet they differed in that they offered more critical and politicized analyses of Liza's life in the age of AIDS. A brief excerpt from a discussion at Dalia's house is exemplary:

LS: What do they tell you at school, in the hospital, etc. about AIDS and how to avoid it?

Foringa: They say, *"Tsy mijangajanga"*—"Don't go sleeping around"—like a prostitute *[makarely]*, or *"Tsy mañano makotipa"* [literally, "Don't do bordellos"].

Dalia pulls out her copy of *Liza* and opens it to the page where she is shown embracing different men (fig. 15b). I ask about their appearance, because, to me, one looks blond and European, whereas the others seem dark but have hairstyles more typical of African-American than Malagasy men.

LS: What are they, *Gasy? Vazaha?* [Malagasy? European/white?]"

[They respond together]: *Gasy jiaby!* ["They're all Malagasy!" I am surprised, and so I ask them to explain.]

Dalia: . . . That's what this is all about. All the characters are Malagasy.

LS: Hmm, OK. Now, can you explain a term for me again? Why, for example, would you say *mijangajanga?* Doesn't *mijanga* imply that one is healthy?

Foringa: You say *mijangajanga* because it is a person who is in great shape—and so they want to go out and about, they want to strut their stuff. . . . But in the end they aren't healthy. And so the message here is "Don't be a prostitute."

Dalia: But you know, it's more complicated than this. It's just a new form of exploitation: foreigners have imposed their fomba, their ways on us from the beginning of colonial contact. They like to tell the Malagasy what to do, and what is wrong with our culture. They don't like our marriage practices, they don't like our ancestral customs [*fombandrazaña*]. And now, look what they are doing—they say we have too many children, we have too much sex. And so they impose the threat of AIDS upon us, too.

Imperialism and the Fear of AIDS

As all of these students' responses make clear, AIDS in Madagascar is framed by broader understandings of foreign invasion. Most frequently, this is articulated in reference to the island's isolated status and recent trespasses across its ocean borders. Yet Dalia adds another dimension, couching her analysis in the deeper historical meanings of conquest and colonization. AIDS emerges in this context as a public health crisis generated from abroad, signifying the hegemony of foreign values and, thus, the associated dangers they impose on the inhabitants of an already marginalized (and, ultimately, intensely vulnerable) African nation. Dalia's arguments thus place the blame for this pandemic squarely in the context of foreign imperialism.

Paul Farmer (1992) similarly underscores the complexity of what he refers to as the "geography of blame" associated with AIDS in Haiti. Briefly, he identifies three concentric rings of accusation that radiate from the center, or village, to the nation as a whole, and then beyond its borders as a legacy of empire. Thus, within each ring, understandings of AIDS are first shaped locally by sorcery accusations; second, by larger national themes of social stratification and racism; and, finally, by globalized fears that ultimately relegate Haiti to pariah status. Dalia's astute comments clearly echo some of these themes in Madagascar as well.[19] But whereas Haiti is blamed for worldwide infection, Madagascar remains vulnerable to AIDS's impending dangers.

Current concerns for Madagascar's vulnerability stem from islandwide understandings of the breakdown of their nation's long-term isolation and, thus, new impending threats to national security.[20] Under Ratsiraka, Madagascar was shielded from the outside. By virtue of socialist isolation, few foreigners ventured to its shores. Furthermore, as a large island that sits virtually alone in the Indian Ocean, it has preserved a protected status of sorts, its watery boundaries making it difficult for unwelcome visitors—along with their practices and ideas—to venture here. Thus, a collective understanding especially throughout the Second Republic was that Malagasy were safe from infection. Under Zafy's Third Republic (and beyond), however, air travel, radio transmissions, and television via satellite opened the nation to a host of foreign forces. By the mid 1990s, ecotourists and other foreign pleasure seekers had begun to flood the northwest, potentially spreading this dreaded disease through sexual encounters with Malagasy women.

By 1994, I found that anxieties surrounding the mysterious and lethal quality of AIDS had begun to generate an elaborate body of folklore, with tales reminiscent of fears of child snatching in Latin America (Campion-Vincent 1997; Leventhal 1994). The tales I heard in Ambanja inevitably exposed the underbelly of foreign relations, with particular emphasis placed on exploitative and predatory practices. Rachida's mother Yvetty, a trader who travels frequently to Antananarivo, offered an especially chilling example:

> Outside Madagascar, a team of foreign scientists has discovered that the AIDS virus can be found clustered prominently in girls' brains. For this reason there is a clandestine trade, a black market, that involves acquiring their heads! A bus driver told me this story: A middle-aged woman gets on a bus, and she's carrying a basket that is very heavy. She's really careful with the basket, and she won't let anyone touch it. It has to stay with her all the time, even though it's big and takes up a lot of room, because she refused to let the driver put it on the roof. When it comes time to pay the bus fare to the driver, however, she doesn't have any change,[21] and so she sets off in search of some, leaving her basket behind. It is during her absence that the contents are discovered: the basket gets in someone's way, and so they disturb it, knocking it over and exposing what's inside. It is full of the severed heads of young women! She has killed them and cut off their heads to sell them to her contact overseas, who wants them for research purposes to develop a serum against AIDS![22]

As Yvetty's gruesome tale underscores, independent girls are now potentially both victims and villains. Although, like Liza, they are warned by elders and friends to be "prudent" sexually, they may nevertheless fall prey to the lures of urban life. Furthermore, they themselves now harbor greater dangers. Whereas the deuxième bureau and makarely have always threatened domestic tranquility, today these young, daring, and unattached women shoulder the blame for undermining the collective health of their own nation. Because the prostitute cannot be controlled, she bears the potential of becoming a Malagasy AIDS Mary. This theme inevitably emerges in the public health messages embedded in such stories as *Liza*, exposing new forms of "scientific imperialism" (Lyons 1997, 136 ff.), as well as the sexist and racist underpinnings of AIDS research in Africa (cf. Harrison-Chirimuuta and Chirimuuta 1997). As Dalia herself asserts, "They say, we have too many children, we have too much sex. And so now they impose the threat of AIDS upon us too." Yvetty's story uncovers an even darker message: that such girls are now the special target for predatory capitalist desires.

Who, then, in the end are the true victims? Yvetty's chilling tale offers one answer. In the international trade in human body parts, those from young women and girls are perceived in northern Madagascar as highly valued commodities (cf. Burke 2000a and 2000b, Comaroff and Comaroff 1999, Masquelier 2000, and White 2000). Herein lie references to the political economy of scarce and precious goods of a macabre nature, where the heads and brains of Malagasy women can be harvested to serve the needs of the wealthy abroad (cf. again Farmer 1993, 230–31). Only once foreign demands for items of quality are exhausted will the remnants perhaps return home, serving the needs of the nation's elite before the final dregs fall to the poor in dangerous and virulent form. Such is, to borrow Michael Taussig's phrasing, the reality of the "magic of [the] modern" (1987, 274–83). As he illustrates, in contexts where medical care is woefully inadequate, one confronts a troubling paradox. What, in the end, is more lethal: inferior products of foreign origin, or imaginative—albeit often life-threatening—local responses to the void left by, at best, mediocre health care? In this vein, Yvetty's story conveys symbolically the nightmarish anger and fears that sometimes characterize Malagasy readings of neocolonial agendas.

Under the imposition of colonial power Malagasy women were prime targets of a very particular form of attention, taken as mistresses by men of foreign origin and thrust into the role of prostitutes or mistresses in ports and other towns. As this chapter has shown, the pairing of guilt and distress plague girls and young women in unique ways unknown to their brothers and male partners: over historical time, and over the course of their lives, they suffer, first, from school failure, rooted in the experience of the unwanted pregnancy; they bear the local shame associated with prostitution; and, now they bear the responsibility of a national death associated with AIDS. In the end, it is girls and women who consistently bear the heavy burden of sexual trespass as they once again fall victim to the predatory nature of foreign desires.

CHAPTER 8

The Social Worth of Children

"Oh, Madamo é, mampalahelo be—misy tsaiky lahy maty. Maty izy. Mampalahelo. Mampalahelo be" ["Oh, Madame, it's so very sad—a boy has died. He's dead. [It makes one] sad, so very sad"], Maman'i'Ricky, a bookkeeper in the county accounts office, said to me one morning. Her office window is low to the ground and overlooks a path I use, and so for several years now I have often stopped by simply to say hello before venturing out on a day of interviews and other research. On this specific day in July 1994, however, Maman'i'Ricky did not greet me in her characteristic fashion, smiling and full of silly jokes and teasing me about my work. Instead, she was clearly disturbed and saddened, and she uttered these words with great difficulty. She nevertheless remained stalwart and shed no tears, for such behavior would be dangerous in the shadow of death. As she explained, her office director's son, Achille, was dead. Everyone who worked at the fivondronana was rattled—how could harm come to so productive and healthy a young man? The accounts office was in complete disarray, everyone appearing dejected and forlorn, and work had come to a near standstill in the director's absence. My heart, too, was heavy for the rest of the day: although I did not know the director well, I, too, mourned his loss.

This chapter explores the social worth of children in Ambanja, my discussion set against the sudden death of a treasured young man cut down in the prime of youth. If, as Ratsiraka and other politicians have repeatedly argued, Madagascar's future rests with its children, then sudden tragedies such as this only further accentuate the lifetime sacrifices made by kin and communities to enable youth to succeed in so precarious a world. Life in Madagascar is rife with danger, and thus elders must be vigilant in their efforts to usher youth beyond their early years, through schooling, and into adulthood. The urban schoolyard emerges as an especially perilous milieu, where the very students who succeed academically may quickly become the targets of virulent forms of jealousy. Thus, their very survival depends upon the care of older kin who ultimately require their labor for their own survival. Because so much hinges on a child's success, some adults or other students may resort to destructive forms of magic that can maim and even kill their victims, who are inevitably the most gifted students. These developments are explored here in reference to larger concerns, where the focus then shifts to an analysis of children as wealth in Madagascar. As I shall show, their value hinges simultaneously on adults' deep emotional and economic investments in their children. Such institutionalized practices as child fosterage offer especially lucrative ways to share this wealth among kin. In the end, the most valued of all are those who successfully integrate knowledge acquired in school and in the domestic sphere. Such children labor carefully, skillfully, and willingly to ensure the economic independence of their own kin; at times, boys' and girls' experiences vary radically within their respective domains.

LOST YOUTH

The Death of a Beloved Son

Within a few days of Achille's death, much of the town was abuzz with the story. Shortly after my encounter with Maman'i'Ricky, I was scheduled to meet with Félix in order to interview him on schooling in Ambanja. As I soon learned, Félix and many of his peers had already heard the news, and they were deeply distressed by Achille's sudden death. Félix lives a stone's throw from the director's house, and he had witnessed much of the comings and goings in preparation for Achille's wake and funeral firsthand. As we sat and talked on Félix's veranda, our conversation was periodically punctuated with the wailing and sobbing of mourning female kin only two houses away.

Félix, like his friend Hasina, is yet another outstanding lycée student. At eighteen, he stands poised to take his bac exams for the first time. He is the son of Tsimihety parents, and the third of seven children (one of whom died in his teens). Félix is currently the eldest of four who now live with their mother, who brought her family here when Félix was seven, following the death of his father. Ever since, she has worked steadily as a clerk at the fivondronana, a job she finds tedious but one that has to be done if she is to feed, clothe, and educate her children. When she first arrived, she sought out the distant kinsman of a dear friend, who soon agreed to watch over her as her *fatidra,* or blood brother,[1] and he offered to rent two windowless yet spacious rooms to her for pittance. Félix's labor is indispensable to his mother, who works long hours, and so when he is not in school, he is inevitably at home working in the family courtyard, perhaps pounding rice with a tiny brother or sister, their pestles beating rhythmically against the inside walls of a large, weathered wooden mortar. When he has leisure time, he is inevitably playing soccer nearby with a few classmates. By virtue of his parentage, Félix is vahiny, but his peers and teachers consider him tera-tany, because he has spent most of his life here and because his mother was born in a village only slightly to the north. As he explained one day, "I've been here a long time and I speak Sakalava like [a local] and so everyone thinks I'm Sakalava. So [my vahiny identity] doesn't matter much when I'm in school." I suspect that his popularity at school plays a part here, too: Félix is quick to assist others with their studies, and he is known for his wacky yet friendly sense of humor.

Félix knew Achille well and was deeply distressed by the death of a young man he considered a friend, peer, and role model. His mother is a longtime friend of Achille's mother, because the two women were schoolmates from an early age. Thus, on the day following Achille's death, she had already ventured to the director's house, taking Félix and his siblings with her so that they might pay their respects. Such visits not only convey sentiment; they also help absolve friends, neighbors, and relatives of any suspicion of guilt or malice. As a close friend of Achille's family, Félix's mother assisted them in a host of ways for, as Félix explained, "because their own [kin] are far away, the two [mothers] are like sisters to each other." His mother took the next day off so that she could mourn with the family during the wake that preceded Achille's entombment.

As Félix and others would repeatedly emphasize, the director's son was well known as one of Ambanja's greatest successes. Achille could claim extraordinary accomplishments, and everyone I encountered struggled to come to terms with how he could have died so suddenly and so young. "Well, see, the way Malagasy think of such things is this: if something bad happens to you, you say it's fate[2] that caused it, while good comes from God," Félix explained. "That's the Malagasy way of thinking. [Then, following a significant pause:] But you know, some are now saying he was poisoned with *fanafody-gasy* [Malagasy medicine][3]—that someone wanted to harm him, and, in the end, well, they succeeded."

Throughout the following week, I heard much about fanafody. When spoken of in positive terms it is, more specifically, referred to as *fanafody tsara*, or "good medicine," involving a host of substances prepared by indigenous healers in order, for example, to cure a sickly child, lure a beloved partner back home, ensure fertility in a barren woman, or generate greater success at work (Sharp 1993, 203 ff.). At other times, however, fanafody is used to cause harm so that the instigator may profit; Sakalava refer to this as *fanafody raty* ("bad medicine"). The vast majority of tromba mediums and other healers based in Ambanja are reluctant to harm others, and so they will only dispense fanafody tsara. Instead, they offer medicines designed to sway another's actions. For example, if a husband has strayed from his wife's bed, a medium might offer the wife love magic that is stronger than the mistress's, but she will nevertheless refuse to dispense fanafody raty that could render the mistress ill. Such responses typify those offered to assuage adult woes. Adult clients understand, too, that attempts to harm others may backfire, because one's adversary may retaliate with even stronger medicines. Thus, clients themselves rarely seek fanafody raty to solve their personal problems. Where their children are concerned, however, they may resort to more drastic and dangerous measures.

A Mother's Investment

The school examinations that fall at the end of the year are a source of great anxiety for students and their adult kin alike, their outcome determining whether a child can continue on in school and, thus, potentially succeed further in life and assist other kin. In 1987, I worked closely with an array of tromba mediums, and I witnessed on a number of occasions consultations with parents who sought spiritual intervention against their children's potential failures in school. As noted in the previous chapter, Yasmine's mother Alida at one time engaged the services of a powerful tromba medium named Marivola in the name of protecting her children. In addition to her worries about Yasmine's sexual encounters, she was deeply concerned for her eldest son, Abel, who stood poised to take his bac examinations, and who she hoped would study medicine like her father. By the middle of the academic term, Alida was making regular, weekly visits to Marivola's home in order to consult with her most powerful spirits (see Sharp 1993, 214–15). As Abel later explained to me quietly and cautiously, Marivola prepared three types of medicine for his mother to use. The first two were designed to shelter Abel from harm: his mother added one to his bathwater, and the other she prepared as an infusion for him to drink for several days before and during the bac examination period. The third consisted of a small bundle of substances that she scattered slowly and secretly in certain locations of his schoolyard and especially near his classroom. These were designed to render tired or ill any students who unknowingly came into contact with them. In the end, Abel not only passed his exams but received among the highest marks in the province; by the following school term, he was enrolled in medical school in Antananarivo.

A general understanding among tromba mediums and their clients is that one only pays for a medium's services if the efforts prove successful. Payment is sometimes in cash, but more often in the form of goods understood to be coveted by the spirits, because it is they who are the healers. Typically, these gifts are body wraps, worn by mediums in trance, and cigarettes and alcohol, which are ingested by the spirits. It is well known, though, that spirits are greedy creatures, whose demands may easily become excessive, as expressed in the proverb "Tromba ny teta, vola miboaka" ("[When a] tromba [spirits sits in] the head [of a medium, inevitably one must] take out [or pay a lot of] money").

Marivola's spirits proved especially demanding, and Alida soon felt terrorized by a medium driven by the insatiable desires of a powerful spirit known for its foul temper and ability even to spit blood. In the end, Alida paid dearly for Marivola's services. When Marivola learned of Abel's success, she began to visit Alida each week, repeatedly threatening Alida with the spirit's wrath unless she paid with precious items. Over the course of several months, Marivola slowly drained Alida of her wealth, returning to her own home with Alida's television, VCR, gold jewelry and, eventually, even pieces of furniture. Only when Marivola tried to take Alida's Italian-made sewing machine—which enabled Alida to generate supplemental income—did the latter put her foot down. "Let her [spirits] kill me, then," said Alida. "She's taken everything. . . . She can't take this too—without it my children and I will starve, so she can go ahead—let her try and kill us if she can." Finally, Marivola's visits ceased. Yet the scars were obvious to anyone who visited Alida's house, now stripped bare by Marivola's raids.

In the end, both women were driven into isolation for their nefarious dealings. Word spread that Alida had used fanafody raty against other people's children so that her own son could succeed; and so eventually her sewing business fell to a near standstill. And when Marivola's landlord learned that she was dispensing dangerous substances as a tromba medium, he evicted her family from their spacious home. When I next encountered Marivola in 1994, she was living in an abandoned community center, which was boarded up and in a sorry state of disrepair, an ugly structure surrounded by gnarled dead fruit trees. To me, the place appeared haunted, as it seems it did, too, to a gang of neighborhood children who referred to it with great bravado as "the witch's house" *(trano ny mpamosavy)*, thus transforming this once powerful medium into the most loathed of social categories. In 1987, I considered both Alida and Marivola to be jovial and sociable women who were also very close friends. By 1994, however, each had grown so paranoid as a result of their contract that neither would venture from her home except when absolutely necessary. Instead, they relied exclusively on trusted kin to run their errands, shop for food, and draw water from distant wells in neighborhoods where no one knew them.

Schoolyard Perils

As this tale illustrates, Alida's desires for Abel's future were so great that she willfully sought to harm other children: as she scattered fanafody raty about the schoolyard, she knew that if her son were to succeed, others would have to fail. Fanafody raty strikes indiscriminately, poisoning anyone who touches it. Thus, Alida's actions defied all rules of sociality: she did not care whom she harmed, as long as Abel's career advanced. She knew the range of possible effects: that it could affect one's memory, slow one's thoughts, or render one physically ill. Fanafody can also derive its power from malicious and dangerous *njarinintsy* spirits, who seize victims' bodies and drive them mad. They can also spread quickly from one victim to another, and in Ambanja, the schoolyard is a favored locale for their attacks. As noted earlier, local schools have in fact periodically experienced epidemics of possessed students.

Throughout 1987, my research focused on tromba, njarinintsy, and other forms of spirit possession, so that by midyear, I was occasionally approached by parents seeking advice on how to treat offspring who had encountered fanafody raty at school. Although this typified experiences in Ambanja, I was similarly approached once in Antananarivo after I gave an academic talk that was publicized in a national newspaper. Shortly afterward an anxious elderly man named Papan'i'Ranja visited the home where I was staying. His demeanor communicated deep sadness; as we sat together in the parlor he slowly unraveled his tale:

> My oldest daughter, Ranja, she's been ill for four years. She's so accomplished—she's very smart, and she has always excelled in her studies. She's so gifted—she passed her bac the first time at age eighteen and then she quickly earned a [coveted] place at the university in [Toliara in the far south]. My wife and I, we worried about her, because [Toliara] is so far away, but it was where she needed to go. But then she fell gravely ill in her first year. She had an aunt who lived there and who looked in on her when she could. But finally her aunt wrote one day and told us that our daughter was sick. I went down there myself to retrieve her. That was four years ago, and she's still gravely ill. In her worst states, she speaks to herself all the time, she can't dress herself properly, and sometimes she throws things or runs out into the street. For years now I've taken her to all sorts of doctors, and to costly healers of all sorts—to herbalists and diviners [HP: *ombiasy, mpisikidy*]. They tell me she is possessed by spirits, but nothing they do helps her. Perhaps you know what to do? I fear she might die. Please tell me, what can this father do to save his lost daughter?

Requests such as this always left me deeply distressed, because I was powerless to offer any immediate solutions. In my own culture, there are no steadfast cures for many of the experiences we label madness. In the course of my research, however, I had been impressed by the work of a group of Lutheran exorcists, and thus I directed Papan'i'Ranja to the central healing retreat headed by their celebrated prophet in Antananarivo (see Sharp 1994). But Papan'i'Ranja was a stranger to me and to my hosts, and I never learned whether he took his daughter there for treatment.

This was not the only story I heard that recounted the dangers of schooling. Two of my dearest friends similarly witnessed the devastating effects of fanafody raty on their own sisters. The parents of the first did in fact seek assistance from local Lutherans, and eventually six exorcists came to live with them full-time for several months, keeping constant vigil by working in two shifts of three healers each. In the end, the daughter emerged from her madness, and her sister, who is my friend, later married one of the exorcists, who then served as a pastor in Ambanja. The sister of my second friend fell mad while enrolled at lycée. She had been at the top of her class and was an exceptional athlete, who had traveled throughout Africa to compete in international tournaments. During her terminale year, she grew haggard, stopped speaking altogether, and barely ate. Under the doting care of her parents, she was cured after two years, and later she passed her bac exams with high marks. Both sisters are now doctors, driven by a shared desire to understand her earlier suffering.

With these experiences in mind, throughout my research for this current project, I regularly asked students in Ambanja about their experiences with or knowledge of schoolroom magic and possession. In contrast to its frequency in the early 1980s, the majority of students now insisted that njarinintsy and other forms of possession sickness were a thing of the past. School officials similarly reported that although one or two cases might occur each year, these no longer reached epidemic proportions. Thus, I was struck by Félix's remarks during an interview shortly after Achille's death. His reflections in the end underscored the gendered nature of fanafody raty:

LS: What can you tell me about the use of fanafody in school? Is possession still a problem as it was a decade ago?

Félix: I've seen njarinintsy in school, but not for a few years.

LS: What causes it?

Félix: Well, generally, a boy really loves a girl, but she doesn't like him. So he does it to her—he uses fanafody to give her a njarinintsy [spirit]. Two years ago we had some [cases], when I was at the CEG. But I've never seen it at the lycée. You know that if one student has it then others will get it, too. . . .

LS: What do the teachers do?

Félix: Oh, they've all been told what to do. They stay calm and get everyone out of the room.

LS: And what about the principal? What does he do?

Félix: He usually comes by to see what's going on. Everyone knows what it is, so it's not a big deal.

LS: With the girls who have it, do they drop out of school? [This was the case in the early 1980s.]

Félix: Oh, they might be gone for a few weeks, but then they come back. You know, though, that njarinintsy [possession] is usually just the first phase of tromba [mediumship].

LS: [I nod in agreement]: Do boys have crises of their own?

Félix: No, nothing like this. They don't have problems like this. [Then, following a long pause:] But then there's Achille, [the director's] son. You see, if, for example, if you're like my [own] brother and you die in puberty, especially if you're, oh, say twelve, eighteen, or even a little older, and then you die suddenly, well Malagasy say it must be fanafody. [But] it is always difficult to know. For example, last year, Achille [passed his] bac at a young age—he was [only] twenty. He then applied for and [was accepted into] a police training program. Then he received further training in Diégo. But then he fell ill—with something, like a fever.[4] The police were really worried about him and so they transported him right away to his parents. He was in the Catholic Hospital by 8:00 [A.M.], but then he was dead by 4:00 [P.M.]. Everyone in the neighborhood is saying someone must have poisoned him with fanafody-gasy. He had already accomplished so much! But this is something the family has not yet considered. They're very religious Protestants, and they refuse to engage in this.

LS: What do they say at the hospital? What did they say he died from?

Félix: They don't know. He had a fever. That's all we know. He has a brother and a sister who will be taking their [own] exams next week.

Perhaps there, I thought, lay these parents' future hopes.

Adults, too, understood Achille's death in similar terms: that is, the sudden death of so successful a student indicates nefarious dealings. When I asked one of Achille's former teachers, Mr. Ernest from the state-run lycée, for his interpretation, he responded as follows:

> *Mr. Ernest:* It must have been fanafody. Look, this was a healthy young man, in excellent shape! He was strong and athletic. When he still lived here in Ambanja you could often see him out running. He was a serious athlete.
>
> *LS:* Why—or who—would do such a thing to him?
>
> *Mr. Ernest:* Someone in Diégo where he was training. Someone who was jealous of his abilities. He was far from home and young. No one—[especially] his parents were not there to protect him. Someone was jealous of him and wanted to harm him because of it. He was alone and vulnerable. And now he is dead.

Félix's account and Mr. Ernest's response together underscore the potential virulence of fanafody raty and its ability to strike down the most accomplished of students. Yet its effects are experienced differently by girls and boys. As Félix explained, girls' experiences are framed by the anger of unrequited love, when a rejected suitor seeks revenge by planting malicious spirits in the schoolyard. These spirits may seize any girls who cross their paths, or they may pass from one victim to others. As Sakalava explain, spirits are drawn to girls more readily than boys because they are "softer" or more "pliable" *(malemy)*, rendering them more susceptible to possession. Although these spirits drive their victims mad, this state is usually temporary in Ambanja. Under the care of kin and skilled healers, most girls are eventually freed of their malicious spirits, and many later assume careers as respected tromba mediums. The jealousy directed at boys like Achille, however, relies upon more potent forms of fanafody that can kill suddenly and mercilessly. It is, ironically, their "hardness" *(mafy)* and thus their valued strength and vitality that ultimately renders boys the most vulnerable schoolyard victims. Furthermore, as Mr. Ernest underscores, the fact that Achille was living alone and unprotected in Diégo further exposed him to attack.

Because children are inherently weak, adults strive to protect them from the dangers of fanafody raty. Thus, parents regularly instruct their children never to accept food from anyone save close kin *(havaña)*. The understanding here is that kin cherish relatives' children far too much to harm them; were they to do so they would risk injuring their own kin group and, thus, themselves. Also, whereas food poisoned with fanafody may temporarily weaken an adult, it can kill a child. The fact that children are so precious inevitably renders them especially vulnerable as targets of jealousy or rage. By harming them, slighted peers or ambitious parents can destroy the future hopes of a rival household, kin group, or even a community.

Missing Children

Among the most difficult experiences for a fieldworker to endure involves witnessing the deaths of the weak and powerless, especially when they are sudden or seem especially unjust. My time in the field has been marked by the joys of births, first haircuttings, circumcisions, and tromba ceremonies, as well as by the deep sadness of children's funerals. Although the heartfelt loss of an older ruler inspired my own sense of catharsis when I witnessed the lively instatement of his son and successor, I have yet to take in stride the deaths of young children I have known. The Sambirano is a region marked by prosperity, yet children still succumb regularly to disease, injury, and death, a fact illustrated by Félix's own life, since he (like Dalia, too) lost an older teenage brother a few years ago. I always find the deaths of children difficult to bear; nevertheless, they harbor important lessons about the inseparability of their emotional and social worth.

Over the course of eight years of research, I have been fortunate: to date I have only witnessed the deaths of three children; I shall speak briefly of two.[5] The first loss, and the first Sakalava funeral I attended, involved a toddler who succumbed one night to malaria (see Sharp 1993, 211–12). I knew the little girl's parents well: they were my next-door neighbors and my landlady's co-workers, and their daughter's sudden death was a terrible shock to us all. She was the glue that held her parents' rocky marriage together; soon afterward her mother, Alice, departed, and within a week, her husband's mistress moved in to take her place. The child's death had other repercussions as well: although Alice was a nurse, she nevertheless sought additional nonclinical answers for why the little girl had died so suddenly. After consulting a host of healers, she accused Mama Rose—an elderly grandmother who lived nearby—of being a witch *(mpamosavy)* who had poisoned her child with fanafody-gasy when she had come to play with Mama Rose's grandchildren. This drama came to a temporary halt when Mama Rose's adult daughter arrived in order to protect her mother. After my own departure from the field, Mama Rose left town for several years, relocating with her grandchildren to her daughter's home in Ambilobe. When she later returned to her dusty home in Ambanja, she was careful never to venture anywhere near the neighbor's compound.

Within months of this little girl's death, I learned of yet another. One afternoon, Tsarahita and I were scheduled to conduct a follow-up interview with Tsifaly, an accomplished tromba medium who was a key informant. We had struggled for weeks to meet with her, arriving twice before, as scheduled, only to find her house empty. Such behavior was uncharacteristic of Tsifaly, and we could only conclude she was avoiding us. On our third attempt, we found her sitting on her porch lost in thought, appearing sad and dejected. As Tsifaly explained, her eight-year-old nephew, who had lived under her care, had died terribly a month before. As Tsifaly described the progression of his illness, I suddenly realized he had had diphtheria. In a panic, I ended the interview and told Tsarahita—who was pregnant at the time—that we must leave at once. We rushed back to her compound where, with her mother's help, we checked everyone's health cards to make sure all been vaccinated against the disease.

Tsifaly's loss was an especially troubling experience for a woman with a rocky past. At sixteen or so, she had run away from her village to Mahajanga, where she had worked as a prostitute for over a decade. She eventually followed her current lover to Ambanja, where they have since settled. Only then did she realize that she was unable to conceive. The burden of this knowledge troubled Tsifaly deeply and became interwoven with the personal narrative of one of her tromba spirits, Mbotimahasaky (cf. Sharp 1995). The boy who died was her beloved foster son, a nephew given to her by an older sister because she was childless. Tsifaly thus experienced the boy's death both as a reminder of her own sterility and as the result of her failure as a mother to care for this cherished child.

CHILDREN AND URBAN PROSPERITY

As the preceding tales of death underscore, raising a child to adulthood is a precarious affair in Madagascar. In addition to the forces of popular culture, as described in chapter 7, urban life is rife with yet other dangers that threaten children's lives, including infectious diseases, automobile accidents, and school magic. As I shall illustrate, children are precious to adults, first, because they inspire deep love in those who care for them, and, second, because in light of their economic potential, they are among the most precious forms of wealth that can be shared among kin. Throughout Madagascar, having many children epitomizes a household's prosperity, and their value is expressed through the ubiquitous blessing showered upon newlyweds: "Miteraha fito lahy [sy] fito vavy" ("May you bear seven boys and seven girls"). I frequently meet people who were raised in households of this size. Let us turn, then, to the social worth assigned to children.

A Kidnapping

At times, adults such as Tsifaly truly hunger for child companionship, and occasionally this can take unusual turns. An extreme version of such hunger was exemplified by a scandalous event that took place in Ambanja in 1987, when a barren woman in her thirties stole a merchant's infant daughter from her market stall and fled to the neighboring hills. For the next three days, nearly everyone I encountered spoke of this event, for the story quickly circulated on the streets and was broadcast by the local radio station as well. Among the most striking reactions was utter disbelief and collective horror. Everyone I spoke to asked, why would someone steal a child? The police were reported to be searching everywhere for the baby—on the valley's back roads, in small rural villages, and in the hillsides surrounding the town. Such efforts were highly uncharacteristic of the local police, who rarely responded to other more common misfortunes, such as burglaries or automobile accidents. Finally, on the fourth day, the kidnapper (*mpangala-zaza*, literally "child thief") was apprehended at her brother's rural compound in the Upper Sambirano. The baby was retrieved unharmed and returned to its mother's arms.

Standing in stark contrast to the typical anger and brutality shown to thieves (see Sharp 2001b), this kidnapper was neither punished nor charged. Once the baby was located, it was simply taken from her, and the woman was left among her own kin, who were expected to address the issue with her themselves. Some informants assumed she must have been crazy *(adala)* to go to such lengths to acquire a child. But more pronounced was the compassion that everyone expressed, for all understood her deep longing to have a child of her own, a terrible desire that drove her to attempt such a bizarre feat. Everyone wondered, too, why she had been unable to acquire a child through fosterage. After all, adult siblings often share or willingly give children to one another. Some hypothesized that perhaps it was her assumed madness that prevented kin from extending such generosity. As subsequent examples will illustrate, fosterage and child sharing are in fact common practices in the Sambirano.

Institutionalized Child Borrowing

Child fosterage and adoption have been documented cross-culturally by anthropologists (Carroll 1970b; Carsten 1991), and have received some attention from scholars of Madagascar as well (see Colburn 2000; Kottak 1986). As Vern Carroll notes, it is essential that such terms as *adoption* and *fosterage* be culturally contextualized. For example, a pervasive assumption in the United States is that adoption generally involves anonymous strangers, yet in the 1970s, approximately half of all cases in this country involved adopting the children of kin (1970, 4–5). A similar pattern is described by Carroll and others for Eastern Oceania (Carroll 1970b), where children are generally adopted by adults who are classificatory siblings or parents. Similar patterns typify current Malagasy practices.

Given this, I wish to define, briefly, essential terminology in order to clarify that which does *not* concern the discussion here. By *adoption* I refer to the legal, institutionalized, and permanent acceptance of another person's offspring as one's own, generally with little expectation of maintaining long-lasting ties of kinship between the adoptive parents and child, on the one hand, and the child's conception parents, on the other (see Carsten 1991, 431 and 440 n. 11). Adoption in this sense is, in fact, rare in Madagascar, and most often involves Malagasy children taken in by foreign couples.[6] *Fosterage*, which is far more widespread, here refers to the incorporation of a child of one's own kin (generally that of a sibling, including classificatory) into one's household on a long-term or, perhaps, even permanent basis.[7] Under such circumstances, both sets of adults are known to the child and all are often addressed as parents. The degree of biological closeness may be reflected in terms of address (e.g., *Mamabe* ["big Mother"] versus *Mamahely* or *Mamakely* ["little Mother"]). Various circumstances encourage the fostering of children. As illustrated by Tsifaly's story above, a woman might give one of her children to a sibling who has none, or to a sister who requires more economic assistance than her own children can give her, or to an aged and solitary grandparent in need of domestic or field labor. Most often it is women who are the instigators of such offers or requests, but men, too, are recognized as givers and receivers of children. In still other cases, a conception parent unable to provide for all of her children may send a child to live with a sibling who is better situated financially, or who may live close to highly valued services, such as medical care or private schooling. I also use the expression *child sharing* to refer to the temporary loaning of one's child, a practice that is pervasive in Ambanja and that most often involves exchanges among kinswomen. Such sharing (through either borrowing or lending) may span a few hours, a day or two, or longer, perhaps several weeks, or months; ultimately, the longer the stay the more akin to fosterage the relationship becomes. Child sharing is the most fluid of these forms of child exchange: as I shall demonstrate, shared children may circulate constantly among households, their movements dependent on the needs of their adult kin or, perhaps, their own personal moods and whims. Within the context of sharing, generally only conception parents are referred to as *Mama* or *Neny* (HP: *Reny*) and *Papa* or *Baba*.[8]

These arrangements reveal the range of intertwined emotional and economic values associated with children. Requests to borrow children are usually driven primarily by economic necessity, yet they also reflect emotional attachments to particular children and among adult kin. In Madagascar, fosterage and adoption have important economic components, driven, too, by strong emotional needs (or even longing or hunger at times) to have children to love in a culture where they are so highly valued. As I shall show, an analysis of child sharing and, ultimately, fosterage, is essential to uncovering the depth of a child's social and, more specifically, economic value. Within such relationships, adults and children alike may thrive, because a child's economic potential can ensure long-term household stability. In northern Madagascar, adults frequently invest significant effort and capital in fostered children in ways that equal or even exceed what they offer to their biological offspring (cf. Colburn 2001).[9] This is especially true when it comes to a child's education, be it in the domestic sphere or schoolyard. Furthermore, given that so few children succeed in school, domestic apprenticeship may prove more lucrative in the long run. In this sense, because of the daily demands placed on them when they are young, girls may in fact receive more comprehensive training than boys. Just as migrant school youth master adult skills earlier and more readily than their urban based peers (see again chapter 3), girls who fail in school are nevertheless often better prepared to survive independently, having been taught how to run a household or even a small business. This enables them in turn to escape wage labor more easily than boys.

The Daily Circulation of Children

It's a hot afternoon in June 1995, and I have stopped by to pay a visit to Mme. Vezo—or, as her kin and I refer to her affectionately, Mama Vé. As I step onto her porch, I am struck by the silence, and I wonder if anyone is at home. One of the front doors is wide open, blocked only by floor-length lace curtains designed to keep out flies, dust, and the prying eyes of passersby on their way to the market or mosque. It is unusually quiet: oddly, no children sit on the porch playing, and as I step inside, I realize that this side of the house is empty. I then enter the dusty court-yard in back, where I find Mama Vé's brother-in-law pouting near a cold cooking stove, surrounded by piles of dirty dishes and yet another, outer circle of motor-cycle parts. He hasn't plucked his beard in days.

"Heh, there, Aly, where are all the children?" I ask.

"At Auntie Mariamo's," he grumbles, never pausing to look up from cleaning rice.

I realize his wife Ivetty must be gone, too, perhaps staying with her latest lover, or en route to the capital, where she'll buy scarce goods to sell back here to her ex-tensive network of clients. I reenter through another back door and find Mama Vé sewing a neighbor's party dress out of brilliant pink polyester satin. A big disco boum is scheduled for tomorrow night, and she's fallen far behind on her sewing projects. Her husband Saidy lounges on their bed, carefully trimming loose threads from a freshly sewn pair of boy's well-tailored trousers.

I repeat my question: "Akory drakô!—Hello, dear friend—I see you are work-ing hard! But where are all your children?" Mama Vé remains focused on her work.

Saidy, in response, looks up drowsily: "Ahh, they're all long gone. They left early this morning for my mother's, before dawn. She's been ill with malaria and needs their help. They'll be back in a few days, or maybe we'll go join them. One of them will come back soon enough to tell us what we need to do for her."

Saidy and Mama Vé, Aly and Yvetty, and Auntie Mariamo and her respective husband Tantely define the more closely linked segment of a highly diversified net-work of extended kin, all of whom live within fifty kilometers of each other (see table 4). These adults, with their children, are long-term inhabitants of the Sam-birano. Two other brothers complete this segment of kin: these are Hassan, a bach-elor merchant, who lives at the far end of town, and the sailor Mohammed, who, when not at sea, lives with his wife and two young children in the bustling port and tourist town of Hellville. Saidy, Aly, Hassan, Mariamo, and Mohammed are the offspring of a now widowed, locally born Sakalava mother, Dady ("Grand-mother") Saidy. Their father migrated from Yemen to Madagascar in the 1920s, eventually settling on a small patch of land in the town's center, where he built both a comfortable home of concrete and, with the help of others of Arab descent, the mosque that now faces this house. The elder Saidy died twenty years ago; once his children began to marry and settle in town, his widow returned to her own mother's farm, leaving the house to her two eldest sons. Dady Saidy, a hardy woman in her seventies, now lives fifteen kilometers away from her offspring in Ambanja. At first glance, her rural home seems to be nothing more than a two-room falafa house, but she is, in fact, surrounded by riches: she keeps a dozen goats and she has an imposing vegetable garden, two hectares of rice fields, and a small plot (approxi-mately half a hectare) of coffee, cocoa, and bananas. Next door lives Maso, a younger female cross-cousin, along with her husband and two sons, all of whom provide the hardy yet aged Dady Saidy with invaluable labor.

Saidy and his brother Aly, at the insistence of their wives, have since jerry-rigged the house in Ambanja to create some privacy for their two nuclear units, consisting on one side of Saidy, Mama Vé, and their four offspring (Alima, Zalifa, Ibrahim, and Zita), and on the other of Aly, his wife Yvetty, and their three children (Rachida, Tina, and Moser). This conjoined household is tightly linked with that of Auntie Mariamo, who lives ten minutes away by foot with her husband, Tantely, and their two unruly sons, Bruno and Abdullah. Mariamo also cares for two of Hassan's children (born to different mothers): the first is Ouardah, a diligent eleven-year-old girl, whom Mariamo now regards as her own daughter, and baby Ishmael, whom Mariamo insists on caring for each time he falls ill with a life-threatening illness.

The movements of their eleven children reflect a highly institutionalized form of child sharing, in which three professional women rely heavily upon the labor of one another's offspring. Together, they constitute a core of economic prosperity. Although two of these women are migrants, all three now regard one another as dear sisters. Whereas Mariamo was born and raised in Ambanja, Mama Vé grew up in the far southwest, and Yvetty was born in a town 300 kilometers directly south of Ambanja. Their closeness is facilitated by the fact that all three are well-educated and hard-working: Mama Vé, a teacher at the local lycée, holds a university degree, and her sisters-in-law, Yvetty and Mariamo, attended school through the lycée level. Although the latter two did not sit for their bac exams, both are fluent in French, a skill that is essential to their success as market women. Their shared prosperity is further enhanced by the fact that all three regularly draw upon the labor power of their eleven children.

Children on the Move

Whenever I try to track the movements of the children of Mama Vé, Mariamo, and Yvetty, I often experience an intense sense of fieldwork vertigo. On any day (particularly once school is out), their eleven children circulate in dizzying fashion. I can never assume I will find any of them "at home" *(an-trano)*—that is, within the house of their conception parents—regardless of whether it is meal or siesta time, market day, or the like. Over the course of only a few days, they might be glimpsed at Mama Vé's and Yvetty's, then be off for a few days to Dady Saidy's in the country, returning later to Mama Vé's, where they will spend the night, then to Auntie Mariamo's for a few days, from where they in turn might radiate out on urgent errands, perhaps venturing to Tantely's market stall or to Uncle Hassan's boutique on the northern edge of town, or maybe carrying little Ishmael to the hospital to be treated for his latest illness.

These children's responsibilities vary widely in each household. Mama Vé is a fastidious housekeeper and her offspring provide much of the labor for a multitude of tasks. Her floors are always beautifully polished, and she makes certain the shared compound's yard, well, and lean-to shower are clean. Linens she herself has

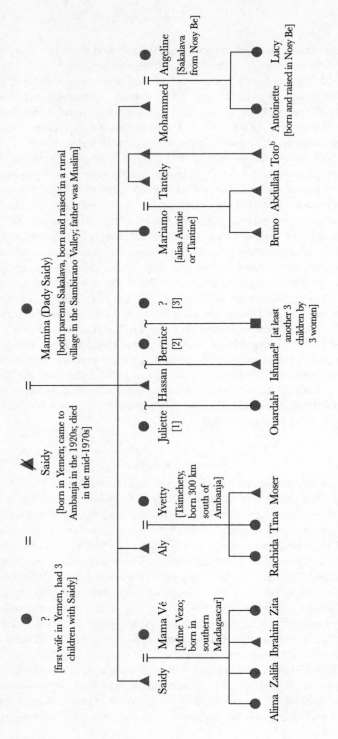

Table 4. A Child-sharing Network of Urban Ambanja

NOTES: All individuals on this chart were born and raised in Ambanja unless specified otherwise.
[a]Designates two children (Ouardah and Ishmael) who have been fostered out —at least temporarily—to Mariamo.
[b]Toto works for Mariamo's husband, Tantely, for wages. Toto is the son of one of Tantely's brothers.

embroidered or crocheted are changed every few days, and delicious meals are served at regular times on tableware given to her on her wedding day. Each of her four children have daily household chores, which they perform without fuss, so that Mama Vé sometimes jokes that she has not been to the market or to the Sambirano River to wash dishes or clothes for years. When she is not teaching high school, Mama Vé can usually be found sewing away at projects commissioned by one of her many customers: sheets and tablecloths, beautiful dresses, blazers, and men's tailored shirts and pants. All of Mama Vé's children also bring her a steady flow of new clients met through their schoolmates.

Next door is the household headed by Yvetty and Aly. Compared to Mama Vé and Saidy's four "well-behaved" (hendry) children, this is a wild, naughty (maditra) brood of three. Aly rarely budges from his back porch, except when he wishes to get his own children out of his hair, and then he loads all three on his motorcycle and drops them off at Auntie Mariamo's. When Yvetty is about, however, this otherwise depressed household bursts into action: three dusty children are transformed into freshly scrubbed, smartly dressed beauties. Even though all are under ten, as described in the previous chapter, Rachida has begun to master their mother's impressive market skills.[10]

One always finds the greatest flurry of activity at Auntie Mariamo's, however, where, ironically, her own sons have grown into two ne'er-do-wells (maditra be or "very naughty" and kamo, "lazy," boys) who often skip school. This problem is especially pronounced in June: each year when the majority of their classmates are studying for their end-of-year exams, Bruno and Abdullah can be spotted on rural roads riding their expensive bicycles in preparation for a local abbreviated version of the Tour de France (Bruno has won this competition three years in a row). When I first met her in 1987, Mariamo spent much of her time working in the market with her husband, nearly always with her two little boys in tow. Once they were in school, however, this couple decided to divide their labor so that Mariamo could tend a second, smaller store on their front porch, now littered with the most basic needs requested of neighboring households, such as matches, kerosene, and candles, as well as Mariamo's delicious cakes and cookies. In 1993, she constructed an impressive brick oven in her front yard with her earnings from this second business, and in 1994, four boys were employed on a regular basis as bakers, while a handful of her nieces and nephews pitched in more informally to help with kneading bread, special orders, or deliveries. Two of the four boys had forfeited schooling for these economic pursuits, whereas her nieces typically lent additional labor before and after school hours. By the end of 1994, Mariamo had acquired a tourist hotel as a client and was supplying its proprietor with croissants and brioches. Three of Mama Vé's children expertly mind Mariamo's store, and Mariamo jokes that perhaps even Yvetty's reckless daughter Rachida will join them soon one day. On the days when Mama Vé's house is empty and still, they are inevitably at Mariamo's. "Where are my children?" she exclaimed one day. "Bah! I sent little Zita there to retrieve a cooking pot; a day later she still hadn't returned, and when I sent the other three after her, the only thing that came back was a message by way of Bruno on a bicycle that they all preferred to stay at Mariamo's! At least I don't have to worry about cooking for them. Maybe we'll go see them ourselves later this afternoon, eh?" As Mama Vé herself knows, Zita's choice to eat and sleep regularly at Mariamo's is a declaration of her love for her lively and affectionate aunt.

The intertwining of the economic and emotional value of children is exemplified by the relationship that has developed between Mariamo and her brother Hassan's daughter, Ouardah. As the mother of two unruly boys, Mariamo has longed for years to have a daughter of her own, but, now that she is thirty-seven, she feels she is far too old to bear another child, and she argues that having another baby of her own, on top of all the work she does, would probably kill her (she expressed this sentiment while simultaneously tending to baby Ishmael). As with all his children, Hassan begrudgingly and sporadically provides for his offspring, yet he shows little emotional attachment to them as their parent.[11] Ouardah's mother in particular has found it financially difficult to care for her daughter, and so she was relieved when Mariamo asked if Ouardah might come to live with her, allowing Ouardah's mother to move further north in search of work. Mariamo maintains a certain level of distance from Ouardah, in that she often gives preference to the immediate needs of her own nagging sons. Ouardah is, however, a far more serious student than are Mariamo's two boys and, thus, while these sons attend the state-run CEG, Mariamo herself pays for Ouardah's tuition at the Catholic Academy, relying heavily on this girl's labor when she is not in school. As Mama Vé once explained, adoption is rare in Madagascar, and, in Ouardah's case, it is unnecessary, because her parents remain nearby and can care for her. Ouardah is instead a niece out on indefinite loan, and so "[It is] Auntie [who] raises [and thus nurtures] Ouardah" ("Tantine *mitarimy* Ouardah") as if she were her own daughter.

Thus, child sharing among adult kin may answer both vital economic and emotional needs, and urban women especially may rely heavily on child labor to sustain their households. The long-term bonds that grow and deepen over time can also prove lifesaving. Were it not for Auntie Mariamo's most recent intervention, baby Ishmael would surely have died from infection after being vaccinated with an unclean syringe by a nurse at a state-run hospital. Ouardah was assigned the daily task of taking Ishmael to Ambanja's Catholic Hospital for penicillin injections and to have his frighteningly deep abscess cleaned. Similarly, children's actions may have saved Dady Saidy's life. Afflicted with a terrible bout of malaria, she was unable to attend to her most basic daily tasks. Maso, who lives next door, had left with her own husband and children in order to attend a funeral. Thanks to a passerby who encountered the aged Dady Saidy, the urgency of her needs was transmitted to her kin in Ambanja. Mama Vé's four children, ranging in age from seven to fifteen, were quickly dispatched to their grandmother's house, only to discover that she was indeed in serious ill health. They remained with her for five days, administering malarial suppressants, carrying water, washing clothes and linens, cooking for her, and tending to her animals and fields. All were habituated to this work, having done so before either as a break from the tedium of town life or at more labor-intensive times, such as the rice or coffee harvest seasons. At first the two middle children took turns walking to and from town each day to inform their parents of their grandmother's condition; by the third day they were joined by Mariamo's son Abdullah, who, on his bike, could easily race between town and country each day bearing news. By the end of the week, Mama Vé, Saidy, Mariamo, and I made the trek to Dady Saidy's, where we found her happily sitting on her porch brewing a pot of deliciously sweetened coffee in anticipation of our arrival.

A Wealth of Children

As the example above illustrates, even young children may prove essential to daily survival and prosperity. Their social worth lies in part in their ability to deepen ties among adult kin: by sharing their children, mothers especially may assert the inclusiveness of kinship, especially with other female kin. Janet Carsten's (1991) discussion of fostering on the Malay island of Langkawi illustrates just how deep the bonds enhanced by children can become, arguing that, through their exchange, children in essence embody kinship, enabling affinal links, over time, to transform into consanguinal ones. Not surprisingly, the circumstances she describes also involve highly mobile (migrant) populations, as is similarly true for much of the population in urban Ambanja. For Mama Vé and Yvetty, both of whom are of vahiny origins, child sharing enhances their social personae, so that after a decade they, together with Mariamo, are "dear friends" *(drakô)* or fictive sisters, bound to one another even in the midst of periodic disputes that erupt between their husbands or brothers. In Ambanja, uterine ties are especially significant for defining a child's identity, and thus, by lending out a child, a woman essentially lends out herself to kin in need. In this sense, child lending offers a powerful means not only for inclusion but for identity extension of adults and children (cf. Goodenough 1970, 392).

The special significance of child sharing within this kin group is thrown into relief when contrasted to the actions that characterize wealthier households. Elite women in town, for example, more often lend out house servants, not children. In such cases, a woman (that is, the employer) likewise gives aid to another. The employer operates on the assumption that she owns her servant's labor. The relationship with the servant is radically different, however, from that which exists between a parent and her offspring. Even in cases where poor country cousins are employed (or virtually enslaved), no emotional bonds are expected to develop between servant and employer or servant and borrower, nor does the lending out of servants create fictive kin ties between elite women. Rather, a servant frees an employer from labor while simultaneously enhancing her prestige and politicoeconomic power among other nonkin members of the elite. In Ambanja, two women whose husbands were in direct competition as the directors of the town's two largest banks regularly shared their servants, slowly transforming competition into friendship. This process was further facilitated by the fact that their young children regularly played together. Through their wives' efforts, the bankers themselves became close business associates, presenting when necessary a formidable united front in the town's more important arenas of power. This lucrative friendship was clearly facilitated by earlier activities involving their wives, servants, and even their children.

Perhaps one of the most compelling aspects of child sharing in this community is the fact that it is a potent economic strategy employed especially by women. As the work of Erika Friedl in Iran (1992) and Enid Schildkrout in northern Nigeria (1981) attests, child labor can be indispensable to women's economic survival, while simultaneously sustaining or enhancing social networks, particularly if, as Muslims, they honor purdah. Similarly, in Ambanja it is (albeit nonconfined and not necessarily Muslim) women who are negotiating these child exchanges. In contrast, men are far more likely to hire assistants: even teenage boys who are kin may be paid wages. Mariamo's husband Tantely, for example, employs two boys, one of whom is Toto, his brother's son. Both boys work at the market stall and then go directly home, for neither have been integrated into the network of children who frequent Mariamo's businesses and home. Girls in contrast, as borrowed children, more often serve as part-time apprentices, learning, often informally, the skills of their older female kin. Thus whereas Mama Vé's three daughters are now mastering Mariamo's marketing skills, their brother Ibrahim and their cousins Bruno and Abdullah more typically are left to play with their friends, and only occasionally are they called upon to run errands[12] (when they may demand minor wages). As a result of these diverse patterns, girls and boys inevitably signify different forms of child wealth. Whereas boys are revered as future wage laborers, girls are invested with expert knowledge that may integrate schooling and domestic skills. As a result, girls are more likely be labeled as economically "clever" *(hendry)* or "capable" *(mahay)* than are boys their own age, so that the skills they develop under adult tutelage may be more comprehensive and specialized. As I have argued throughout part 3, colonial practices singled out young men as exploitable manual laborers; today in Ambanja this legacy now drives the assumption that poorly trained urban boys may be forced to shoulder the demands of unskilled labor to generate precious wages.

An Indispensable Education

In the end, such gendered contrasts expose the weaknesses that characterize current discussions of education in Africa, where schooling and homebound activities are far too often described as discretely occupying *either* formal *or* informal realms of learning. In other words, these are considered mutually exclusive domains (cf. Serpell 1993). When girls' and boys' trainings are so different, girls may in fact acquire more comprehensive forms of schooling than do their male peers. In other words, girls may experience a more integrative education, where the schoolroom and home together expose them to deeper forms of both intellectual *and* practical urban knowledge; this is especially true of town-based children raised in adult-headed households. Although boys are exposed to the same curricula in the classroom, their out-of-school experiences are shaped by older colonial assumptions: that is, they ultimately must be the primary breadwinners of their households. As unemployed young scholars, they may inevitably be bound for less skilled and sometimes back-breaking urban employment. Among their few escapes may lie in farming (skills that girls also acquire), a destiny that is almost a certain reality if they stand to inherit fertile land from kin in the countryside. Migrant school youth—if they survive town life—stand as well to develop a more integrated education, because from the start they have been burdened with the demands of schoolroom, household, and rural homestead. Whether they do in fact succeed is yet another matter entirely.

Members of the cohort that defines the central focus of this book are currently too young to generate any definitive answers. Yet those who are slightly older than they do nevertheless reveal preliminary possibilities for post-lycée success. Survival and prosperity frequently rest upon a seamless integration of careful schooling *and* homebound abilities. Mama Vé, for example, is not only a respected schoolteacher, but her gifted sewing abilities generate a significant supplementary income for her household. In turn, her sisters-in-law Mariamo and Yvetty are both highly success-ful merchants. They are literate, fluent in French, and also skilled in math—all of these being abilities they developed in school and that have subsequently enabled them to build small mercantile empires in the north. Together, all three women rely heavily on children to maintain their urban and rural ties: their offspring provide in-dispensable labor, and through their movements and associations, they generate new links to clientele and sustain established ones. The social and economic survival—and prosperity—of all three women clearly depends on the myriad skills of their children. Their prosperity demands ceaseless efforts and investments; in the end, though, these may guarantee economic freedom and, thus, independence from the drudgery of the brutish labor demands of the valley's plantations.

Myriad sacrifices inevitably characterize the process of raising children when life is fraught with daily perils. Even schooling itself may be laced with danger, espe-cially in urban contexts where children must live far from loving kin. In Ambanja and elsewhere, the most accomplished students can inspire the greatest wrath, their lives sometimes cut short at the very moments when they succeed. Perhaps they have already survived the trials of school migration, later accomplishing nearly im-possible feats by completing terminale and passing their bac examinations. Yet some of this nation's most promising students succumb to the dangerous strategies of others, encountering forces that can destroy their minds, bodies, and, ultimately, the hopes and dreams of their parents, their communities, and the nation as a whole. Others who fail to acquire advanced degrees or coveted posts may never-theless succeed through other means, integrating skills they acquire at school and at home to generate lucrative independent businesses. In a community that shuns wage labor, and where strangers are potential enemies, true success and economic freedom are defined not by the wealth generated by alienating wage labor, but, rather, through the combined efforts of loving and supportive kin.

Conclusion:
Youth in an Age of Nationalism

We have sacrificed our children, an entire generation, massacred! And now what?
Well, we're going to have to wait—our hope [now] lies in [a future] generation.

MR. PASCAL *(1993)*

DESPAIR

As I neared the completion of this book, an American colleague whose professional
pursuits focus on grassroots community organizing offered an emotionally charged
response to my research. To paraphrase (and expand a bit on) his remarks, Why
must the teaching of agricultural and other pragmatic skills be linked to destructive colonial policies? What good, after all, are lessons in philosophy, history, and
geography, when life's more immediate concerns in Madagascar are shadowed by
hunger and poverty? Isn't farming, after all, the most basic, valuable, and essential
form of self-sufficiency in a nation such as this? Schooling inevitably ends in failure for the majority of Malagasy youth, because no jobs await even the most gifted
students. Why, then, shouldn't Madagascar heed the wisdom of colonial pedagogy
and exchange pencils, pens, and paper for seeds and hoes, and classroom time for
school gardening?

In my darker moments I think perhaps my colleague is right. As this study has
shown, schooling most certainly entails enormous sacrifices and frequently ends
prematurely in scholastic failure. Thus, as a lifetime endeavor for both youth and
their parents, schooling seems to reaps few gains, save for an elite minority who can
draw on impressive private resources and personal contacts so that their own children may be placed in schools abroad or in lucrative posts back home. For the majority of coastal students, however, advanced schooling has far too many perils, and
urban life can be difficult and unforgiving, facts understood all too well by Ambanja's youth. Unwelcome by adult tera-tany, young migrants frequently are forced
to live independently in town, bearing the double burdens associated with the demands of home and school. If they are to survive, they must be truly serious about
and capable in their studies, and be competent in fulfilling their daily needs. Many
also provide constant field labor to kin in the countryside, while the less fortunate

work at local plantations during their school breaks to make ends meet. Town-based peers face other obstacles: although some are freed from domestic demands, many must manage school requirements alongside a host of household chores, while perhaps also assisting adult merchant kin. I have often wondered how any of Ambanja's students ever manage to complete their lessons and advance in school, when economic restraints only exacerbate the limitations they face in a bankrupt educational system. Miraculously, a handful do excel, as this study's exceptional cohort of lycée level students attests.

I am, however, unable to embrace my colleague's stance for long. Although he certainly underscores many of the realities of survival in Ambanja and Madagascar as a whole, his questions nevertheless disregard the long-term devastation wreaked by less than seventy years of colonial occupation. Are schooling opportunities limited in Madagascar? Indeed, yes. Do coastal students suffer more than highland students? Certainly. Would this nation's schools profit if flooded with curricular materials? Without question. But this staunchly materialist approach seems mundane and shallow when set against the larger ideological quandaries uncovered by this project.

As I argue throughout this work, members of Madagascar's sacrificed generation are deeply cognizant of the burdens they shoulder as the inheritors of a colonial legacy, one that affects their daily survival, their dreams, as well as their periodic despair. Their critical vision, or what Paulo Freire (1985) refers to as *conscientização*, is rooted in a politicized reading of the past, a process that has characterized a lifetime of schooling guided by Ratsiraka's socialist vision. Thus, to ignore the weight of history would be to deny the sacrifices that they themselves have made throughout their brief lives. Their awareness of their own predicament, however, nevertheless exposes the great paradox of pedagogical praxis: Where lies the hope when resources are so scarce, successful schooling ends with little chance of employment, and Mr. Pascal and other now aged activists declare malagasization to have been a national travesty? As I shall argue in these final pages, the predicaments that plague Madagascar also typify other countries; in response, the critique I offer below insists on the inseparability of history and political consciousness as the bedrock that informs an understanding of the agency of African youth.

YOUTH AND MEMORY POLITICS
Colonialism Deconstructed

In a discussion of the European conquest of Africa, V. Y. Mudimbe underscores the centrality of conversion as a potent strategy employed both by foreign states and myriad religious orders that together strove to "domesticate" colonized peoples (1994, 105 ff.; cf. Comaroff and Comaroff 1997, 63 ff.). Of particular concern was the desire within each territory to undermine indigenous institutions, a process that would in turn initiate the invention of a new, cohesive colonial culture. As such, this project was an inherently moral one that privileged, for example, patrilineality, Christian values, European linguistic hegemony, and, further, the professionalization of colonized subjects. As this study of Madagascar illustrates, too, indigenous institutions were at times appropriated in answer to colonial needs. Mudimbe also asserts that European strategies of domination and subjugation engendered the "invention of a new colonial memory," an insidious form of colonial violence that has borne long-term, devastating consequences for those who now inhabit much of Africa (1994, 126, 130–34).

Linguistic policies were pivotal to this "metamorphosis of memory" (Mudimbe 1994, 134). More specifically, as Johannes Fabian argues, early colonizers were frequently bewildered by the array of local languages they encountered in their African colonies, and thus they sought to impose linguistic order through the use of a lingua franca within specific domains (1986, 71). As my data from Madagascar demonstrate, indigenous languages were also regularly devalued; these were then reordered within a racialized hierarchy that privileged those cultures that exhibited only certain forms of economic productivity and political organization. Thus, both French and Merina were rapidly promoted as the two legitimate languages for this island colony. As the Tunisian nationalist Albert Memmi notes, "linguistic dualism" emerged as an essential component of foreign rule throughout the colonized world (1965:106).

If linguistic policies were a fundamental colonial strategy, then schooling defined a locus of power that facilitated transformation. In African contexts, youth clearly emerge as the primary targets for colonial conversionary practices. As Memmi further argued, educated youth thus "suffer the tortures of colonial bilingualism" (1965, 106); clearly this has proved true not only for the colonial era, but for contemporary Africa as well. If we turn specifically to Madagascar, French and Merina worked in tandem as a form of bilingual hegemony, a process consistently enabled by schooling. Furthermore, the problems (or, in Memmi's words, "tortures") associated with sanctioned bilingualism are easily exposed when viewed from a coastal perspective. First, coastal students, unlike their highland Merina counterparts, must be at least *tri*lingual if they are to survive simultaneously on the street and in the schoolroom. Second, both French and Merina expose how politically charged hegemonic bilingualism can be: on the one hand, both languages emerge as emblematic of oppression, since each awakens painful memories of former conquests; on the other, the refusal by coastal inhabitants to speak one or the other works as a potent form of localized resistance. In an attempt to unify the nation, the architects of malagasization sought to create a third, more neutral language, but official Malagasy, too, soon emerged as yet another sorry reminder of highland oppression. Similar quandaries of course characterize colonial projects in other regions of Africa that paired French, English, German, or Portuguese with, perhaps, Wolof, Arabic, kiSwahili, and Shona to the exclusion of Fulani, Berber, Luo, Makua, and myriad other indigenous tongues.

Sanctioned bilingualism bears other perils for those literate enough to comprehend school texts and lectures. Again, as Memmi further asserted, bilingualism "creates a permanent duality" within and thus disrupts the psyches of school youth, for whom village and school define radically different worlds. As they internalized this duality, educated youth in the colonies found they were never fully at home in either indigenous or foreign contexts (Memmi 1965, 106). Yet another potent colonial weapon that affected youth profoundly involved a deliberate obscuring of the past, a process that privileged European ways while attempting to erase all traces of local knowledge. As a result, students were soon alienated from their own history and, thus, they lost all sense of who they were. It is through this process that the minds of youth were colonized. As Memmi explained:

> [H]e who has the wonderful good luck to be accepted in a school will not be saved nationally. The memory which is assigned him is certainly not that of his people. This history which is taught him is not his own. . . . He and his land are nonentities or exist only with reference to the Gauls, the Franks or the Marne. In other words, with reference to what he is not. (Memmi 1965, 104–5).

Marc Ferro (1981), citing similar examples from colonial school lessons, likewise argues that such practices were standardized throughout the colonies (as they are frequently during the postindependence era as well). Children scattered across the globe were obliged to share a mythical past that asserted the exclusive legitimacy of European history while erasing indigenous ones. Thus, children inhabiting francophone territories all studied the same history, their lessons inevitably beginning with "Our ancestors, the Gauls" (1981, 17). Memmi describes this process as the effective "emasculation" or "calcification" of colonized societies or, stronger still, as the "social and historical catalepsy of the colonized" (1965, 102). Thus, colonial dominance depends heavily on the control of history, where only contemporary indigenous knowledge is allowed to persist. Without a knowledge of their own past, the colonized are indeed lost: "As long as he tolerates colonization, the only possible alternatives for the colonized are assimilation or petrification. . . . Planning and building his future are forbidden. He must therefore limit himself to the present, and even that present is cut off and abstract . . . [and] he draws less and less from his past. The colonizer never even recognized he had one; everyone knows that the commoner whose origins are unknown has no history" (Memmi 1965, 102).

For Memmi, the most troubling effects of all involved the "mummification" of youth who, possessing little local knowledge, would retreat to the safety of their homes and villages, in the end assuming dependent and passive roles because they remained unable to overcome the hopelessness of colonial domination. Ferro similarly underscores the deadening power of historical illiteracy. If, indeed, "the history we are taught as children . . . marks us for life," then critical pedagogy is crucial, for Ferro, like Memmi, insists that "to control the past is to master the present" (1984, vii).

Pedagogy, Politics, and Praxis

Thus, radical social transformation is dependant on the politicization of youth, a process most readily addressed through pedagogical praxis. In Paulo Freire's words, one must grasp that one "exists *in* and *with* the world," a stance that necessitates the simultaneous awakening of subjective self-knowledge and an objective under- standing of the world beyond. From this dialectic springs the possibility of critical reflection and, ultimately, true political consciousness, or conscientizição (Freire 1985, 67–70). Within this framework, youth emerge as crucial actors for instigating deliberate, thoughtful, and radical change. Frantz Fanon, too, considered youth crucial to the success of anti-colonial movements: as he described in his "Letter to the Youth of Africa," his hopes for Algerian independence lay in the global unifi- cation of students drawn from the West Indies, the African continent, and the is- land of Madagascar (Fanon 1967, 119).

If, then, as Mudimbe maintains (and as echoed by Memmi), the colonial proj- ect strove to "domesticate" the colonized through the invention of new histories and, thus, "a new colonial memory," this project was, nevertheless, far from flaw- less. Even in the context of colonial schooling, there was a seepage of information that then radicalized school youth. "In attempting to find a way beyond colonized forms of knowledge, one has to be careful not to imagine that they invariably col- onize the learner," John Willinsky observes. "Students can and do turn to their own advantage what they are taught. We need to recognize that for all the cultural dom- ination that Western education came to represent, it proved a useful resource for resisting that very domination" (Willinsky 1998, 109).

One need only consider the life trajectories of such nationalists as Ny Avana in Madagascar, Fanon in Martinique and, later, Algeria, and Memmi in Tunisia to grasp the full significance of Willinsky's warning. Although formal schooling may have silenced all discussions of an indigenous past in the schoolroom, elders nev- ertheless have long preserved and transmitted their personal memories of colonial oppression to their progeny. In Madagascar at least, youth have not discredited their elders' knowledge (see Fanon 1963, 206–7); rather, they have consistently drawn upon it to generate their own precise readings of island history. In essence, then, through its own oppressive policies, the colonial project crafted its own demise.

Thus, if we consider the arguments of such radical theorists as Memmi, Fanon, Freire, and Ferro, we find that they in fact reach fruition in Madagascar. Pedagogi- cal praxis certainly characterized schooling throughout Ratsiraka's socialist era (and curricula may even have been inspired by at least the writings of Fanon, if not oth- ers like him). Furthermore, throughout the twentieth century, Malagasy school youth have defined the political vanguard for nationalist movements on the island. Whether they were the founders of VVS, proponents of malagasization, or are the members of the current sacrificed generation, for all of them, the dialectic of school-derived knowledge and subjective experience has always been pivotal to shaping informed political critique and collective action (cf. Bloch and Vavrus 1998, after Escobar 1995;

James and Prout 1990, 218–19). As the tales they tell attest, in Madagascar, it is youth—be they students, poets, rulers, laborers, or foot soldiers—who are the makers of history.

Subaltern Youth

Against this background of writings by Marxist revolutionaries and radical pedagogists stands the rather flaccid treatment of youth by many North American and anglophone social scientists. Within anthropology in particular, youth rarely emerge as political actors, and, thus, the current literature sadly subverts the revolutionary project. Fortunately, though, a few critics now seek to expose current oversights. As they all assert, far too often children—and, because of my concerns here, I underscore youth—remain "objects of adult activity" and can be understood only through the lens of their elders' experiences. Furthermore, if and when youth are described in politicized terms, they emerge merely as vulnerable victims or reckless instigators of structural or political violence (Wulff 1995; see also Jackson and Scott 1999). Youth are constantly portrayed as cultural receptors but not as cultural producers, for they are assumed to be incapable of generating sustainable cultural meanings. Young people are thus currently described by such critics as defining "elusive," "distanced," "marginal," and "muted" social categories (James and Prout 1990a, 1990b; Kline 1998; Lave and Fernandez 1992; Hardman 1973, 85; Stephens 1995; Reynolds 1985, 1989, 1995a; Wulff 1995). They thus remain, in Virginia Caputo's (1995) words, "anthropology's silent others."

As such, youth emerge as a provocative subaltern category that demands more careful and critical examination. The now historicized experiences of Third and Fourth world women offer important parallels for analysis, since their potential for political agency has invariably hinged on the merging of voice and collective action (see Caputo 1995; Hardman 1973; Mohanty et al. 1991; Ortner 1996, 1–20; Tabachnick and Beoku-Betts 1998). Pamela Reynolds (1989, 114), quoting Jean Baudrillard (1987, 97–98), offers this comparison as a means to address with greater care the unique characteristics of children as a neglected category of analysis:

> [Like women, children] have a kind of objective ironic presentiment that the category into which they have been placed does not exist.... The child always has a double strategy. He has the possibility of offering himself as object, protected, recognized, destined as a child to the pedagogical function; and at the same time he is fighting on equal terms. At some level the child knows that he is not a child, but the adult does not understand that. This is the secret.

For the sake of this current study, this secret does in fact prove crucial to transforming an understanding of the political agency of Malagasy and other Africa school youth. Gayatri Chakravorty Spivak, in writing specifically of the subaltern, argues that "in the context of colonial production, the subaltern has no history and cannot speak"; furthermore, that colonized women in particular are doubly and even triply "effaced," for, "clearly, if you are poor, black and female you get it in three ways" (Spivak 1988, 287, 294). What, then, are we to make of the *subaltern child* who, by current definition, has no history, is consistently denied an independent voice, and, when African (or even more marginal in anglophone texts, Malagasy), is poor, black, young, and, at times, female, too?

The answer lies, I believe, in the politicization of youth as a social category. This necessitates a radical paradigmatic shift not only in anthropology but in the social sciences more generally (as also argued by Hardman 1973; Reynolds 1995a; Stephens 1995; and Wulff 1995, among others). Rather than assuming that youth are incomplete or only "partially cultural" beings, this new paradigm asserts instead that youth "have a different kind of knowledge" (Caputo 1995, 10). They are not passive receptacles for established wisdom; instead, we must establish their generative power as cultural and, potentially, politicized actors in their own right (cf. Jiang and Ashley 2000; Reynolds 1995b; Richards 1996; Rosen 2000; Wulff 1995; Lave et al. 1992). Just as Freire insists on the centrality of the subjective-objective dialectic in sustaining conscientizição, critical reflection should similarly inform the theorizing of youth. As Sherry Ortner argues, anthropology must recover the subject in its analyses of women as a subaltern category (1996, 11); similarly, the discipline must rethink current myopic paradigms that deny youth a voice. Following Allison James's lead, anthropologists must "learn . . . to 'talk'—again" with and about youth (1995, 47).

Thus, we must return once again to questions of language, history, and expression. As this book reveals, an inevitable result of postcolonial existence is a conflict of memories. Formerly colonized subjects must now grapple with the complex problem of how to represent, criticize, speak of, and transform their memories of the past. This is, in short, what Mudimbe identifies as "the political discourse of independence" (1994, 145–46). Reformulations of the past must reach far beyond the mere autobiography; as Reynolds (1985, 16) emphasizes specifically in reference to youth, the danger inherent here is that this form of storytelling easily romanticizes individual lives. To this I would add that it also leaves them untheorized. As should be clear from this study of coastal Malagasy youth, politicized historical narratives are more deeply textured than personal stories, for they readily expose the political agency of youth as they shape their own lives and their nation's independent trajectory.

In this light, memory politics emerges as a crucial framework for understanding the paradoxes that plague the lives of contemporary youth in Madagascar, in Africa, and elsewhere. As revealed in this study, students' personal and historical narratives are clearly inseparable and, thus, they are most powerful when read in tandem and recognized as defining their own dialectic. Their power also lies in the fact that political critique and activism spring not simply from the mundane trials of personal suffering in the schoolyard, but that they are intrinsically linked to their heightened awareness of much larger political and economic disparities (cf. Bundy 1986, 1987). Thus, a crucial aspect of this intensely difficult project is the need to think critically about history. What renders the colonial project of such pronounced scholarly interest is, after all, the potency of its transformative powers; in Africa, this frequently occurred within less than a century of formal occupation. In the end, such an analysis is greatly enriched when history is viewed through the lens held specifically by articulate African school youth, whose tales and analyses uncover a deep comprehension and clear collective consciousness of the weight of colonial history, the theme of the colonized mind, and the ever-evolving potential for national transformation.

Finally, then, school youth are crucial to comparative social analysis. As Helena Wulff underscores, youth must also be privileged in theoretical debates that center on global and transnational concerns, since, after all, "their ideas and commodities move easily across national borders" (1995, 10). Here one only need recall the pictures that grace Dalia's walls and the deep-seated fears that trouble Ambanja's adults when they contemplate the effects of foreign mass media on their children's psyches. With such concerns in mind, we are clearly far removed from my colleague's staunchly materialist approach, where schooling is valued simply as a source of future human capital (Schultz 1961; cf. Bloch and Vavrus 1998). Certainly, the nation must be fed, but this should not require as a consequence the deadening or "mummification" of the minds of its children. We need only consider the fact that more students have been killed by police in independent African states than in colonial contexts (Atteh 1996, 38; cf. Bundy 1987) to realize how critical it is to examine with care the political potency of school youth in this age of renewed nationalism.

Thus, we must even think critically about how the labels we employ ultimately shape how we perceive youth. As Stanley Rosen (2000) seems to imply in his review of children who grew up during China's Cultural Revolution, such labels as "Mao's Children," China's "Red Guard," or the "Third," "Thinking" or "Lost Generation" all bear serious repercussions for how we understand the political and historical relevance of this special category of youth. In Africa, too, the concept of the "lost generation" is far too quickly assigned to students (see, e.g., Donal Cruise O'Brien 1996), a label that immediately dispels all possibility of organized, collective action or agency. It is for this reason that members of Madagascar's sacrificed generation have seized upon this category and claimed it as their own: in their minds, they are not the helpless victims of a failed political experiment; rather, they have willingly sacrificed themselves for the nation and for future generations of children.

FUTURE DESIRES

If, in Madagascar, youth embody the future of the nation, then it is essential that I turn once more to the lives of those students who are so central to this study. As always, definitions of sacrifice, survival, and success remain simultaneously complex and contradictory in the Malagasy context. As a result, two final questions must be addressed: What, in fact, happened to Ambanja's lycée students? And how do their desires and dreams correspond with or converge from daily realities? In answer, I begin with the results of the bac exam, using this as an anchor for exploring their complicated futures.

As noted earlier, Olive, the intensely tutored temporary resident from Antananarivo, passed her bac examinations in 1993; although she had hoped to study medicine, her scores were too low and, so, a year later she was admitted to a program in agricultural science at the university in Antananarivo. The following year was one of remarkable achievement for the state-run lycée, when 23 percent (18 of 77) of those students who sat for their bac examinations passed, heralding the school's highest success rate since 1991. Among those who passed were Dalia, Félix, Foringa Josef, Hasina, Jaona, and Pauline. Lucien, however, did not; and Hazaly and Sidy decided to forego the process altogether that year, feeling they were ill prepared. Foringa, Félix, and Hasina were all admitted to university for the 1994–95 academic year after excelling on yet another set of entrance exams. Foringa enrolled at the eastern coastal campus in Toamasina; Félix instead accepted a place at a new and highly competitive training program in computer science in the north in Diégo-Suarez; whereas Hasina entered the central metropolitan university in Antananarivo. Jaona submitted an application to the southern campus at Toliara but was rejected; his mother then gathered her savings so that he, too, might go to Antananarivo. There, Jaona moved in with an older maternal uncle and enrolled in a private school specializing in business administration. His mother insisted that he concentrate not only on management skills, but also on French and English; in the meantime, he submitted yet another application to Toliara, where he was accepted in late 1995.

Still others made a variety of alternative choices. Dalia did not have the financial means to continue her schooling, and so she relocated to Diégo where she could live with and work among close kin while seeking a place at the local university campus. Pauline, too, left Ambanja, much to the dismay of her parents: with her bac certificate in hand she boarded a bus bound for the west coast city of Mahajanga, where she hoped to live with a close girlfriend. Sidy decided to repeat his terminale year, but Hazaly did not; thus Hazaly, as well as Lucien, continue to live with their parents, providing full-time labor in their homesteads, shops, and fields. In 1995, Antoine, who had been enrolled in the state-run Technical Lycée, also took his bac exams, but he failed. He then began a search for an apprenticeship in town where he could simultaneously develop a lucrative technical trade while still being able to watch over his younger brother Jacques. The two seminary students who figure most prominently in this study are Ignace and Christian: in 1995 they, too, took their bac exams and passed. Ignace then entered the priesthood, through which he would acquire an advanced education, whereas Christian returned home to work with his uncle the photographer, hoping to generate some income to help his widowed mother. He planned to enter university the following year; as late as 1997, however, financial problems still prevented him from doing so.

The final question that arises, then, is how might failure and success be understood in such contexts? An astounding majority of students followed most closely in this study excelled scholastically at the end of their lycée careers. More specifically, of the twelve students named here, ten sat for their bac examinations, nine passed, six of whom then went on to university or entered other programs for advanced training, all between 1993 and 1995. When analyzed against a broader cohort of peers, their scholastic histories are obviously exceptional, for very few students indeed ever even make it to the terminale year of lycée, much less pass the bac and enter university. The future possibilities that may exist for this small group of exceptional students remain unknown at this point, yet certain preliminary trends warrant mention here. Dalia, for example, despite her advanced training and proficiency in both French and official Malagasy, might search in vain for specialized employment; Lucien now offers full-time economic assistance to adult kin in the Sambirano, such responsibilities running contrary to his personal desires; and the prospects that await such university students as Foringa and Hasina cannot be predicted: after all, Madagascar, like many African nations, is flooded with unemployed university students. In this light, their stories seem bleak indeed.

Yet even greater dangers, however, threaten the well-being of Madagascar's younger students. If the nation's curricula are forged once again by French advisors, the ideological concerns so central to this current study may be obliterated, undermining hopes for the sustained radical politicization of youth. Perhaps, then, it is these latest pedagogical reforms that mark the onset of an even greater travesty in Madagascar, since they herald the reintroduction of a European-driven moral education. Nearly four decades later, independence remains an ongoing struggle. Such are the ideological border wars so intrinsic to schooling in Madagascar, Africa, and beyond. It is to be hoped that foreign infringements on island schooling and, ultimately, constructions of local history, will not, as Memmi, Fanon, and others feared half a century ago, once again anesthetize Malagasy youth, destroying the future potential for their astute reflections on the colonized mind.

A Guide to Key Informants

Name	Details	Chapter(s)
	Lycée Level School Youth	
Abel	Approximately 19 (in 1987);[#] the son of Alida, who used school magic *(fanafody gasy)* to ensure his success on his bac exams and his subsequent placement in medical school.	7, 8
Achille	20 (in 1993); the son of a mid-level bureaucrat, he had attended the state-run *lycée* in Ambanja, where he excelled as a student. He passed his bac examinations in 1993 and then he was awarded a place at a police training academy in Diégo-Suarez. He died suddenly in July, 1994. Many in Ambanja assumed he had been poisoned by a rival who was jealous of his accomplishments.	8
Alphonse, Bert, David, Edmond, Florent	Seminary students enrolled in their final *(terminale)* year at the Catholic Academy. They are classmates of Christian and Ignace.	7
Antoine	19 (in 1993); a school migrant who lives in Ambanja with his younger brother, Jacques (17), in a house owned by their parents. Although they have spent much of their lives in town, their parents have since separated	3, 4, C[+]

Name	*Details*	*Chapter(s)*
	Lycée Level School Youth (*continued*)	
Antoine (*continued*)	and settled in two separate rural villages. In 1994 Antoine was in his second year (*première*) at the state-run Technical *Lycée*; in 1995 he made his first attempt at the bac but failed. He has since sought out an apprenticeship in a technical trade. His brother Jacques attends middle school at the Catholic Academy.	
Christian	17; a seminary student at the Catholic Academy since 1991, enrolled in his second year (*première*). He is the son of Tsimihety parents from a small village near Bealanana, 350 kilometers south of Ambanja. His father died five years ago and so during the summers he works with a paternal uncle who is a traveling portrait photographer. He hopes some day to be the director of a tourist agency.	3, 7, C
Clement	18; in the first year (*seconde*) at the state-run *lycée*, he is an avid fan of the poet Ny Avana.	5, 6
Dalia	21; enrolled in her final (*terminale*) year at the state-run *lycée*. She is a school migrant who lives with a younger sister Flora who also attends the *lycée*. Together they moved to Ambanja in 1990. Their house belongs to a maternal aunt; a grandmother lives nearby. Her father is Antankaraña, her mother the offspring of Sakalava and Tsimihety parents; both are retired school teachers. Dalia was born in Antalaha on the northeast coast, yet her peers consider her to be *tera-tany* because she has lived in the Sambirano since 1979. Her boyfriend is Foringa Josef.	1, 2, 3, 4, 5, 7, C
Félix	18; a town-based student whose work is exceptional: at this young age he is in his final (terminale) year at the state-run *lycée*. The offspring of Tsimihety migrants, he currently lives with his mother, who works at the county seat (*fivondronana*) (his father died when he was young). As he explains, because his mother was born in a village slightly to the north, and because he has lived in	1, 3, 5, 6, 7, 8, C

Name	Details	Chapter(s)
	Lycée Level School Youth *(continued)*	
Félix *(continued)*	Ambanja for a decade, his peers consider him to be *tera-tany* and even Sakalava.	
Foringa Josef	23; A school migrant who lives with his sister and brother-in-law at the edge of town. He is enrolled in his final *(terminale)* year at the state-run *lycée*. His grandfather, Andrianambinina, was conscripted as a soldier during World War I. Foringa is Dalia's boyfriend.	appears throughout
Hasina	19; Hasina was born outside Antananarivo, although he has lived in northern Madagascar since he was 5 and in Ambanja since age 8. His father (from whom his mother has long been estranged) is Merina; his mother is of Tsimihety origin and works at the local courthouse. Hasina considers himself to be a *tsaiky ny Sambirano* or a "child of the Sambirano," as do his peers, although some teachers assume he is Merina. Hasina is an exceptional student: he is currently in his final *(terminale)* year at the state-run *lycée*.	1, 4, 5, 6, 7, 8, C
Hazaly	24; his mother is Sakalava royalty *(ampanjaka)*. Enrolled in his final *(terminale)* year at the state-run *lycée*.	1, 2, 4, C
Ignace	19; a seminary student enrolled in his second year *(première)* at the Catholic Academy; he comes from a village 120 kilometers north of Ambanja.	3, 7, C
Jaona	19; a town-based student enrolled in his final *(terminale)* year at the state-run *lycée*. His parents are separated; his mother, who is a midwife, is Betsimisaraka of royal descent from the east coast. His father is Antankaraña from north of Ambanja. Jaona is an avid soccer player who hopes to combine this passion with medicine.	1, 3, 4, 5, 6, 7, C
Lucien	20; enrolled in his final *(terminale)* year at the state-run *lycée*. He is of royal descent on his father's side.	1, 2, 4, C
Olive	19 (in 1993) a student from Antananarivo who lived temporarily with an aunt in Ambanja so that she could study for the bac exam for	3, C

Name	Details	Chapter(s)
	Lycée Level School Youth *(continued)*	
Olive *(continued)*	the second time. This year she succeeded; in 1994 she began her university studies in agricultural science in Antananarivo; she had hoped, however, to study medicine, although her bac scores were not high enough to allow her to do this.	
Pauline	20; a town-based student in her final *(terminale)* year at the Catholic Academy. Her father works for a local merchant; her mother is a postal clerk.	1, 2, 3, 4, 5, 7, C
Sidy	20; enrolled in his final *(terminale)* year at the state-run *lycée*. Both parents are Sakalava royalty *(ampanjaka)*.	1, 2, 4, C
Vonjy	15; daughter of elite Betsileo parents stationed in Ambanja. Schooled in elite private (and especially Catholic and "French") schools her entire life. Fluent in French (the language she speaks at home as well as in the classroom), she struggles with written and spoken Malagasy.	2, 7
	Other Youth (younger and older than *Lycée* Level)	
Andriatahiry Parfait	24; enstated as *Ampanjakabe* Tsiaraso Rachidy IV in 1994. The son of the preceding Bemazava ruler, he spent much of his childhood in exile in Toliara and then joined the national army. As a soldier he was stationed in the high plateaux.	4
Doda	26; a university student from Antananarivo. For his National Service he worked in the office of a government minister. Whereas he celebrated the ending of National Service, his older sister Suzy and her husband, Rommy, were saddened by this news because they had found their National Service posts more rewarding (they had worked as teachers in a rural school).	6
Ketsy	18, completed *quatrième* at the middle school level at the Catholic Mission Academy in 1994. Born in a village sixty kilometers southwest of Ambanja on the Ampasindava Peninsula. She lives in Ambanja with a	3

Name	*Details*	*Chapter(s)*
	Other Youth (younger and older than *Lycée* Level) *(continued)*	
Ketsy *(continued)*	maternal aunt (Mamahely) who works as a maid for a European employer. In the summers Ketsy works a host of jobs at local plantations. She hopes some day to be a pop singer.	
Ouardah	The fostered daughter of the merchant Mariamo. She attends the Catholic Mission Academy and then helps her aunt when she is not in school.	8
Rachida	7 (she had just turned 8 in 1995); her mother is the skilled merchant Ivetty. Rachida can often be seen carousing with other children in the courtyard of her Aunt Mariamo's house; although previously a bit of a hellion, she has quickly begun to master rudimentary marketing skills.	7, 8
Rova	6 (she turned 7 in mid-1995); the oldest of two children in an elite Betsileo household in Ambanja. Her father is a plantation director, her mother a housewife and part-time petty merchant. She attends the exclusive and private French Elementary School, where she is referred to as Rosalie. She speaks only French at home with her parents.	7
Tata	8 years old in 1987, the live-in domestic servant in a pastor's household. The offspring of Tsimihety migrants, her mother died from post-partum complications. Her father was a parishoner in the pastor's church. He agreed to let Tata work for the pastor's family (and eventually move with them to Diégo-Suarez) with the understanding that she could attend school.	3
Yasmine	22 in 1993; met initially in 1987 at age 16. The sister of Abel and daughter of Alida. In 1987 her mother sought the assistance of a powerful tromba medium to curb Yasmine's carousing about town. By 1993 Yasmine had dropped out of school and was now the mistress of a powerful older man.	7, 8

Name	*Details*	*Chapter(s)*
	Teachers and Other School Officials	
Mme. Chantal	31; a part-time French teacher at the Catholic Academy. Born and raised in Nosy Be, she accompanied her husband, Mr. Prosper, to Ambanja following university studies in Antananarivo. Her mother is Sakalava; her father was French-Betsileo métis from the high plateaux.	3, 7
Mr. Ernest	A school teacher who knew Achille when he was a student at the state-run *lycée*.	8
Sister Estelle	A history and geography teacher at the *lycée* level at the Catholic Academy. Of highland origin, she nevertheless favors Sakalava hairstyles and other markers of local identity.	5, 6
Mme. Honorine	Headmistress of the state-run *lycée* (a post she shares with another headmaster). She teaches history and geography. She and her husband (also a teacher at a state-run *lycée* in Ambilobe, a town north of Ambanja) are active on the board of the *Alliance Française*.	2
Mr. Jaozara	A history teacher at the state-run *lycée*. He also moonlights at a local remedial school, and he farms as well to help make ends meet.	3, 7
Mr. Léon	Principal of Ambanja's largest *CEG* (State-run middle school).	2
Mme. Lucie	A school teacher at the Catholic Academy's *lycée*. She grew up in the Sambirano.	6
Mr. Prosper	34; Husband of Mme. Chantal; Betsileo from the central highlands, he spent his childhood in Morondava on the southwest coast. He teaches philosophy at the state-run *lycée*.	3, 7
Mr. Saidy	In his thirties; he teaches math at the state-run *lycée*. The son of a Yemeni migrant father and Sakalava mother, he is the husband of Mme. Vezo and brother of Mariamo.	3, 7, 8
Mme. Tsarahita	35; born and raised in Ambanja, she attended the Catholic Academy and passed her bac in 1986. Her parents could only afford to send one of their nine children to university; this brother is now a school administrator in a town north of Ambanja.	appears throughout

Name	*Details*	*Chapter(s)*
	Teachers and Other School Officials (*continued*)	
Mme. Tsarahita (*continued*)	Tsarahita works part-time at the Catholic Academy teaching classes in Official Malagasy; she is also the mother of three children. She is the primary research assistant to this project.	
Mme. Vezo [alias Mama Vé]	36; she teaches history, geography, and Official Official Malagasy at the *lycée*; she is also a gifted seamstress. Her husband Mr. Saidy is also a school teacher who specializes in math; they have four children, Alima, Zalifa, Ibrahim, and Zita. Mme. Vezo is very close to her sisters-in-law Mariamo and Ivetty, both of whom are merchants.	1, 2, 3, 6, 7, 8
Mr. Victor	In his thirties; as a teacher at the state-run *lycée* he initially struggled to learn to teach in Official Malagasy.	1, 2
	Other Adults (Parents, Professionals, etc.)	
Said Achimo	Elder cousin of Mme. Fatima; of royal descent, he rose to the level of Assistant Governor in the indigenous colonial administration in Ambanja in 1935; active in royal politics, he challenged the selection of Rachidy I as Bemazava-Sakalava ruler. Rachidy's supporters triumphed, and he reigned 1935–1945.	2
Alice	In 1987 her two-year-old daughter died of malaria; Alice, a nurse by training, sought advice from a host of indigenous healers for other explanations for her daughter's sudden death. She later accused her elderly neighbor Mama Rose of poisoning the child.	8
Mme. Alida	A nurse, seamstress, and part-time petty merchant born and raised in Ambanja. In 1987 (and subsequent years) she paid dearly for services rendered by a powerful tromba medium named Marivola. Her primary concerns were for her son Abel, whom she hoped would do well enough on his bac exams to gain entrance to medical school;	7, 8

Name	*Details*	*Chapter(s)*
	Other Adults (Parents, Professionals, etc.) (*continued*)	

Name	*Details*	*Chapter(s)*
Mme. Alida (*continued*)	and for her daughter Yasmine, who showed more interest in boys than schoolwork.	
Andrianam- binina	94; the grandfather of Foringa Josef; born in 1900 on the east coast (he is of Betsimisaraka royal origins), he arrived in Ambanja when he was sixteen. He was soon conscripted as a soldier during WWI and then remained in the army for twelve years.	5, 6
Antoinette	34; landless petty merchant who was born and raised in Ambanja; the daughter of Sakalava and Tsimihety parents. She is suspicious of the wealth reaped by peasants.	6
Mme. Fatima	Royal woman in her late sixties; attended Catholic boarding school in Antananarivo during the colonial era. Younger cousin of Said Achimo.	2
Fleur	32, from Nosy Be. She expresses great bitterness towards the travesty of her own experiences with her late schooling during the 1970s. She sees herself as a member of the Sacrificed Generation because she endured the early effects of malagasization.	1
Gérard	30 in 1987. Worked as an engineer at a local enterprise (state-run plantation). He attended the Catholic Academy eight years before and then continued on to university. He had been a school migrant from the Ampasindava Peninsula; later he convinced his parents to allow his younger sister to continue her studies in town while living under his supervision.	7
Mr. Laurent	35; a bank employee of highland origins.	6
Lydia	In her late 20s. She became pregnant in the same year that she studied for and passed her bac exams; as a result she abandoned her desire to continue her schooling at the university level.	2

Name	*Details*	*Chapter(s)*
	Other Adults (Parents, Professionals, etc.) (*continued*)	
Maman'i'Ricky	She works in a bureaucratic office based in Ambanja; in July, 1995, her boss's son, Achille, died suddenly while studying at a police academy in Diégo-Suarez.	8
Mama Rose	An elderly grandmother accused in 1987 of poisoning Alice's two-year-old daughter. She later left Ambanja to live in Ambilobe with her daughter (and with the two grandchildren who had been under her care). By the mid-1990s she had returned to Ambanja.	8
Mariamo	37; a skilled merchant and baker who is the daughter of a Yemeni migrant father and a Sakalava mother. Her husband is Tantely; her sons are Bruno Abdullah. She also has two fostered children living with her, Ouardah and Ishmael (their father is Mariamo's brother Hassan). She grew up in Ambanja, and she is the sister-in-law of Mme. Vezo and Yvetty. She completed *lycée* and is fluent in French.	3, 8
Marie	A tromba spirit medium who, in 1987, inhabited what is currently Dalia's house. She specialized in treating young (and sometimes pregnant) school girls who were afflicted with possession sickness.	7
Marivola	A powerful tromba spirit medium known for dispensing *fanafody raty* or harmful magic. Among her clients in 1987 was Alida, who first sought spiritual intervention that would help her son succeed on his bac exam and, subsequently, enter medical school; she later brought her daughter, Yasmine, hoping to curb her carousing about town with older men.	7, 8
Mélanie	Earned her bac certificate in the 1980s; she works hard to put her two sons through the Catholic Academy.	2
Papan'i'Ranja	Encountered in 1987 in Antananarivo. After his eldest daughter Ranja passed her bac exams, she went on to study at the university at Toliara in the far south; he was impelled to bring her back home after she fell gravely ill from madness or possession sickness.	8

Name	*Details*	*Chapter(s)*
	Other Adults (Parents, Professionals, etc.) (*continued*)	
Mr. Pascal	60; father of 8 children, a former school teacher; studied law and economics in France and Israel; worked much of his life as personal secretary to the owner of a large plantation in the Sambirano; also practices law.	1, 2, C
Salima and Abdul	Petty merchants who worked hard to send their two sons to the Catholic Academy. When they showed little scholastic promise they reluctantly transferred them to the state-run *CEG*.	2
Tsifaly	Met in 1987; medium possessed by the spirit Mbotimahasaky; her sister's fostered boy died of diphtheria that year while under her care.	8
Yvetty	In her 30s; a highly skilled merchant who travels frequently between Antananarivo, Nosy Be, and Ambanja. Rachida is her daughter, Mme. Vezo and Mariamo her sisters-in-law. Her husband is Aly; her two other children are Tina and Moser. Yvetty grew up 300 km south of Ambanja, where she completed *lycée*. She is fluent in French.	7, 8

\# All ages provided here are for 1994 unless noted otherwise.

\+ "C" designates "Conclusion."

Population Figures for Madagascar, 1900-1994

Year	M	F	Total
1900			2,245,000
1911	1,501,000	1,652,000	3,154,000
1921			3,388,000
1931			3,759,000
1940			4,087,000
1950			4,260,000*
			4,560,000**
1960			5,390,000*
			5,470,000**
1970			6,800,000
1985			9,985,000
1990			11,197,000
1994			14,303,000

Sources: Mitchell (1982:39) for 1900-1940; and United Nations (1979:80) and (1996:148) for 1948-1978 and 1985-1994, respectively. Mitchell provides a gender breakdown for 1911 only. For 1950 and 1960, estimates generated by Mitchell and the United Nations differ, and so I include both here. The totals are identified as follows: * = Mitchell; ** = United Nations.

APPENDIX THREE

Population Figures for Ambanja
and the Sambirano Valley

I. Census Results for 1986

| | Malagasy Citizens | | | | | |
| | 0–6 yrs. | | 6–17 yrs. | | 18–59 yrs. | |
Region	M	F	M	F	M	F
Ambanja Town	2,622	2,560	5,769	5,913	4,122	4,185
Rest of Valley	5,408	5,808	9,928	9,712	15,049	15,137
Totals:	8,030	8,368	15,697	15,625	19,171	19,322

Source: Service du Planification, Ambanja 3.7.87, assembled 1986.
* These figures reflect minor adjustments made to correct for calculation errors
  on the original census form; the total figure for foreign nationals is 3 points higher
  and the total population figure is 1 point higher than the original copy's calculation.

Malagasy Citizens			Foreign Nationals				
60+ yrs.		Mal.	M		F		FN	Grand
M	F	Total	(> 21 yrs.)		(> 21 yrs.)		Total	Totals
479	277	25,927	221	(155)	122	(77)	343	26,270
3,131	3,198	67,371	109	(61)	42	(13)	151	67,522
3,610	3,475	93,298*	330*	(216*)	164	(90)	494*	93,792*

II. Subsequent Censuses for 1993 and 1995

	1993	*1995*
Ambanja Town	24,358	27,524
Rest of Valley	78,384	82,574
TOTAL:	102,742	110,098

Source: Ambanja Fivondronana, July 1996.

NOTE: Beginning in the 1990s, attempts were no longer made to distinguish the Valley's population along ethnic lines, as had been done in 1986 (and thus it is unclear, too, whether these figures include foreign nationals). Furthermore, no records were available that specified sub-categories of the population by age.

Several factors may account for the apparent drop in Ambanja's population from 1986–87 to 1993: censuses are generally conducted in anticipation of elections; given that this is a migrant town, Ambanja's population waxes and wanes according to the season. In 1993 especially, county (Fivondronana) staff sought to exclude migrants from their survey, even though a significant proportion of the town's (and Valley's) population consists of settlers from other parts of the island. It is unclear, too, whether the figures above include foreign nationals.

Schools in Ambanja
and the Sambirano Valley

	Primary (primaire)	Middle School (collège)	High School (lycée)
classes:	11ème–7ème	6ème–3ème	seconde, première, terminale
equivalent grades in the U.S.:	1st–5th	6th–9th	10th–12th

Public			

STATE-RUN:

* in town:	6	1	2
* regional, within the valley:	4	6	0

Six *neighborhood schools* in Ambanja; four others are scattered throughout the valley (the county or *fivondronana*) placed for the most part on plantation lands to serve the needs of workers' children. Primary education for Malagasy children in Ambanja began in the colonial era with the first school

Ambanja has 1 *CEG*; another 6 are scattered throughout the valley, typically 20-30 km apart. 2 others shut down in 1990 for lack of State funding. Ambanja's *CEG* is the largest and best staffed in the region. *No. of students*: approx. 400 in Ambanja.

Lycée Tsiaraso I (also referred to as the *Lycée Mixte* because it is co-ed). First classes held in 1986–87; a smaller *lycée* had existed previously and opened around 1980. *No. of students*: shrinking over time from 300 to 145. *Cost*: As with the *CEG*, beginning with the 1994–5 academic year,

Primary (primaire)	Middle School (collège)	High School (lycée)
	Public (continued)	

Primary (primaire)	Middle School (collège)	High School (lycée)
being built in 1908. It then expanded significantly in the 1970s under President Ratsiraka, but by the mid-1980s several small village schools in the Sambirano were closed because of budgetary constraints. *No. of students*: approx. 800 alone in the town's largest primary school. Estimate for the entire valley: 12,500. *Cost:* none, save for basic school supplies.	Estimate for the entire valley: 1,450. *Cost*: Beginning with the 1994–5 academic year, each student was charged FMG 2,500 plus FMG 3,000 for the services of a parent-teacher association and for miscellaneous operating costs, plus FMG 100 for institutional insurance. Prior to 1994, middle school education was free, save for basic school supplies.	each student was charged FMG 5,000 plus FMG 3,000 for a parent-teacher association and for miscellaneous operating costs, plus FMG 100 for institutional insurance.

A small Technical School is located at the outskirts of town and serves students from throughout the valley, as well as from the neighboring counties *(fivondronana)* of Ambilobe and Nosy Be. *No. of students*: approx. 80. *Cost*: unreported [assumed similar to the *lycée*].

[In 1987 there was also an Agricultural School about a half-hour drive from Ambanja; by 1993 it had closed.] |

	Primary (primaire)	Middle School (collège)	High School (lycée)
Private: Licensed			
* in town:	2	1	1
* regional, within the valley:	1	1	1

FOREIGN: (ELITE)

French Elementary School. This primary school also includes a kindergarten. In operation since the mid-1980s. Established through the efforts of the town's foreign and highland elite in order to satisfy the educational needs they had identified for their own young children. It is staffed primarily by foreign nationals, especially by university students from France. Some instructors are Malagasy.

No. of students: approx. 75.

Cost: FMG 25,000 in 1993–4, by 1994–5 FMG 37,500 x 10 months. French citizens receive a discount so that they pay approximately half the amount charged for the children of Malagasy citizens.

	Primary (primaire)	*Middle School (collège)*	*High School (lycée)*
	Private: Licensed *(continued)*		
CATHOLIC:	*Catholic Mission Academy.* This school also has a kindergarten. Primary school in operation since 1938. *No. of students:* approx 1,300. *Cost:* FMG 4,000 x 10 months.	The Academy's middle school opened in the 1950s. *No. of students:* approx. 550. *Cost:* FMG 6,000 x 10 months.	The Academy introduced a *terminale* class in 1979. *No. of students:* under 200. *Cost:* FMG 7,000 x 10 months for *seconde* and *première*; FMG 9,000 x 10 months for *terminale*.
	Catholic School of the Upper Sambirano (CSUP). Located approximately 25 km southeast of Ambanja in the region referred to as the upper Sambirano Valley. A sister school of Ambanja's Catholic Academy, it serves almost exclusively children from this more isolated region. *No. of students at primary level:* unknown, but considerably smaller than Ambanja's Catholic Academy. *Cost:* approx. the same as Ambanja's Catholic Academy.	*No. of students at middle school:* unknown, but considerably smaller than Ambanja's Catholic Academy. *Cost:* approx. the same as Ambanja's Catholic Academy.	In conjunction with the Academy's *lycée*, there is a parallel Seminary program for young men; these students prepare for the priesthood while simultaneously enrolled in *lycée*. Few actually become priests. *No. of students:* under 20. *Cost:* approximately the same as the Academy's regular *lycée* level classes. The majority are on scholarships. *No. of students at* lycée *level:* 70–90. *Cost:* approx. the same as the Catholic Academy.

	Primary (primaire)	Middle School (collège)	High School (lycée)
		Private: Unlicensed	
* in town:	1	3	0
REMEDIAL:	*Salvation School.* Started admitting primary school students in the mid-1990s. *No. of students*: approx. 200. *Cost:* FMG 5,000 x 10 months.	Salvation was opened originally in the 1986–7 academic year to serve the needs of students who had failed at the *collège* level at the State-run *CEG* or at the Catholic Academy. *No. of students*: approx. 150. *Cost:* FMG 7,500 x 10 months.	
		School of Courage. In 1992 this second remedial school opened. *No. of students*: unreported. *Cost:* unreported (approx. the same as Salvation).	
		Helping Hand of Hope. At the beginning of the 1993–4 academic year this third remedial school opened. *No. of students*: unreported. *Cost:* FMG 8,000 x 10 months.	[In 1995 staff at Helping Hand had begun to consider expanding the school to include a *lycée* curriculum.]

	Primary (primaire)	Middle School (collège)	High School (lycée)
		Other	

* in town: 3

Koranic Schools. The most
recent of these schools
was established in the
late 1980s and catered to
the needs of Muslim
children from a wide
array of ethnic and
national backgrounds.
Two other well-
established Islamic
schools already exist in
town: one is connected
to a mosque whose
membership is primarily
Comorean; the other is
part of the imposing
Indo-Pakistani mosque.
Two other small
communities (one based
at the old "Arab"
mosque, another defined
by a small splinter group
that encourages veiling
and purdah) provide less
formalized instruction
for their children.
Students enrolled at all
three Islamic schools are,
for the most part, of
primary school age, and
their pupils are both girls
and boys.

NOTE: Enrollment figures are approximations based on information supplied for the 1993, 1994 and 1995 school years. Tuition costs reflect 1995 rates.

Enrollment Figures
for Select Ambanja Schools

(Primary, CEG, and Lycée, 1993-94, 1994-95)

The bureaucratic sources for statistical data on education in the Sambirano change frequently. By 1994–95 they were as follows: Government of Madagascar, Firaisana of Ambanja: Fiches D'Enquéte Lycée, Programme de Renforcement du Système Educatif Malgache (PRESEM), Ministère de l'Education Nationale, Direction de l'Inspection Générale de l'Education Nationale, Direction de la Planification de l'Education, Direction des Ressources Humaines, Direction de l'Enseignement Secondaire.

Enrollment Figures for Ambanja's Largest State-Run Primary School 1994–95

Classe	U.S. Grade	Boys		Girls		Total	Gender Difference
		Total	Repeat	Total	Repeat		
11ème	first	79	(32)	90	(18)	169	11 more girls than boys
10ème	second	71	(28)	78	(26)	149	7 more girls than boys
9ème	third	47	(21)	78	(28)	125	31 more girls than boys
8ème	fourth	104	(32)	133	(48)	237	29 more girls than boys
7ème	fifth	52	(20)	75	(30)	127	23 more girls than boys
Total students:		353		454		807	101 more girls than boys

Number of students who passed the *CEPE* exam at the end of this school term: unknown; the national average is around 32–35%.

TOTAL ESTIMATED PRIMARY SCHOOL ENROLLMENTS FOR THE SAMBIRANO:

Institutional Category	*Pupils*
State-run Schools: (includes enrollment figures for Ambanja's largest primary school)	12,500 (this figure typifies enrollment figures in the 1990s; 1991–92, however, was exceptionally high with a registration rate of over 17,000)
Private Schools: (licensed and unlicensed/remedial)	1,100–1,300
Total:	approximately 13,700

Enrollment Figures for Ambanja's Largest State-Run Primary School
By Class, Age, and Gender, 1994–1995

Age	*11ème* Boys	Girls	*10ème* Boys	Girls	*9ème* Boys	Girls	*8ème* Boys	Girls	*7ème* Boys	Girls
six	29	55	2	5						
seven	30	17	7	17		1				
eight	10	11	25	15	2	10	1	1		
nine	7	2	15	19	10	24	6	4		
ten	1	3	13	19	11	13	17	24	1	
eleven	1	1	2	2	10	14	20	36	1	4
twelve	1	1	5		5	10	22	32	5	9
thirteen				1	1	3	19	20	16	17
fourteen			1		6	2	14	11	8	21
fifteen and over			1		2	1	5	5	22	23
Average Age:*	7.1	6.8	9	8.6	10.9	10.1	11.9	11.7	13.9	13.6
Totals:	79	90	71	78	47	78	104	133	52	75
= 807 pupils	169		149		125		237		127	

* Age averages have been rounded to the nearest tenth. Also, all students who fall into the category of "fifteen or over" were computed as being fifteen years old when, in fact, several students may have been considerably older, especially in the *8ème* and *7ème* classes.

Enrollment Figures for Ambanja's Largest State-Run Middle School (*CEG*)
1993–1994

Classe	U.S. Grade	New	Boys Repeat	Total	New	Girls Repeat	Total	Grand Totals	Average* Age
6ème	6th	41	(34)	75	21	(37)	58	133	15.3
5ème	7th	48	(10)	58	51	(6)	57	115	14.98
4ème	8th	25	(7)	32	29	(7)	36	68	15.89
3ème	9th	22	(14)	36	32	(21)	53	89	16.87
Totals:		136	(65)	201	133	(71)	204	405	

* No tables were available that showed the breakdown of students' individual ages.

Number of students drawn from all of the
Sambirano's middle schools (both public
and private) who sat for the *BEPC* exam the
previous academic year (1992–93):   546

Those who passed: 26% (approximately 142 students)

TOTAL ESTIMATED MIDDLE SCHOOL (CEG) ENROLLMENTS FOR THE SAMBIRANO:

Institutional Category	Pupils
State-run *CEG*s: (includes enrollment figures for Ambanja's *CEG*)	approximately 1,450
Private Schools: (licensed and unlicensed/remedial)	approximately 800
Total:	approximately 2,250

Enrollment Figures for the State-Run *Lycée* Tsiraso I 1993–1994

Classe	U.S. Grade	Boys New	Boys Repeat	Total	Girls New	Girls Repeat	Total	Grand Totals	Average Age
Seconde	10th	26	(5)	31	5	(2)	7	38	18
Primière (Séries A & D)	11th	15	(8)	23	7	(0)	7	30	19.5
Terminale A (humanities & social sciences)	12th	5	(16)	21	11	(15)	26	47	20.5
Terminale D (natural sciences)		15	(8)	23	4	(3)	7	30	19.5*
				44			33	77	
Totals:		61	(37)	98	27	(20)	47	145**	

* This was an exceptional class of girls in terms of their average age; see the following chart for details.

** By the end of the school term the initial enrollment of 145 had dropped to 130.

TOTAL ESTIMATED LYCÉE ENROLLMENTS FOR THE SAMBIRANO:

Institutional Category	Pupils
State-run Schools	
Lycée Tsiaraso I	145
Technical School	80 (approximate)
Private Schools	
Catholic Mission School Academy	184
Catholic School of the Upper Sambirano	80 (approximate)
Total:	489 (approximate)

Class Enrollments for the State-run *Lycée* Tsiraso I
By Class, Age, and Gender 1993–1994

Age	Seconde		Première		Terminale A		Terminale D		All Terminale	
	Boys	Girls	Boys	Girls	Boys	Girls	Boys	Girls	Boys	Girls
Unknown: 3			1				2		2	
fourteen	1									
fifteen	3									
sixteen	5	1	2					1		1
seventeen	2	1	1	2	1				1	
eighteen	5	1	2		1	4	5	1	6	5
nineteen	9	3	7	1		4	2	3	2	7
twenty	4	1	1	2	2	1	3	1	5	2
twenty-one	2		3	1	5	8	3	1	8	9
twenty-two			3		2	2	1		3	2
twenty-three			3		6	1	6		12	1
twenty-four (and over)					4	6	1		5	6
Average Age:*	17.9	18.3	19	18.4	21.8	21	18.9	18.9	20.3	20.4
Totals:	31	7	23	7	21	26	23	7	44	33
= 145 pupils	38		30		47		30		77	

* Age averages have been rounded to the nearest tenth.

Enrollment Figures for the Catholic Mission Academy *Lycée* 1993–1994

Classe	U.S. Grade	New	Boys Redo	Total	New	Girls Redo	Total	Grand Totals	Average* Age
Seconde	10th	24	(0)	24	25	(0)	25	49	20
Primière (Séries A & D)	11th	35	(0)	35	20	(0)	20	55	20
Terminale A (humanities & social science)	12th	18	(8)	26	10	(14)	24	50	20
Terminale D (natural science)		13	(9)	22	5	(3)	8	30	19
				48			32	80	
Totals:		90	(17)	107	60	(17)	77	184	

* No tables were available that showed a breakdown of students' individual ages.

Bac Results at the State-Run Lycée Tsiraso I, 1990-1994

Terminale Class:*	A		C		D		Totals		
	Boys	Girls	Boys	Girls	Boys	Girls	Boys	Girls	
1990–91 exam students:	27	17	11	1	33	11	71	29	(T=110)
Number who passed:	4	5	0	1	5	0	9	6	(T=15)
Percent who passed:									14% **
1991–92 exam students:	27	36	—	—	52	16	77	52	(T=131)
Number who passed:	2	3	—	—	4	0	6	3	(T=9)
Percent who passed:									7% **
1992–93 exam students:	29	26	—	—	16	9	45	35	(T=80)
Number who passed:	0	0	—	—	1	0	1	0	(T=1)
Percent who passed:									1% **
1993–94 exam students:	21	26	—	—	23	7	44	33	(T=77)
Number who passed:	9	7	—	—	2	2	11	9	(T=18)
Percent who passed:									23% **

* *Terminale Série A*: humanities and social science track.

Terminale Série D: natural science track, necessary for medical school training.

Terminale Série C: track that emphasizes advanced mathematics and physics. Beginning in the 1990–91 academic year Ambanja's schools no longer offered schooling or bac exams in *Terminale Série C*.

** These percentages have been rounded to the nearest whole number.

Students' Aspirations

Overall Distribution of Completed Student
Questionnaires Concerning Personal Background and Future Aspirations

Level of Schooling	State-run Schools			Private						Totals		
				Catholic Mission Academy			Remedial Schools					
	Girls	Boys	Total	Girls	Boys	Total	Girls	Boys	Total	Girls	Boys	Total
Primary	7	15	22	—	—	—	—	—	—	7	15	22
Middle School	13	11	24	47	30	77	38	28	66	98	69	167
Lycée	6	19	25	22	16	38	—	—	—	28	35	63
										133	119	252

STUDENTS' PROFESSIONAL DREAMS

NOTE: A total of 252 questionnaires were completed by 133 girls and 119 boys. These questionnaires were distributed as follows: 22 at the primary, 167 at the middle school, and 63 at the *lycée* levels. Students often provided more than one answer to the question of relevance here (FR: "What do you hope [to be] when you are an adult?", *Qu'est-ce que c'est tes aspirations quand tu sera adulte?*; OM: "What things do you wish for when you grow up [are big]?", *Inona no zavatra tianao hatao rehefa lehibe ianao?*). Thus, the total number of responses recorded below far exceeds 252.

I. ADVANCED EDUCATION

(lycée level a minimum; generally requires a passing grade on the bac exam and/or advanced schooling at, for example, a university or seminary)

	Primary			Middle School			Lycée			Totals		
	Girls	Boys	Total	Girls	Boys	Total	Girls	Boys	Total	Girls	Boys	Total
EDUCATION												
Teacher:	1	6	7	16	8	24	—	1	1	17	15	32
More specific goals:												
— teach Malagasy							—	1	1	—	1	1
— teach philosophy and/or history/geog.							1	1	2	1	1	2
—teach science							1	—	1	1	—	1
—teach math							1	—	1	1	—	1
—teach English				1	—	1				1	—	1
University Professor				1	—	1				1	—	1
Teacher Totals:	1	6	7	18	8	26	3	3	6	22	17	39
Advanced study at the university level:												
—philosophy							—	1	1	—	1	1
—history/geog.							1	1	2	1	1	2
School Director	—	1	1	1	—	1				1	1	2
Education Totals:	1	7	8	19	8	27	4	5	9	24	20	44

	Primary			Middle School			Lycée			Totals		
	Girls	Boys	Total	Girls	Boys	Total	Girls	Boys	Total	Girls	Boys	Total
HEALTH CARE												
Doctor	1	4	5	19	19	38	2	13	15	22	36	58
— Surgeon				1	—	1	—	1	1	1	1	2
Dentist				2	—	2	—	1	1	2	1	3
Midwife	3	—	3	49	—	49	5	—	5	57	—	57
Nurse	1	—	1	4	1	5	1	—	1	6	1	7
Health Care (unspecified)	1	—	1							1	—	1
Pharmacy							—	1	1	—	1	1
Health Care Totals:	6	4	10	75	20	95	8	16	24	89	40	129
SCIENTIFIC RESEARCH AND SUPPORT												
Agricultural Science							—	1	1	—	1	1
Scientific Research							—	1	1	—	1	1
Lab Technician				1	—	1				1	—	1
Scientific Totals:	—	—	—	1	—	1	—	2	2	1	2	3
ENGINEERING												
Engineer				1	2	3	1	1	2	2	3	5
Electrical Engineer				—	1	1	—	1	1	—	1	1
Engineering Totals:	—	—	—	1	3	4	1	1	2	2	4	6

	Primary			Middle School			Lycée			Totals		
	Girls	Boys	Total	Girls	Boys	Total	Girls	Boys	Total	Girls	Boys	Total
WRITING/JOURNALISM												
Journalist	—	—	—	—	—	—	3	—	3	3	—	3
CLERGY												
Catholic Nun/Priest	—	—	—	3	2	5	2	—	2	5	2	7
LAW/GOVERNMENT												
Judge	—	1	1	—	3	3	—	1	1	—	5	5
Lawyer	—	—	—	—	—	—	—	1	1	—	1	1
Provincial Head	—	—	—	—	1	1	—	—	—	—	1	1
President of Madagascar	—	—	—	—	1	1	—	—	—	—	1	1
Law/Government Totals:	—	1	1	—	5	5	—	2	2	—	8	8
TOURISM OR TRAVEL/WORK ABROAD												
Ambassador	—	—	—	1	1	2	—	—	—	1	1	2
Flight Attendant	—	—	—	12	—	12	7	—	7	19	—	19
Airplane Pilot	—	—	—	2	—	2	—	6	6	2	6	8
Director of a Tourist Agency	—	—	—	—	—	—	—	1	1	—	1	1
Hotel Services	—	—	—	—	—	—	1	—	1	1	—	1
Model	—	—	—	1	—	1	—	—	—	1	—	1

	Primary			Middle School			Lycée			Totals		
	Girls	Boys	Total	Girls	Boys	Total	Girls	Boys	Total	Girls	Boys	Total
Work Abroad												
—in France							2	1	3	2	1	3
—in U.S.					2	2					2	3
—office work oversees				1		1				1		2
—engineer in France					1	1		1		1	1	1
—international business							1	1	2	1	1	2
Study Abroad								1	1		1	1
Tourism/Work	1				1		1				1	
Abroad Totals:	—	—	—	19	5	24	11	10	21	30	15	45
BUSINESS (DOMESTIC)												
Bank Teller				3	1	4				3	1	4
Bank Director				1		1				1		1
Secretary/Office Staff	1		1	9	1	10				10	1	11
Business							1	1	2	1	1	2
Business Manager								1	1		1	1
Insurance					1	1					1	1
Business Totals:	1	—	1	13	3	16	1	2	3	15	5	20
I. ADVANCED TOTALS:	8	12	20	131	46	177	30	38	68	169	96	265

II. MID-RANGE EDUCATION

(requires specialized skills; training often occurs through apprenticeships, etc.; *lycée* education not required, although a high literacy level is important)

	Primary			Middle School			Lycée			Totals		
	Girls	Boys	Total	Girls	Boys	Total	Girls	Boys	Total	Girls	Boys	Total
COMMERCE												
Independent Merchant				1	—	1	—	1	1	1	1	2
SUPERVISORY ROLES IN MILITARY, MARINE, AND LAW ENFORCEMENT												
Boat Captain				—	2	2				—	2	2
Head of Police				—	1	1				—	1	1
Supervisory Military, etc. Totals:	—	—	—	—	3	3	—	—	—	—	3	3
SPECIALIZED TRADES REQUIRING ADVANCED TRAINING AND LITERACY												
Electrician				—	3	3				—	3	3
Mechanic/Technician				—	4	4				—	4	4
Specialized Trades Totals:	—	—	—	—	7	7	—	—	—	—	7	7
II. MID-RANGE TOTALS:	—	—	—	1	10	11	—	1	1	1	11	12

III. LOW LEVEL EDUCATION

(requires specialized skills, yet little formal education is required. Minimal literacy requirement.)

	Primary			Middle School			Lycée			Totals		
	Girls	Boys	Total	Girls	Boys	Total	Girls	Boys	Total	Girls	Boys	Total
NON-SUPERVISORY MILITARY AND MARINE (including lay jobs)												
Marine				—	2	2	—	2	2	—	2	2
Soldier	—	1	1	—	1	1	—	1	1	—	4	4
Sailor							—	2	2	—	3	3
Non-Supervisory Military and Marine Totals:	—	1	1	—	3	3	—	5	5	—	9	9
SPECIALIZED SKILLS AND TRADES (often require apprenticeships)												
Furniture Maker				—	1	1				—	1	1
Tailor/Seamstress	—	2	2	3	1	4	2	—	2	5	3	8
Driver				—	2	2				—	2	2
Hairdresser				1	—	1				1	—	1
Artist/Singer				1	—	1	1	1	2	2	1	3
Athlete							—	1	1	—	1	1
Specialized Skills Totals:	—	2	2	5	4	9	3	2	5	8	8	16
III. LOW LEVEL TOTALS:	—	3	3	5	7	12	3	7	10	8	17	25

IV. NO FORMAL EDUCATION
(specialized skills, but no formal education required, nor is high literacy)

	Primary			Middle School			Lycée			Totals		
	Girls	Boys	Total	Girls	Boys	Total	Girls	Boys	Total	Girls	Boys	Total
LOW SKILL/SERVICE TRADES (no extensive formal training)												
Factory Worker				1	1	2				1	1	2
Cook							1	—	1	1	—	1
Low Skill/Service Trades Totals:	—	—	—	1	1	2	1	—	1	2	1	3
SUBSISTENCE ECONOMY												
Peasant/Farmer	—	2	2	1	4	5	—	1	1	1	7	8
Fisherman				—	2	2	—	—	—	—	2	2
Subsistence Economy Totals:	—	2	2	1	6	7	—	1	1	1	9	10
IV. NO FORMAL EDUCATION TOTALS:	—	2	2	2	7	9	1	1	2	3	10	13

NOTES

INTRODUCTION

1. My friend communicated this idea by playing on a local idiomatic expression, saying that radio had become "*fady* [taboo] like *tromba* [royal spirit possession]," tromba being the focus of my research throughout 1987. In essence, then, radio has come to seem a remnant of the past, no longer viable in the newly commercialized environment of the Fourth Republic. As such, it is now considered unfashionable by urban youth in Antananarivo.

2. I intentionally reject the term "postcolonial," relying instead on "postindependent." Although post*colonial* operates as a powerful tool for underscoring the complexity of modernity (and thus of post*modern* existence), such terminology nevertheless belittles the power—be it actual or potential—of African states and their people following independence. For a compelling discussion of the problematics of such terminology, see Appiah 1991.

3. I wish to thank Thomas Miller for encouraging me to view this exhibit, following his own remarks on its ambiguous status.

4. I should note that this characterization was far more true in the 1970s, when I began my research. In the past few years, there has been a burgeoning of young scholars working throughout the island and outside of the highlands.

5. Malagasy naming practices are complex. The surname is often given first and the personal name second, although this rule is loosely followed at best. Malagasy typically provide the full names of presidents Tsiranana and Ratsiraka with their personal names first, but they do the opposite with Zafy. Honoring national custom, I order their names as do the island's citizens.

6. As noted earlier, the time frame of this study ends in 1995, two years after President Zafy resumed office (he was removed in late 1996). Ratsiraka has done little to disrupt Zafy's pedagogical reforms, and schooling continues to be conducted in French. Given that this study focuses on a cohort of students schooled during the Second Republic's socialist era, it concludes in the mid 1990s. In January 2002, while this book was in press, Ratsiraka's standing as president was being challenged in preliminary national elections.

7. The anthropological literature on indigenous reconstructions of history is widespread; for discussions of personal histories as social critiques, see Abu-Lughod 1993; Halbwachs 1925, 1968; Hejaiej 1996; and Kenyon 1991; other texts that underscore the intersection of history, collective memory, and politics include Battaglia 1990; Bloch 1989; Boyarin 1994; Casey 1987; Connerton 1989; Comaroff and Comaroff 1991, 1992; Foster 1988; Geertz 1980; Gell 1992; Hobsbawm 1983; Obeyesekere 1992; Price and Price 1991; Rosaldo 1980; Sahlins 1985; Vansina 1985; and Wolf 1982.

8. For the impact of Fanon on other theorists, see Asad 1973; Memmi 1965; Ngugi 1986; Fisher 1985; and Balandier 1951. For Fanon's critique of Mannoni's assessment of the colonized mind, see Fanon 1967, ch. 4.

9. In recent years, nationalism has defined a rich terrain for studies by anthropologists and other social scientists. See, e.g., Apter 1992; Anderson 1991; Bayart 1993; Chatterjee 1993; Gellner 1983, 1987; and Mbembe 1992.

10. An exceptional and comprehensive collection has evolved under the editorship of Beatrice B. and John W. M. Whiting. See Whiting 1963; Whiting, Whiting, and Longabaugh 1975; and Whiting and Edwards 1988. And see also, e.g., Burbank 1988; Condon 1987; Davis and Davis 1989; Hollos and Leis 1989; Gottlieb et al. 1966; Lebra 1995; Le Vine 1974; LeVine and White 1986; and LeVine et al. 1994.

11. Numerous standard anthropological techniques have been employed throughout this work to protect informants' identities. These include the use of pseudonyms and, at times, composite case studies.

12. The lack of attention given to the 1947 insurrection may spring in part from the fact that Ambanja's inhabitants were not as heavily involved as were people living on the east coast, for example. There were, nevertheless, activists living in the north, and, as colonial documents attest, many people were arrested, interrogated, and tried in the northern province of Antsiranana. As noted, elders with personal knowledge of these events are sometimes reluctant to speak of them in detail. For a detailed account of 1947, see Tronchon 1982. For contemporary perspectives on the politics of memory from the east coast of Madagascar, see Cole, 2001.

CHAPTER 1. YOUTH AND THE COLONIZED MIND

Epigraph: Ratsiraka 1975, 117.

1. Even the nation's first constitution made direct reference to its indebtedness to France: the preamble declared "that the Malagasy believe in God and in the eminent dignity of the human person, to demonstrate the will of Madagascar to remain attached to . . . Western Civilization" (Paillard 1979, 302). Under Ratsiraka's Second Republic, references to (a Christian) God were removed and a commitment was instead declared to "the condemnation of the exploitation of man by man as well as all forms of domination, oppression and alienation that might ensue" (ibid., 354, n. 93).

2. In my choice of the term *moral,* I wish to underscore the manner in which a colonial ideology inevitably denigrated the collective sense of self among the colonized (cf. Fisher 1985; Fanon 1967), not unlike what Erving Goffman has labeled the "mortification" of the self in the context of total institutions (1961, 14 ff., 127 ff.).

3. In Madagascar, there is no single word that refers collectively to the people of the high plateaux (in French, *les gens des hauts plateaux* or *les habitants des hautes terres*), as for the in-

habitants of the coast *(côtiers)*. For the sake of symmetry, I have therefore adopted the English term *highlander*. In Ambanja, a highlander is assumed to be Merina, Betsileo, or Vakinankaratra. The major urban centers of this region are Antananarivo, Fianarantsoa, and Antsirabe.

4. This pattern typifies much of urban Africa; see, e.g., Hansen 1997 on Lusaka.

5. The Zatovo Western Andevo Malagasy, or ZWAM, young "cowboys" (of slave descent) who assumed a style of dress and attitude reminiscent of Clint Eastwood, a loner recognized as "the champion of real justice" over "the venal guardians of formal law" (Covell 1987, 39, citing Althabe 1980 and Leymarie 1973), were one of the most striking groups to form during this period. By 1972, they had renamed themselves the Zatovo Orin'asa Anivon'ny Madagasikara (Young Unemployed of Madagascar), or ZOAM (Covell 1987, 47; Paillard 1979, esp. 353, n. 75; Raison-Jourde 1997, 35–38).

6. The Mouvement National pour l'Indépendance de Madagascar (National Movement for the Independence of Madagascar), or MONIMA, was founded by Monja Jaona in 1958 and was a major opposition party during President Tsiranana's First Republic. The party was renamed Madagasikara Otronin'ny Malagasy (Madagascar Supported by the Malagasy) in 1967 (Covell 1995, 150–51).

7. For more details on these events, see Archer 1976; Covell 1987, 41–49, 51–57, 167–68; Paillard 1979, 328–46; and Rajoelina 1988.

8. AREMA was not the sole political party in Madagascar during the period of the socialist revolution, but it was the dominant one. In fact, as Covell explains, there was greater party diversity under Ratsiraka than there had been during the Tsiranana years. For a discussion of AREMA and Madagascar's one-party system, see Covell 1987, 119 ff.; on AREMA more generally, see ibid., 59, 60–61; Bunge 1983, 11; and Paillard 1979, 345.

9. I was also in Madagascar for a month in 1981, but I was not particularly well informed of the political situation at that time and I hesitate to comment on my impressions.

10. Zafy, a surgeon by training, was educated in France, beginning in 1954, and remained there until 1971. From 1972 to 1975, he was the minister of health under General Ramanantsoa. After campaigning against Ratsiraka's proposed constitution, Zafy then returned to his post as a professor at the University of Madagascar, where he remained throughout much of the Second Republic. Zafy reemerged as a clear presidential candidate during the late years of Ratsiraka's regime (Covell 1995, 254–55). On the failings of the Ratsiraka regime, see Ramanandraibe 1987.

11. The evolution of corruption is a complex process. I do not mean to imply that Ratsiraka's regime was solely responsible for the rise of corruption in Madagascar: bribery and black market trade had existed long before, with current practices often stemming from those introduced by the French as part of the destructive patron-client relationship so common in colonized territories. The hybridization of Malagasy and European-derived practices is aptly expressed in a phrase that came into vogue in the late 1980s: underhanded dealings that generated enormous wealth were often referred to in Ambanja and elsewhere as *manao business* ("doing business"), simultaneously implying corrupt practices and shrewd business sense.

12. Ratsiraka 1975, 9: "L'indépendance, et plus précisément l'indépendance politique, n'entraîne pas ipso facto, et loin s'en faut la fin du colonialisme et l'avènement d'une société plus juste." The *Boky Mena* has been published within Madagascar in both official Malagasy and French. I have chosen to use the French translation so as to highlight the manner in which it echoes and contests colonial rhetoric. My informants generally

preferred to use French rather than Malagasy for key terms such as *sacrificed generation, revolution, colonized mind,* and *metropole,* because they, too, recognized that the origins of these ideas lay in colonial and revolutionary French writings.

13. More specifically, what Ratsiraka referred to as "*social et culturel autonome*" ("social and cultural autonomy") (1975, 9).

14. Covell 1987, 28. In Covell's opinion, Tsiranana was an appropriate choice for a first president from the point of view of his French contemporaries: he had already proved himself as a national leader in Madagascar; as a student in France, he had challenged the legitimacy of Merina nationalist groups, advocating the needs of *côtiers;* in 1947, he had been in France and thus was unassociated with the turmoil on the island during that year; he was a member of the French Socialist Party, as was the governor-general of Madagascar; and he was opposed to immediate independence, seeing it as running contrary to coastal needs. He also expressed the necessity of maintaining close ties with France. By the early 1950s, he had already entered the political arena, serving as a member of Mahajanga's provincial assembly and later as a deputy of the French national assembly (Covell 1987, 30).

15. Ratsiraka 1975, 9: "La Révolution est un combat de tous les jours."

16. Ibid., 9, 12: "Ceci suppose en particulier une révolution des mentalités, une cohérence entre la doctrine et la réalité, entre les paroles et les actes, entre l'action du gouvernement et celle du peuple, bref une cohésion et une unité de toutes les forces vivres de la Nation tendues vers un même but—faire l'homme malgache nouveau, réaliser une société plus heureuse sous la direction des masses laborieuses des villes et des campagnes. Que la lutte soit difficile et qu'elle exige des sacrifices, nous le savons. Que la route soit parsemée d'obstacles, c'est évident. Qu'il faille aborder et vaincre ceux-ci tour à tour, un à un, cela est hors de contestation.... Nous n'avons qu'un choix: être ou disparaître. Nous avons choisi d'être, dans l'indépendance, la liberté, la dignité, la justice et la paix-quoiqu'il nous en coûte....

...La révolution nationale malgache n'est pas le fruit d'une parthéno-genèse; elle prend ses racines dans l'âme malgache, elle est conditionnée (conditions objectives) par son environement historique (domination coloniale) et géographique (position stratégique)."

17. This is very much a part of Madagascar's history as a whole: highland as well as coastal Malagasy were heavily involved in the Indian Ocean slave trade for centuries prior to French conquest; the island's shores were dotted with ports well known to Swahili and Arab traders who sailed the Mozambique Channel and beyond; and it served as a place to replenish supplies by pirates and by merchants' ships that sailed as far as East Asia with African goods (for detailed analysis of Chinese knowledge of Africa, see Chittick and Rotberg 1975; Freeman-Grenville 1962). The significance of the coastal slave trade is a focus of chapter 5.

18. In this, as in other writings (Sharp 1981, 1993), I rely here on the spelling *malagasization,* because it corresponds with the term used during my own tenure in Madagascar in the late 1980s and incorporates an indigenous spelling of the term for the island's people and language.

19. French continued to be the primary language of instruction in biology, medicine, and mathematics because of the highly technical language involved, which is recognized as being somewhat universal. In the words of one instructor, "imagine how difficult, frustrating, and counterproductive it would be to create a whole new vocabulary for ex-

plaining cell structure!" Clignet and Ernst provide an apt example of the difficulties encountered in mathematics: should the Malagasy word bear a meaning similar to the French technical term or sound like it? For example, should *tsilo* or *vekotora* be chosen for *vecteur* ("vector")? (Clignet and Ernst 1999, 75; see 65–78 for a broader discussion). This sort of secular linguistic dilemma has much in common with the predicaments that have characterized the translation of Christian values and concepts, as Rafael 1992 describes for Castilian-Latin-Tagalog renderings in the Philippines. In both contexts, new ideas are introduced that are, in essence, untranslatable in a local tongue, and thus the local culture becomes dominated by foreign ideas.

20. The name Vazimba is generally used to refer to (a perhaps mythical) people who inhabited the island prior to the early occupation by Austronesian people. The term is also equated locally with distant ancestral *(razana)* status. Because the Vazimba are believed to have been short, the label is used as well to describe a reclusive category of small nature spirits.

21. The region near the Sambirano was one such site, since the offshore island of Nosy Be (and, it is thought, the neighboring island of Nosy Komba) were locations of early—albeit unsuccessful—European settlements. British settlers arrived under the leadership of Colonel Robert Hunt in early 1649, with partial backing from the East India Company. Mervyn Brown argues that the timing of this settlement was "unfortunate," because "the middle of the seventeenth century saw the foundation of the Sakalava military empire which was to be the most powerful force in the island for nearly two centuries." Sakalava expansionist activities were well known to the inhabitants of another French settlement at Fort Dauphin, at a distant location on the southeastern tip of the island (it ended in a massacre in 1674). For discussion of early European settlements (including Portuguese, Dutch, English and French) between the early sixteenth and late eighteenth centuries, and even earlier activities of Arab traders, see Brown 1978, 46–54, 72–109; Escamps 1884, 1–64; Descartes 1846, 1–26; La Vaissière 1884, vol. 1; and Verin 1986.

22. Literacy in Madagascar did not hinge upon European penetration. A much older form of written Malagasy, found in texts known as *Sorabe*, employs Arabic script and was developed on the southeast coast. Some of these texts date as far back as the sixteenth century. Today, sorabe are employed primarily in ritual and healing contexts, although some contain historical narratives (Mack 1986, 33–38, 52).

23. For reasons that will become clear here and in subsequent chapters, neither Ranavalona I nor any other Merina ruler figures prominently in coastal reconstructions of history, at least in a heroic and nationalist sense.

24. More specifically, Queen Tsiomeko reigned over the northern Bemihisatra-Sakalava of Nosy Be. The Bemihisatra define a separate dynastic branch from the Bemazava of the Sambirano.

25. The sultan mandated that northern rulers convert to Islam, which they did; in the region of this study, they did not receive guns, however, but only hats. (Lisa Gezon [1995] reports that the Antankaraña to the north fared better.) According to my informants, it is this alliance that lies behind the fact that royal Bemazava-Sakalava of the Sambirano (as well as other neighboring rulers of Nosy Be and the Antankaraña kingdom) are Muslim. Commoner Bemazava-Sakalava, however, are more likely to be Catholic and/or adhere to practices associated with the *fombandrazaña*—that is, tromba and other royal rituals. For a detailed discussion of this, see Sharp 1993.

26. The independent Fiongonana Jesosy Kristiany Malagasy (FJKM), or the Malagasy Church of Jesus Christ, is by far the largest Protestant group in Ambanja, its membership swelling with Tsimihety and Betsileo migrants.

27. Ratsiraka 1975, 83: "impératifs de la Révolution, c'est-à-dire l'édification d'un État socialiste et véritablement malgache."

28. Although the breakdown of education in Madagascar may be more widespread, such conditions are, of course, unique neither to the island nor even to Africa. What is described here parallels the experiences of children in many countries. There are underrepresented, underfunded, and thus abandoned populations in even the most affluent nations, as I have learned from former students and colleagues working for voluntary organizations based in East Palo Alto in California, on Indian reservations in the Southwest, and in inner-city New York schools, where there may be few books or supplies, where bathrooms are converted into ramshackle classrooms, and where undertrained teachers themselves struggle to comprehend the curriculum, or where others simply do not care about the purposes of pedagogy (cf. Kozol 1991).

29. Official Malagasy, high plateaux, and Sakalava renderings of this and several other Malagasy terms that appear in this section are identical (save for *fombandrazana*, which in Sakalava is *fombandrazaña*), so I have not specified OM, HP, or SAK here.

30. My concern here is specifically with northern Sakalava understandings of sacrifice and, in turn, the metaphorical associations it generates in reference to the sacrificed generation. For discussions of sacrifice from elsewhere in Madagascar, see Bloch 1986, 1992; Cole 1997; and Graeber 1996.

31. There are several ways to pronounce—and write—this term. Northern Sakalava speak of the *tanindrazaña* and the *razaña* (ancestors), whereas in High Plateaux dialects and official Malagasy there is no *ñ*, and when spoken aloud the final two syllables are typically dropped. Given that these two variations, when written down, are so similar, I have opted to use the high plateaux (HP) spelling of these terms throughout much of this chapter in order to avoid confusing readers. Informants in Ambanja, however, typically used the word *tanindrazaña*, as did I in my questions, because we were speaking the northern Sakalava dialect. Thus the *ñ* appears below in interview excerpts.

32. The Loza River lies approximately 200 kilometers south of Ambanja, near Analalava.

33. Official French reports estimated that in the 1947 insurrection 60,000–89,000 Malagasy died (later reduced to 11,200), but Simone de Beauvoir, writing to Nelson Algren in November 1948, gives the much higher figure of 90,000 ("On a massacré 90 000 Noirs dans la rébellion, où 150 Blancs ont trouvé la mort" [*Lettres à Nelson Algren: Un amour transatlantique, 1947–1964* (Paris: Gallimard, 1997), 373–74]; I wish to thank Peter Dreyer for drawing my attention to de Beauvoir's account). As many as 5,000–6,000 Malagasy were convicted, and their military leaders were tried and condemned to death or life imprisonment (Bunge 1983, 23; Covell 1995, 211–13; Rakotomalala 1983; Tronchon 1982).

34. Some of the arguments and data presented here draw in part on Sharp 2001a.

35. F. Hawkins, personal communication, June, 1998.

36. Young informants in Ambanja often searched for alternative models, clamoring for a copy of the U.S. Bill of Rights (which I located, with great difficulty, in French translation, ironically in the home of someone I considered to be among the most corrupt men in Antsiranana Province). Our discussions often turned to such topics as Abraham Lincoln and the Civil War, and the Civil Rights Movement of the 1950s and 1960s.

37. For a concise discussion of the significance of these and other related terms in the French context, see Conor Cruise O'Brien 1988 and Kamenka 1988.

38. The French Revolution also permeates discussions of precolonial Imerina. Raison-Jourde 1990, for example, argues that the English and French alike envisioned the Merina ruler Radama I as a Malagasy Napoleon (cf. M. Esoavelomandroso 1990), whereas Domenichini 1990 describes Radama II (r. 1861–63) assuming command of Imerina at a revolutionary moment following the overthrow of the isolationist Queen Ranavalovana I.

39. Rambeloson-Rapiera 1990, 30: "Le regard porté sur l'Autre ramène toujours à soi-même." Cf. Kramer 1993.

40. The fact that Ratsiraka did not take up residence in Tsiranana's former palace can also be read in these terms: by occupying the former French embassy, he redefined this captured space as belonging to the revolution. By assuming a new residence different from his predecessor, he followed a pattern typical of Malagasy rulers, who generally build new palaces following the deaths of their predecessors (see chapter 4).

41. I employ the concept of ethnicity loosely here, since current constructions are in fact rooted in categories of difference as originally conceived of by the French. For discussions of the expansion of the Merina state in the late eighteenth and early nineteenth centuries, see Brown 1978; Heseltine 1971; and Labatut and Raharinarivonirina 1969. Brown 1978, 146, provides a map designed to show the expansions of the kingdom under Andrianampoinimerina and Radama I. Radama's territory encompassed much of northern and Sakalava territory, contradicting indigenous (and at times his own) accounts. The original notion of an islandwide Malagasy government (that is, a Merina one) was solidified by French agreement. The Franco-Malagasy treaty of 1868 recognized Queen Ranavalona I as the sovereign of the entire island of Madagascar. This is repeated in a subsequent treaty of 1881 with Queen Ranavalona II. Ranavalona II, when confronted with the news of French naval attacks on Nosy Be (Sakalava territory) in 1883, described the island as a whole as the land of her ancestors in a *kabary* she addressed to her troops (Brown 1978, 223–27). Merina hegemony over the entire island is likewise asserted by a portrait of the ruler Radama II (fig. 3); the original is labeled "Mpanjaka ny Madagascar" or "King of Madagascar."

42. It is no wonder, then, that (reelected) Ratsiraka's earliest revisionist platform included a federalist agenda that would have granted greater political and economic autonomy to all provinces. This was a topic of great debate when I was on the island from 1993 to 1995. I wish to stress here, too, that on the coast especially, national policies frequently favor Merina hegemony. Although Tsiranana, Ratsiraka, and Zafy in fact all hail from the different regions of the coast (they are Tsimihety, Betsimisaraka, and Antankaraña, respectively), they are, nevertheless, assumed to be in cahoots with Merina elite said to control much of the nation's political apparatus. In response, elite Merina professionals living in Ambanja often pass as Betsileo so that they may work peacefully in town.

43. Nigel Heseltine's (1971) detailed study focuses heavily on Merina history, for example; and see also Frederica Bunge's "Unification under the Merina, 1810–95" (Bunge 1983, 16) and Valette 1979. In contrast, Labatut and Raharinarivonirina 1969, a school text still in circulation today, provides a more inclusive or decentralized rendering of history, as does Stratton 1964, an oddly chatty and often blatantly racist travelogue.

44. This holiday is most frequently referred to in Madagascar as "le 26 juin" (June 26). This wording is again reminiscent of French nationalism, since it so clearly references "le quatorze juillet," Bastille Day (July 14).

45. The Lycée Mixte Tsiaraso I is co-educational, hence the *mixte*. In order to avoid the cumbersome quality of its name, I shall refer to it as the Lycée Tsiaraso I, or simply as "the state-run lycée."

46. Their entrance heralded an elite and primarily highlander-led takeover of institutions previously dominated by French and *métis* (that is, of mixed Malagasy and foreign origins). The first to fall was the Alliance Française, a battle that had ensued the year before.

47. French soldiers do not, in fact, goose-step, although the Foreign Legion does have its own particular march style, approximating a slow and highly abbreviated goose-step movement. My assumption, however, is that Malagasy soldiers, scouts, and students have probably incorporated a Soviet marching style, one that may have come into vogue under Ratsiraka. I have been unable, however, to confirm this theory.

48. Faranirina Esoavelomandroso 1990, 145: "la fête de tout un peuple libre."

49. Red and white are also important symbols of Sakalava dynastic power, although no coastal informant ever made this connection in reference to the national flag. Instead, its Merina origin is always underscored.

50. Throughout this book, *la mentalité colonisée* is glossed as "the colonized mind," even though this is not the language used, e.g., by Mannoni 1990 or Bouillon 1981. Official Malagasy distinguishes between *saina* (mind, intellect) and *fanahy* (spirit or soul), and my informants in Madagascar regularly used the term *mentalité* (for example, when a young informant spoke of Malagasy identity as being defined by one's soul). Only in a few instances did informants use the French word *esprit* (spirit or mind), and rarely *âme*. I have encountered similar uses of *mentalité* and *esprit* in colonial documents that focus on education. (At times, too, *esprit* was used by students as a means to gloss the notion of life essence in a manner reminiscent of spirit possession.) For a discussion of what distinguishes *mentalité* (mentality, or state of mind) from *âme* (soul), see Bouillon 1981, esp. 144 ff.

51. For an interesting critique of the value of ethnocentrism in anthropology, see Mudimbe 1988, 19.

52. Colonial Senegalese, Malagasy, and Algerian foot soldiers (FR: *tirailleurs*) served on their own as well as on one another's soil and were often commanded to commit violent acts against other colonized people. As a pair of disturbing photos in Rasoanasy 1976 (17–18; see also 101) make clear, such orders included the execution of nationalists who fought for the liberation of France's African subjects.

53. Students' ages are provided along with a word on their backgrounds as a means to introduce key informants who will appear repeatedly throughout this book. Appendix 1 provides a succinct overview of all informants who figure prominently in this study.

54. Adherence to these work-day taboos implies unequivocally that one follows royal custom. As a result, they were a source of great aggravation for colonial employers. They are a sign among Malagasy that one accepts local royalty as one's superiors and, thus, that one also embraces Sakalava identity (see chapter 4).

55. Rabenoro 1986, 146 ff., and Mangalaza 1977 identify *fihavanana* as a central philosophical concept in Malagasy culture. Given that both of these men are also well-known university professors in Madagascar, it is possible that Hasina's inspiration came partly from one or more of his own teachers, who might have studied with either of these scholars.

56. Mr. Q had lived in the Sambirano for decades and was the director of a large plantation. His father had been a Frenchman in the colonial service, and his mother was from

the highlands. He was generally identified as a *vazaha* and made a point of describing himself as French or, sometimes, as French *métis,* but he had married in the Sambirano and spoke Sakalava fluently. Although he certainly had his enemies, he differed from the rest of the local elite in that he was respected and even loved by most of the valley's inhabitants. Unlike other powerful, wealthy men in the region, he had a strong sense of justice and fairness. Two mornings a week, he sat in his private office with the doors to the outside open wide and received any and all visitors, whom he would often assist administratively, financially, or otherwise when he could. As a result, workers from his own and other plantations often came to his office when all other authorities had failed them. He has, since, sadly, passed away.

CHAPTER 2. THE SACRIFICED GENERATION

1. Clignet and Ernst were astonished that so little had been written on educational policy in Madagascar, given the number of qualified social scientists they encountered on the island. They clearly did not take into account that an investigation into educational shortfalls would soon become dangerously ensnared in a critique of nationalist ideology.

2. In earlier publications (e.g., Sharp 1993), I followed the Malagasy example and referred to the Sambirano Valley's plantations as enterprises (FR: *entreprises*) to underscore the fact that what had once been large-scale privately owned farms established in the early years of the colonial period had subsequently been nationalized under Ratsiraka during the Second Republic. During the 1991–93 transitional period, many were once again privatized and, as will become clear, it was often their highland Malagasy directors who purchased them. To avoid confusion, I refer to them in this book simply as plantations, regardless of the era.

3. Aside from experiencing a shortage of building materials, a rich man in Madagascar was a poor one abroad, because the Malagasy franc (FMG) had no foreign exchange value, and it was illegal to accumulate more than a very small amount of foreign currency. Numerous strategies were used to circumvent the rules, of course, including black market trade with foreigners and foreign bank accounts.

4. The theme of lost children is addressed in chapter 8.

5. Earlier efforts were instigated during the transitional period under the new minister of education, Fulgence Fanony (see Clignet and Ernst 1995).

6. To further complicate matters, the numbering system was reversed during the Ratsiraka years, so that one began with "T1" in primary school and advanced through "T12" (terminale) at the end of lycée. Inasmuch as the French system in principle persisted into the 1990s, and because it is familiar to all educated Malagasy, I have opted to exclude the "T" numbering system.

7. Under Ratsiraka, the names for the CEPE and BEPC qualifying exams changed, but as with *classe* (grade) names, all my informants remained familiar with the older French abbreviations, so to avoid confusing readers, I use CEPE and BEPC throughout this book. The exam taken at the end of the lycée years continued to be known as the bac under Ratsiraka.

8. This then subdivides into *série* A1, which is more literary, and *série* A2, which stresses the social sciences.

9. Until the end of the Second Republic, there were two bac sessions, so that if a student failed on the first try, he or she could make a second attempt that same year. Under Zafy, students were required to reenroll in the terminale year of lycée.

10. Madagascar already had an impressive education infrastructure when compared to other African colonies at independence. Of a population of approximately 5.3 million, about 5,000 Malagasy had passed the BEPC and 1,500 had passed the bac. Antananarivo had a medical school (founded in 1897), and a newly established university boasted an enrollment of 4,000 students. In contrast, in Zambia, a British territory of 3.7 million, only eighty inhabitants had secondary school certificates and there were fewer than a hundred university graduates, the majority of whom had studied in South Africa; furthermore, only ten graduates from the University of Zambia were indigenous Zambians. Nevertheless, a significant concern in Madagascar at independence was that educational opportunities beyond primary school were severely limited, and 60 percent of all facilities were in and around Antananarivo. In response, state-run lycées were established in all provincial capitals under President Tsiranana (Covell 1995, 44; Heseltine 1971, 12–13; Mathieu 1996; Serpell 1993; Thompson and Adloff 1965, 261).

11. A few gifted students are awarded scholarships. In 1994–95, I encountered two in Antananarivo who received FMG 21,000 a month. Both lived with kin and commuted to school, since their scholarships did little more than cover the cost of school supplies, transportation, and allow them to make a contribution to the household food budget (it could not begin to cover the cost of rent if they were to live elsewhere). One of my informants reported that the most promising of students might receive FMG 63,000 a month. These were rare exceptions, however, and thus most students were required to work to pay for their studies or rely heavily on kin to support them. Those students who were fortunate enough to acquire dorm space were charged no rent and held responsible only for the cost of electricity and buying their own food. As one student in Antananarivo explained, however, much of this space at his campus was in fact inhabited by police and gendarmes. When the government attempted to expel them to make room for students, these angry tenants stole everything they could, including the doors from their rooms. Reflecting on this state of affairs, this young man explained "It's nothing more than a dead city now." For a discussion of the shortage of university housing elsewhere in Africa, see Atteh 1996, 37, and Kirkaldy 1996.

12. Andriamanaitriarivo is this ruler's praise name, granted to him after his death. Its full significance will be discussed in a later chapter.

13. See appendix 3 for population information for Ambanja and the Sambirano Valley. In summarizing population data, I am forced to rely heavily on census materials that are well over a decade old, because data gathered in 1986 (and tallied in 1987) have proven to be far more detailed and reliable than those collected in the first half of the 1990s. For example, in 1987, the total population of Ambanja was calculated at 26,270, but in 1993, another local census showed that it had shrunk to approximately 24,358 (in contrast to my own impression that the town had expanded considerably, especially along its northern and eastern borders). Two years later, in 1995, it was calculated as 27,524. Two factors may account for these discrepancies: censuses in Madagascar are inevitably conducted in anticipation of elections, and thus a shift in several thousands may be shaped by polling strategies; second, since the Sambirano attracts migrants from throughout the island, the season in which a census is conducted will affect total numbers. I was told by a government employee who was involved with all three censuses

that in 1993 in particular they had made an attempt to exclude all transitory migrants from the census (which was not true in 1986). For the purposes of my research, the 1986 census serves as a baseline: in my earlier work from the 1980s (Sharp 1993), I reported the population of Ambanja as approximately 27,000. For the period covered by this study (1993–95), I estimate it to have been approximately 30,000 in the dry season, when migration is at its peak.

14. As noted earlier, by 1993, government employees, including schoolteachers, began to experience substantial salary raises. In 1987, CEG teachers usually made about FMG 30,000 a month; by 1994, they earned around 100,000. A friend who worked at the lycée level at the Catholic Academy also reported that she made FMG 110,000 a month. A senior instructor at the state-run lycée could potentially make as much as FMG 150,000 a month. Teachers' monthly rents in 1993–95 typically ranged anywhere from FMG 25,000 for the simplest of dwellings to 60,000 or more (two informants reported that their landlords had doubled their rents when they received posts at the Catholic Academy). Some civil servants were fortunate enough to pay little or no rent, since long-term service in Ambanja often allowed them access to housing in a few state-owned buildings (this was true of postal clerks, for example). Many manual laborers had also received significant raises by 1994. In 1987, a full-time male plantation laborer earned approximately FMG 30,000 a month (women earned less, since they were paid by the piece or kilo for sorting and cleaning produce). Night watchmen also did well, especially since they were in greater demand by the 1990s because of an increased fear of thieves (see Sharp 2001b). A number whom I knew well in 1987 made as little as FMG 10,000 a month; this forced them to take second and even third jobs during the daytime. By 1994, some of these same men were making as much as FMG 60,000 to 100,000 a month, as were manual laborers. Rents paid by watchmen and laborers were usually much lower than those paid by teachers (and their dwellings were often much simpler). Live-in domestic house servants experienced little improvement over this same period of time. Typically, they were either young unmarried women or widows with adult children. They generally made little more than FMG 40,000 a month in 1994, and thus they had received raises of FMG 30,000 or less since 1987. Schoolteachers (like other civil servants) as well as some better-paid manual laborers could conceivably afford to send one or more children to the Catholic Academy, especially if they had other sources of supplemental income (through tutoring, farming, trading, or cattle herding, for example) and/or spouses (or children) who worked.

15. As Covell 1997, 36, notes, a frequent complaint about schooling under Tsiranana was that the state system charged fees, which, although minimal, "were onerous for poorer families." In other words, this is yet another aspect of First Republic schooling that was reinstated under President Zafy.

16. Only one out of fourteen terminale level seminary students I encountered in 1995 was over the age of twenty. Among the remaining thirteen were three seventeen-year-olds.

17. The national survey of state-run primary schooling reported in Clignet and Ernst 1995, 82–83, 88, gives the average distance between the nation's primary schools as 35 kilometers. To inspect their regional schools, 12 percent of all school directors surveyed travel by bicycle, and another 7 percent use small boats. In Ambanja, the bicycle (often borrowed) is the rule. Clignet and Ernst 1995 found that many schools seemed to observe no regular class schedules, and William Lambert, who worked in the Sambirano

as a Peace Corps volunteer in the mid 1990s, likewise reported that rural CEGs typically were not in session if he arrived unannounced.

18. I have chosen to rely on the 1993–94 and, to a lesser extent, the 1994–95 academic school years for a number of reasons. First, statistics are most complete for primary schooling in 1993–94, and in 1994–95 for middle school and lycée enrollments. Second, these two academic years follow one of pronounced political turmoil, when many schools closed and exams were canceled, making 1992–93 and even 1991–92 difficult years in terms of providing reliable data. The survey offered in this book ends with the 1994–95 academic year (and thus includes the end of the 1991–93 transitional period), by which time aggressive measures had been introduced to replace official Malagasy with French. For details, see appendix 5.

19. As Colonna 1997 illustrates for colonial Algeria, however, excellence is not necessarily so much a question of ability as of preferred performance and, ultimately, social conformity. Exam performance is clearly an important criterion in evaluating the "seriousness" of schoolgirls in Ambanja, but there is no denying that conformity—and, therefore, moral behavior—may also play a part.

20. Similar trends are reported for much of sub-Saharan Africa by Bledsoe et al. (1993). An impression I have, based on informal observations in Ambanja, is that boys are more likely to find wage labor at an earlier age than girls. In other words, their sisters generally stay at home to assist mothers and other female kin with daily tasks, and if they work in a relative's store, for example, they are not paid but take part in a reciprocal exchange of child labor. Sons, on the other hand, may work part-time for a family friend or relative and bring home their meager wages to their parents (see chapter 8). More careful investigation is called for in order to confirm whether such practices are widespread in Madagascar. By the time sons and daughters reach their twenties, however, both are likely to be seeking wages, especially if they are parents themselves.

21. Chapter 7, however, notes the arrival of one version of *Plume* devoted to AIDS education, targeted specifically at lycée students.

22. Maps were so scarce that I brought them as gifts throughout the course of my fieldwork.

23. See CAOM, DS 0330 (1937).

24. See ibid. and Sharp 1996.

25. Colonna 1997, 352. In his typically flippant way, Arthur Stratton describes the aim of these combined missions, as originally formulated by Gallieni, as follows: "to instruct the Malagasy in modern methods of agriculture and stock-breeding—to teach them how to work regularly and systemically *[sic]*, so that they could go out and put more of the uncultivated land into production, thus to populate the almost empty island, and thus to enlarge the oil spot," a mission that was then to be promoted by the stalwart "soldier-teacher-farmer-worker-spreader of French civilization" (Stratton 1964, 224). In a more serious tone, the Comaroffs, writing of southern Africa, summarize it thus: "The poetic bridge between cultivation and civilization was not coincidental . . . the African garden was to be part of the imperial marketplace. After all, commerce, like money, was an integral—even sanctified—aspect of civilization. [And from a missionary perspective,] . . . commercial agriculture was the panacea that would establish both the material and the moral infrastructure of the Kingdom of God" (Comaroff and Comaroff 1991, 80).

26. As Françoise Raison-Jourde (1997, 34–35) indicates, a favorite expression coined by Malagasy youth in the 1960s was "*Samy Malagasy*": "[We're] all Malagasy" or "All

Malagasy are the Same" (the former is her translation, the latter mine). I do not know, however, if Vonjy was aware of this.

27. Even today, this theme still dominates the exhibit on Madagascar at the Musée de l'Homme in Paris, which contains numerous old photos of bridges, ports, laboratory facilities, and factories built during the First Republic.

28. "Une démocratie effective, dit-on, ne peut exister dans une société socialiste. Qu'en pensez-vous?"

29. "Peut-on parler de liberté sans égalité sociale?"

30. Jean Lacroix, Panorama de la philosophie française contemporaine (Paris: Presses universitaires de France, 1966, 1968).

31. "Les pays riches et ceux du Tiers monde interviennent respectivement dans les principales productions mondiales. Comment?"

32. "Les répercussions économiques, sociales et politiques de la deuxième guerre en Afrique."

33. "Expliquer l'évolution de l'économie américaine depuis la Seconde guerre mondiale jusqu'à nos jours, et quels sont ses problèmes actuels?"

34. "Commentaire de texte: Les problèmes économiques de la reconstruction post-coloniale."

35. "Les malaises de la société américaine sont indissociables de son système économique."

36. "Étude comparée de l'agriculture en URSS et aux États-Unis: importance, organisation, performances."

37. "Le plan Marshall passera à la postérité comme l'une des contributions essentielles apportées par l'Amérique à la cause de la paix mondiale."

38. "L'ex-URSS a toujours été considérée comme une grande puissance. Cependant on y rencontre la pénurie, méme si elle dispose de tous les atouts pour l'éviter."

CHAPTER 3. THE LIFE AND
HARD TIMES OF THE SCHOOL MIGRANT

1. The category of "school migrant" as used here includes students who were not from Ambanja and who, for the purposes of schooling, lived alone with schoolmates, siblings, or older kin other than their parents, most often a maternal grandmother. I refer to those who lived alone or only with other young people (siblings or friends) as "solitary" or "independent" migrants. Of nine classes surveyed, ranging from troisième through terminale at three different schools (Salvation, the Catholic Academy, and the Lycée Tsiaraso I), in four instances, school migrants accounted for approximately 50 percent; in one case, for closer to 40 percent; and in the remaining four, for approximately 30 percent of the total class enrollment.

2. Occasionally, the Catholic Academy makes arrangements for migrant schoolgirls to be housed with the sisters in their own building, but this is an exception and not a rule. In the course of three seasons of fieldwork, I encountered four such schoolgirls, as opposed to several dozen male seminarists.

3. Seminarists are permitted, however, to attend the special disco events hosted by the Catholic Academy; these are organized by students and staff as school fund-raising events.

4. For discussions of the effects of clock time in transforming social and economic aspects of life, see Comaroff and Comaroff (1991, xi, 64, 191 ff); Cooper (1992) and Thompson (1967).

5. As the discussion in chapter 8 will reveal, the caring relationship between Tata and her employers more closely approximates fosterage, even though they are not kin.

6. As I later learned, this partnership consisted of two brothers (the elder was seventeen in 1995) and a third classmate, who lived together independently. I was unable to locate the girl. For a discussion of this partnership, see Sharp 1996, 38.

7. In her study of education and economic transformation in Melanesia, Alice Pomponio encountered a similar attitude, reflected in the title of her book *Seagulls Don't Fly into the Bush* (Pomponio 1992).

8. The gendered nature of town diversions is addressed in chapter 7.

9. See CAOM, DS 0422 (1930), PM 0014 (1932–54).

10. As described below, two school officials distributed some questionnaires for me at the primary and middle school levels. I was not present when they did so, and so I do not know whether any students they encountered actively refused to complete the form. I was fully responsible for the distribution of all questionnaires at the lycée level.

11. Students rarely distinguished between whether they aspired to teach at the primary, middle, or lycée level. Although distinctions can be made in French through the use of such terms as *instituteur* and *professeur,* most students used a generic official Malagasy term, such as *mpampianatra.* In other words, it is possible that some imagine acquiring teaching posts below the lycée level that only require a bac certificate, for example, and not a university degree. Because I do not know their actual intent, I have chosen to place "teaching" as a profession under the first main category, "advanced education."

12. To work as a flight attendant for Air Madagascar, one has to be able to speak official Malagasy, French, and English.

CHAPTER 4. THE RESURGENCE OF ROYAL POWER

1. The focus of this chapter necessitates using a name for the indigenous inhabitants of the Sambirano Valley that is more specific than Sakalava. I therefore use Bemazava-Sakalava, or its abbreviated form, Bemazava, when referring to the local royal dynasty and the subjects of its kingdom.

2. Sakalava society honors hierarchy. First are those of royal descent *(ampanjaka)*, members of related lineages whose offspring may potentially become rulers *(ampanjakabe,* where *-be* means "big" or "great"). Beneath them are the general populace, commoners *(ny olo* or "the people") or citizens of the kingdom, who are referred to simply as Sakalava. All may be distinguished by clan membership, although many have forgotten their affiliations, designations that are especially important in determining modes of participation during royal rituals, given that it is through the demands of royal service, or *fanompoaña,* that one declares or asserts one's loyalty to the ruler. Among the most significant group in this regard are the Sambarivo, men and women born into a highly specialized caste whose primary duties in life involve serving royalty. It is they, for example, who guard the royal tombs at Nosy Faly, who direct and coordinate royal feasts, and who handle, guard, and clean the royal body of a deceased ruler and who ultimately collect relics from it once it has decomposed. Today, they are almost exclusively associated with villages far from Ambanja.

3. More literally, "the king has turned around" or, essentially, averted his gaze. In the northern Sakalava dialect, rulers are never spoken of as "dead" *(maty),* but imagined instead as somewhat removed from the living. The bodies of the royal dead are prepared with

care and placed in special tombs grouped within a walled, gated enclosure, where they join other royal ancestors, who collectively watch over their subjects. These ancestors may communicate with the living in the form of powerful (or, literally, the "greatest," or *maventibe*) *tromba* spirits, who possess an elite category of mediums known as *saha*.

4. When Sakalava rulers die, they shed the names they bore during their lifetimes, and these are replaced with praise names (*fitahiaña*, from *mitaha*, "to protect" [see Baré 1980, 290]), which make reference to events or achievements that characterized their lives. It is generally considered taboo *(fady)* to use any name but the praise name following death. However, the Bemazava are "proud of their liberal attitudes that relate not only to the birth and elaboration of royal lines, but also to the death of royalty" (Feeley-Harnik 1982, 36–7). For example, the Bemazava of the Sambirano apply these rules about naming very loosely, for they continue to utter the living names of rulers after their deaths (albeit with lowered voices). Since praise names can be long and cumbersome for non-Malagasy speakers, I have chosen to follow contemporary custom, so that in most cases I use the living names of rulers. The one exception is the founding ancestor, Andriantompoeniarivo, whom I refer to only by his praise name. Henceforth, the first time a ruler's name appears in the text, it is given as follows: living name (praise name; years reigned). This chapter is dedicated to the memory of Tsiaraso Victor III (Andriamanaitriarivo, "The Ruler Who Surprised Many").

5. For a detailed discussion of these events see Sharp 1997.

6. The Sakalava ritual calendar is dictated by a complex set of rules associated with lunar phases. For a discussion of this in reference to *tromba* possession, see Sharp 1993, 190 ff.

7. It is important to note here, however, that the majority of Sakalava dynasties might be conceived of as being established by strangers of a particular sort, since they involve movement away from established royal kingdoms following disagreements over succession. The founding ancestor settles elsewhere (generally by moving north), accompanied by a retinue of faithful supporters. This is, in fact, how the Bemazava dynasty of the Sambirano was founded in the early nineteenth century. Furthermore, by residing in Toliara, Parfait had in fact lived on the fringes of the oldest of Sakalava dynasties.

8. The term *tsiñy* is associated with royal wrath, although in the Sambirano it is most often used as a label for a category of forest sprits (cf. Feeley-Harnik 1991, 160). Their close association with royalty is evident during possession ceremonies, when their mediums assume attire highly reminiscent of royal *tromba* spirits.

9. In this reconstruction of the Bemazava past, I rely heavily on oral historical accounts offered by local elders, school youth, and schoolteachers based in Ambanja, as well as the tomb guardians on Nosy Faly. This knowledge is further embellished by information culled from archival sources. For a more detailed account of the reign of Tsiaraso I, see Sharp 1997.

10. Brief portions of the following are revisions of earlier arguments that appear in Sharp 1997.

11. For more details on the life of Andriantompoeniarivo, see Verin 1986, 133.

12. Baré 1980, 72: "une atmosphère de violence assez inconcevable."

13. Paillard 1983–84, 366: "la vallée du Sambirano était la région la plus menacée par l'intrusion de la colonisation agricole."

14. A hectare is equal to 2.47 acres.

15. Today in Madagascar the name Sénégal (or, more properly, in Malagasy, Sonegaly) is laced with xenophobic overtones. In everyday speech, it is used to describe anyone who originates from the African continent, regardless of nationality, and it frequently connotes distrust and fear: children are told, for example, that if they misbehave, the Sonegaly will come and eat them. The title of the compact disk *Son Egal* (Equal Sound) issued in 1997 by the Malagasy pop group Tarika, and their song "Sonegaly," combine to convey the message "We're all equal," whether Malagasy or Senegalese in origin.

16. See Gillian Feeley-Harnik's *A Green Estate: Restoring Independence in Madagascar* (1991) for a comprehensive study of royal Sakalava rituals that reclaim indigenous territory and, as her subtitle asserts, restore independence in the aftermath of French occupation.

17. Local informants are uncertain as to the exact date when Bemazava royalty were forced to relocate to Ambanja. In 1907, the French established a new military post, along with a prison and cemetery for whites, at what is now the center of the town of Ambanja. Informants say that as late as 1912, Tsiaraso I was still living in Ankify and, at times, in Ankatafa (Ankazotelo). Baré, in a footnote to an informant's description of the building of Tsiresy's palace, describes Ankify as the location "that served as the royal residence for Bemazava aristocrats before their final move to Ambanja and Ankatafa" ("qui servait de résidence royale aux aristocrates Benazava *[sic]* avant leur installation définitive à Ambanja et Ankatafa" [1980, 289]). Contemporary town inhabitants are certain that by 1945 (if not earlier) the *ampanjakabe* was living full-time in Ambanja.

18. According to Lisa Gezon (personal communication, September 1995), throughout this century the Antankaraña to the north likewise have not built new royal residences (*doany* or *zomba*) following the deaths of former rulers. Only one did so at the turn of the century, but he was involved in a dispute over succession. The current ruler's two residences, however, were required to be purified before he could inhabit them.

19. As described in a previous chapter, however, Ratsiraka did eventually secure reelection in 1997 following the impeachment of Zafy Albert.

20. For example, as one elderly royal man explained, Bemazava tend to name their rulers in succession as Europeans do (thus, Tsiaraso I, II, III, IV), whereas the royal house of Nosy Be is wedded to such "archaic" names as Binao and Amada.

CHAPTER 5. OUR GRANDFATHERS WENT TO WAR

1. I do not know whether the French military in fact used flatbed trucks in Madagascar during World War I (oxcarts seem more likely), but this detail shows that Foringa associates his grandfather's forcible impressment into the army with the plantation labor he fears he will have to do if he fails his bac again.

2. A play on "Ny Ady Lehibe," "The Great War," the name Malagasy—like many Europeans—give World War I.

3. For simplicity's sake, I have chosen to focus exclusively on World War I, but young Malagasy emphasized similar themes of entrapment and enslavement during World War II, which was, of course, crucial to the development of nationalism in the final decades of the colonial era.

4. Work done by wartime laborers included "unloading on the docks, building roads, quarrying, farming, working on railways and in factories, in the construction of military camps, and in forestry work" (Clarke 1986, 10).

5. Why did Andrianambinana remain a soldier once he had returned to Madagascar? Perhaps he could not afford to leave the army or did not know that he could do so. West African soldiers were similarly confused and ambivalent about their roles as soldiers, and especially as esteemed warriors, in the French army (Lunn 1987). In order to keep them in Europe for the duration of the war, the colonial government of Madagascar first sidestepped and then modified a 1904 decree limiting wartime conscription of Malagasy men to four years (CAOM, SG c 316, d. 822 [January 1919]). The French minister of war proposed that Malagasy troops be incorporated into Somali units in Djibouti, so that new rules for Madagascar would not have to be created. Even before the war, Malagasy soldiers had been mustered together with Senegalese troops, and Somali soldiers had been shipped to France via Madagascar. See CAOM, SG c. 316, d. 822 (May 19, 1917), issued by the French cabinet's Bureau Militaire, for the official guidelines for *recrutement indigène*.

6. Given the increased zeal of local authorities, "the conception of 'volunteer' evolved toward a [form of] enrollment that was increasingly forced" *(la conception du 'volontariat' évolua vers un enrôlement de plus en plus forcé)*, Gontard observes (n.d. a, 15).

7. Gontard n.d. a, 9: " . . . une grandiose manifestation patriotique dans la capitale. Trente mille personnes se rassemblent avenue de France pour acclamer les tirailleurs à qui l'on distribue des fleurs et des friandises."

8. Gontard n.d. a, 9: "Après la mort d'un jeune malgache en France, il envoie le chef de la province annoncer le malheur à la famille avec les ménagements d'usage. Le chef de la province trouve réunis la mère, la femme, le frère du disparu. 'La femme du militaire indigène fondit en larmes. Alors la mère lui dit: "Tu ne dois pas pleurer ton mari. Il est mort glorieusement." Et se tournant vers l'administrateur, elle ajouta "J'ai un autre fils ici présent; je vous le donne pour qu'il aille en France remplacer celui qui n'est plus." Et le jeune homme s'engage incontinent.' " Garbit, a military man by training, was governor-general of Madagascar from October 1914 to June 1917 and again briefly in January 1918; he was replaced in the interim by Martial Merlin. During his absence from Madagascar, Garbit was in charge of Malagasy troops and wartime laborers in France (Gontard n.d. b, 273; CAOM, MAD 3 annexes, pt. IIB, 212).

9. Historical and fictional accounts from elsewhere in Africa describe scenes that bear an uncanny resemblance, not to Garbit's narrative, but, rather, to Foringa's recounting of his grandfather's experiences. Richard Rathbone (1978) describes recruiting drives in French West Africa as especially brutal. (Citing an unpublished piece by Robert Archer, though, he argues that such harshness did not characterize French practices in Madagascar.) Joe Harris Lunn, who also writes of French West Africa during World War I, emphasizes capture as a form of conscription, where men would flee to the mountains and forests, so that villages were populated only by women and the elderly (1987, 32). British conscription drives in Africa during World War II also suggested enslavement. In *The Joys of Motherhood* by the Nigerian novelist Buchi Emecheta, the protagonist's husband is captured at work and fears enslavement is imminent, only to learn he has been conscripted by force as a soldier (1979, 144–45). Peter B. Clarke provides an array of print material generated for West African audiences that describes Hitler as one who enslaves others (1986, 41–57). Hitler was perceived by Malagasy as an enemy for similar reasons.

10. The account I offer here draws upon schoolteachers' and elders' narratives (two of the latter had served in World War I). Unless otherwise specified as direct quotations, local

accounts are complemented by data drawn from Aderibigbe 1989; Gerbera 1979; Gow 1979, 3–4, 25; Handyman 1964; McLeod 1969, 54–56; Mutibwa 1974, 11–12, 229–32, 335–36, 348; Slipchenko 1989; Stein 1978; and Verin 1986, chs. 6 and 7.

11. As Marcia Wright (1993, 8) stresses, "Arab" is a problematic label: throughout East Africa, this blanket term encompasses a wide array of Islamicized traders. I therefore use it loosely here.

12. These may have been Merina, and not Sakalava raiders, because by the early nineteenth century, the Merina had established a coastal trading center south of the Ampasindava Peninsula.

13. Most notably, these are the British Abolition Act of 1807; British and French prohibitions in 1810 and 1817, respectively; the Anglo-Malagasy Treaty of 1817, in which the Merina kingdom agreed to outlaw the slave trade within Madagascar; the 1877 edict that liberated all slaves introduced into Madagascar, under which the British estimated that approximately 150,000 slaves were freed; and a further legal reform of 1881, which again outlawed slavery in Merina territory. Finally, in 1896, the year the island was officially proclaimed a colony, 500,000 slaves were again freed. See Gerbeau 1979, 197; Gow 1979, 4; Mutibwa 1974, 21, 244, 335–36, 348; Slipchenko 1989.

14. Captain F. Moresby to T. F. Buxton, April 18, 1826 in *British Parliamentary Papers on the Slave Trade*, 1: 79, as cited in Aderibigbe 1989.

15. The mass suicide of Zafin'i'fotsy royalty does not figure prominently when their tale is told in other parts of Madagascar (Maurice Bloch, personal communication, 1998).

16. See CAOM, DS 0479, 1938–48; PM 56, 1939.

17. This fear was even more pronounced during the post–World War II era and was actualized in the 1947 insurrection.

18. See Gontard n.d. a, who details the progression of this realization among both the Malagasy and the French in Madagascar.

19. Most authors refer to this as a revolt, rather than an insurrection. Since the latter term implies more widespread participation, I have opted to use it throughout this book, following Tronchon 1982.

20. For detailed discussions of the Menalamba, see Ellis 1985 and Rasoanasy 1976; on 1947, consult Cole 1996, 200, and Tronchon 1982.

21. During my fieldwork in 1995, I encountered strong local reluctance to discuss the events of 1947. For example, one afternoon, Tsarahita and I sought to interview an uncle of hers, a man in his sixties who had witnessed firsthand many of events as they unfolded in the Sambirano. This is a man I know well, and one who had at first expressed enthusiasm in recounting details to us. Following a few minutes of lively discussion, however, he became increasingly quiet; after a substantial pause he then said, "You know, many of us were very frightened. We often didn't fully understand what these [local] men were doing, and the response from the French was so immediate and so harsh." When prodded a bit more by Tsarahita, who was frustrated by the fact that she knew so little about local events in 1947, he then briefly continued, "One day we learned that they had arrested [a man I knew] and a few days later many arrests were made [father north in the city of] Diégo-Suarez. It was frightening. My dears, [let's] not talk about it anymore."

22. Recall that the Malagasy concept of *fihavanana* is inspired both by the French nationalist sentiment of "fraternity" *(fraternité)* and Christian "brotherly love" (see chapter 1).

23. In identifying the founding members of the VVS as young Malagasy intellectuals, I follow Thompson and Adloff (1965, 2). For example, the poet Ny Avana, described below, was a young man when arrested by the French for his association with VVS.

24. Several key leaders of the VVS who were freed in the 1920s later became instrumental in subsequent nationalist movements. Key sources here include Covell 1987, 23–24; Thompson and Adloff 1965, 21–23; and CAOM, SG c. 316, d. 822 (December 1917), letter from Merlin to the minister of colonies in Paris.

25. Poem by Ny Avana Ramanantoanina (Source: Ramanantoanina [1993:182]). I wish to thank Tiana Ralaizonia and Annie Rabodoarimiadana for their assistance with this translation. I am no poet and, thus, I have preserved neither the rhyme scheme nor the rhythm. Furthermore, as several informants have stressed, Ny Avana's poetry is difficult to explain, since the references, metaphors, and multiple meanings do not translate well. For example, I suspect that when he describes the ship as *sambatra* or "fortunate" in the first line, he simultaneously alludes to his own "captive" (*sambotra*) status. I have nevertheless attempted to preserve some semblance of the rich imagery and melancholy tone for which Ny Avana is so famous.

26. This reconstruction of Ny Avana's life is drawn from the following sources: Adejunmobi 1994; Rajemisa-Raolison 1966, 86–87; and Rakotonaivo in Ramanantsoanina 1983, 7–8. Note that Adejunmobi 1994, 1, gives 1890 as the year in which Ny Avana was born; both Rajemisa-Raolison 1966, 86, and Rakotonaivo (the editor of Ramanantoanina 1993), however, record the date of his birth more specifically as February 26, 1891.

27. Both Covell 1987 and Adejunmobi 1994 unfortunately ignore the hurdles presented by differences in dialect. Adejunmobi especially downplays the limited number who might actually have been able to read and write in Malagasy or French. Nevertheless, Malagasy in print form most certainly gave nationalists a significant level of linguistic freedom.

CHAPTER 6. LABORING FOR THE COLONY

1. As noted earlier, Malagasy students are frequently required to repeat at least one grade in the course of their academic careers, as is common under the French system. Many of Hasina's peers, too, are making their second or even third attempt to pass their bac.

2. CAOM, PM 0011, 1926; PM 0168, 1946.

3. Gallieni and Olivier, as cited in Thompson and Adloff 1965, 443, 286; CAOM, AP 2942: 1 (1938–39), March 5, 1907, arrêté.

4. CAOM, AP 2942: 1, "Décret: Travail indigène" (1925).

5. Brown 1978, 261.

6. Stratton 1964, 97.

7. For concise and informative discussions of SMOTIG's founding and demise, see Covell 1987, 20, and Thompson and Adloff 1965, 444 f.

8. The French consistently justified their colonial programs by citing a genealogy of measures and decrees in the text of each new policy, and Gallieni's actions are frequently referenced as the origins for most labor policies. In addition to the decree of October 1, 1896, those of December 11, 1895, and July 30, 1897, appear with great frequency. See CAOM, PM 0089: 048, *Journal officiel de Madagascar et dépendances,* October 4, 1941, 730.

9. See Thompson and Adloff 1965, 310, 443; Heseltine 1971, 160–61; and CAOM, AF 2942: 1 (1919–1939).

10. As noted in chapter 5, this lecture formed part of a review session Sister Estelle offered in preparation for end-of-the-year examinations in history at the lycée level at the Catholic Academy. Officially age sixteen marked the onset of labor requirements; yet many older Malagasy today do not know their exact ages, and colonial records reveal that the French even actively recruited workers under sixteen, as they did during wartime.

11. Governor-General Marcel Olivier held office in Madagascar from May 1924 to January 1926, and then from March 1927 until May 1930 (CAOM, MAD3, annexes to IIB, pp. 212–13 [n.d.]).

12. See CAOM, PM 0093: 0487 (n.d.); Covell 1995, 222–23; Labatut and Raharinarivonirina 1969, 159–60; Stratton 1964, 97; Thompson and Adloff 1965, 286. On the Brussels exhibition, see CAOM, FOM 83: 2919 (1935).

13. CAOM, AP 2942: 1 (1919–1949): "une grande masse d'indigènes pour transformer progressivement la mentalité des races autochtones."

14. See CAOM, AP 2942: 1, draft letter dated July 10, 1926, proposing the creation of SMOTIG; cf. CAOM, PM 0605 (1935 and 1940); PM 0168 (1946). The kcal. values of these rations would vary according to whether, for example, these are dry or cooked weights, as well as the quality of rice, meat, and "condiments" served. My impression, however, is that these would have been substandard rations for full-time manual laborers. (I wish to thank Heather Fisher and Lisa Colburn for their assistance.)

15. *Bureau International du Travail* (1925), in CAOM, AP 2942: 1; CAOM PM 0168: 0561 (1946).

16. At one point Olivier suggested that some male laborers should be allowed to bring their families with them, and he considered the possibility of creating "family" work camps. A few women were allowed in regular camps to do the cooking, housework, and laundry and, one may assume, to satisfy men's sexual desires. See CAOM, AP 2942: 1 (1925–29) and DS 0604 (1943–48) on their role in SMOTIG.

17. CAOM, PM 0168: 0561 (May 9, 1946): "travail forcé ou obligatoire." Labatut and Raharinarivonirina 1969, 163 contradict other sources, stating that SMOTIG came to an end in 1938.

18. Heseltine 1971, 162. Governor-General Cayla (1930–39) wrote to the minister of colonies in France in 1938 noting that a shortage of labor in the north was due in part to the fact that laborers from points south received no advances for travel expenses, so that many were forced to stop repeatedly during their journeys to earn enough money so that they could eat (CAOM, AP 2942: 1 [1938]; CAOM, MAD 3, annexes to pt. IIB, p. 213 [n.d.]).

19. Other sources for this discussion are Brown 1978, 262; *Bureau International du Travail* (1925), in CAOM, AP 2942: 1; CAOM, PM 0605, arrêté of March 17, 1945, as published in the *Journal Officiel de Madagascar,* no. 3104, p. 148. Covell 1987, 24–25, and 1995, 222–23; and Thompson and Adloff 1965, 446–47.

20. CAOM, PM 0168: 0561 (1946): "Le travailleur doit être: bien payé, bien nourri, bien vêtu" / "prix rémunérateur, ration abondante, distributions de tissus." See also this source for additional examples from Analalava and Antalova. Archival records reveal that much debate focused on what defined fair forms of compensation for workers. In the north, no single wage standard existed. Instead, individual districts bargained more or less successfully for daily wages, food rations, and cloth allotments, the dominant argument given each time by French being that provincial payments should not exceed or even approach those paid in the urban metropole of Antananarivo.

21. The last three towns continue to be key sources of seasonal migrant labor today for the plantations of Nosy Be and the Sambirano. The farthest, Bealanana, lies approximately 350 kilometers from Ambanja.

22. CAOM, PM 0168: 0561 (1946): "les chantieres publics ont été désertés."

23. Prison labor had already been employed as an early strategy in the Sambirano and Nosy Be. Other documents detail the practice at work in Namakia: 125 men were recruited from Tulear (Toliara) in 1944, bound for the Sucreries Marseillaises de Madagascar, followed by the return of another 285 to prison (CAOM DS158 [1944]).

24. See CAOM, PM 0168: 0561, letter dated May 8, 1946.

25. For references to women and children as laborers, see CAOM, AP 2942: 1 (1938–39); DS 0604 (1943–48). The inclusion of children in the documents generated under the title "Mission Wintrebert" is particularly interesting in light of the focus of my study. Children were listed as receiving different wages according to age (12 and 15, for example), and boys were to be paid more than girls. Colonial officials instructed the author to delete these references in subsequent versions of the proposal. Clearly young children were considered a significant part of plantation labor at this time, but such practices contradicted ILO guidelines that accompanied earlier responses to SMOTIG and thus references to them did not belong in official documents.

26. CAOM, PM 0168: 0561, letter of May 11, 1946: "il est à craindre qu'il Port-Bergé qui, j'en ai peur, reflète bien la pensée de nombreux malgaches même parmi les côtieres: 'Les Vazaha sont vaincus—Ils ne peuvent plus nous commander. Ils ne peuvent plus nous forces à travailler ni nous mettre en prison. Nous sommes maintenant libres de faire ce qui nous voulons.' . . . Sans doute allons-nous nous efforcer tous de lutter contre l'expansion de cet état d'esprit." Port-Bergé is located approximately 300 kilometers by road from Majunga (Mahajanga).

27. Ratsiraka 1975, "Les Forces Armées Populaires, La Jeunesse et le Service National."

28. Ibid.: "démocratisation, décentralisation, révolution des mentalités, etc."

29. "Citoyens privilégiés de la Nation pour lesquels le peuple a consenti un lourd sacrifice (bourse, écoles, université . . .), il est normal qu'ils donnent à leur tour 18 mois à 2 ans de leur vie presque gratuitement au service du peuple."

30. Ratsiraka 1975, 111–15: "l'unité nationale du peuple malgache."

31. Gallieni in fact devoted a significant amount of energy to creating a sophisticated educational system within the first few years of colonization. As Covell explains, he established French schools that competed with those run by English missionaries; he sought to establish administrative training schools beyond the highlands for future non-Merina administrators (a program discontinued by future colonial officials); and he founded both the medical school at Befeletanana and the celebrated teacher training academy, the École Le Myre de Vilers (Covell 1995, 108–9). These institutions, however, did not touch the lives of the majority of manual laborers, although they were attended, for example, by such nationalists as Ny Avana, a number of Ambanja's own Sakalava elite, and, as reflected in the story of Victorien Tombo below, Malagasy who served in the colonial administration.

32. Today, these survive in the archives as documents labeled "*Proces-Verbal*" by their original authors.

33. See, e.g., CAOM, PM 0011 (1926).

34. CAOM, AP 2942: 1 (1938–39): "négligence, paresse, absence injustifiée et refus d'obéissance."

35. Throughout the colonial literature, groups from the south are often lumped together under one ethnic label. Antandroy, Bara, and Mahafaly, for example, are used interchangeably to encompass what is, in fact, a variety of southern pastoral peoples.

36. Dubois 1931, 5: "plus sauvage, caractère plus indépendant, esprit moi[n]s assimilable à notre civilisation."

37. Perrier de la Bathie 1931, 1–2: "La Grande Ile est un vaste pays assez pauvre, à population clarsemée. Sans travail, sans ordre, sans main-d'oeuvre, ce pays resterait ou redeviendrait ce qu'il était lorsque nous l'avons pris en charge, c'est-à-dire une immense terre ravagée et stérile, sur laquelle vivaient quelques peuplades indolentes et chétives, décimées de temps à autre par des famines, ne sortant de leur indolence que pour s'égorger ou se piller mutuellement. La paix française, celle de Gallieni, a heureusement changé tout cela. Mais ce n'est pas assez." The author also goes so far as to suggest that much could be solved by "exterminating" certain undesirable and lazy members of the population using machine guns or alcohol, since the majority of the island's subjects do in fact care about the development of the colony (2).

38. Ibid., 11: "vivant dans des conditions précaires."

39. Ibid., 2: "des indigènes qui sont rebelles à tout travail, qui ne s'y livrent que contraints et forcés par la faim ou différentes causes, se contentant pour vivre, très misérablement, lorsqu'on les laisse libres, de quelques cultures très extensives, aussi vagues qu'aléatoires."

40. Ibid., 12: "Cette grande tribu, qui avait jadis conquis la moitié de l'Ile, est aujourd'hui, en effet, en voie manifeste de régression et d'extinction."

41. For a more general, islandwide discussion of these themes, see Thompson and Adloff 1965, 442.

42. CAOM, AP 2942: 1, Décret: Travail Indigène (1925).

43. CAOM, DS0162 (1918): "Fanampona *[sic]* . . . corvée de reparation des tombeaux Royaux août 1918." Later in this same document, she describes this "little royal service" *(une petite fanompoana)* as corvée labor. Thus, just as the French appropriated indigenous terms, Binao used French to justify her own actions.

44. CAOM, PM 006 (1930–33), DS 0162 (1918): "serieux, actif, intelligent, parlant et écrivant en notre langue très courramment."

45. Ibid.: "Monsieur l'Administrateur, / J'ai l'honneur de vous prièr de vouloir bien transmettre ma demande d'enrôlement volontaire pour la guerre en France, je consens à donner ma vie pour la France, je serais très content d'être un seul Sakalava au milieu des [*sic*] tous ces peuples en guerre. / Je vous prie de transmettre ma demande avec avis très favorable. / Befotaka à 12.2.1915 / le chef de canton V. Tombo."

46. It is important to note here that Tomba does not ask Moana "Who are you" but, rather, "What are you?" In other words, he is not interested in her personal identity, but rather in the significance of her status in reference to royal affairs.

47. *D:* Qu'avez vous fait à Mahabo?

   R: Je suis venu à Mahabo depuis quatre mois pour faire ma plantation et ma récolte de riz.

   D: Est-ce qu'il y a avait beaucoup de gens qui se reunissaient à Mahabo la nuit du 11 au 12 août? Et quel était à but de cette réunion?

   R: Oui: ils étaient reunis à l'effet de reparer la toiture des "Fantsina [*sic*] royal" mais comme cette soirée au apprenait que la demande d'autorisation n'avait pas été accordé la fieule [*sic*] se dispersait le lendemain de bonne heure.

D: Qu'est ce qu'au [*sic*] faisait cette nuit-là?

R: On dansait en face du Mahabo jusqu'au lendemain.

D: Qu'est ce que vous êtes?

R: Je suis la "saha" d'Andriamamalikarivo, le regrette [*sic*] propriétaire du Mahabo.

D: Quels rôles jouez-vous en votre qualité de "saha"?

R: Je remplis à peu près les mêmes fonctions que celles des "rangitry ampanjaka" (conseillers de la Reine) et je janis [*sic:* jouis?] pas finis de mêmes privilèges.

48. CAOM, DS 0163 (1904–14): "contre la civilisation française."
49. Today, Hellville is sometimes referred to by northern Sakalava as Andoany, or "The Place of the Royal Palace." It is marked as such, too, on contemporary maps of Madagascar.
50. Sources for this section and this phase of Tombo's life more generally are CAOM, PM 0533 (1930–31) and 76 (1935–39, 1941).
51. These words are particularly surprising given that Antoinette's grandparents were themselves peasants of mixed Sakalava and Tsimihety origins. The reasons for her lack of access to arable land are complex and extend beyond the focus of this discussion; briefly, however, she has long been in dispute with two siblings over land inheritance, a development further complicated by the actions of a now estranged spouse who squandered away her earnings and other possessions.

CHAPTER 7. GIRLS AND SEX AND OTHER URBAN DIVERSIONS

1. Some of the data and arguments presented here appear in abbreviated form in Sharp 2002.
2. More specifically, this is referred to locally as *toko-telo*, where the tenant gives the proprietor one-third of his or her harvest.
3. Many of the so-called "American" films are actually produced outside the United States exclusively for non-Western audiences. Two genres are worth mentioning. The first consists of Indian-produced cowboy films staring American actors who have become well-known popular heroes throughout Madagascar. (For a discussion of the popularity of Indian films in West Africa, see Larkin 1997.) Many of my informants were shocked that I had never heard of them and took this to mean that I did not know much about the movies. The second are Italian-produced "commando" films, again starring American actors, modeled heavily on Sylvester Stallone's *Rambo*. Typically, these follow a group of American soldiers lost in the jungles of Vietnam who courageously continue to fight the war for many years afterward until every man is killed. On a number of occasions, it was explained to me that these films were products of a (my) nation that still hurt from losing this war. James Bond films also qualify as a subset of "commando" films, although in these the hero always survives.
4. Mme. Vezo (alias Mama Vé), a schoolteacher who loves going to the movies, once said with great humor, "We little people [*ny olo madiniky*] prefer the westerns, kung-fu and commando films because you don't have to speak a word of French to understand them! All you have to do is watch the action! Ha ha!"

5. Elsewhere I have referred to Alida as Fatima; I have opted for a new pseudonym here to avoid confusion with the different Mme. Fatima who appears in chapter 2 and Sharp 1996.

6. The fate of her possessions is the subject of chapter 8.

7. Informants cite several origins for this slang term: most frequently they link it to the French term *maquereau* ("mackerel") in reference to the fishy smell that lingers after sexual intercourse (the term also means "pimp" in French). Another possibility is *maquerelle*, a French term for a madam (Feeley-Harnik, personal communication, 2000). Note here, too, the distinctions made between mistresses and prostitutes. For a detailed study of the intricacies of categories within prostitution in colonial Kenya, see White 1990.

8. For a succinct literature review focusing on pregnancy and abortion in school contexts throughout Africa, see Bledsoe et al. 1993, 110–13.

9. Similarly, Bledsoe et al. 1993 speaks of the paradoxes that plague adolescent fertility in Africa, especially among girls, underscoring the "serene normalcy with which most adolescent childbearing is received in many parts of Africa" (p. 7). Although educational and employment opportunities have increased for young women, adolescent pregnancy inevitably forces them to terminate their studies and training. Such trends clearly characterize the experiences of girls as well.

10. One informant reported that injections of *"noristera"* were also given; I do not know if this is the same as or related to Norplant.

11. For a discussion of ritual play in the colonial literature, see Camo 1931.

12. In 1987, I knew a woman who had worked for a decade as a prostitute in Diégo and who had come home to Ambanja, essentially, to die in her mother's home. At the time I suspected that she might have had AIDS, but this possibility was vehemently denied by local health professionals, because at the time it was accepted as fact that AIDS did not exist in Madagascar.

13. As Ebron 1997 reminds us, European women are invisible partners in the sexual trade in Africa.

14. "Quoi?! J'ai le sida, Moi? . . . Mais, je ne me suis jamais droguée! . . . je n'ai jamais eu de transfusion . . . !!! . . . Vous êtes sûr? . . . Refaites les tests!!!"

15. For a discussion of the intimacy between siblings, see Feeley-Harnik 1991, 186–89, 210 ff., 225–29, and Bloch 1995, 73 ff.

16. These materials consisted of photos of female Asian models taken from calendars that are ubiquitous in Ambanja's homes and shops; another showing two European children with a tricycle; one of the opera singer Kiri te Kanawa; another of soldiers and a flag beside President Clinton in the Philippines; an ad for a Toyota four-wheel-drive vehicle; Arnold Schwarzenegger wielding a gun; Nelson Mandela from the cover of *Newsweek;* the French African comic book *Kourakou;* and the comic book about Liza. Clinton, Mandela, and *Liza* were the most popular topics of discussion, in ascending order.

17. I was unable to confirm whether this story was true or local folklore. Several other informants could give me fairly similar accounts of this man's tale, the most important being that he was a European who had not been in town very long when he died. He had no local family, and so some say he was buried locally; others say his body was transported elsewhere where he had kin. None of the health professionals I know could confirm the story. The significance of potential folklore will be discussed below.

18. This is, unfortunately, common practice in state-run clinics and hospitals in the region. Medical staff may be in too big a rush (or too lazy) to resterilize equipment during vaccination campaigns and so it is not unusual for young children especially to suffer the consequences. One baby I knew was treated for several months at the Catholic Mission Hospital for a terrible abscess that followed a vaccination administered with an unclean needle at another town's state hospital (see chapter 8).

19. For the relevance of these themes elsewhere, see Treichler 1989, 43, as cited in Farmer 1992, 235; on the "geography of blame" in Africa and associated racist premises, see Harrison-Chirimuuta and Chirimuuta 1997.

20. The political metaphors associated with AIDS operate in both directions. "By the 1990's, our security was further undermined by the worldwide emergence of new and resurgent epidemic diseases [such as AIDS and other diseases]," Shirley Lindenbaum writes, for example, of Western perceptions of world epidemics (1997, 191); for a detailed discussion of such metaphors, see Martin 1994.

21. This was a chronic problem in 1994, a year plagued by a nationwide shortage of coins and small bills. The local post office, for example, would often resort to giving change in stamps. Merchants altered their prices by rounding up or down, or else they would provide candy as change.

22. Farmer similarly offers other "conspiracy tales" from Haiti (1992, 230–21, 239 ff.).

CHAPTER 8. THE SOCIAL WORTH OF CHILDREN

1. *Fatidra,* or blood brother- or sisterhood, is practiced throughout Madagascar as a form of fictive kinship. Migrants employ it frequently in order to establish local ties in a community where they spend a significant amount of their lives.

2. Here Félix uses the Malagasy term *lahatra*. More typically, one might say *lahatra rat[s]y,* or "bad fate," where destiny is determined by *vintana,* the indigenous system of predestination that is anchored in part to one's day and time of birth.

3. *Fanafody* is typically translated by Sakalava speakers into French as *poison* or *magique* ("poison," "magic"). The term itself encompasses a range of substances and actions—including medicinal plants, as well as sacred items such as silver *(vola fotsy)* and kaolin *(tany malandy)*, and gestures that may involve blowing or breathing on healing substances or on patients themselves—all of which evoke significant physical and emotional responses. Although in Ambanja the French term *medicament* is reserved for pharmaceuticals, I use the corresponding English terms "medicine" and "magic" interchangeably here since, when paired, they best communicate the way Sakalava themselves employ the term *fanafody* in daily discourse. Malagasy often speak of *fanafody vazaha* ("European medicine") and *fanafody-gasy* ("Malagasy medicine," as does Félix here), each with its own realms of potency (recall the discussion on abortifacients with Dalia in chapter 7). Here I am concerned with the latter only, which in turn can be described as *fanafody tsara* ("good," "helpful," or "curing" medicine) and *fanafody raty* ("bad," "evil," or "harmful" medicine).

4. Fever (FR: *la fièvre*) is a blanket term applied to a host of illnesses, although it is most often used to describe malaria.

5. The third child is Zoko who died in early 1995 after wasting away for years from cancer. This book is dedicated in part to him.

6. Conrad Kottak's discussion of adoption among Betsileo informants reveals the importance of formal adoption by childless adults who are in need of heirs. Such a practice
can also strengthen alliances across kin groups, villages, etc. As he stresses, "Adoption
of an outsider, however, is viewed by Betsileo as a profoundly selfish act" because
through such actions "adopters flout a collectivist ethos by asserting their independence
of their own community and relatives. Simultaneously, they make an *individual* matter
out of inheritance and land—which traditionally and appropriately are *group* concerns.
Not surprisingly, lands transferred through adoption have led to extended litigation"
(1986, 287). Thus, legal adoption remains fairly unusual, although fosterage occurs frequently among kin. The beauty of fosterage lies in the fact that "in such cases the preexisting kinship bond is *re-modeled* by analogy to the rights and obligations that characterize the parent-child relationship" (1986, 288). He reports from his highland field sites
that in instances children were fostered out to other adult kin because their own destiny *(vintana)* was seen to conflict with that of (and thus endanger the life of) a conception parent. The child was then placed with a relative whose destiny was divined to be
more compatible. Often such relatives were older, childless, or better off economically.
Today, economic considerations more often shape such decisions among couples with
many children (this happens in communities where the ability to maintain dependents
is a reflection of wealth). Kottak's data also highlight the significance of schooling in
the transfer of children between households. These children may be sons or daughters
(although sons appear to be fostered more often). With virilocal residence being the
norm, fosterage patterns also work to ensure a hold on uterine rights, particularly in the
form of land holdings in the mother's natal village (1986, 290–96). Kottak does not consider the care of resident school children to be true fosterage (1986, 296), a distinction
which I find irrelevant for Ambanja, as the examples of Ketsy in chapter 3 and
Ouardah, in this chapter, illustrate.

7. Vern Carroll offers these definitions: "Adoption: any customary and optional procedure
for taking as one's own a child of other parents" (p. 3), acknowledging the assumed
formal legal aspects of the relationship (pp. 5–6), or again "permanently assuming the
major responsibilities of natural parents" as opposed to fosterage, which involves "temporarily taking care of others' children as an obligation of kinship" (p. 7). Also of note
is Carroll's discussion of what he identifies as a "universal desire for children throughout Eastern Oceania" (p. 12) and, later, why it is "difficult for parents to refuse requests
for the adoption of a child" (p. 13)—in other words, the obligation to answer a kins-
man/woman's needs. Goodenough, in his discussion of parenthood in this same volume, also inserts into this discussion the significance of guardianship and household
headship, stressing the relevance of psychological and jural meanings for kin-based relationships (1970, 391 ff.). Goodenough also speaks of "physical," "natural," "jural," and
"psychic" (emotionally bound) degrees of motherhood (392 ff.).

8. Urban Sakalava kinship in Ambanja is typically classificatory, and thus a child usually
refers to his/her parents' same sex siblings and cousins as "little mothers" and "little
fathers," and to their respective children as "brothers" and "sisters." Some, however,
rely on French terms of address, such as *Tantine* ("Aunt") and, less often, *Oncle* ("Uncle").
In rural areas and among elderly Sakalava, distinctions are more often drawn between
consanguinal and affinal kin as well as same sex versus opposite sex siblings of one's
parents (for a detailed discussion, see Sharp 1993, 98–108). Children also learn at an
early age to use teknonyms when addressing their elders (including their parents). Thus,

Mama Vé's urban-raised children interchange "Tantine" and "Maman'i'Bruno" ("Bruno's Mother") for their father's sister Mariamo.

9. Strong kin ties define the bedrock of the sentimental attachment between adults and fostered children. A striking contrast is offered by Mary Moran's (1992) work in Liberia, where fosterage serves as the idiom for more distanced relations between employers and their unrelated servants.

10. For a more detailed discussion of this, see Sharp 1996 (cf. May 1996; Bass 1996).

11. Hassan is not necessarily neglectful of his children. From a Sakalava point of view, by having Mariamo care for Ouardah and Ishmael, he is at least structurally satisfying a father's obligations, albeit through the labor, earnings, and attention of his sister.

12. On the demands placed on girls versus boys in the domestic sphere in many parts of sub-Saharan Africa, see Bledsoe et al. 1993, 72.

GLOSSARY

Unless otherwise specified, all Malagasy terms are in the Sakalava dialect (and generally defined from a northern Sakalava point of view); sometimes these correspond to terms in French or other dialects of Malagasy. FR: French; HP: high plateaus (esp. Merina); OM: official Malagasy; SAK: Sakalava.

ampanjaka: royalty

ampanjakabe: ruler

ampanompo: "those who work for royalty" or who perform royal service; see also *fanompoaña*

an-banvolo: "from near the forest," rural

andafy: overseas

Andevo (HP): applied in Merina territory to refer to people assumed to be of slave origin; associated with the HP term *mainty* (dark-skinned); see also Makoa

Ankify: seaside royal village of the Bemazava-Sakalava. Also referred to as Andoany, "[the place] At the Royal Palace *[doany]*"; see also Palais Royal

an-tanambe: "from town," urban

Antandroy, Tandroy: pastoralists from southern Madagascar who migrate to the Sambirano and who work primarily as manual laborers. *Tandroy* is the adjectival form; it also refers to the dialect spoken

Antankaraña: northern Malagasy neighbors of the Sakalava of the Sambirano

AREMA, or Antokin'ny Revolisiona Malagasy (OM): Vanguard of the Malagasy Revolution, the national political party of Madagascar during the Second Republic. (FR: Avant-Garde de la Révolution Malgache)

bac: (FR: *baccalauréat*) examination students must pass at the end of their *terminale* year at lycée in order to go on to the university

Bemazava: the northern dynastic branch of the Sakalava

Bemihisatra: a northern Sakalava dynastic branch located to the south of the Sambirano Valley and on the smaller offshore island of Nosy Be

BEPC: (FR: *brévet d'études du premier cycle*) examinations that follow a middle school (CEG) education; one must receive a passing score in order to continue on to the lycée level

Betsileo: central highland group of Malagasy centered around Fianarantsoa

Betsimisaraka: Malagasy speakers associated with the central and northern band of the east coast of Madagascar

Boky Mena: "the Red Book"; the socialist treatise of President Didier Ratsiraka's Second Republic

CEG: (FR: *collège d'enseignement général*) a state-run middle school; see also *collège*

CEPE: (FR: *certificat d'études primaires élémentaires*) the national examination following primary schooling; one must receive a passing score in order to continue on to the middle school (collège or CEG) level

collège (FR):   middle school; also referred to as CEG (FR: *collège d'enseignement général*) when it is a state-run school

côtier (FR):   someone from the coast; coined during the colonial period, this term is used to encompass all Malagasy save for those of the high plateaux (which refers primarily to the Merina and Betsileo)

deuxième bureau: mistress; in French it also refers to the branch of government concerned with national security, especially in the realm of covert actions and sabotage

diversion (FR):   distraction, amusement, what one does for fun

doany: Sakalava royal palace; see also *zomba*

drakô: "my dear friend," affectionate term of address used between women

fady: taboo

falafa: palm fiber used to construct the simplest dwellings in Ambanja and the Sambirano

fanafody: medicine, magic; *fanafody tsara:* "good medicine," used to bring about a positive change in one's life; *fanafody raty,* or *ratsy:* "bad medicine" used to harm an adversary; *fanafody-gasy:* "Malagasy [indigenous] medicine" as opposed to *fanafody vazaha:* medicine of foreign (biomedical) origin

Fandroana (HP):   Royal Bath, the annual renewal ceremony when subjects of Imerina proclaimed their allegiance to the monarch; last performed in November, 1896 and thereafter prohibited by the French, its end corresponding to the downfall of the Merina monarchy under colonialism

fanjakana: the (authority of the) royal state or kingdom; (OM): "government" or more specifically the state of Madagascar

fanompoaña: royal service

firaisana (OM):   city government, city hall; (FR: *hôtel de ville*)

First Republic: (FR: Première République) corresponds with the tenure of President Philibert Tsiranana (1960–72)

FISA: Fianakaviana Sambatra ("Happy Family"), Madagascar's state-run family planning program

fitahiaña: commemorative praise name given to a deceased Sakalava ruler (from *mitaha,* "to protect")

fivondronana (OM):   county government or seat

fokon'olona (HP, OM):   community, collective

fomba: custom

fombandrazaña: royal ancestral customs; see also *razaña* and *tanindrazaña*

Fourth Republic: (FR: Quatrième République) corresponds with Didier Ratsiraka's second presidency (1997–)

havaña: kin

hendry: wise, clever, prudent, socially intelligent, well-behaved; applied as a strong form of praise for children; see also *mahay*

Imerina: the central highland kingdom of the Merina peoples, centered around the city of Antananarivo; from the late eighteenth through much of the nineteenth century, the Merina were a formidable force, conquering much of Madagascar

joro: the sacrifice—generally of cattle—to honor, commemorate, request of, or thank ancestors for their blessing

kabary: speech, royal oratory; (OM:) official government oratory

kamo: lazy

karazaña: "kind" or "group," a term used to refer to ethnicity; see also *razaña* and *tanindrazaña*

katramy: (HP from FR:) *quatre amis* ("four friends") or *quatre murs* ("four walls") because they lack friends and/or homes; the homeless of Antananarivo

laklasy mandry: "the[servant] class that sleeps [in the house]," a live-in servant

lambahoany: a cotton print body wrap; see also *salovaña*

lolo: spirit[s] of lost or displaced dead

lycée (FR):   high school

maditra: naughty; term applied to children who misbehave

mahay: capable, knowledgeable, skilled; to know how to do something well

makarely: prostitute (from FR: *maquereau,* "mackerel" or "pimp," or *maquerelle,* "madam")

Makoa: blanket term applied to west coast inhabitants assumed to be of slave origin; from Makua, an ethnic label of Portuguese East Africa (Mozambique); may also be used more generally to refer to someone considered dark-skinned *(joby)* and thus assumed to be of African origin

malagasization: (FR: *malgachisation*) although the term was used during the French era and in the first decade following independence in 1960, *malagasization* is generally associated with national reforms by President Didier Ratsiraka during the Second Republic. Its purpose was to replace or transform all French policies, customs, and practices with Malagasy ones; see also official Malagasy

Malagasy: the general term applied to the indigenous inhabitants of Madagascar, it encompasses a host of subgroups, including, for example, the Antandroy, Antaimoro, Antankaraña, Betsileo, Betsimisaraka, Merina, and Sakalava; the term also refers to the Austronesian language spoken by all Malagasy peoples (and thus their dialects)

Malagasy iombonana: "official Malagasy" or OM; national language created in 1975 under President Ratsiraka to unite the nation linguistically (*iombonana,* "joint effort"). The primary language of instruction until the 1991–93 transitional period.

mampalahelo, mamaplahelobe: "to [make one] sad"; *-be* further intensifies the sentiment: "[to make one] very sad [indeed]"

manantany: the primary advisor to a Sakalava ruler; sometimes referred to as the "prime minister"

Merina: highland Malagasy group that established the central kingdom of Imerina, with Antananarivo as its capital; considered to be the dominant group of Madagascar by northern Sakalava

métis(se) (FR):   of mixed origins, more specifically involving pairings of Malagasy and non-Malagasy parents; for example, a woman one of whose parents is Arab (in northern Madagascar, Yemeni) and the other Malagasy is called Arab-métisse; since foreign migration to Madagascar has primarily involved men, the father is most often the non-Malagasy parent

mihilaña: a sacred verb form used exclusively for royalty meaning "to die" (lit. "turn [one's] back" or avert one's gaze); in contrast, the proper term used for commoners is *maty*

mitsangantsangana: to promenade, stroll about with friends or kin as a form of leisure activity

mpañarivo: "those who have thousands"; the rich, elite, wealthy

mpangalaza-zaza: kidnapper

mpitsabo: peasant

njarinintsy: malicious possessing spirit that must be driven from its victim; if not, it causes serious illness, madness, or even death

Nosy Be: "Big Island"; located off the northwest coast of Madagascar near Ambanja; the seat of the northern branch of the Bemihisatra-Sakalava

Nosy Faly: "Taboo Island"; sacred island where the northern Bemazava-Sakalava of the Sambirano Valley entomb their royal dead

Nosy Lava: "Long Island"; located along the northwest coast of Madagascar near Analalava; site of a French prison

Official Malagasy: see *Malagasy iombonana.*

olo ambañy: "the people below," i.e., most Malagasy, as opposed to the wealthy elite, or *olo ambony*

olo ambony: "the people above," the wealthy elite, as opposed to *olo ambañy*; see also *mpañarivo olo madiniky:*   "the little people," the poor; often used to encompass most Malagasy

Palais Royal (FR):   Royal Palace; name given to the new *doany* built in the royal village of Andoany at Ankify Beach, near Ambanja

première (FR):   the first of three years of a *lycée* education; see also *terminale* and *seconde*

primaire (FR):   primary or elementary school

razaña: (royal) ancestors; see also *fombandraña* and *tanindrazaña*

rebiky: a celebratory dance performed at royal ceremonies

saha: a medium for the most powerful of the royal *tromba* spirits

Sakalava: Malagasy speakers whose string of kingdoms span much of the western coast of Madagascar

salovaña: a woman's body wrap

Sambarivo: caste of royal retainers responsible for a host of duties associated with Sakalava royal service

sambatra: happy, blessed; can also imply wisdom or that one is in good health (see FISA)

Sambirano *ambañy:*   the Lower Sambirano Valley, located near the coast

Sambirano *ambony:*   the Upper Sambirano Valley, located in the cooler hilly area away from the coast

seconde (FR):   the second of three years of a *lycée* education; see also *terminale* and *première*

Second Republic: (FR: Deuxième République); Didier Ratsiraka's first presidency (1975–91); an era also referred to as the socialist revolution

Service National Révolutionnaire, or SN: a youth corps program established under the Second Republic by President Ratsiraka in 1975 and eliminated during the 1991–92 transitional period; SN was required of all *bac* graduates who wished to go on to university

sida: AIDS (FR: *syndrome d'immunodéficience acquise*)

SMOTIG (FR):   Service de la Main d'Oeuvre des Travaux d'Intérêt Général ("Manual Labor Service for Works of General Interest"); colonial-era corvée labor program

socialist revolution: corresponds to the Second Republic of Didier Ratsiraka's first presidency (1975–91)

soma: play, game; from the verb *misoma,* "to play"

taloha: the past, long ago

tanindrazaña: (HP: *tanindrazana*) ancestral land, e.g., the Sambirano Valley is the *tanindrazaña* of the Bemazava-Sakalava kingdom; (OM:) homeland, the nation; see also *fombandrazaña, razaña*

tanora (HP, OM):   youth

tany: land, soil

tera-tany: "children" or "offspring of the soil"; in the Sambirano, it refers to indigenous Sakalava; see also *vahiny*

terminale (FR):   final year of *lycée;* see also *seconde* and *première*

Terminale séries A, D, C (FR):   The three tracks that characterize the final two years of a *lycée* education; A focuses on humanities and social sciences, D is a natural science core suitable for premedical training, whereas C is an advanced science program, with an especially strong emphasis on mathematics and physics

Third Republic (FR):   Troisième République; Zafy Albert's presidency (1993–96)

tirailleur (FR):   foot soldier

transitional period: the 1991–93 interlude between the Second and Third republics

tromba: possessing spirits of royal ancestors; the most powerful are referred to by a host of names, including *razambe* ("great ancestors"), *dady* ("grandparents" or "royal relics"), and *tromba maventibe* ("the greatest tromba")

tsaiky lahy: boy, man-child

tsaiky ny Sambirano: "children of the Sambirano," or those born and raised in the Sambirano who speak the local dialect with ease and are familiar with local cultural norms

tsangam-bato: "standing stone," a memorial erected in the memory of lost dead. At times these are raised in honor of migrants who have died outside of their *tanindrazana;* in many cities and towns in Madagascar they have also been erected by the state to commemorate those who died during insurrections or as soldiers abroad during the two world wars.

Tsangantsaiñy: royal ceremony of the Antankaraña kingdom located to the north of the Sakalava of the Sambirano Valley

Tsimihety: sedentary and pastoral Malagasy of western Madagascar, Tsimihety have long migrated to the Sambirano Valley and intermarried with Sakalava

tsiñy: forest spirits; sometimes regarded as ancient royal ancestors or as the agents of royal wrath

tsy an'asa: "[those] without work"; the unemployed

vahiny: guest; in the Sambirano this term is applied to labor migrants; see also *tera-tany*

vazaha: stranger, a white European

VVS (HP: Vy Vato Sakelika, or "Iron Stone Network"):   nationalist movement founded in 1912 by medical students, intellectuals, and journalists in Antananarivo

Zafin'i'fotsy: dynastic branch of living Sakalava royalty and their *tromba* spirits; in Ambanja, it is associated most closely with Analalava, a town south of Ambanja

zomba: royal residence; see also *doany*

REFERENCES

ABBREVIATIONS

AP	Affaires politiques
c	carton
CAOM	Centre des Archives d'Outre-Mer, Aix-en-Provence
d	dossier
DS	Diégo-Suarez
MAD	Madagascar
PM	Province Majunga
SG	*Série géographique*

UNPUBLISHED GOVERNMENT MATERIALS

(A) Colonial Archival Documents

Sources from the Centre des Archives d'Outre-Mer (CAOM) in Aix-en-Provence

MAD *3*

Annexes for part IIB

PM 56 (1939)

DS 0479 (1938–1948)

MAD *4*

DS 0158 (1944), 0162, 0163, 0170 (1946), 0330 [Enseignement 1937]; 0422 [1932–1942–1954: "Censure cinématographique et theâtral" (*sic*)], 0526 [Notables 1935], 0604 (1943–44).

PM 0006, 0089, 0093, 0168 (1946), 0605 (1935–40, 1945), 0014 [1930: "Pièces de thèâtres représentées sans autorisations"].

MAD 5

PM 0010 [1926], 0168 [1946]
Affaires politiques
AP 2942:1 (1925, 1938–39)
Série géographique (assorted materials)

(B) Government of Madagascar

- Madagascar-FTM:

  1986 Sarintanin-Dàlana/Carte Routier, Madagascar [Road map for Madagascar]. Antananarivo: Foiben-Taosarintanin'i Madagasikara (FTM) [National Geodetic and Cartographic Institute].

- Service des Statistiques de l'Éducation:

  1987–90 Annuaire statistique. Direction de la Planification de l'Orientation de l'Enseignement, Ministère de l'Enseignement Secondaire et de l'Education de Base.

  1990–91 Annuaire statistique. Direction de la Planification et de l'Orientation de l'Enseignement, Ministère de l'Instruction Publique.

- [Census Data]:

  1950–71 Monographies. Census data, Province de Diégo-Suarez, Préfecture de Diégo-Suarez, Sous-Préfecture d'Ambanja. Antananarivo: Ministère de l'Intérieur, Service des Affaires Générales et Territoriales; and Archives Nationales, Tsaralalana.

  1986 [Census for the town and county (fivondronana) of Ambanja.] Ambanja: Service du Planification.

- Firaisana [City Government] of Ambanja:

  Statistical information on schooling in the Sambirano was drawn from the following sources for the years spanning 1986–95: Programme de Renforcement du Système Éducatif Malgache (PRESEM), Ministère de l'Éducation Nationale, Direction de l'Inspection Générale de l'Éducation Nationale, Direction de la Planification de l'Éducation, Direction des Ressources Humaines, Direction de l'Enseignement Secondaire.

PUBLISHED SOURCES, DISSERTATIONS, AND PAPERS

Abu-Lughod, Lila. 1993. *Writing Women's Worlds: Bedouin Stories.* Berkeley and Los Angeles: University of California Press.

Adejunmobi, Moradewun. 1994. African Language Writing and Writers: A Case Study of Jean-Joseph Rabearivelo and Ny Avana in Madagascar. *African Languages and Cultures* 7, 1: 1–18.

Aderibigbe, A. B. 1989. Slavery in South-West of Indian Ocean. In *Slavery in South West Indian Ocean,* ed. U. Bissoondoyal and S. B. Servansing, 320–29. Moka, Mauritius: Mahatma Gandhi Institute.

Akony ny Sambirano. 1994. Mensuel independant d'informations [publication produced by the Catholic Mission], 8 (December): 27. Ambanja: Association Hafaliana.

Althabe, Gerard 1969. *Oppression et libération dans l'imaginaire: Les Communautés villageoises de la Côte Orientale de Madagascar.* Paris: François Maspero.

———. 1972. Les Manifestations paysans d'avril 1971. *RFEPA,* June, 71–77.

———. 1980. Les Luttes sociales à Tananarive en 1972. *Cahiers d'Études Africaines* 20: 407–47.

Amit-Talai, Vered, and Helena Wulff, eds. 1995. *Youth Cultures: A Cross-Cultural Perspective.* New York: Routledge.

Anderson, Benedict. [1983] 1991. *Imagined Communities: Reflections on the Origin and Spread of Nationalism.* Rev. ed. New York: Verso.

Andrew, C. M. and A. S. Kanya-Forstner. 1978. France, Africa and the First World War. *Journal of African History* 19, 1: 11–23.

Andriamihamina, R., N. Trevet., T. de Commarmond, J-L. Rabenandrasana, and R. Perier. 1987. *Ambanja, État Actuel.* Projet Urbain dans les Faritany, Service de l'Urbanisme et de l'Aménagement, Direction de l'Architecture de l'Urbanisme et de l'Habitat, Direction Générale de l'Équipement, Ministère des Travaux Publics. Antananarivo.

Appiah, Kwame Anthony. 1991. Is the Post- in Postmodernism the Post- in Postcolonial? *Critical Inquiry* 17: 336–57.

Apter, Andrew H. 1992. *Black Critics and Kings: The Hermeneutics of Power in Yoruba Society.* Chicago: University of Chicago Press.

———. 1993. Atinga Revisited: Yoruba Witchcraft and the Cocoa Economy, 1950–1951. In *Modernity and its Malcontents: Ritual and Power in Postcolonial Africa,* ed. J. and J. Comaroff, 111–28. Chicago: University of Chicago Press.

Archer, Robert. 1976. *Madagascar depuis 1972: La Marche d'une révolution.* Paris: L'Har-mattan.

Ariès, Philippe. 1960. *L'Enfant et la vie familiale sous l'ancien regime.* Paris: Librairie Plon.

Asad, Talal, ed. 1973. *Anthropology and the Colonial Encounter.* Atlantic City, N.J.: Humanities Press.

Astuti, Rita. 1995. *People of the Sea: Identity and Descent among the Vezo of Madagascar.* Cambridge: Cambridge University Press.

Atteh, Samuel O. 1996. The Crisis in Higher Education in Africa. *Issue: A Journal of Opinion* 24, 1: 36–42.

Balandier, George. 1951. La Situation coloniale: Approche théorique. *Cahiers internationaux de sociologie* 11: 44–79.

Balesi, C. J. 1976. From Adversary to Comrades in Arms: West Africans and the French Military. Ph.D. diss. University of Illinois.

Barbusse, Henri. 1920 [. . .]. *Foreign Affairs* 1: 12. June supplement.

———. [1926?] 1974. *Under Fire.* Translated by W. F. Wray. New York: Dutton.

Baré, Jean-François. 1980. *Sable Rouge: Une Monarchie du nord-ouest malgache dans l'histoire.* Paris: L'Harmattan.

———. 1986. L'Organisation sociale Sakalava du nord: Une Récapitulation. In *Madagascar: Society and History,* ed. C. P. Kottak, J.-A. Rakotoarisoa, A. Southall and P. Vérin, 353–92. Durham, N.C.: Carolina Academic Press for the Wenner-Gren Foundation for Anthropological Research.

Bass, Loretta E. 1996. Beyond Homework: Children's Incorporation into Market-based Work in Urban Areas of Senegal. *Anthropology of Work Review* 7, 1–2: 19–25.

Battaglia, Debbora. 1990. *On the Bones of the Serpent: Person, Memory, and Mortality in Sabarl Island Society.* Chicago: University of Chicago Press.

Baudrillard, Jean. 1987. Forget Foucault and Forget Baudrillard. An Interview with Sylvere Lotringer. *Semiotexte* (New York).

Bayart, Jean François. 1993. *The State in Africa: Politics of the Belly*. London: Longman. Originally published as *L'Etat en Afrique: La Politique du ventre* (Paris: Arthème Fayard, 1989).

Behrend, Heike, and Ute Luig, eds. 1999. *Spirit Possession, Modernity, and Power in Africa*. London: James Currey.

Belrose-Huyghues, Vincent. 1974. At the Origin of British Evangelization: The Dream of Madagascar. In *Madagascar in History: Essays from the 1970s*, ed. R. Kent, 252–68. Albany, Calif.: Foundation for Malagasy Studies.

Benolo, François. 1992. Le Lolo ou le problème de la reviviscence des morts dans l'Androy (l'extrême-sud de Madagascar). Thesis, doctorat en science théologique. Institut catholique de Paris.

Bledsoe, Caroline H. 1999. *Critical Perspectives on Schooling and Fertility in the Developing World*. Washington, D.C.: National Academy Press.

Bledsoe, Carolina H., Andrew J. Cherlin, Anastasia J. Gage-Brandon, Jane I. Guyer, and Daniel M. Sala-Diakanda. 1993. *Social Dynamics of Adolescent Fertility in Sub-Saharan Africa*. Washington, D.C.: National Research Council.

Bloch, Marianne, and Frances Vavrus. 1998. Gender and Educational Research, Policy, and Practice in Sub-Saharan Africa: Theoretical and Empirical Problems and Prospects. In *Women and Education in Sub-Saharan Africa: Power, Opportunities, and Constraints*, ed. M. Bloch, J. A. Boeku-Betts, and B. R. Tabachnick, 1–23. Boulder, Colo.: Lynne Rienner.

Bloch, Maurice. 1971. *Placing the Dead: Tombs, Ancestral Villages, and Kinship Organization in Madagascar*. New York: Seminar Press.

———. 1982. Death, Women and Power. In *Death and the Regeneration of Life*, ed. M. Bloch and J. Parry, 211–30. Cambridge: Cambridge University Press.

———. 1986. *From Blessing to Violence. History and Ideology in the Circumcision Ritual of the Merina of Madagascar*. Cambridge: Cambridge University Press.

———. 1989. *Ritual, History and Power: Selected Papers in Anthropology*. LSE Monographs on Social Anthropology No. 58. London: Athlone Press.

———. 1992. *Prey into Hunter: The Politics of Religious Experience*. Cambridge: Cambridge University Press.

———. 1994. The Slaves, the King, and Mary in the Slums of Antananarivo. In *Shamanism, History, and the State*, ed. N. Thomas and C. Humphrey, 133–45. Ann Arbor: University of Michigan Press.

———. 1995. People into Places: Zafimaniry Concepts of Clarity. In *The Anthropology of Landscape: Perspectives on Place and Space*, ed. E. Hirsch and M. O'Hanlon, 63–77. Oxford: Clarendon Press.

Bouillon, Antoine. 1973. Le MFM malgache. *RFEPA*, November, 46–71.

———. 1981. *Madagascar: Le Colonisé et son "âme": Essai sur le discours psychologique colonial*. Paris: L'Harmattan.

Boyarin, Jonathan. 1994. Space, Time, and the Politics of Memory. In *Remapping Memory: The Politics of Time and Space*, ed. id., 1–37. Minneapolis: University of Minnesota Press.

Brooks, Alan, and Jeremy Brickhill. 1987: The Soweto Uprising, 1976. In *The Anti-Apartheid Reader: The Struggle against White Racist Rule in South Africa*, ed. D. Mermelstein, 228–35. New York: Grove Press.

Brown, Mervyn. 1978. *Madagascar Rediscovered: A History from Early Times to Independence*. London: Damien Tunnacliffe.

Bundy, Colin. 1986. Schools and Revolution. *New Society* 75, 1202: 52–55.

————. 1987. Street Sociology and Pavement Politics: Aspects of Youth and Student Resistance in Cape Town, 1985. *Journal of South African Studies* 13, 3: 303–30.

Bunge, Frederica M., ed. 1983. *Indian Ocean, Five Island Countries.* 2d. ed. Department of the Army Area Handbook Series, Publication No. DA Pam 550–154. Washington, D.C.: American University for the Secretary of the Army.

Burbank, Victoria K. 1988. *Aboriginal Adolescence: Maidenhood in an Australian Community.* New Brunswick, N.J.: Rutgers University Press.

Bureau International du Travail. 1925. *Décret: Travail indigène; Madagascar et dépendances.* Série législative. 16 pp. Geneva: E. Birkhaeuser. Reprinted from *Journal Officiel,* 1925, no. 229, p. 9488, and no. 247, p. 10,090.

Burke, Charlanne. 2000a. Dangerous Dependencies: The Power and Potential of Youth in Botswana. Ph.D. diss. Anthropology Department, Teachers College, Columbia University.

————. 2000b. They cut Segametsi into Parts: Ritual Murder, Youth, and the Politics of Knowledge in Botswana. *Anthropology Quarterly* 73:4: 204–214.

Callet, R. P. [1908] 1974. *Histoire des rois: Tantaran'ny Andriana.* Translated by G.-S. Chapus and E. Ratsimba. Antananarivo: Librairie de Madagascar. Originally published in 1908 in Malagasy (Edition de l'Imprimerie Officielle).

Camo, Pierre. 1931. *La Protection de la vie locale à Madagascar.* Proceedings of the Congrès International et Intercolonial de la Société Indigène, Exposition Coloniale Internationale de Paris, October 5–10. 14 pp.

Campion-Vincent, Véronique. 1997. *La Légende des vols d'organes.* Paris: Les Belles Lettres.

Caputo, Virginia. 1995. Anthropology's Silent "Others." A Consideration of Some Conceptual and Methodological Issues for the Study of Youth and Children's Cultures. In *Youth Cultures: A Cross-Cultural Perspective,* ed. V. Amit-Talai and Helena Wulff, 19–42. New York: Routledge.

Carnoy, M. 1972. *Education as Cultural Imperialism.* New York: McKay.

Carroll, Vern. 1970a. Introduction: What Does "Adoption" Mean? In *Adoption in Eastern Oceania,* ed. id., 3–17. ASAO Monograph No. 1. Honolulu: University of Hawaii Press.

————, ed. 1970b. *Adoption in Eastern Oceania.* ASAO Monograph No. 1. Honolulu: University of Hawaii Press.

Carsten, Janet. 1991. Children In Between: Fostering and the Process of Kinship on Pulau Langkawi, Malaysia. *Man,* n.s., 26: 425–43.

Casey, Edward S. 1987. *Remembering: A Phenomenological Study.* Bloomington: Indiana University Press.

Cerny, Charlene, and Suzanne Seriff, eds. 1996. *Recycled Re-Seen: Folk Art from the Global Scrap Heap.* New York: Harry N. Abrams in association with the Museum of International Folk Art, Santa Fe.

Césaire, Aimé. [1955] 1970. *Discours sur le colonialisme.* Paris: Présence Africaine.

Chatterjee, Partha. [1986] 1993. *Nationalist Thought and the Colonial World.* Minneapolis: University of Minnesota Press.

Chazan-Gillic, Suzanne. 1983. Le Fitampoha de 1968; ou l'efficacité symbolique du myth de la royauté Sakalava dans l'actualité politique et économique malgache. In *Les Souverains de Madagascar: L'Histoire royale et ses résurgences contemporaines,* ed. F. Raison-Jourde, 452–76. Paris: Karthala.

Chittick, Neville H. and Robert I. Rotberg, eds. 1975. *East Africa and the Orient: Cultural Syntheses in Pre-Colonial Times.* New York: Africana Publishing.

Clarke, Peter B. 1986. *West Africans at War, 1914–18, 1939–45: Colonial Propaganda and its Cultural Aftermath*. London: Ethnographica.

Clignet, Rémi, and Bernard Ernst. 1995. *L'École à Madagascar: Evaluation de la qualité de l'enseignement primaire public*. Paris: Karthala.

Cohen, David William. 1994. *The Combing of History*. Chicago: University of Chicago Press.

Colburn, Lisa L. 2000. Nurturing Social Networks as a Household Resource: A Comparative Study of Child Nutrition in Fishing Villages in Northwest Madagascar. Ph.D. diss. Department of Anthropology, University of Connecticut, Storrs.

Cole, Jennifer. 1997. Sacrifice, Narratives and Experience in East Madagascar. *Journal of Religion in Africa* 26, 4: 401–25.

———. 2001. *Forget Colonialism? Sacrifice and the Art of Memory in Madagascar*. Berkeley and Los Angeles: University of California Press.

Coles, Robert. 1971. *Children of Crisis: A Study of Courage and Fear*. Boston: Little, Brown.

———. 1986. *The Moral Life of Children*. New York: Atlantic Monthly Press.

Colonna, Fanny. 1997. Educating Conformity in French Colonial Algeria. In *Tensions of Empire: Colonial Cultures in a Bourgeois World*, ed. F. Cooper and A. L. Stoler, 346–70. Berkeley and Los Angeles: University of California Press.

Colson, Elizabeth. 1971. *The Social Consequences of Resettlement*. Manchester: Manchester University Press for the Institute for African Studies, University of Zambia.

Comaroff, Jean. 1985. *Body of Power, Spirit of Resistance: The Culture and History of a South African People*. Chicago: University of Chicago Press.

Comaroff, Jean, and John Comaroff. 1991. *Of Revelation and Revolution*, vol. 1: *Christianity, Colonialism, and Consciousness in South Africa*. Chicago: University of Chicago Press.

———. 1992. *Ethnography and the Historical Imagination*. Boulder, Colo.: Westview Press.

———. 1993a. Introduction. In *Modernity and Its Malcontents: Ritual and Power in Postcolonial Africa*, ed. id., xi–xxxvii. Chicago: University of Chicago Press.

———, eds. 1993b. *Modernity and Its Malcontents: Ritual and Power in Postcolonial Africa*. Chicago: Chicago University Press.

———. 1997. *Of Revelation and Revolution*, vol. 2: *The Dialectics of Modernity on a South African Frontier*. Chicago: Chicago University Press.

———. 1999. Occult Economies and the Violence of Abstraction: Notes from the South African Postcolony. *American Ethnologist* 26:2:279–303.

Condominas, Georges. 1960. *Fokon'olona et collectivités rurales en Imerina*. Paris: Berger-Levrault.

Condon, Richard G. 1987. *Inuit Youth*. New Brunswick, N.J.: Rutgers University Press.

Connerton, Paul. 1989. *How Societies Remember*. New York: Cambridge University Press.

Coombe, Rosemary J. 1991. Beyond Modernity's Meanings: Engaging the Postmodern in Cultural Anthropology. *Culture* 11:1–2: 111–24.

Cooper, Frederick. 1992. Colonizing Time: Work Rhythms and Labor Conflict in Colonial Mombasa. In *Colonialism and Culture*, ed. N. B. Dirks, 209–45. Ann Arbor: University of Michigan Press.

Covell, Maureen. 1987. *Madagascar: Politics, Economics and Society*. London: Frances Pinter.

———. 1995. *Historical Dictionary of Madagascar*. African Historical Dictionaries No. 50. Lanham, Md.: Scarecrow Press.

Cruise O'Brien, Conor. 1988. Nationalism and the French Revolution. In *The Permanent Revolution: The French Revolution and Its Legacy: 1789–1989*, ed. G. Best, 17–48. Chicago: University of Chicago Press.

Cruise O'Brien, Donal B. 1996. A Lost Generation? Youth Identity and State Decay in West Africa. In *Postcolonial Identities in Africa,* ed. R. Werbner and T. Ranger, 55–74. London: Zed Books.

Dalmond, Pierre. 1840. Mission saclave 1840. Manuscript in the Archives of the Institut Supérieur de Théologie et de Philosophie de Madagascar, Antsiranana.

———. n.d. *Exercices en langue sakalava et betsimisaraka, 1841–1844.* Recherches et Documents No. 3. Antsiranana: Institut Supérieur de Théologie et de Philosophie de Madagascar.

Dandouau, A., and G.-S. Chapus. 1952. *Histoire des populations de Madagascar.* Paris: Larose.

Davidson, James West, and Mark Hamilton Lytle. 1992. *After the Fact: The Art of Historical Detection.* 3d ed. New York: McGraw-Hill.

Davis, Susan Schaefer, and Douglas A. Davis. 1989. *Adolescence in a Moroccan Town.* New Brunswick, N.J.: Rutgers University Press.

Deschamps, Hubert. 1959. *Les Migrations intérieures à Madagascar.* Paris: Berger-Levrault.

———. 1972. *Histoire de Madagascar.* Paris: Berger-Levraut.

Dijk, Rijk van. 1998. Pentecostalism, Cultural Memory and the State: Contested Representations of Time in Postcolonial Malawi. In *Memory and the Postcolony: African Anthropology and the Critique of Power,* ed. R. Werbner, 155–81. London: Zed Books.

Dirks, Nicholas B. 1992. Introduction: Colonialism and Culture. In *Colonialism and Culture,* ed. N. B. Dirks, 1–25. Ann Arbor: University of Michigan Press.

Domatob, Jerry Komia. 1996. Policy Issues for African Universities. *Issue: A Journal of Opinion* 24, 1: 29–35.

Domenichini, Jean-Pierre. 1990. Le Règne de Radama II: Un Règne sous le signe de la Révolution? In *Ravao ny "La Bastille": Regards sur Madagascar et la Révolution française,* ed. Guy Jacob, 97–109. Actes du colloque d'Antananarivo, June 5 and 6, 1989. Antananarivo: CNAPMAD.

Dubois, H. (Père). 1931. La Connaissance des mentalités indigènes à Madagascar. Presented at the Congrès international et intercolonial de la Société indigène, Exposition coloniale internationale de Paris, October 5–10, 1931. 16 pp.

Durham, Deborah, ed. 2000. Special issues on Youth and the Social Imagination in Africa. *Anthropology Quarterly* 73:3 and 4.

Ebron, Paulla. 1997. Traffic in Men. In *Gendered Encounters: Challenging Cultural Boundaries and Social Hierarchies in Africa,* ed. M. Grosz-Ngate and O. H. Kokole, 223–44. New York: Routledge.

Ellis, Stephen. 1985. *The Rising of the Red Shawls: A Revolt in Madagascar, 1895–1899.* Cambridge: Cambridge University Press.

Emecheta, Buchi. 1979. *The Joys of Motherhood.* Portsmouth, N.H.: Heinemann.

Ennew, Judith, and Brian Milne. 1990. *The Next Generation: Lives of Third World Children.* Philadephia: New Society.

Epstein, A. L. 1958. *Politics in an Urban African Community.* Manchester: Manchester University Press.

Escamps, Henry d'. 1884. *Histoire et géographie de Madagascar.* Paris: Firmin-Didot. Revised edition of a work originally published under the pseudonym Macé Descartes, Histoire et géographie de Madagascar depuis la découverte de l'île, en 1506, jusqu'au récit des derniers événements de Tamatave (Paris: P. Bertrand, 1846).

Escobar, Arturo. 1995. *Encountering Development: The Making and Unmaking of the Third World.* Princeton, N.J.: Princeton University Press.

Esoavelomandroso, Faranirina V. 1990. Les 14 juillet à d'Antananarivo au temps de la colonisation. In *Ravao ny "La Bastille": Regards sur Madagascar et la Révolution française,* ed. Guy Jacob, 145–58. Actes du colloque d'Antananarivo, June 5 and 6, 1989. Antananarivo: CNAPMAD.

Esoavelomandroso, Manassé. 1990. La génération de Rainandriamampandry et la Révolution Française. In *Ravao ny "La Bastille": Regards sur Madagascar et la Révolution française*, ed. Guy Jacob, 113–19. Actes du colloque d'Antananarivo, June 5 and 6, 1989. Antananarivo: CNAPMAD.

Fabian, Johannes. 1986. *Language and Colonial Power.* Berkeley and Los Angeles: University of California Press.

Fahrner, Charles. 1937. *Manuel de Sakalava: Dialecte de la région nord-ouest de Madagascar.* Paris: René Roger, Librairie Africaine et Coloniale.

Fallers, Lloyd A. 1965. *Bantu Bureaucracy: A Century of Political Evolution among the Basoga of Uganda.* Chicago: University of Chicago Press.

Fanon, Frantz. 1963. *The Wretched of the Earth.* Translated by C. Farrington. New York: Grove Weidenfeld. Originally published as *Les Damnés de la terre* (Paris: François Maspero, 1961).

———. 1966. The Ordeal of the Black Man. In *Social Change: The Colonial Situation*, ed. I. Wallerstein, 75–87. New York: Wiley.

———. 1967. *Black Skin, White Masks.* Translated by C. L. Markmann. New York: Grove Weidenfeld. Originally published as *Peau noire, masques blancs* (Paris: Seuil, 1952).

Farmer, Paul. 1992. *AIDS and Accusation: Haiti and the Geography of Blame.* Berkeley and Los Angeles: University of California Press.

Feeley-Harnik, Gillian. 1982. The King's Men in Madagascar: Slavery, Citizenship and Sakalava Monarchy. *Africa* 52, 2: 31–50.

———. 1984. The Political Economy of Death: Communication and Change in Malagasy Colonial History. *American Ethnologist* 11, 1: 1–19.

———. 1991. *A Green Estate: Restoring Independence in Madagascar.* Washington, D.C.: Smithsonian Institution Press.

Feinberg, Richard. 1994. Contested Worlds: The Politics of Culture and the Politics of Anthropology. *Anthropology and Humanism* 19, 1: 20–35.

Ferro, Marc. 1984. *The Use and Abuse of History, or, How the Past is Taught.* London: Routledge & Kegan Paul. Originally published as Comment on raconte l'histoire aux enfants : À travers le monde entier (Paris: Payot, 1981).

Fisher, Lawrence. 1985. *Colonial Madness: Mental Health in the Barbadian Social Order.* New Brunswick, N.J.: Rutgers University Press.

Freeman, Derek. 1983. *Margaret Mead and Samoa: The Making and Unmaking of an Anthropological Myth.* Cambridge, Mass.: Harvard University Press.

Freeman-Grenville, G. S. P. 1962. *The East African Coast: Select Documents from the First to the Earlier Nineteenth Century.* Oxford: Clarendon Press.

Freire, Paulo. 1970. *Pedagogy of the Oppressed.* Translated by M. B. Ramos. New York: Herder & Herder.

———. 1985. *The Politics of Education: Culture, Power, and Liberation.* Translated by D. Macedo. New York: Bergin & Garvey.

Friedl, Erika. 1992. Moonrose: Watched Through a Sunny Day. *Natural History*, August, 34–45.

Furley, Oliver. 1995. Child Soldiers in Africa. In *Conflict in Africa*, ed. O. Furley, 28–45. New York: I. B. Tauris.

Gallieni, Joseph Simon. 1900. See Hellot.

———. 1908. *Neuf ans à Madagascar.* Paris: Hachette.

Geertz, Clifford. 1980. *Negara: The Theatre State in Nineteenth-Century Bali.* Princeton, N.J.: Princeton University Press.

Gell, Alfred. 1992. *The Anthropology of Time: Cultural Constructions of Temporal Maps and Images.* Oxford: Berg.

Gellner, Ernest. 1983. *Nations and Nationalism.* Oxford: Blackwell.

————. 1987. *Culture, Identity, and Politics.* Cambridge: Cambridge University Press.

Gerbeau, Hubert. 1979. The Slave Trade in the Indian Ocean: Problems Facing the Historian and Research to be Undertaken. In *The African Slave Trade from the Fifteenth to Nineteenth Century,* 184–207. Reports and Papers of the Meetings of Experts Organized by UNESCO at Port-au-Prince, Haiti, January 31–February 4, 1978. Paris: UNESCO.

Gezon, Lisa L. 1995. The Political Ecology of Conflict and Control in Ankarana, Madagascar. Ph.D. diss. Department of Anthropology, University of Michigan.

Goffman, Erving. 1961. *Asylums: Essays on the Social Situation of Mental Patients and Other Inmates.* New York: Doubleday.

Gontard, Maurice. N.d.a. La Contribution de Madagascar à l'effort de guerre Français: le recrutement des volontaires malgaches pendant la guerre de 1914–1918. Annales de la Faculté des Lettres de Madagascar 5: 7–25.

————. N.d.b. Une année critique à Madagascar pendant la Première Guerre mondiale: 1917. Source unknown; but see CAOM B. 6404.

Goodenough, Ward. 1970. Epilogue: Transactions in Parenthood. In *Adoption in Eastern Oceania,* ed. Vern Carroll, 391–410. ASAO Monograph No. 1. Honolulu: University of Hawaii Press.

Gottlieb, David, Jon Reeves, and Warren D. TenHouten. 1966. *The Emergence of Youth Societies: A Cross-Cultural Approach.* New York: Free Press.

Gow, Bonar A. 1979. *Madagascar and the Protestant Impact: The Work of the British Missions, 1818–1895.* New York: Africana Publishing.

Graeber, David. 1995. Dancing with Corpses Reconsidered: An Interpretation of *Famadihana* (in Arivonimamo, Madagascar). *American Ethnologist* 22, 2: 258–78.

————. 1996. The Disastrous Ordeal of 1987: Magic and History in Rural Madagascar. Ph.D. diss. University of Chicago.

Grant, Nicole. 1995. From Margaret Mead's Field Notes: What Counted as "Sex" in Samoa? *American Anthropologist* 97, 4: 678–82.

Gueunier, Noël J. 1991–92. Une Copie de la lettre de Tsiomeko, reine des Sakalava à Louis-Philippe, roi des Français (1840). *Omaly sy Anio (Hier et Aujourd'hui),* no. 33–36: 513–31.

————. 1993. Parler blanc: Le Français à Madagascar. In *Une Francophonie différentielle,* ed. S. Abou and K. Hadad, 300–315. Paris: L'Harmattan.

Gueunier, N. J., with J. M. Katupha. N.d. *Contes de la côte ouest de Madagascar.* Antananarivo: Ambozontany. Based on a 1985 Université de Paris thesis.

Guillain, Charles. [1845] 1856. *Documents sur l'histoire, la géographie et le commerce de la partie occidentale de Madagascar.* Paris: A. Bertrand.

Halbwachs, Maurice. 1925. *Les Cadres sociaux de la mémoire.* Paris: F. Alcan.

————. 1968. *La Mémoire collective.* 2d ed. Paris: Presses Universitaires de France.

Hall, Kathleen. 1995. "There's a Time to Act English and a Time to Act Indian": The Politics of Identity among British-Sikh Teenagers. In *Children and the Politics of Culture,* ed. S. Stephens, 243–64. Princeton, N.J.: Princeton University Press.

Hansen, Karen Tranberg. 1997. *Keeping House in Lusaka.* New York: Columbia University Press.

Hardman, C. 1973. Can There Be an Anthropology of Children? *Journal of the Anthropological Society of Oxford* 4, 1: 85–99.

Hardyman, J. T. 1964. The Madagascar Slave-Trade to the Americas (1632–1830). In *Colloque de Lourenço-Marquès sur Océan Indien et Méditerranée*, 501–21. Paris: SEVPAN.

Harrison-Chirimuuta, Rosalind J., and Richard Chirimuuta. 1997. AIDS from Africa: A Case of Racism vs. Science? In *AIDS in Africa and the Caribbean*, ed. G. Bond, J. Kreniske, I. Susser, and J. Vincent, 165–80. Boulder, Colo.: Westview Press.

Hejaiej, Monia. 1996. *Behind Closed Doors: Women's Oral Narratives in Tunis.* New Brunswick, N.J.: Rutgers University Press.

Hellot, Frédéric. 1900. La Pacification de Madagascar: Operations d'oct. 1896 à mars 1899. Edited by General Joseph Simon Gallieni. Paris: R. Chapelot.

Heseltine, Nigel. 1971. *Madagascar.* New York: Praeger Publishers.

Hobsbawm, Eric. 1983. Introduction: Inventing Traditions. In *The Invention of Tradition*, ed. E. Hobsbawm and T. Ranger, 1–14. Cambridge: Cambridge University Press.

Hollos, Marida, and Philip E. Leis. 1989. *Becoming Nigerian in Ijo Society.* New Brunswick, N.J.: Rutgers University Press.

Holmes, Lowell. 1987. *Quest for the Real Samoa: The Mead/Freeman Controversy and Beyond.* South Hadley, Mass.: Bergin & Garvey.

Hostetler, John A., and Gertrude Enders Huntington. 1992. *Amish Children: Education in the Family, School, and Community.* 2d ed. Fort Worth, Tex.: Harcourt Brace Jovanovich.

Jackson, P. H. 1890. "Sketches in Madagascar." *Illustrated London News*, August 9, 181.

Jackson, Stevi, and Sue Scott. 1999. Risk Anxiety and the Social Construction of Childhood. In *Risk and Sociocultural Theory: New Directions and Perspectives*, ed. D. Lupton, 36–107. Cambridge: Cambridge University Press.

Jacob, Guy. 1990. Le Madécasse et les Lumières: *Voyage à Madagascar* d'Alexis Rochon. In *Ravao ny "La Bastille": Regards sur Madagascar et la Révolution française*, ed. id., 43–61. Actes du colloque d'Antananarivo, June 5 and 6, 1989. Antananarivo: CNAPMAD.

———, ed. 1990. *Ravao ny "La Bastille": Regards sur Madagascar et la Révolution française.* Actes du colloque d'Antananarivo, June 5 and 6, 1989. Antananarivo: CNAPMAD.

James, Allison. 1995. Talking of Children and Youth. Language, Socialization, and Culture. In *Youth Cultures: A Cross-Cultural Perspective*, ed. V. Amit-Talai and H. Wulff, 43–62. New York: Routledge.

James, Allison, and Alan Prout. 1990a. A New Paradigm for the Sociology of Childhood? Provenance, Promise and Problems. In *Constructing and Reconstructing Childhood*, ed. id., 7–34. New York: Falmer Press.

———. 1990b. Re-Presenting Childhood: Time and Transition in the Study of Childhood. In *Constructing and Reconstructing Childhood*, ed. id., 216–37. New York: Falmer Press.

Jinadu, Adele. 1980. *Fanon: In Search of the African Revolution.* [Lagos?]: Fourth Dimension Publishers.

Kamenka, Eugene. 1988. Revolutionary Ideology and "The Great French Revolution of 1789–" ? In *The Permanent Revolution: The French Revolution and Its Legacy: 1789–1989*, ed. G. Best, 75–99. Chicago: University of Chicago Press.

Kent, Raymond K. 1968. The Sakalava, Maroseranana, Dady and Tromba before 1700. *Journal of African History* 9, 4: 517–46.

———. 1979. Religion and the State: A Comparison of Antanosy and Sakalava in the 1600s. In *Madagascar in History: Essays from the 1970s*, ed. id., 80–101. Berkeley, Calif.: Foundation for Malagasy Studies.

Kenyon, Susan M. 1991. *Five Women of Sennar: Culture and Change in Central Sudan.* Oxford: Clarendon Press.

Kirkaldy, Alan. 1996. History Teaching in Rural Areas: The University of Venda. *Issue: A Journal of Opinion* 24, 1: 17–23.

Kline, Stephen. 1998. The Making of Children's Culture. In *The Children's Culture Reader,* ed. H. Jenkins, 95–109. New York: New York University Press.

Koerner, F. 1968. La colonisation agricole du Nord-Ouest de Madagascar. *Revue Economique de Madagascar,* 165–93. Cujas-Université de Madagascar.

Kottak, Conrad. 1986. Kinship Modeling: Adaption, Fosterage, and Fictive Kinship among the Betsileo. In *Madagascar: Society and History,* ed. C. P. Kottak, J.-A. Rakotoarisoa, A. Southall, and P. Vérin, 276–98. Durham, N.C.: Carolina Academic Press.

Kozol, Jonathan. 1991. *Savage Inequalities: Children in America's Schools.* New York: Harper Perennial.

Kramer, Fritz. 1993. *The Red Fez: Art and Spirit Possession in Africa.* Translated by M. R. Green. London: Verso.

Labatut, F., and R. Raharinarivonirina. 1969. *Madagascar: Étude historique.* [Antananarivo?]: Fernand Nathan-Madagascar.

Lambek, Michael, and Andrew Walsh. 1997. The Imagined Community of the Antankaraña: Identity, History, and Ritual in Northern Madagascar. *Journal of Religion in Africa* 27, 3: 308–32.

Larkin, Brian. 1997. Indian Films and Nigerian Lovers: Media and the Creation of Parallel Modernities. *Africa* 67, 3: 406–40.

La Vaissière, Camille de (Père). 1884. *Histoire de Madagascar, ses habitants et ses missionnaires.* 2 vols. Paris: Victor Lecoffre.

Lave, J., P. Duguid, and N. Fernandez. 1992. Coming of Age in Birmingham: Cultural Studies and Conceptions of Subjectivity. *Annual Review of Anthropology* 21: 257–82.

Lebra, Takie Sugiyama. 1995. Skipped and Postponed Adolescence of Aristocratic Women in Japan: Resurrecting the Culture/Nature Issue. *Ethos* 23, 1: 79–102.

Leventhal, Todd. 1994. The Child Organ Trafficking Rumor: A Modern "Urban Legend." Report submitted to the United Nations Special Rapporteur on the Sale of Children, Child Prostitution, and Child Pornography. Washington, D.C.: United States Information Agency.

LeVine, Robert A. 1974. *Culture and Personality.* Chicago: Aldine.

LeVine, Robert A., and Merry I. White. 1986. *Human Conditions: The Cultural Basis of Educational Development.* New York: Routledge & Kegan Paul.

LeVine, Robert A., et al. 1994. *Child Care and Culture: Lessons from Africa.* Cambridge: Cambridge University Press.

Leymarie, P. 1973. Madagascar: Une "Seconde indépendence"? *RFEPA,* July, 21–23.

Lindenbaum, Shirley. 1997. AIDS: Body, Mind, and History. In *AIDS in Africa and the Caribbean,* ed. G. Bond, J. Kreniske, I Susser, and J. Vincent, 191–194. Boulder, Colo.: Westview Press.

Liza. 1994. *La Plume, Journal pédagogique à destination des maîtres,* Ministère de l'Education Nationale, no. 5.

Lunn, Joe Harris. 1987. Kande Kamara Speaks; An Oral History of the West African Experience in France in 1914–18. In *Africa and the First World War,* ed. M. E. Page, 28–53. London: Macmillan.

Lyons, Maryinez. 1997. The Point of View: Perspectives on AIDS in Uganda. In *AIDS in Africa and the Caribbean,* ed. G. Bond, J. Kreniske, I Susser, and J. Vincent, 131–46. Boulder, Colo.: Westview Press.

Mack, John. 1986. *Madagascar: Island of the Ancestors.* London: British Museum Publications.

Mandel, Ruth. 1995. Second-Generation Noncitizens: Children of the Turkish Migrant Diaspora in Germany. In *Children and the Politics of Culture,* ed. S. Stephens, 265–81. Princeton, N.J.: Princeton University Press.

Mangalaza, E. 1977. La Philosophie malgache. *Tsiokatimo* (CUR, Toliara) 3: 4.

Mangin, Charles. 1911. *La Force noire.* 3d ed. Paris: Hachette.

Mannoni, Octave. [1956] 1990. *Prospero and Caliban: The Psychology of Colonization.* Translated by Pamela Powesland. Reprint. Ann Arbor: University of Michigan Press. Originally published as *Psychologie de la colonisation* (Paris: Seuil, 1950).

Masquelier, Adeline. 2000. Headhunters and Cannibals: Migrancy, Labor, and Consumption in the Mawri Imagination. *Cultural Anthropology* 15, 1: 84–126.

Martin, Emily. 1994. *Flexible Bodies: Tracking Immunity in American Culture from the Days of Polio to the Age of AIDS.* Boston: Beacon Press.

Mathieu, James T. 1996. Reflections on Two African Universities. *Issue: A Journal of Opinion* 24:1: 24–28.

May, Ann. 1996. Handshops and Hope: Young Street Vendors in Dar es Salaam, Tanzania. *Anthropology of Work Review* 17:1–2: 25–34.

Mbembe, Achille. 1992. Provisional Notes on the Postcolony. *Africa* 62:1: 3–37.

McLeod, Lyons. [1865]. 1969. *Madagascar and Its People.* New York: Negro University Presses.

Mead, Margaret. 1939. *From the South Seas: Studies of Adolescence and Sex in Primitive Societies.* New York: William Morrow.

———. [1928] 1961. *Coming of Age in Samoa. A Psychological Study of Primitive Youth for Western Civilization.* New York: Dell.

Memmi, Albert. 1965. *The Colonizer and the Colonized.* Translated by Howard Greenfield. New York: Orion Press. Originally published as *Portrait du colonisé, précédé du portrait du colonisateur* (Paris: Buchet/Chastel, 1957).

Mendelievich, E., ed. 1979. *Children at Work.* Geneva: International Labour Office.

Metcalf, Peter, and Richard Huntington. 1991. *Celebrations of Death: The Anthropology of Mortuary Ritual.* 2d ed. Cambridge: Cambridge University Press.

Michel, M. 1974. Un Mythe: La Force noire avant 1914. *Relations internationales* 2: 83–90.

Minge, Wanda. 1986. The Industrial Revolution and the European Family: "Childhood" as a Market for Family Labor. In *Women's Work: Development and the Division of Labor by Gender,* ed. E. Leacock and H. Safa, 13–24. New York: Bergen & Garvey.

Mitchell, B. R. 1982. *International Historical Statistics: Africa and Asia.* New York: New York University Press.

Mohanty, C., A. Russo, and L. Torres, eds. 1991. *Third World Women and the Politics of Feminism.* Bloomington: Indiana University Press.

Molet, Louis. 1956. *Le Bain royal à Madagascar: Explication de la fête malgache du Fandroana par la coutume disparue de la manducation des morts.* Tananarive: Imprimerie Luthérienne.

———. 1974. Le Vocabulaire concernant l'esclavage dans l'ancien Madagascar. In *Perspectives: Nouvelles sur le passé de l'Afrique noire et Madagascar,* 45–65. Paris: Publications de la Sorbonne.

Moran, Mary H. 1992. Civilized Servants: Child Fosterage and Training for Status among the Glebo of Liberia. In *African Encounters with Domesticity,* ed. K. T. Hansen, 98–115. New Brunswick, N.J.: Rutgers University Press.

———. 1994. *The Idea of Africa.* Bloomington: Indiana University Press.

Mudimbe, V. Y. 1988. *The Invention of Africa: Gnosis, Philosophy, and the Order of Knowledge.* Bloomington: Indiana University Press.

———. 1994. *The Idea of Africa.* Bloomington: Indiana University Press.

Mutibwa, P. M. 1974. *The Malagasy and the Europeans: Madagascar's Foreign Relations, 1861–1895.* Atlantic Highlands, N.J.: Humanities Press.

Ndebele, Njabulo. 1995. Recovering Childhood: Children in South African National Reconstruction. In *Children and the Politics of Culture,* ed. S. Stephens, 321–33. Princeton, N.J.: Princeton University Press.

Nelson, Charles M. 1996. PAT 101: Principles of Patronage. *Issue: A Journal of Opinion* 24, 1: 45–51.

Nérine-Botokeky, Elénore. 1983. Le Fitampoha en royaume de Menabe: Bain des reliques royales. In *Les Souverains de Madagascar: L'Histoire royale et ses résurgences contemporaines,* ed. F. Raison-Jourde, 211–19. Paris: Karthala.

Ngugi wa Thiong'o, ed. 1986. *Decolonizing the Mind: The Politics of Language in African Literature.* Portsmouth, N.H.: Heinemann.

Nordstrom, Carolyn. 1997a. *A Different Kind of War Story.* Philadelphia: University of Pennsylvania Press.

———. 1997b. *Girls and War Zones: Troubling Questions.* Uppsala: Life and Peace Institute.

Obeyesekere, Gananath. 1992. *The Apotheosis of Captain Cook: European Mythmaking in the Pacific.* Princeton, N.J.: Princeton University Press.

Okoth, P. G. 1993. The Creation of a Dependent Culture: The Imperial School Curriculum in Uganda. In *The Imperial Curriculum: Racial Images and Education in the British Colonial Experience,* ed. J. A. Mangan, 135–46. London: Routledge.

Ortner, Sherry B. 1996. *Making Gender: The Politics and Erotics of Culture.* Boston: Beacon Press.

Paes, C., M.-C. Paes, J. F. Rabedimy, N. Rajaonarimanana, and Velonandro. 1991. *L'Origine des choses: Recits de la côte ouest de Madagascar.* Série Arts et Culture Malgache. Antananarivo: Foi et Justice.

Page, Melvin E. 1987. Introduction: Black Men in a White Men's War. In *Africa and the First World War,* ed. id., 1–27. London: Macmillan.

Paillard, Yvan-Georges. 1979. The First and Second Malagasy Republics: The Difficult Road to Independence. In *Madagascar in History: Essays from the 1970s,* ed. and trans. R. Kent, 298–354. Albany, Calif.: Foundation for Malagasy Studies.

———. 1983–84. Les Mpanjaka du nord-ouest de Madagascar et l'insurrection anticoloniale de 1898. *Omaly sy Anio (Hier et Aujourd'hui)* 17–20: 339–74.

Perrier de la Bathie, H. 1931. *Le Salariat indigène à Madagascar.* Presented at the Congrès International et Intercolonial de la Société Indigène, Exposition Coloniale Internationale de Paris, 5–10 October. 16 pp.

Pomponio, Alice. 1992. *Seagulls Don't Fly into the Bush: Cultural Identity and Development in Melanesia.* Belmont, Calif.: Wadsworth.

Population Reference Bureau. 1990. *1990 World Population Data Sheet.* Washington, D.C.: PRB.

Pred, Allan, and Michael John Watts. 1992. *Reworking Modernity: Capitalisms and Symbolic Discontent.* New Brunswick, N.J.: Rutgers University Press.

Price, Richard, and Sally Price. 1991. *Two Evenings in Saramaka.* Chicago: University of Chicago Press.

Rabenoro, Césaire. 1986. *Les Relations extérieures de Madagascar de 1960 à 1972.* Paris: L'Harmattan.

Rafael, Vicente L. 1992. Confession, Conversion, and Reciprocity in Early Tagalog Colonial Society. In *Colonialism and Culture,* ed. N. B. Dirks, 65–88. Ann Arbor: University of Michigan Press.

Rahajarizafy, Remi. 1973. *Mey 1972.* Antananarivo: Ny Nouvelle Imprimerie des Arts Graphiques NIAG.

Raison-Jourde, Françoise, ed. 1983. *Les Souverains de Madagascar: L'Histoire royale et ses résurgences contemporaines.* Paris: Karthala.

————. 1990. L'Échange des hommes illustres entre Madagascar et l'Europe ou la Révolution masquée par Bonaparte. In *Ravao ny "La Bastille": Regards sur Madagascar et la Révolution française,* ed. Guy Jacob, 89–95. Actes du colloque d'Antananarivo, June 5 and 6, 1989. Antananarivo: CNAPMAD.

————. 1997. L'Ici et l'ailleurs dans la construction identitaire: Le *Look* des jeunes urbains à Madagascar. In *Le Lieu identitaire de la jeunesse d'aujourd'hui: Études de cas,* ed. J. Létourneau, 27–45. Paris: L'Harmattan.

Rajemisa-Raolison, Régis. 1966. *Dictionnaire historique et géographique de Madagascar.* Fianarantsoa: Librairie Ambozontany.

Rajoelina, Patrick. 1988. *Quarante années de la vie politique de Madagascar, 1947–1987.* Paris: L'Harmattan.

Rakotomalala, Joëlson. 1983. *Zava nafenin'ny 29 Marsa 47.* [Antananarivo?]: Sosaiety Madprint.

Ramamonjisoa, J. 1984. Langue nationale, français et développement. *Cahier des Sciences Sociales* (Antananarivo) 1: 39–74.

Ramanandraibe, Lucile Rasoamanalina. 1987. *Le Livre vert de l'espérance malgache.* Paris: L'Harmattan.

Ramanantoanina, Ny Avana. 1993. *Ny diam-penin' Ny Avana Ramanantoanina,* ed. François Rakotonaivo. Fianarantsoa: [Librarie/Baingan'] Ambozontany.

Rambeloson-Rapiera, Jeannine. 1990. Madagascar et les Malgaches dans la pensé des Lumières. In *Ravao ny "La Bastille": Regards sur Madagascar et la Révolution française,* ed. Guy Jacob, 29–41. Actes du colloque d'Antananarivo, June 5 and 6, 1989. Antananarivo: CNAPMAD.

Randrianja, Solofo. 1990. Les Valeurs de 89 et leur utilisation par les forces politiques à Madagascar durant l'entre-deux-guerres. In *Ravao ny "La Bastille": Regards sur Madagascar et la Révolution française,* ed. Guy Jacob, 159–66. Actes du colloque d'Antananrivo, June 5 and 6, 1989. Antananarivo: CNAPMAD.

Rasoanasy, Jeanne. 1976. *Menalamba sy Tanindrazana: Ny Lasan'i Madagasikara (Ny ady nataon'ny tia tanindrazana eran'ny nosy teo anelanelan'ny taona 1895 sy 1905).* Antananarivo: Trano Printy Loterana.

Rathbone, Richard. 1978. World War I and Africa: Introduction. *Journal of African History* 19, 1: 1–9.

Ratsiraka, Didier. 1975. *Ny Boky Mena: Charte de la Révolution socialiste malgache tous azimuts.* Antananarivo: Imprimerie d'ouvrages éducatifs.

Razafimpahanana, Bertin. 1972. *Le Paysan malagasy.* [Antananarivo?:] T.P.L. [Trano Printy Loterana?].

Reynolds, Pamela. 1985. Children in Zimbabwe: Rights and Power in Relation to Work. *Anthropology Today* 1, 3: 16–20.

————. 1989. The Double Strategy of Children in South Africa. *Sociological Studies of Child Development* 3: 113–38.

————. 1995a. "Not Known because Not Looked For": Ethnographers Listening to the Young in Southern Africa. *Ethnos* 60, 3–4: 193–221.

————. 1995b. Youth and the Politics of Culture in South Africa. In *Children and the Politics of Culture*, ed. S. Stephens, 218–40. Princeton, N.J.: Princeton University Press.

Reynolds, Pamela, and Sandra Burman, eds. 1986. *Growing Up in a Divided Society: The Contexts of Childhood in South Africa.* Johannesburg: Ravan Press.

Richards, Paul. 1994. Videos and Violence on the Periphery: Rambo and War in the Forests of the Sierra Leone-Liberia Border. *IDS Bulletin* 25, 2: 88–93.

————. 1996. *Fighting for the Rain Forest: War, Youth and Resources in Sierra Leone.* Oxford: James Currey for the International African Institute.

Rosaldo, Renato. 1980. *Ilongot Headhunting, 1883–1974: A Study in Society and History.* Stanford, Calif.: Stanford University Press.

Rosen, Stanley. 2000. Foreword. In Y. Jiang and D. Ashley, *Mao's Children in the New China: Voices from the Red Guard Generation.* London: Routledge.

Rousseau, Jean-Jacques. [1755] 1992. *Discourse on the Origin of Inequality.* Translated by D. A. Cross. Indianapolis: Hackett.

Sahlins, Marshall. 1985. *Islands of History.* Chicago: University of Chicago Press.

Said, Edward W. 1979. *Orientalism.* New York: Vintage Books.

Schapera, Isaac. 1956. *Government and Politics in Tribal Societies.* London: Watts.

Scheper-Hughes, Nancy, ed. 1987. *Child Survival: Anthropological Perspectives on the Treatment and Maltreatment of Children.* Boston: D. Reidel.

————. 1992. *Death without Weeping: Everyday Violence in Northeast Brazil.* Berkeley and Los Angeles: University of California Press.

————. 1995. Who's the Killer? Popular Justice and Human Rights in a South African Squatter Camp. *Social Justice* 22, 3: 143–64.

Scheper-Hughes, Nancy, and Carolyn Sargent, eds. 1998. *Small Wars: The Cultural Politics of Childhood.* Berkeley and Los Angeles: University of California Press.

Schildkrout, Enid. 1979. The Ideology of Regionalism in Ghana. In *Strangers in African Societies,* ed. W. A. Shack and E. P. Skinner, 183–207. Berkeley and Los Angeles: University of California Press.

————. 1981. Young Traders of Northern Nigeria. *Natural History* 90, 6: 44–53.

Schlegel, Alice. 1995a. Introduction [to the Special Issue on Adolescence]. *Ethos* 23, 1: 3–14.

————. 1995b. A Cross-Cultural Approach to Adolescence. *Ethos* 23, 1: 15–32.

Schultz, T. W. 1961. Investment in Human Capital. *American Economic Review* 51: 1–17.

Scott, James C. 1985. *Weapons of the Weak: Everyday Forms of Peasant Resistance.* New Haven, Conn.: Yale University Press.

Serpell, Robert. 1993. *The Significance of Schooling: Life-Journeys in an African Society.* Cambridge: Cambridge University Press.

Sharp, Lesley A. 1990. Possessed and Dispossessed Youth: Spirit Possession of School Children in Northwest Madagascar. *Culture, Medicine and Psychiatry* 14: 339–64.

————. 1993. *The Possessed and the Dispossessed: Spirits, Identity, and Power in a Madagascar Migrant Town.* Berkeley and Los Angeles: University of California Press.

————. 1994. Exorcists, Psychiatrists, and the Problems of Possession in Northwest Madagascar. *Journal of Social Science and Medicine* 38, 4: 525–42.

————. 1995. Playboy Princely Spirits of Madagascar: Possession as Youthful Commentary and Social Critique. *Anthropological Quarterly* 68, 2: 75–88.

————. 1996. The Work Ideology of Malagasy Children: Schooling and Survival in Urban Madagascar. *Anthropology of Work Review* 17, 1–2: 35–42.

————. 1997a. Royal Difficulties: A Question of Succession in an Urbanized Sakalava Kingdom. *Journal of Religion in Africa* 27, 3: 270–307

————. 1997b. Sewing and Sowing the Ties that Bind: Child Sharing by Entrepreneurial Malagasy Women. Paper delivered in the session "Women Helping Women: A Cross-Cultural Perspective on their Cooperative and Supportive Behavior," American Anthropological Association Annual Meetings, Washington, D.C.

————. 1999. The Power of Possession in Northwest Madagascar: Contesting Colonial and National Hegemonies. In *Spirit Possession, Modernity, and Power in Africa,* ed. H. Behrend and U. Luig, 3–19. Mainz and London: James Currey.

————. 2000. Royal Affairs and the Power of (Fictive) Kin: Mediumship, Maternity, and the Contemporary Politics of Bemazava Identity. *Taloha* (Madagascar) 13: 111–34.

————. 2001a. Youth, Land, and Liberty in Coastal Madagascar: A Children's Independence. *Ethnohistory* 48, 1–2: 205–36.

————. 2001b. Wayward Pastoral Ghosts and Regional Xenophobia in a Northern Madagascar Town. *Africa* 71, 1: 38–81.

————. 2002. Girls, Sex, and the Dangers of Urban Schooling in Coastal Madagascar. In *Contested Terrains and Constructed Categories: Contemporary Africa in Focus,* ed. G. Bond and N. Gibson, 321–44. Boulder, Colo.: Westview Press.

Shiraishi, Saya S. 1995. Children's Stories and the State in New Order Indonesia. In *Children and the Politics of Culture,* ed. S. Stephens, 169–83. Princeton, N.J.: Princeton University Press.

Silverman, Milton, Philip R. Lee, and Mia Lydecker. 1982. The Drugging of the Third World. *International Journal of Health Services* 12, 4: 585–95.

Silverman, Milton, Mia Lydecker, and Philip R. Lee. 1990. The Drug Swindlers. The *International Journal of Health Services* 20, 4: 561–72.

Simpson, Anthony. 1998. Memory and Becoming Chosen Other: Fundamentalist Elite-Making in a Zambian Catholic Mission School. In *Memory and the Postcolony: African Anthropology and the Critique of Power,* ed. R. Werbner, 209–28. London: Zed Books.

Sklar, Richard L. 1994. Social Class and Political Action in Africa: The Bourgeoisie and the Proletariat. In *Political Development and the New Realism in Sub-Saharan Africa,* ed. D. Apter and C. Rosberg, 117–41. Charlottesville: University Press of Virginia.

Slipchenko, S. A. 1989. Three Main Periods in the History of Slave Trade. In *Slavery in South West Indian Ocean,* ed. U. Bissoondoyal and S. B. Servansing, 397–400. Moka, Mauritius: Mahatma Gandhi Institute.

Spivak, Gayatri Chakravorty. 1988. "Can the Subaltern Speak?" In *Marxism and the Interpretation of Culture,* ed. C. Nelson and L. Grossberg, 271–313. Urbana: University of Illinois Press.

Stein, Robert. 1978. Measuring the French Slave Trade. *Journal of African History* 19, 4: 515–21.

Stephens, Sharon. 1995a. Preface and Introduction: Children and the Politics of Culture in "Late Capitalism." In *Children and the Politics of Culture,* ed. id., vii–viii, 4–48. Princeton, N.J.: Princeton University Press.

————, ed. 1995b. *Children and the Politics of Culture.* Princeton, N.J.: Princeton University Press.

Société Malgache. 1973. *A Glance at Madagascar.* Antananarivo: Librarie Tout pour l'École.

Soyinka, Wole. 1993. *Art, Dialogue, and Outrage: Essays on Literature and Culture.* New York: Pantheon Books.

Stoler, Ann L. 1985. *Capitalism and Confrontation in Sumatra's Plantation Belt, 1870–1979.* New Haven, Conn.: Yale University Press.

Stratton, Arthur. 1964. *The Great Red Island.* New York: Charles Scribner's Sons.

Sylla, Yvette. 1990. Un Envoyée de l'Assemblée nationale à Madagascar en 1792: La mission de Daniel Lescallier. In *Ravao ny "La Bastille": Regards sur Madagascar et la Révolution française,* ed. Guy Jacob, 63–69. Actes du colloque d'Antananarivo, June 5 and 6, 1989. Antananarivo: CNAPMAD.

Tabachnick, B. Robert, and Josephine A. Beoku-Betts. 1998. Using the Past to Fashion an Expanding Future. In *Women and Education in Sub-Saharan Africa: Power, Opportunities, and Constraints,* ed. M. Bloch, J. A. Boeku-Betts, and B. R. Tabachnick, 299–311. Boulder, Colo.: Lynne Rienner.

Taussig, Michael. 1977. The Genesis of Capitalism amongst a South American Peasantry: Devil's Labor and the Baptism of Money. *Comparative Studies in Society and History* 19: 130–55.

———. 1987. *Shamanism, Colonialism, and the Wild Man: A Study in Terror and Healing.* Chicago: University of Chicago Press.

———. 1993. *Mimesis and Alterity: A Particular History of the Senses.* New York: Routledge.

———. 1997. *The Magic of the State.* New York: Routledge.

Thompson, E. P. 1967. Time, Work Discipline, and Industrial Capitalism. *Past and Present* 38: 56–97.

Thompson, Virginia, and Richard Adloff. 1965. *The Malagasy Republic: Madagascar Today.* Stanford, Calif.: Stanford University Press.

Thorne, B. 1987. Revisioning Women and Social Change: Where Are the Children? *Gender and Society* 1, 1: 85–109.

Treichler, Paula. 1989. AIDS and HIV Infection in the Third World: A First World Chronicle. In *Remaking History,* ed. B. Kruger and P. Mariani, 31–86. Seattle: Bay Press.

Tronchon, Jacques. 1982. *L'Insurrection malgache de 1947: Essai d'interprétation historique.* Fianarantsoa: Ambozontany Fianarantsoa.

———. 1990. Le Modèle républicain français et ses interprétations à Madagascar de la conquête à la IIe République. In *Ravao ny "La Bastille": Regards sur Madagascar et la Révolution française,* ed. Guy Jacob, 133–43. Actes du colloque d'Antananarivo, June 5 and 6, 1989. Antananarivo: CNAPMAD.

United Nations. 1979. Demographic Yearbook. Histoical Supplement. Department of International Economic and Social Affairs, Statistical Office. New York: United Nations.

———. 1995. The United Nations Convention on the Rights of the Child. In *Children and the Politics of Culture,* ed. S. Stephens, 335–55. Princeton, N.J.: Princeton University Press.

———. 1996. Demographic Yearbook (46th issue). Department for Economic and Social Information and Policy Analysis. New York: United Nations.

UNICEF [United Nations Children's Fund]. 1987. *Children on the Front Line: The Impact of Apartheid, Destabilisation and Warfare on Children in Southern Africa.* New York: UNICEF.

UNICEF-U.K. 1988. *The State of the World's Children.* Oxford: Oxford University Press.

Valette, Jean. 1979. Radama I, the Unification of Madagascar and the Modernization of Imerina (1810–1828). In *Madagascar in History: Essays from the 1970s,* ed. R. K. Kent, 168–96. Albany, Calif.: Foundation for Malagasy Studies.

Vansina, Jan. 1985. *Oral Tradition as History.* Madison: University of Wisconsin Press.

Verin, Pierre. 1986. *The History of Civilisation in North Madagascar.* Translated by D. Smith. Rotterdam: A. A. Balkema.

Vincent, Joan. 1971. *African Elite: The Big Men of a Small Town.* New York: Columbia University Press.

Wanquet, Claude. 1990. Joseph-François Charpentier de Cossigny, et le projet d'une colonisation 'éclairée' de Madagascar à la fin du XVIIIe siècle. In *Ravao ny "La Bastille": Regards sur Madagascar et la Révolution française,* ed. Guy Jacob, 71–85. Actes du colloque d'Antananarivo, June 5 and 6, 1989. Antananarivo: CNAPMAD.

White, Luise. 1990. *The Comforts of Home: Prostitution in Colonial Nairobi.* Chicago: University of Chicago Press.

———. *Speaking with Vampires: Rumor and History in Colonial Africa.* Berkeley and Los Angeles: University of California Press.

Whiting, Beatrice B., ed. 1963. *Six Cultures: Studies of Child Rearing.* New York: Wiley.

Whiting, Beatrice B., and Carolyn Pope Edwards. 1988. *Children of Different Worlds: The Formation of Social Behavior.* Cambridge, Mass.: Harvard University Press.

Whiting, Beatrice B., John W. M. Whiting, and Richard Longabaugh. 1975. *Children of Six Cultures: A Psycho-Cultural Analysis.* Cambridge, Mass.: Harvard University Press.

Willinsky, John. 1998. *Learning to Divide the World: Education at Empire's End.* Minneapolis: University of Minnesota Press.

Willis, Paul. 1977. *Learning to Labor: How Working Class Kids Get Working Class Jobs.* New York: Columbia University Press.

Wilson, Peter J. 1992. *Freedom by a Hair's Breadth. Tsimihety in Madagascar.* Ann Arbor: University of Michigan Press.

Wolf, Eric R. 1982. *Europe and the People without History.* Berkeley and Los Angeles: University of California Press.

World Bank. 1980. *Madagascar: Recent Economic Developments and Future Prospects. A World Bank Country Study.* Washington, D.C.: Eastern Africa Regional Office, World Bank.

———. 1989. *Education in Sub-Saharan Africa: Policies for Adjustment, Revitalization, and Expansion.* Washington, D.C.: World Bank.

Wright, Marcia. 1993. *Strategies of Slaves and Women. Life-Stories from East/Central Africa.* New York: Lilian Barber Press.

Wulff, Helena. 1995. Introduction: Introducing Youth Culture in Its Own Right: The State of the Art and New Possibilities. In *Youth Cultures: A Cross-Cultural Perspective,* ed. V. Amit-Talai and H. Wulff, 1–18. New York: Routledge.

Yarong, Jiang, and David Ashley. 2000. *Mao's Children in the New China: Voices from the Red Guard Generation.* New York: Routledge.

INDEX

Compositor:	Impressions Book & Journal Services, Inc.
Text:	10/12 Baskerville
Display:	Baskerville
Printer and binder:	Edwards Brothers, Inc.